DATE			

HISTORIES
OF A PLAGUE YEAR

Studies on the History of Society and Culture
Victoria E. Bonnell and Lynn Hunt, Editors

HISTORIES
OF A PLAGUE YEAR

THE SOCIAL AND THE IMAGINARY
IN BAROQUE FLORENCE

GIULIA CALVI

Translated by

DARIO BIOCCA and BRYANT T. RAGAN, JR.

With a Foreword by

RANDOLPH STARN

University of California Press
Berkeley · Los Angeles · Oxford

Originally published as
Storie di un anno di peste
© 1984 Bompiani, Milan

University of California Press
Berkeley and Los Angeles, California

University of California Press, Ltd.
Oxford, England

Library of Congress Cataloging-in-Publication Data

Calvi, Giulia, 1948–
    [Storie di un anno di peste. English]
    Histories of a plague year : the social and the imaginary
in baroque Florence / Giulia Calvi ; translated by Dario
Biocca and Bryant T. Ragan, Jr. ; with a foreword by
Randolph Starn.
        p.   cm. — (Studies on the history of society and
culture)
    Translation of: Storie di un anno di peste.
    Bibliography: p.
    ISBN 0-520-05799-6 (alk. paper)
    1. Plague—Italy—Florence—History—17th century.
I. Title. II. Series.
RC178.12.F 1989
614.5'732'009455—dc 19   88-29549
                                                       CIP

Printed in the United States of America
1   2   3   4   5   6   7   8   9

To my mother

Contents

Foreword to the
English-language Edition
by Randolph Starn

Coming nearly three hundred years after the black death, the terrible
plague that ravaged Italy in 1630–31 was only one of a long series of
European epidemics that finally tapered off late in the seventeenth century. The death toll of 20–60 percent of the population was "normal"
for such visitations; the plague hospitals, the rituals of expiation, the
flight of the well-to-do, the suffering crowd were all too familiar. The
grim irony of the situation in northern and central Italy is that the
authorities were so well prepared. Since the middle of the fifteenth
century public health commissions had gradually extended their responsibility for quarantines, hospitals, and burials in times of emergency until they exercised wide-ranging supervision over practically
every aspect of daily life. These measures followed from the dominant
medical opinion that the plague was an infectious disease transmitted
by "venomous atoms" through "miasmatic air"; not until late in the
nineteenth century, with the discovery that the plague bacillus actually
passes from infected rats to fleas and so under certain conditions to
human hosts, was this view laid to rest. The one certain result of the
combination of false science and largely irrelevant institutional controls was a detailed archival record. The plague of 1630–31 is one of
the best documented in early modern Europe, and nowhere better
than in Florence.

Historians have always been drawn to misery and disaster—presumably because happy histories would be uneventful ones. The analogy between writing history and charting the course of a disease goes
back to antiquity, together with the idea that the "illnesses" of society
ultimately break out in actual epidemics. As far back as the Bible and
the Greek historians, and as recently as newspaper accounts on AIDS,

the standard version has remained fundamentally unchanged through any number of variations: "A historical actor (the leader, the city, the Christian people, the nation) receives from an outside source (God, foreign lands, the Jews, social deviants) an infection (punishment, test) for which the actor must seek the proper remedy (prayer, science, exile, extermination)."[1] This scenario supplies the sense of an over-arching plot and a definable process, the rhetorical and analytical framing that historians need to make the past intelligible—and this coherence is, or should be, the nagging problem of such accounts. How can anyone presume to do justice either to the immensity or to the immediacy of so much suffering? Or, for that matter, to the numbing capacity of people to resist or to tolerate tremendous losses? The plague is one of the classic subjects of historical writing in part because it forces such fundamental questions and elicits answers in which the purpose and intelligibility of history are at stake.

It is all the more striking, then, that historical epidemics have become a major focus of some of the more self-consciously "new" forms of historical inquiry. Twenty years ago, Bartolome Bennassar outlined a research agenda divided into topics and subtopics and ranging from the medical, demographic, and economic to the social and religious aspects of the "great epidemics" of the Mediterranean world. The latest bibliographies list dozens of studies on these subjects.[2] As a result of these investigations, much more is known about general patterns as well as specific details, and this knowledge has begun to transform some long-standing assumptions. On the graphs of historical demographers and economic historians, which extend over generations and even centuries, recurrent epidemics are likely to appear less the exception than the rule, all the more so when "lesser plagues" are identified in the company of the greater ones or in the intervals between them: sickness rather than health thus becomes the "normal" human condition. This chronic presence of disease suggests that we should not think of medieval and early modern societies as caught in the grip of plague-year panics or as waiting passively to be delivered by modern medicine.[3] The newer accounts speak of "experienced populations," of well-organized institutional responses, of resourceful strategies for survival. Epidemics are in this sense social, not just biological, phenomena. It has been shown, for example, that the model antiplague system of the old regime, with its public health regulations, pesthouses, and so on, was put on a regular footing in Italy only a century *after* the black death and that it was specifically directed against the poor at a time when the urban lower classes were more segregated in their own districts and, in the perceptions of their betters, more threatening. Plague controls, in short, were also social controls, a blueprint for the great absolutist projects of confinement for the sick, the poor, the criminal, and the uprooted. As a social drama the plague was the supreme theater of the old regime, in which the binding ties and the divisive conflicts, the assumptions, rituals, and symbols of the afflicted community, were acted out.[4]

Giulia Calvi pitches her account of the Florentine plague of 1630–31 on the margins of the more recent research—and challenges old and new ways of understanding such an event by experimenting with radical alternatives that bring the shattering experience of a human catastrophe into sharp focus. As the original Italian title suggests more precisely than the English translation, Calvi is concerned with the kaleidoscopic relationship of *storie* ("stories" or "histories"), *comportamenti sociali* ("social behaviors" in the plural), and *l'immaginario* (the "imaginary" or "symbolic"). What emerges from this careful triangulation of perspectives is a world of human choices, feelings, and perceptions that, like the black rats the pre-Pasteur doctors hardly noticed, has never quite been seen before.

Storie, like its equivalent in other languages (the French *histoires* or *Geschichten* in German, for example), can just as well refer to stories or tales, histories in the sense of what happens over time, or the books that historians write. "Histories" is a rather inadequate substitute, but the translators were surely right to keep the plural form in the title of Calvi's book, awkward as it may be in English. Her book is a book of "histories," not only because it is composed of any number of particular cases, but also because it presents history as a tissue of tales that construct, rather than merely report, a complex reality. This format reflects in part the author's choice of sources, the most important of which are the detailed criminal records of the Public Health Magistracy in Florence and the testimony from the canonization proceedings for the Dominican nun Domenica da Paradiso, which were initiated at the height of the epidemic. More than simply rehearsing tales from the archives, however, Calvi distinguishes the plot structures and narrative codes of quite different versions of the same events. The "naturalistic version" of the official chronicles likens the body of the community to the body of a stricken individual, so as to impose a narrative order on impending chaos and to justify the harsh cures of official regulation. The trajectory of these accounts is relatively consistent, somehow even reassuring—or would be except for sudden turns of events, unforeseen circumstances, and furtive connections in which the plague might be found lurking. The history of the plague becomes in this view a story of little intrigues, of cases to be investigated and mysteries to be solved. Then, too, there are the traces of collective imagination and memory, which break into the record to paint the present in the colors of the past and to draw upon the symbolic defenses and practical remedies of earlier times.

Calvi goes on to show how these more or less formal narrative structures are embedded in concrete political and social interests. In other words, the account of forms of discourse about the plague merges into a kind of retrospective ethnography of Florentine behavior. The official set of analogies between physical and social maladies is anything but remote from practical concerns when it justifies a policy of official surveillance and control. Moreover, the official obsession with the pathological generates an almost surreal record of the normal, compiled by bureaucrats intent on tracking the spread of the plague through the mundane encounters of everyday life. So, for example, the long chain of events that—in the eyes of the authorities, at least—linked the chance meeting of an infected poulterer and a thieving acquaintance in the village of Trespiano to certain bales of wool brought by Sisto the wool merchant from Trespiano to Florence, to the deaths of Sisto and his Florentine neighbors, to the infection of an anonymous widow and her four children in the house of Maddalena del Garbo, to del Garbo's own death from the plague. The apparatus of the emergency maps the minute contours of the ordinary social landscape.

Since the poor and the uprooted were especially suspect as carriers of the plague, this mapping operation extended from the depths to the margins of Florentine society. Bennassar doubted twenty years ago whether it would be possible to penetrate to the lowest social levels where "the silence of the texts reigns, logically so since we enter here into the domain of the collective silence of the masses."[5] To break this alleged silence, Calvi began her research by concentrating on the criminal archives of the Florentine Public Health officials. What she found there was a cast of individuals who were alternately cagey, assertive, and obstinate in protecting their interests: hardly an anonymous mass suffering in silence from forces beyond their control. Understanding their testimony means learning how to decipher its codes and reading between the lines. Acts that the official paradigms interpreted as criminal, if not diabolical, violations deserving punishment turn out to have been strategies of survival and self-help for the poor. The authorities imposed their quarantines, and the people of Florence, both men and women, broke them in order to continue working at their trades, to find ways to feed their families and tend the sick, to retrieve their belongings from covetous neighbors and meddling bureaucrats. Most cases of assault or theft investigated by the Public Health officials were committed by relatives and friends of plague victims trying to preserve their rights and property. To avoid the desecration and disgrace of mass burials, doctors, priests, bailiffs, and gravediggers were bribed and threatened, the sick were hidden from the authorities, the dead were laid secretly to rest. Calvi's patient and caring reconstruction of the stories of little people who were determined and resourceful despite the great odds against them is a brilliant tour de force.

Although the "imaginary" comes last in her title and "the universe of symbols" is reserved for the second part of her book, Calvi does not mean to suggest that the symbolic dimension of her "histories" belongs to a separate realm, least of all that it is a "superstructure" to some more material "base." Here again she follows the lead of the archives, in this case the Vatican records of the proceedings for the canonization of Domenica Nardini da Paradiso (d. 1553), founder of the Dominican convent of Santa Croce in the plain of Ripoli a few miles from Florence. Hearings began at the height of the epidemic in November 1630 and, as Calvi shows, were practically inseparable from the Florentine response to the crisis. The proceedings were, in the first place, a kind of political theater—to use the organizing metaphor that Calvi draws as much from her sources as from her reading in cultural anthropology. The drama of votive masses, of the exhumed body and relics, of the parade of distinguished witnesses, was an offering from the Medici court to the community, a deliberate attempt to proclaim the legitimacy of the embattled regime through an appeal to "its" plague saint, who had been at once popular, Medicean, and renowned as a saintly administrator during an epidemic two generations earlier.

The political gesture, however, soon takes on the aura of a utopian vision, in which the radiant sanctity of the holy woman, her body reputedly unsullied by death, illuminates a dark world of disfiguring disease and death, together with their metaphorical extension, moral and spiritual corruption. The official testimony tells of her own suffering from the plague and of how she recovered by trusting to prayer and to the simple ministrations of the sisters in the convent. Spurning the doctors, she protected her people even as the plague raged within her body and throughout the city at large. The court, clerics, patricians, doctors, notaries, and artists swear that her relics and her remedies had performed miracles in the past and continued to bring relief to her devotees in the present. Thus, while Domenica da Paradiso herself embodies the virtues claimed by the Medici regime—sanctity, healing power, and good government—the retelling of her story reveals the outlook of people at a higher social level than those who fell afoul of the Public Health officials. The saint of the court is also the saint of a privileged transgression of the health ordinances, a transgression that leads in the case of the upper classes not to arrest and punishment but to the signs of divine favor to which the elite no doubt felt entitled.

Giulia Calvi's book invites reading from perspectives as diverse as the shifting patterns of narrative, action, and symbolism that run through it. Readers interested in Florence will see the city in the garish sunset of what Eric Cochrane called "the forgotten centuries" after the fall of the Florentine republic in 1530; those who know their Florentine history and Florentine historians may compare the views from below in the criminal archives and from above in the testimony on Domenica da Paradiso with Carlo M. Cipolla's studies of the demographic and administrative aspects of the same epidemic.[6] As a portrait of a baroque world, the book is charged with the high and low dramas, the glaring contrasts, the fantastic juxtapositions of setting, scale, and sensibility of the age of the baroque. As an analysis of the impact of the plague, Calvi's work opens up registers of historical experience that have hardly been explored in so many dimensions and in such vivid detail. But whatever its bearing on any particular topic, this book should also be read as an unsettling challenge to the conventional scenarios and distancing formulas of most historical writing on the all too human encounters with catastrophe in the past. In this larger sense, Calvi makes her own contribution to a major reassessment of aims and methods that has gained momentum in various fields of historical inquiry in recent years.

I do not want to exaggerate the consistency of the latest moves along a broad and irregular front. Whether one is inclined to welcome the creative ferment or lament the passing of some imagined scholarly consensus, the boundaries of historical study are in some disarray— not for the first time, of course. Even so, shared claims are being staked out by an otherwise diverse group that includes "historical anthropologists," some of the more innovative social and cultural historians, and the so-called new historicists in literary studies. The perspective of these scholars is interdisciplinary, not simply because they cross disciplinary lines freely, but also because they often focus on phenomena that are themselves polyvalent—so, for example, representations of the human body, public rituals, judicial records, patterns of communication in speech, writing, and images, and practices of everyday life, from eating and drinking to fashions in manners and dress. For all the differences in method, there are fairly consistent preferences for detailed description over abstract analysis, for interpretation in terms of a given society's norms and values over explanation in terms of causal "trends" or "factors" that contemporaries would hardly have recognized, and for a dynamic understanding of culture as an arena of conflicting constructions of reality over hierarchical distinctions between "high" and "low" culture. Taken together, these interpretive strategies point toward a methodological pluralism based on the conviction that there is no single, objective truth to history, or at least no truth that lies outside interpretation both by those who live through it and by those who come to write about it. The ambiguity of this view can be seen in the literature: some critics worry that the interdisciplinary approach is too obsessed with the historical limits of "great works" of literature and art, while others fear that it is not historical enough because it denies the ontological status of history. The fact remains that these views here are producing some of the most stimulating historical work being done these days, not least of all by Italian historians.[7]

Calvi is a member of the advisory committee and a regular contributor to the pages of *Quaderni storici,* and her work grows out of the community of interests that has made this journal the most vital forum of historical research and debate in Italy since its founding in

1966. Committed to social and cultural history with strong interdisciplinary ties to anthropology and semiotics, open to controversy and experiment, receptive to the work of younger historians marginalized in the hierarchical and highly politicized Italian academic world, the journal combines lively discussion of methodological questions with highly specific, close-grained archival studies. This concern for large issues on a small scale has become virtually—if not exclusively—programmatic in the form of "microhistory," which is best known outside Italy through the work of Carlo Ginzburg, an editor of *Quaderni storici,* but was first elaborated as a research agenda by Ginzburg's co-editor Edoardo Grendi. Microhistory takes as its unit of study the single incident, life, or artifact. Its preferred sources are the archival dossier, its distinctive subjects the marginal figures or cases that historians would ordinarily regard as insignificant; its methods are eclectic, critical, and theoretically informed.

Although these commitments may not seem especially radical, they point up by contrast the more traditional preoccupation of historians with the *grande histoire* of nations, elites, and abstract ideas in which phantasmic entities such as the State, Society, and Culture take on lives of their own. At the same time, microhistory is explicitly a critique of the modern forms of structuralism imported into history from the social sciences, particularly from economics, sociology, and structural anthropology; more precisely, it is a "poststructuralist" critique which accepts the proposition that history is acted out within the constraints of long-term structures of practice and perception, while insisting on the multiple dimensions of historical experience and the capacity of human beings for creative choices. Finally, microhistory represents, for some of its practitioners at least, a self-conscious Italian rebellion against the French school of historians associated with the influential historical journal *Annales.* In professional jargon, it heralds a return to the "third level" of human actors and historical events, which the "second generation" of *Annales* historians dismissed, in the words of Fernand Braudel, as "mere disturbances, crests of foam that the tides of history carry on their strong backs."[8]

Full agreement can hardly be expected or desired from historians who emphasize diversity and individual choice. In a recent issue of *Quaderni storici* Calvi was taken to task for leaving her premises mostly implicit and for resisting categorical distinctions between structure and event, analysis and narrative, and social "reality" and the symbolic elaboration of social interests—in short, for practicing what the journal has often preached. Calvi responded with a pointed critique of the persistent failure of historians of the plague to break out of arbitrary categories and a moving account of her debts to the historians and social theorists who helped her to see the stubbornly creative opposition of human beings to forces that would determine their fate.[9] Whether or not she has made her case, readers of this book may decide for themselves. What they will surely find here are not litanies of death, but histories of life precariously poised—as human existence always seems to be—between the powers of necessity and the resources of free will.

NOTES

1. See Jean-Pierre Peter and Jacques Revel, "Le corps: L'homme malade et son histoire," in *Faire de l'histoire: Nouveaux objets,* ed. Jacques Le Goff and Pierre Nora (Paris, 1974), 3:170.

2. Cf. Bartolome Bennassar, *Recherches sur les grandes épidémies dans le Nord de l'Espagne à la fin du XVIe siècle* (Paris, 1969); and the bibliographical essay by Ann G. Carmichael, *Plague and the Poor in Renaissance Florence* (Cambridge, Mass., 1986), pp. 166–75.

3. See esp. William H. McNeill, *Plagues and Peoples* (New York, 1976), pp. 180–215.

4. Jean-Noël Biraben, *Les hommes et la peste en France et dans les pays européens et méditerranéens,* 2 vols. (Paris, 1975–76), devotes the second volume of his massive synthesis to these themes. For plague ordinances as social controls in the Italian case, see Carmichael, *Plague and the Poor,* pp. 108–26; and John A. Henderson, "Epidemie nella Firenze del Rinascimento: Teoria sanitaria e provvedimenti governativi," in *Sanità e società,* ed. A. Pastore (Udine, 1987), pp. 39–64.

5. Bennassar, *Recherches,* p. 44.

6. Eric Cochrane, *Florence in the Forgotten Centuries, 1527–1800* (Chicago, 1973). Carlo M. Cipolla's important studies on the plague include *Cristofano and the Plague* (Berkeley and Los Angeles, 1973); *Faith, Reason, and the Plague in Seventeenth-Century Tuscany,* trans. Muriel Kittel (Ithaca, N.Y., 1979); and *Fighting the Plague in Seventeenth-Century Italy* (Madison, Wis., 1981).

7. See, for example, Peter Burke, *The Historical Anthropology of Early Modern Italy: Essays in Perception and Communication* (Cambridge, 1987); *The New Cultural History,* ed. Lynn Hunt (Berkeley, 1989); and Jean E. Howard, "The New Historicism in Renaissance Studies," *English Literary Renaissance* 16 (1986): 13–43.

8. Fernand Braudel, *The Mediterranean and the Mediterranean World in the Age of Philip II,* trans. Sian Reynolds (New York, 1972), 1:21. On *Quaderni*

storici and "microhistory," see the full bibliography and excellent analysis by Edward Muir, "'The Observation of Trifles': Microhistory as Detection and Ethnography," in *Microhistory: Essays from Quaderni Storici,* ed. Edward Muir and Guido Ruggiero (Baltimore, forthcoming).

9. Edoardo Grendi, "Storia sociale e storia interpretativa," *Quaderni storici* 21, no. 1 (1986): 201–10; Giulia Calvi, "A proposito di *Storie di un anno di peste,*" *Quaderni storici* 21, no. 3 (1986): 1009–18.

Preface

I intended that this book be a comparative study of three great episodes of urban crisis in the baroque age: the plagues of Milan, Florence, and Naples. The vastness and the originality of the Florentine sources that, despite their fragmented nature, slowly grew in my hands finally convinced me to orient my work in another direction.

I am grateful to many friends who followed this book through its stages by reading part or all of the manuscript: Sergio Bertelli, Alberto Caracciolo, Paola Di Cori, Anna Foa, Paolo Preto, Adriano Prosperi, Lucetta Scaraffia, and Anna Scattigno. I especially want to thank Romeo De Maio for his insistence on the importance of using the canonization hearings as a primary source for social history. This material led me to uncover the story of Domenica da Paradiso.

Introduction:
The Florentine Plague of 1630–1633

Compared to the great plagues of baroque Italy, the Florentine pestilence of 1630–33 followed a quiet course. It arouses our interest more from its silences, its absences, and its grey tones, than from the choreographic spectacle of the contemporary epidemics of 1656 in Milan or Naples. There were neither riots nor killings of reputed plague spreaders, nor were there moments of collective panic or revolt; even the mortality rate was not particularly high. In contrast to the decimation that took place in the plague-stricken cities of the Po valley, the ten thousand deaths during the peak periods of the Florentine epidemic—which first struck in summer 1630, then slacked off in early 1631, and thereafter reappeared briefly in the spring of 1633—seemed to contemporaries almost a "blessing."[1]

Naturally, all of the apparatus that invariably accompanied epidemics appeared: the Public Health Magistracy, the hierarchy of functionaries created ad hoc, the lazarets, the mass graves, the barred doors, the quarantine. The defensive and offensive tools used by the state to reorganize urban space and the minute grammar of social life created a theatrical setting identical to that of the other baroque plagues. If the background is similar, however, the scene represented here is different.

Grand Duke Ferdinand II ordered his librarian, Francesco Rondinelli, to compile an official record of the epidemic.[2] This account serves as the principal source for investigating the structures and mechanisms of the political authorities and the public health administration, the mood of the court, the accomplishments of religious orders in their ministrations to the ill, and the conflict between physicians and magistrates. Like many memoirs written during times of plague, the text can be read in fixed sequences following the movement of a double curve: from a peak of good health to a precipitous decline marked by disease and death to the return of good health. The body of the city supposedly followed the same parabola of physiological decline and renewal experienced by the bodies of those who survived. The emphasis throughout is on cyclical and natural processes. Just as the disease appeared at regular intervals, so too was the opposite route toward health repeated. Imposing a naturalistic reading upon events, the official script assimilated the course of the city's history to that of the inevitable trajectory of the illness. Within the descending and ascending curves of epidemic and recovery, the text offers a series of interlocking motifs: the arrival of the pestilence in the city; the conflicting efforts to cover it up; the slow establishment of a regimen of separation between the healthy, the suspect, and the diseased, culminating in a dictatorship of the Public Health Magistracy; and the street processions upon the arrival of the image of the Madonna of Impruneta. In official memory the forms of social reorganization mobilized to counter the threat to the city are as inevitable and natural as the course of the contagion itself.

Within this official path, however, there is also a minor register, a long chain of minute details. In Rondinelli's pages, the outbreak of the contagion coincides with the cataloguing of long sequences of behavior believed to be the cause of the epidemic. Its development runs like a rigmarole, attentive to a rapid and arbitrary evolution of relationships between characters. Thus, the official view of the epidemic was accompanied by a symptomatic reading of daily life which attempted to recapture events in the city, the streets, and the homes of common people. The etiology that links the disease to an invasion of Milanese mercenaries and to the war of succession over Mantua parallels the story of a poor infected poulterer who came down from the Bolognese in early August and, exhausted, entered Florence. At the San Gallo Gate, he, "very weak, painfully putting one foot ahead of the other, and lackluster eyes lowered," met Viviano, an acquaintance from Trespiano. The latter, "torn between pity . . . and the danger to which he might expose himself, stood still, uncertain what to do. Just as concern for his own life was overcoming his sympathy, . . . the blinding shine of some gold coins made him begin to lose sight of that danger, and he surrendered to the growing desire for wealth."[3]

Viviano's greed was punished by the death of his entire family. The chain continues, and the thread broken by the death of the poulterer and his acquaintance is joined again in a different social milieu. A widow with four children lived in a "large old house" along the road linking Trespiano and Florence. On 6 August, Grand Duchess Christine of Lorraine celebrated her birthday by "dispensing alms to poor widows." The widow bought a bushel of flour with her portion. "Having made a mush of it, she and her children ate their fill"; but shortly afterwards they all seemed to lose their minds. By the following day, they were dead. Both Signora Maddalena del Garbo and her servant died in the same house.

How had the plague (for that was the cause of these sudden deaths) traveled so far? Coincidence keeps unraveling the account: "On the corner near the square" a certain draper, Sisto, who had bought some bales of wool in Trespiano also died; so did his weavers. A window in Sisto's shop faced the courtyard where the widow and her four children had entered and left the building.[4]

The poulterer Viviano's greed, Sisto the draper, the bales of wool, the window, and the widow and her four children: it is a rigmarole that killed.

The underlying logic of these chains of contingency lies in the linkage of environment and disease. In the chronicle, the incidence—or coincidence—of the details of daily life was considered responsible for the spread of the disease. The cause of so many deaths was embedded in a highly personalized scenario, where any sign—the shuffling step of the poulterer, the uncertain oscillations of a body through the gate, the courtyard dividing the draper from the widow, the shop's window—could be discerned. These were the indicators of everyday life, the passages where people communicated, met, spoke, worked, and ate. The plague hid there among chickens and bales of wool. Such an abundance of details, meticulous descriptions, and the reconstitution of domestic scenes all recall the fixed luminosity of contemporary still lifes and link the written and the spoken word, things seen and things heard. Francesco Rondinelli gathered information from the registers of the Public Health Magistracy, but he also went down into the streets of Florence to listen to the voices, rumors, and chatter of the survivors. "When one can see a chain, such as the one we have just recounted, of ten people whom we know to be related," he comments, "one can be justifiably suspicious."[5]

Narrative chains and punctilious cataloguing seem to me the best means of conveying the way the epidemic was considered, imagined, and feared by those who found themselves in its midst. The apparent nonsense of events obscures a secret code that can be uncovered in the density of the social fabric. If the contagion was spread by those who behaved normally, one had to investigate this behavior; the attention of the Magistracy was absorbed in reading the social world. To host a relative who had traveled through dangerous territories, to buy infected wool in Trespiano, and to glance into a courtyard opened a chain of death among neighbors and relatives: even a minor detour might prime unpredictable spirals. The usual forms of communication were transformed into symptoms of a lethal diffusion in which the pattern of the spread of disease converged with the network of social exchange.

The printed chronicle interrupts the narrative chain at the moment when it begins to involve an important person. The chain culminates in a sudden flash and then becomes silent; but by illuminating the last link, it makes an entire sequence of events and cast of characters visible. Let us follow such a narrative for a moment in a specific case.

At 3 Via de' Calderari, the bricklayer Antonio, Francesco Giannelli's son, emptied the well of the Poverine nuns. "Because of his fatigue and a stench, he was suddenly overcome with pain and discovered somewhat later a nut-sized bubo between his thigh and trunk." Doctor Lorenzi visited him and granted permission for the farm laborers of the house to circulate freely, both inside and outside the dwelling. On 2 February Antonio's sister-in-law, Caterina, died, and seven days later he lost his father, two brothers, and six of their farm laborers. Just when Antonio was himself bedridden, probably with the plague, a servant "of the Signor Ambassador of the Most Serene Lord of Modena" bought a pair of old sleeves from a second-hand dealer who, coincidentally, turned out to be one of Antonio's tenants. The servant then infected his master's family. Carlo, the ambassador's son, died first, soon followed by Madonna Leonora and Livio, Carlo's brother. Don Tranquilo Cerpelli, vicar of the Monastery of San Michele Bisdomini, ordered the neighborhood parish "to bury the dead in the cemetery of Santa Maria Nuova."[6]

The disease in the ambassador's family brings the narrative chain to a close. In order to reconnect the threads that link the top of the social scale to the bottom (the bricklayer Antonio recovered!), it is necessary to follow the path of the narrative backward, descending the social hierarchy step by step and tracing those links and exchanges that hid the disease.

The narratives interrupted in the printed chronicle can be reconstructed from the criminal trials recorded in the archives of the Public Health officials. The proceedings typically include denunciations, interrogations of witnesses and defendants, sentences passed in the vast majority of cases, appeals by the convicted, and judgments subsequently revised, which sometimes led to pardons granted by the grand duke. A few days generally passed between the trial and the promulgation of the sentence. The extraordinary rapidity and efficiency with which these procedures were carried out was due to the emergency powers granted to a special Public Health Magistracy, which co-opted criminal jurisdiction during epidemic outbreaks.

Fulvio Giubetti, chancellor of the Florentine Public Health Magistracy at the outbreak of the epidemic, explained in a small volume his jurisdiction throughout the whole territory as follows:

> to commence and prepare trials against those who either commit fraud in the realm of public health or disobey regulations; to make necessary proposals to the Magistracy when accompanied by solid evidence and reason; to refer matters to the prince that only he can ultimately resolve, to write the resolutions and reports of the Magistracy to local officials and foreign correspondents, clearly on paper so as to maintain the dignity and the decorum of the Magistracy.[7]

I have examined more than three hundred trials, including those leaving only fragmentary interrogations or denunciations in the record. It is a vast collection so far as the characters and witnesses who belonged to the popular classes are concerned. Having been caught breaking Public Health regulations, artisans, workers, women employed in the silk and wool industries, unskilled hospital laborers (not including physicians), cobblers, coachmen, printers, grocers, herbalists, servants, surgeons, and traveling salesmen talked in their interrogations about themselves, their families, and their work.

The trial reports trace paths of perception different from those of the chronicle. Here the epidemic acts as a social indicator, a filter through which specific groups, behavior, times, and places are made transparent. In the words of those under investigation, the emergency underlines and brings to light the various stages of daily life, patterns of community, and rhythms of work. During the virtual dictatorship of the Public Health officials, habitual routines became infractions of numerous regulations, motivated by the fear of contagion and designed to interrupt and block the common channels of communication.

A familiar step outdoors or movement through a passage or courtyard constituted, in and of itself, a crime. A room locked to prevent contagion prevented the circulation of affection and household goods. The Public Health officials would examine, confiscate, and most likely burn the objects belonging to the person who lived there. For the neighbors, family members, apprentices, and shop masters wanting to preserve their belongings, that nailed door became the target of infractions. They hoped to redistribute those goods according to their own rights and priorities and to activate those familiar circuits of exchange between the living and the dead which, through the rituals of mourning, diminished the terrifying unknown of disease and death.

Everyday life was therefore acted out, as the official chronicler of the plague had immediately grasped, as a kind of intrigue. Almost all of the defendants used the weapons of pressure, insult, vulgar and vivacious familiarity, and denunciation of superiors.[8] The preoccupation of defendants and witnesses with goods, the shop, and anything that remained of normal existence broke through official restraints. The future counted more than the present, and the official edicts were circumvented to preserve whatever could be hidden and accumulated for better times. Therefore, the trials deconstruct the temporal axis of the official version of the plague. The dense collection of testimonies around the event ultimately dissolves in a network of parallel stories. Listening to the words of those who came to testify, the plague fades away (or, at a minimum, its prime role in official chronicles tends to vanish) and we are caught up in the systematic play of characters and values set in motion by the interrogations. In the witness's memory, for example, the story of a blacksmith's knife is what conveys the drama of disease and death.

I have grouped the trials according to the crimes indicated by the denunciations and charges. They consist of violations against property (thefts or the transport and relocation of household items from infected houses); crimes committed by Public Health workers (abuse of power, corruption, theft, fistfights, or rapes); and unlawful hiding of the stricken or dead. Each of these three categories was tightened by emergency measures designed to protect the city. Action took place in the houses and streets of the popular quarters of Florence, those that were then called "the extremities": the quarters of Santa Croce and Prato, the streets of San Zenobi and Tedesca, the neighborhood behind the Basilica of San Lorenzo, and two quarters across the

Arno River, San Niccolò and Santo Spirito. While examining the large collection of documents in the Public Health Archive, I decided to confine my research to the city, passing over the papers concerning the comparatively minor centers in the countryside and the Florentine hinterland. Before permanently shutting the doors of research, however, I peered beyond the urban walls to gather documents that preceded and thereby announced the epidemic.

I refer specifically to the trials of ten travelers who were detained at roadblocks along the main arteries from the north. Guards monitored the movements of visitors from Milanese territory, not only at the gates of the city of Florence itself, but also at the numerous police barricades set up on the main routes between the Po valley and Tuscany. The Po valley was the epicenter from which the plague radiated. Mercenaries from the war of Mantua and Montferrat, who climbed the steep paths of the Apennines and descended its passes, carried the disease and certainly transmitted the contagion. These travel reports moved the plane of the narrative backward, far from Florence. Originating in distant lands, they lead us to different contexts, including the Italian arena of the Thirty Years' War.

Three reports in particular involved deserters from the army of the grand duke of Tuscany, which was then engaged in combat in Casale and the Genoese Alps. These reports provide precise biographical details of the deserters, described by the authorities as having "the bad appearance of soldiers." The soldiers obstinately insisted on discussing the war rather than talking about the plague. For enlisted men, the physical discomforts of the battleground and hatred of their superiors, combined with low salaries and unsavory food, were much more interesting than the plague. These trials of travelers constitute a framework for understanding the epidemic; they link the chronicle of this particular city to the general history of Europe through the testimony of obscure characters mediated by private anxieties, domestic affections, and a sense of adventure, an unusual link between the history of relatively unimportant people and that of great men. These testimonies follow an oscillating rhythm from private to public vicissitudes. Thus, the soldier Michele di Paolo crossed the Genoese Alps and the entire war zone in order to rejoin his evicted wife and son. Similarly, the Roman deserter Giuseppe Gallo fled from the encampment of Cassano because he loathed Captain Stinca, a Neapolitan who gambled with his soldiers' salaries.[9] When an official chronicle high-

lights mortality or fighting armies, these testimonies bind the narrative sequence to a viscous net of minute imperatives.

The relationship between these elements varies greatly in propor-
tion and significance. What the magistrates defined as criminal behavior, the protagonists saw as a coagulation of actions, interests, beliefs,
and strategies of survival. In this sense, the trials conducted by the
Public Health authorities introduce us to a mental universe orienting
the crimes, explaining their configuration, and delineating a horizon
of social adaptation in this period of epidemic emergency. Reactions,
whether concerned with property, hiding sick people, a night of passion, or a perilous return from the battlefield, encompassed a combination of biological and cultural resources mobilized against the
spread of disease.[10] The manner in which a human group reacts to
disease and death is an indicator of the cultural values shared by that
entire community, since both good health and sickness are rooted in
the fundamental elements of the reproduction, quality, and preservation of life. Infractions against Public Health laws therefore expose a
social ecology in which conflicts with juridical ordinances were at-
tempts at self-expression.

It is immediately evident that the social life of common people was
especially affected and that official documents blamed these people
above all for the outbreak of the epidemic. Otherwise, how can we
explain the great quantity of criminal trials which deal exclusively
with the lower orders? The presence of these social strata in the records of the Public Health Magistracy suggests ipso facto a causal
reading, a particular etiology within which trials were inscribed and
understood. In contrast, when the plague hit the upper levels of society we hear little of the living conditions of commoners, that is, of
crowding, malnutrition, and stench.

In the specific case of Florence, however, environmental causes
were particularly accentuated. Even when those working and living in
alleyways were not charged with potentially subversive activities, they
were brought to the attention of the grand duke and listed among
those who were to receive a mattress stamped by the Public Health
Magistracy and whose courtyards were to be cleaned.[11] In this sense
the Florentine plague was atypical, because it did not provoke the conspiracy theories that, in Milan and Naples, translated the plague into
a frontal opposition of social classes and then personalized the etiology
of the disease.[12] The absence of an analogous political codification of

social relations explains in part the persistence of a state of never-ending social brinkmanship within the lower orders of Florentine society. In addition to the arrests carried out by corporals and security forces, the judicial machinery was also activated by an interplay between acquaintances and neighbors. Denunciations moved horizontally rather than vertically. Thus, these trials belong to a semantic process of bargaining and, consequently, of social exchange. On the one hand, emergency legislation claimed to establish new regulations governing social relations; on the other hand, infractions were oriented by preexisting social relationships and values.

During periods of epidemic and accelerated collective mortality, the actions, memories, hopes, and anxieties of the community center on the bodies of the living, the sick, and the dead. What Victor Turner calls a "community of the suffering" forms in the liminal situation produced by the disease. The vulnerable human group redefines its own internal structures and amplifies them to include all those who have been subjected to the passage of disease. Thus redefined, the community encompasses the living and the dead, the professional, amateur, and mythical healers.[13] Memory and hope alternate in the experience of individual and collective time and act as dynamic motives in the social world of the stricken community.[14] Memory and hope, therefore, are deeply entrenched in the individual "crimes" registered in the archives of the Public Health Magistracy. Let us look at some examples.

Crimes against property constitute one of the largest categories in the archival record. They comprise various behaviors, ranging from relocating household items to pilfering objects from quarantined houses and stealing the clothes of the dead. The trials involve different social groups. The first, and by far the largest, includes family members, neighbors, and co-workers of the deceased who are charged with the clandestine removal of furniture and objects falling into the sphere of family, neighborhood, and work. Far from appearing as mere expressions of hostility, these crimes signify the desire to preserve and guarantee the safekeeping of the material possessions within a definable horizon of daily habits and proximity. These goods, no matter how insignificant, were taken away to be spared the destructive disinfections carried out by the authorities; they were subsequently redistributed according to precise priorities and rights. Even in the absence of a will, whoever stole household items from a relative's estate claimed legitimacy for his or her action. The young baker Salvatore Tortorelli, for example, was charged with the theft of some jewels from his brother-in-law's house. He was accused of having covertly entered the house with his younger sister, Caterina. Swinging from a rope in the torture chamber, he exclaimed, "All these things belong to us!"[15]

To say that relocations and thefts took place only in the houses of family members is, however, too simple. The baker Salvatore, for instance, focused on a more exact strategy. Among family members, the horizontal relationship between brothers-in-law was more important when it emerged in conjunction with the death of a father and a sister (the wife of one of the two men). The hostility of brothers toward their relatives by marriage, especially over the rights of a deceased wife's dowry, interrupted the compact transmission of their father's inheritance. Brothers often broke into the house of their (in this case, presumably childless) widowed brother-in-law, in an attempt to exclude their brother-in-law from the redistribution of what by right belonged to the original nuclear family and to prevent him from claiming his right over the dowry.[16]

Membership in the same guild led to other violations of the Public Health regulations. Ludovico Puccetti, a silk weaver, was appointed custodian and head administrator of the lazaret of San Miniato and assigned the task of overseeing the disinfecting of fabrics. Although he gave some unfumigated bales of silk to his fellow workers to keep them working, he himself refused to weave the silk.[17] In another example, Paolo Varnesi, a tailor, was arrested for having forcibly entered the shop of the deceased Bartolomeo. Paolo, to help the family of his friend and fellow guild member, wanted to inventory Bartolomeo's goods and preserve them from indiscriminate requisitioning by the authorities.[18] In a similar case, the blacksmith Niccolò Vannozzi, worrying about his own shop, managed to obtain three hundred pounds of iron from the officials of the lazaret of Bagno a Ripoli.[19] The crimes of the silk weaver Ludovico, the tailor Paolo, and the blacksmith Niccolò trace a path linking their work to members of their respective guilds, their families, and their shops. These priorities bent the apparatus of the epidemiological emergency to the opportunities offered by the plague for safeguarding the personal and the private.

At the same time, there are many examples that testify to a widespread ability and willingness to incorporate the imperatives of healthier periods into the new tasks that the epidemic imposed on everyone. Whoever managed to save themselves—in other words, whoever managed to get well—first inventoried material losses and then denounced wrongdoers, pointing the finger at those reputed to be responsible. Inventories and denunciations were the countersigns on which the desire for the return to normalcy was engraved.

Such activity suggests that common people believed the administration of justice could be activated from below. It also highlights their confidence in the upper echelons of the Magistracy—although certainly not in either the pages or the manservants temporarily wearing official uniforms. Thus, the neighbors of Angelica, who had recently been hospitalized, directly contacted the magistrate of Public Health to obtain permission to dry clothes she had left out in water. The magistrate responded by sending two pages to take the clothes out of the water. Several neighbors kept an eye on the pages and became suspicious when they stayed in Angelica's rooms for an inordinate amount of time. They reported their suspicions to Angelica, and she denounced the pages as soon as she recovered.[20] This case clearly demonstrates a series of evaluations establishing relative rank and competence. How could one fail to realize that a page commissioned to quarantine houses, a sulphur miner, or a gravedigger who had only recently donned the uniform of the Public Health Magistracy and traded clothes like everyone else would immediately try to make some money? It was probably because of these considerations that Angelica's neighbors entrusted her clothes to Public Health personnel while nevertheless watching over her rooms to protect them from the pages' rapacious zeal.

But even opinions about these servants of the Public Health Magistracy varied according to circumstances. A denunciation was merely the last act of a long bargaining process that involved haggling, applying pressure, and exchanging favors. There was, for example, an element of complicity in the relationship between the survivors and the gravediggers. Until the black death of 1348, the physicians' and herbalists' guild, to which gravediggers belonged, sanctioned the recompense of the removal of the dead with a gift of the deceased's clothes made on behalf of the family members.[21] A successive revision of the articles concerning removal and burial of the dead demonstrated the survival of this tradition, which the guild consuls deprecated and attempted in vain to eliminate by proposing various countermeasures.

Despite periods of epidemic, the relationship between family members and gravediggers remained imbued with complicity for centuries, and the gift of clothes continued to legitimize this bond. Thus, what the Magistracy punished as theft appeared to the defendant as a prerogative. The traditions affecting the strategies of family members, including brothers-in-law, founded in the statutes of the guild, erected an obtrusive barrier to public health legislation.

Therefore, a complicated universe of property, most notably involving the covert relocation of goods and clothes, characterized community relations and dictated the modification in the network of social communication produced by disease, hospitalization, and death. It is not coincidental that the only death sentence was the one passed on Andrea Passignani, an unemployed youth who confessed to the crime of looting. Because of the viscous connections between neighbors and family members, as well as the intrigue of complicity and bargaining, Andrea stands out as a desolately modern character who had broken all ties with his native land. He moved fleetingly among those who died, opening doors closed by Public Health officers with his switchblade. A little money here, some iron there, he stole indiscriminately, selling the goods in the ghetto where he was finally arrested. Unlike those who helped their friends circumvent the police measures promulgated by the Public Health Magistracy, Andrea stole only for money, and for this reason he was punished.[22] It is a unique case, different from those crimes committed against property which delineated a convergence between memory and hope.

Another substantial group of crimes involves efforts to hide diseased bodies from the Public Health authorities. Once the sickness hit a member of an artisanal or shopkeeping family, the family unit would divide into two parts to circumvent edicts more easily. On the one side, the father and other adult males would leave the house covertly. Moving into their shop, they would begin a purposeful cohabitation to continue production and trade, aided by their neighbors and co-workers. Typically, the comings and goings of a father or brother to check on the ill family member were what aroused the authorities' suspicions. Sometimes shop owners would help young apprentices who had been struck by the deadly disease, bringing them medicine and food and abandoning them only at death. In these cases a neighbor generally lodged a complaint with the authorities because the stench emanating from the closed room had become unbearable. The charge pressed in these cases ("to work despite the contagion") was anchored in the sociality of the shop and the street, which not even the disease or death of a family member could interrupt.

In the few cases involving members of important guilds or court functionaries, the attempt to hide the disease or death of a relative was brought to light by a certificate signed by the neighborhood surgeon. When the doctor guaranteed the "nonsuspect" nature of the illness, the magistrate's suspicions were aroused. Anybody hoping for a church burial needed a signed certificate. To begin the process, the surgeon would pass the certificate to the parish priest (or his deputy) for permission to bury the body in consecrated land. Some trials began with investigations of corrupted surgeons or unclear transit bills and of certificates linking the hiding of the body to its honorable burial.

During the plague, dead bodies were perceived as degrading, a conviction borne out by the barbaric mass graves in which thousands of anonymous bodies were layered and by the weak fences that barely kept the hungry stray dogs at bay. The texts highlight the acute sense of perplexity and the loss of civic respect that these precautions provoked among the people. Most likely, having enough money to corrupt a surgeon could in and of itself have signaled the difference between those who were able to maintain their family's honor and those who could not afford to circumvent the regulations demanded by the emergency. The will of Orazio Vanni, a goldsmith on the Ponte Vecchio, demonstrates the link between substantial wealth, and consequently social status, and the acknowledgment of status after death. It took many years of work before Orazio was finally able to buy a family plot in Santa Maria Novella, "in front of the Ricasoli family chapel." This purchase epitomized the Vanni family's social climbing and signified the clearly defined and now-successful identity of a family group and its shop.[23]

Individual and collective strategies aimed at providing a dignified death subverted institutional mechanisms. To the grand duke's functionaries and the members of the most important guilds, the bodies of relatives symbolized membership; what could be seen on a grave or under a tombstone found its place in a precise genealogical memory. In the testimonies of ordinary people, in contrast, defendants admitted that their dead had been secretly buried in some unknown location. Occasionally a co-worker or relative would lovingly assist the ill, thereby challenging the edicts. After death, the body would be transported by night and abandoned on a street or on some pallet, and nobody would worry about burying the body. Here, transgression was defined as the timely separation from the family nucleus and the subsequent continuation of work in the shop on the part of the adult males. Common people, as Boccaccio noted, neither owned family plots nor enjoyed elaborate burials; rather, they were primarily concerned with life and the physical body, which, even fatigued, must earn bread for all. What mattered most was vigor, the ability to withstand the exhaustion of loom, lathe, and scalpel.[24]

At the peak of the epidemic, in November 1630, the canonization hearings concerning Domenica da Paradiso, a Dominican tertiary nun and founder of the Convent of Santa Croce, began. The discovery of the canonization documents was an unexpected and welcome surprise in the course of my work. No chronicle, diary, or official document mentions Domenica or her role as mythical thaumaturge during the plague. Her significance was obscured by the holy image of the Madonna of Impruneta, which was carried in a procession to Florence, as it always was during calamities.[25] Among the papers gathered in the Negozi collection of the Public Health Archive, one document in particular captured my attention. It was a request by the nuns of the Crocetta Convent to testify at the hearings for the canonization of their founder, the Reverend Mother Suor Domenica. In addition, there were documents of a procedural nature, such as those indicating that the pope had granted the "letters of remission." Others explained how Father Ascanio dell'Ascensione, a mendicant Augustinian, had been "appointed procurator of the hearings in Florence." Father Ascanio went to Rome in person to receive the letters from the pope. He then began an exhausting journey back to Florence. The nuns outlined the various stages of his journey and the difficulties he faced at the checkpoints along the way. Guards stationed at these checkpoints stopped the priest to ensure that he "had never been suspected of carrying the infection," as he had left Florence during the previous Lent. When he was detained in Siena, the sisters and "the Most Serene Mother, very concerned about the beatification," implored the magistrates to grant Father Ascanio permission to continue his journey. Grand Duke Ferdinand II approved their request.[26]

This journey differed greatly from the clandestine itineraries of escape by other defendants. Even Grand Duchess Christine of Lorraine followed Father Ascanio's progress with apprehension. Intrigued by the attention that this trip received, I tried to verify the outcome of the nuns' request. Consulting the inventory of the canonization hearings of the Holy Congregation of the Rituals at the Vatican Archive, I discovered in series 776 the procedural acts concerning Domenica da Paradiso, initiated at the peak of the Florentine plague of 1630. A new phase of my research began.

Domenica Nardini was born at the end of the fifteenth century in Paradiso, a town in the plain of Ripoli. She was a peasant who had migrated from the countryside to Florence, where she found employment as a domestic servant.[27] Propelled by strong mystical and prophetic inclinations, she and a few faithful friends founded the Convent of Crocetta (as it was commonly known) in 1513. As vicar for life, Domenica directed this female community with prudence and attention through years of intense political crises, calamities, and wars. She became such a model of political and administrative ability that Grand Duchess Christine of Lorraine, regent of Tuscany, tried to follow her example.

After all, the sacred Medicean government of Florence had been founded in the city's glorious past; indeed, the testimonies of government officials and members of the court all revolved around this metaphor. The convent Domenica ran with unfailing consistency was analogous to the political state in the hands of the reigning family. Just as her administrative capabilities compared to the governance of the young Grand Duke Ferdinand II, so was Domenica's prompt intervention, which rescued Florence from the political fractures caused by the siege of 1530, likened to the Medicis' actions that saved the city from the epidemic crisis one hundred years later.

The Florentine hearings began during a period of political change, when the two female regents, Grand Duchess Christine of Lorraine and Mary Magdalen of Austria, turned over the reins of government to Ferdinand II. In 1628 Ferdinand attained his majority, taking charge of the state and displacing the oppressive influence of his mother, grandmother, and the Council of Regency. The great epidemic was the first test of political responsibility which the young grand duke underwent, and the need to prove himself compelled him to return to Florence as soon as he heard about the contagion.[28]

During this period, the duchy experienced a general decline—economically, agriculturally, and industrially—and in these particular years it was at its lowest point.[29] The tendency to focus political life on the court did not change with Ferdinand's government. His court consisted of abbots, nobles, and individuals of no particular value who agreed to surrender the principal secretariat of the grand duchy to the old Florentine aristocracy.[30] The uncertain balance between the young head of state and the two intolerant women was made even more precarious by the epidemic.

The sudden crisis required an intervention by those in charge of the newly legitimized regime, and the transfer of political power activated a universe of symbols.[31] During the middle of the epidemic, the official emphasis on the image of Domenica da Paradiso, the courtly Medicean saint, responded to the political and ideological vacuum by clarifying and making socially explicit the sacred roots of the reigning family. In order to reassure the hysterical city, the dynasty confirmed its ability to govern by drawing on the collective memory of past crises and their positive outcomes. To recall the critical year of 1527, when the city, besieged by both the plague and Imperial troops, overcame the double threat and succeeded in restoring civil harmony, meant to recall a precedent for overcoming the present danger. From this interconnection of three spaces, the enclosed city, the convent, and the palace, a mythical scenario of good government was born.

The ruling classes hoped to create a milieu of peaceful reintegration in Florence and to put an end to disorder, disease, and death.[32] On the initiative of the reigning family, Domenica became an integral part of the "community of the suffering." As a mythical healer, her efficacy had been repeatedly tested by the entire body social. Her heroic capacity to withstand physical as well as moral pain made her capable of finding a release for those who suffered from the epidemic: Domenica herself had passed through such painful suffering. The plague had caused her to lose a great quantity of blood, and afterwards she had experienced unceasing, acute fevers, ultimately emerging stronger, albeit more exhausted, than before. The venerated body of Domenica burst into the memories of those who testified at the hearings. The memory of pain, of bubos that suddenly appeared, of fever, and of insomnia lowered the extraordinary powers of the venerated mystic into a devotional private plane. The words of these urban inhabitants illuminate domestic scenes, individual suffering, intimate anguish, and spaces defined by headboards and stoves.[33] The discourses pronounced within the holy perimeter of Domenica's power were linked to and activated by the social practices of resistance and response to the epidemic.

At the first reading, the testimonies from the canonization proceedings seem to stand in sharp contradiction to the experience of most Florentines in the epidemic. The important details represented a systematic and consistent pattern of inversion. To the blackened bodies of the plague's victims corresponds the healthy and rosy body of the saint; to their nudity, her glistening clothes; to the stench of their putrefaction, her aroma of sanctity; to the deadly contagion transmitted by domestic objects and clothes, the healing contact with her food and holy vestments. Against the criminal charges and professional remedies pressed by the Public Health Magistracy, domestic cures associated with the saints meant life, lying to doctors, and systematically hiding sick people. Angelica del Macchia, prioress of Crocetta, for example, testified that Domenica's life had been endangered by doctors. According to her, "On 20 July 1534 the Mother drank certain potions prescribed by doctors. In one of them, there were poisonous cantharides, perhaps put there by mistake. Immediately after she had swallowed the medicine, she began to vomit, her blood pressure increased, she became swollen, and her vision blurred. She soon collapsed and almost died." Doctors tried to help her, but they only increased the danger. Indeed, she fell "into the same condition three times."[34] As soon as she placed herself in God's hands, Domenica regained her health.

The belief that doctors sometimes poisoned the stricken was confirmed at that time by the trial against Leandro Ciminelli, a doctor at the Florentine hospital of Bonifazio. While "assisting the sick, the magistrate charged him . . . with having administered medicines made of dirt which killed people."[35] The charge was later dropped, and the story concludes with a footnote that Doctor Leandro accused some unknown "jealous" individuals of having left in his workbag "some things that we will explain at the proper place and time so that we will not insult the ears of Your Most Illustrious Persons."[36] Murderous doctors were a common theme, one linked to the more general conflict between traditional (folkloric) medicine and the jealous professionalism of the physicians.[37]

A second example illustrates once again this symbiotic relationship between practice and symbols. At the canonization hearings, several witnesses, notably Albiera de' Guiducci, Ottavio Ammoni, and Lisabetta Centenni, agreed that they had experimented with one of the most effective remedies against the plague. They claimed that bread made from dough brought from Domenica's burial site had curative powers. In an anonymous manuscript entitled *Antidotario di medicamenti di più autori,* written in 1632 and now housed in the Magliabechi Collection at the National Library of Florence, there are medicinal recipes for treating plague victims. One in particular suggests that doctors administer to the sick "bread cooked in a wineless meat broth" and pointed out that this recipe had healed Ferdinand II, grand duke of Tuscany.[38] Again we encounter a new reading that acts on more than one level: although the holy bread was a relic from Domenica's grave, it was also a lay medicine mentioned among numerous other secret recipes. That it was given in the exact year of the plague and had apparently healed the grand duke suggests the diffusion of what was originally a peasant tradition, in which the lay elements converged with religious ones.

The beatification of Domenica da Paradiso and the questions raised by the criminal acts are neither unrelated episodes nor mere coincidences linked by an identical context of crisis. Rather, the behavior and values of witnesses delineate reciprocal processes—the hiding of bodies, the attachment to and contact with objects that were potential death carriers, the diffidence toward doctors, and the interconnection of neighborhoods and families—reflecting a circularity between commoners and the upper-middle classes, between different levels of cultural and social practices. We can comprehend these patterns of behavior if we decipher them and if we penetrate their significance from both the top and the bottom of the social structure.

The biological given of death lies within a socially negotiable order and within human values.[39] Witnesses to the plague in Florence remembered and recounted; they moved readily between various levels of memory to discuss disease, healing, attachment to money and family, rivalries, property, death, and glory. Great passions stimulated the interconnected parabolas of private stories and public life, whether sacred or profane. Literature sometimes tries both to articulate what cannot be adequately told and to translate the absolutism of sentiment into a narrow thread derived from many stories. The story of the plague serves as a theater of collective behavior in which the sentimental education of a society, with all its acutely emotional and disruptively uneven quality, is rooted.

I

The Path
of Contamination

than a month since the gates were closed." Francesco responded that he did not know, while reiterating that he had gone to Pistoia with his father and that he had been in the hospital for one month. As soon as he was released, he continued to beg for money throughout the countryside. "Questioned whether he had a mother, any brothers or sisters, or any other relatives in Bari, he answered that he had no one."

The father and son left in midwinter by themselves and reached Pistoia during the carnival festivities; their story of misery and solitude stands in sharp contrast to the celebrating city, then enveloped in lights and sound. Obviously, the magistrate wanted to know only about their journey: their exhausting and dark hike in the cold mountains; the fact that "they had chosen an unusual route"; and finally, that unusual bite, whose general description and healing were not convincing.

The register of the Ceppo, the hospital of Pistoia, verified that Antognone and Francesco had indeed been released. It recorded their names under the entry date, 24 May, and the exit date, 3 June. On the one hand, Antognone had declared that his son had been hospitalized for eight days, approximating the ten days recorded on the official register. On the other hand, Francesco's claim that he had been hospitalized for nearly one month contradicted his father's testimony and thereby aroused the suspicions of the magistrate. Francesco had simply introduced the subjectivity of his perception of disease and subsequent hospitalization into the spatial account of time, translating them into a painful dilation of days.

In addition, the testimony of Baccio helped to release Antognone and Francesco. After some initial doubts and resistance, this city shopkeeper remembered that he had given some money to "someone who was followed by a child, . . . and I think that the man had a red beard and was around forty-three or forty-four years old."

The threat of contagion could be diverted by paying attention to both symptoms and clues. Could a bandage covering a knee disguise the disease? A precedent had already been set in the same Pistoian hospital where Francesco had been interred and where Lucrezia Vestri had died of the plague. The neighbor who had dressed Lucrezia's body for the burial told the Public Health magistrate that the woman had fallen ill, "just because of a little blister, the size of a coin, on her left knee."[5] The two wounds delineate two opposite human stories, and their similarities substantiate the magistrate's prudence. Considering

Lucrezia's death, the story of Antognone and Francesco illuminates the caution that should be exercised in evaluating and collecting testimonies and in then verifying their internal structure and possible external contradictions.

"I AMUSE MYSELF WITH LITERATURE"

The first sign of the plague at the border forced travelers to surface. Mountain passes and, of course, town gates were checkpoints where travelers' tales shed light on the minute geography of their various activities. One of the most unusual cases was Maddalena, who was immobilized by ill-fated love for her seducer. She was, a corporal of the Bargello guard in Florence reported, "a young pregnant woman" who had come to deliver the baby in Antonio and Lucia's house. They sheltered her in a thatch-roofed hut nearby in exchange for money. Accompanied by one Rinaldo, Maddalena crossed the Apennines from the forbidden region of Valsana di Tassignano to Firenzuola, where she was arrested. Taken to a jail, she delivered a son and was later released.[6]

There were also people who, like Jacopo Teracini, went to Florence for the sake of art and simple curiosity.[7] He was "a tall, thin man with walnut hair and a Nazarene hat. He was dressed in white socks, a large jacket, and the rest in black." When he was taken to the chancellor of the Florentine Public Health Magistracy, he took an oath and recounted:

> My name is Jacopo di Giovanni Teracini, and I'm a gold beater from Palermo. As there is so little work, I amuse myself with literature. I compose pieces which I donate to gentlemen who are nice to me. . . . I live alone in the house of Francesco Pazzi on the via San Zenobi and don't have a wife or any children. I moved to Florence twenty months ago and first lived in the Albergo del Moro. . . . I was in Palermo during the plague. Not wanting to catch the disease, I vowed to go to Oreto. So I went to Rome, then to Oreto, and finally came here. . . . I wanted to see the city of Florence; upon arriving, I fell in love with the city and resolved never to leave. I'm now a groom, and everyone knows me, including my neighbors on the street where I live. I was arrested last night at the Gate of San Miniato upon returning from a visit. I had gone to speak to Signor Alessandro de Albenza. I had given him a composition and was waiting for him in the cool weather for two and one-half hours. While resting in the Church of San Miniato, someone approached me and asked, "What are you doing here?" I answered that I

was enjoying the fresh air. He ordered me to leave, and I was arrested as soon as I left.

Solitude and a variety of contingencies made traveling easy: such trips served to avoid plague and resulted in the man from Palermo's pilgrimage, Maddalena's guilt, and Francesco and Antognone's misery. The following are the stories of itinerants—such as the dangerous tale of Bastiano Giannelli.

THE POISONER OF THE HOLY WATER

Volterra, 31 August 1630. "As it was rumored that a certain foreigner had poisoned the holy water of the city's piles, the six deputies requested the Bargello guard to arrest him immediately."[8] According to those rumors, this foreigner had "poisoned the holy water of the cathedral and of other churches. He had been discovered carrying a sack of soil with His Majesty's seal, alum of burned rocks, pilaster, and two small pots of broken glass. There had been vegetable oil in one of the pots."

It was the first time that the terrible charge had been articulated so clearly: he was a plague spreader and was thereby indicted. On 4 September, the magistrate of Volterra questioned Giannelli.

I am named Bastiano di Girolomo Giannelli, and I come from Borgo a Buggiano in the valley of Nivole. I'm a shoemaker. . . . I left Borgo on 19 August, and I have no other family, save my mother. She's sixty-one years old and a beggar. After leaving, I stayed in Canneto for one day to sell some goods that I had previously bought in Lucca and Pescia. They were mostly needles, agora, and lace. With the money I made, I bought some knives. . . . After selling the knives, I bought a shirt and some other clothes. I was arrested next to the church wall by the security forces of the Bargello guard. I don't know why. . . . They found my pilaster from Ripomarance, which was for toothaches.[9] I still had some vegetable oil from Volterra and some soil from Empoli. I also had some alum, which I used as water to clean ice. The soil, I was told, was good for curing fevers, and I sold it. I came to Volterra last Friday, 30 August, from San Gimignano, and I spent the night there before leaving the following Saturday morning. . . . When I arrived in Volterra, I spent some time in the main square but only sold nine pieces of agora. Then I took all my things and went to the duomo, where I recited the Pater Noster and the Ave Maria. As soon as I entered the cathedral, I passed through a large door and took some holy water from the pile. I kept going and left by the same door.

The magistrate insisted that Bastiano was lying. The court knew that he had been seen loitering in the duomo and that he had discussed "the many items which he carried with him." "I did spend some time near the confessional," Bastiano admitted, "and laid my bag there." The magistrate remained dissatisfied. Bastiano had "to specify precisely why he had come to Volterra and what he had wanted to do in the church." "I didn't want to do anything," Bastiano asserted, "and the items that I had were for profit alone."

Yet the entire city believed that he had come to poison the holy water of Volterra!

"That is not true; it cannot be proven," he protested. "I have never bothered anyone, nor has anyone bothered me. It is true that when I was sitting near the church the police arrived and arrested me, screaming, 'You! Stop!' I have been in Volterra once before, my name has always been Bastiano, and I do not know how to read or write. I only worked with Rosaccio for a few days, as a handyman." [10]

Because he lived in Borgo a Buggiano, Bastiano worked between Lucca and Pescia. These two cities were close to Madonna di Monsummano, where Antognone and Francesco had gone on their pilgrimage and then encountered the mean dog. Sometimes routes crossed, despite Bastiano's usual choice of secondary roads to Pomarance, where he had bought the root of Saint Apollonia for toothaches. Being an illiterate shoemaker, he perhaps learned some notions of medicine from Rosaccio, the man whom Bastiano remembered as his only master.

This name provides us with one more small clue, an unexpected element in the profile of the traveler Bastiano. First of all, it suggests previous journeys. Giuseppe Rosaccio was a physician from Padua; he rarely left his Pordenone office. At the beginning of the century, for example, he had visited the grand duchy of Tuscany, there dedicating some of his works to various members of the Medici family. Rosaccio dedicated his *Microcosmo,* printed in Florence, to Antonio Medici. This manual, directed at a general audience, for curing and diagnosing the most common illnesses was part of a vast body of pamphlet literature full of remedies and secrets that enjoyed widespread circulation. These pamphlets were particularly common in the countryside, where the lack of doctors, difficulties in communication, and the great distances from towns made them useful. Rosaccio's words provide us with the opportunity to listen to his handyman Bastiano as he knocked on country house doors in Maremma, a box full of needles and medicines hanging from his neck. In fact, *Microcosmo* was a summary of common sense mixed with scientific knowledge: physiognomy was oriented by the models of perfection and Christian beauty, and the future was predicted by dreams linked to humoral theory. It also contained several anatomy lessons and a corpus of recipes designed to relieve toothaches, sterility, baldness, infant anemia, and dropsy, as well as suggestions on how to conceive male children.[11]

Bastiano decided to become a street vendor of pins and needles, just as many others who wandered the countryside had done. Like Jacopo, the gold beater from Palermo who posed as a poet, Bastiano viewed the church as a place where he could rest, reflect, consider his accounts, and gossip. Yet to remain there longer than necessary meant running the risk of arousing the suspicions of either the faithful or those who, like Jacopo and Bastiano, simply desired some cool air and quiet. Both men were arrested as they left the church, the former targeted by a bystander and the latter in a wave of collective panic.

Apart from the wells that provided the city's lifeline supply of water, only the stores of holy water, the embodiment of spiritual life, attracted the immediate and widespread fear of possible contamination. The transparency and purity of water were vulnerable to the opacity of a poisoner's weapon, whether in the form of dust or liquid. In Milan, for example, the vases of holy water in the duomo had been the first targets of poisoners.

For the first time, then, the episode in Volterra explicitly depicted the portrait of a plague spreader. The description allows us to understand some elements of such a person's past: a journey; the sunny countryside; dusty roads, villages, and towns; the locales of a street vendor or charlatan. People in Volterra considered anyone from Borgo a Buggiano to be a foreigner: could that particular individual be spreading the deadly dust?

The same charges were pressed somewhat later against a physician from the Florentine hospital of Bonifazio. Such ancient suspicions converged around Doctor Leandro Ciminelli, a native of Naples. We will discuss the case of the "Neapolitan doctor," as the magistrates called him, later; here, it need only be stressed that by connecting distant places and situations, these stories of travel and of foreigners with secret identities tend to eliminate differences between individual cases and instead present similar stereotypes.

SEARCHING FOR THE FATHER-IN-LAW

People sometimes journeyed within more familiar contexts, without exhibiting signs of chronic rootlessness. For example, some were forced to leave Florence to look for relatives who had fled creditors. For individuals who had never ventured beyond the city walls, their trajectory had a definite destination, and their prompt return was expected by those remaining. In the adventure of Michele and Antonio, the two brothers-in-law who left home to find Bartolomeo, Michele's father-in-law and Antonio's father, we follow a path in the geography of sentiments. Like all the other characters we have encountered thus far, these two began to relate their story when "extracted from jail" on 3 September 1630. They were questioned by the chancellor of the Public Health Magistracy.[12]

Michele responded first: "I'm a milliner and work for Mastro Andrea in Florence at San Tommaso. . . . I was arrested at the gate; I thought it was a creditor who wanted me arrested." Thus, this is a story of creditors and money.

> Last Thursday my brother-in-law, Antonio di Bartolomeo Barilli, and I left Florence at one o'clock in the afternoon to go to Pisa to look for my father-in-law, Bartolomeo. He fled Florence one week ago because of a debt he owed to the wool trader Vangelista Artimini. Vangelista was the one who wanted my father-in-law, telling us, "Bring him to Florence any way that you can, and tell him that we have agreed on the payment of one *scudo* per week." That evening my mother-in-law confirmed Artimini's story when we arrived at a tavern—I have forgotten its name—across the Pontadera, where we passed the night.

Michele recalled that the two had spent fifteen *crazie* for dinner and accommodations. They left the next morning and reached Pisa on Friday "at five o'clock in the afternoon. They refused to permit us to enter the city because we were Florentines. So we decided to go to Leghorn to look for our father-in-law. Since we arrived in the evening, they would not let us in. . . . We had no choice but to sleep under two haystacks with seven or eight day laborers. These men told us that they slept there every night."

The cautious Pisan guards transformed travel into an adventure for those used to shops and houses; now such people were forced to spend the night in a haystack under the stars with seven or eight day laborers. "Who were they?" the magistrate asked Michele.

I don't know; however, according to what they told us, two of them were from Pistoia. The following morning, Saturday, the guards didn't let us enter the city because we were from Florence. So I sent for my brother Benvenuto, a cook at the Cartoncino Tavern in old Leghorn. He met us at the gate, and I asked him to look for my father-in-law. He left and returned only to say that he could not find him. He gave us a bottle of wine, three pieces of bread, eight or perhaps twelve small fish, and an onion. After we had eaten, we went back to Pisa. This time we succeeded in entering the city by the Florence Gate, the very gate where we had been denied entrance before, because there were different guards there now. I found lodging at the Piazza dell'Ortagio in a house bearing the insignia of a dragon. My father-in-law had stayed in the house of a nobleman from Pisa; this friend had given him a letter for Florence. Yesterday morning we began our journey to Florence. At the first tavern we drank a half carafe, and we had yet another half carafe at the Pontadera. We arrived at Empoli in the evening. It was late, however, and as the gates were closed, we had to stay in an outlying neighborhood. We ate two pieces of bread and some cheese that we had bought in a shop in Borgo. At the well, a shoemaker gave us a copper bucket to dip for some water, and we stayed there until the moon rose, at five o'clock. We started to walk to Florence and arrived at the Gate of San Frediano at one o'clock. We were arrested (I first, since my brother-in-law was lagging half a mile behind me because his feet hurt), and we do not know what crime we have committed.

The magistrate asked for more information on their itinerary and the stops they had made along the way. "At about one o'clock, we rested for a while at Malmantile," Michele responded. "I had to put a bandage on my blistered toe, and my brother-in-law had to clean the dust off his shoes. Then we stopped beyond Lastra, at a place close to a little bridge—I think it is called Mulinaccio—and I rested for about fifteen minutes. My brother-in-law lounged nearby. . . . We then continued our trip very slowly, and nobody spoke to us."

Antonio was questioned immediately after his brother-in-law. He worked in the same shop as his father, Bartolomeo, and under the same master, Vangelista Artimini. In general, Antonio confirmed the testimony of his brother-in-law but added a few details. In Pisa, for example, he spent the night at the house of his friend Piero. Piero was not a nobleman but a servant. Antonio continued, "Earlier, Piero had stayed in Florence on the via de' Bardi with a gentleman. I don't know the name of that man, but he sells wine and lives near the bakery." Antonio's language was more humble; he was captivated by the novelty of exploring unknown territories while listening to the advice of his more experienced brother-in-law. "I stopped beyond Lastra and took off my shoes because I was so tired. My brother-in-law continued ahead and promised to wait for me in Florence. I don't know where I was because it was the first time that I had been so far from Florence. I stopped to relieve myself and then ate some figs in Legnaia."

In the two testimonies, the guards and the roadblocks near Pisa and Leghorn were the only clues of impending danger; the suspension of trade announced the epidemic. The rhythm of a picaresque causality, however, marked the serene wandering, the "very slow" journey, of Michele and Antonio. Stops in taverns, drinks, nights spent under the stars in haystacks and along the roads, encounters and chats—rather than concern over the fate of a relative or the danger of contagion, what surfaced in the two men's accounts was the simple pleasure of travel, a sense of interrupted daily work, habits, and closed city life, and the stupefying dilation of space and time. The walled perimeter of the enclosed cities of Pisa and Leghorn punctuated the itinerary; for those travelers who understood it, urban space could easily be controlled. At the Gate of Leghorn, Michele recounted, "I sent for my brother Benvenuto. I asked him to go look for my father-in-law. He went, returned, and told me that he couldn't find him." Thus, the spatial perception of the enclosed city is translated into a sequence of three verbs: he went, he returned, he told.

Space in the countryside, in contrast, can be measured by carafes in a tavern. We know from their ill-timed arrival at the gates of cities, already closed at nightfall, that the two travelers failed to estimate rural distances very exactly. They walked during the day and usually slept under the stars, unable to predict the length of the trip. Beyond dawn and dusk, only personal exigencies—that is, hunger, thirst, sleepiness, fatigue, and a full bladder—marked the stops of the journey and measured the length of the trip.

To wander around at night, to sleep in improbable places, to stop in taverns, to meet and travel with strangers is also what the protagonists of many novels did. Yet these activities generally characterized victims of tricksters or thieves: stupid people, generally the urban—or, more frequently, the rural—poor. In this sense, the picaresque dimension works as well for characters of literature as for the protagonists giving these testimonies. Michele and Antonio searched for their father-in-law and father, Bartolomeo, who had escaped from his creditors. Thus they repeated the journey of others who, poor like themselves, had disappeared to escape justice. Because, however, they traveled far from Florence and were unfamiliar with the type of journey involved, their itinerary differed from that of their relative. They were forced to detour by obstacles encountered only by those who walked slowly and laboriously. Yet these obstacles could open unusual paths and make for a pleasurable trip. The journeys of soldiers, beggars, and the urban poor, also the protagonists of picaresque novels, were uncertainly delineated in the midst of unpredicted obstacles, such as those that drew the attention of the guards and the Public Health magistrates in times of epidemic.

THE TORN TRAVEL DOCUMENTS

Literary texts and trial records report that travelers often met people who suggested safe routes to avoid danger, as the case of Andrea di Girolomo demonstrates. While journeying back to his native village of Lavagna in Genoa, Andrea was arrested in Pietrasanta on 11 July 1630. The records describe him as "a short man with a blond beard, black eyes, wearing a hat and a grey, shabby coat."[13] Again we have a poor man, confused and helpless. He started his trip at Civitavecchia and had traveled through Leghorn and Pisa. He was trying to return to Genoa when he was arrested in Viareggio by Public Health guards, their suspicions aroused by his travel document, which was smeared with too much ink.

During his journey the illiterate Andrea had met a man who promised to save him from the guards. In exchange for money, Andrea said, "the man wrote some kind of document for me and then explained the route I should take. I swam across a creek and arrived at Pietrasanta, where the guards told me that my documents were invalid. They said that I had to go back the same way." While retracing his steps, Andrea met a second person, "who told me that my documents were fake. He tore them in half and told me to go through an enclosed vineyard. But it was precisely in that vineyard that I was arrested by the guard and thrown in jail."

The guards laughed at Andrea's adventures and took him for a very simple man: simple people deserved to be victimized by tricksters or villains. These exploiters appeared as almost magical helpers who lured a hero into a trap. From his cell, the young man from Lavagna described the two tricksters. The first "was a big man with a black beard, dressed in black, and about forty-five years old." The second, the one who had torn his documents, "was a man of normal height with a black and white beard, somewhat fat, and dressed in various colors." Perhaps the differences in age, clothes, and their respective heights, or maybe even simple fear alone, pushed the young man to trust them. This episode easily highlights the consciousness of danger and helps to explain the itinerary through the creek and the vineyards.

THE SACK OF MANTUA AND THE
MARQUIS DE' ROSSI'S BAGS

The bitter profiles of the Apennines offered shelter to those returning from war. Soldiers, deserters, or even simple travelers who went through the cities of the lower Po valley and descended the mountain passes toward the grand duchy scared Public Health guards. Invading troops spread the plague in the Po valley.

Early signs of the Thirty Years' War, then raging throughout Europe, appeared in the testimony of prisoners who had reputedly come from the battlefields. The Valtellina and the Genoese hinterlands, strategically vital territories, were necessary additions to the Habsburg possessions. They became particularly important upon the death of Duke Vicenzo Gonzaga of Mantua and Montferrat, when Olivares and Richelieu, the rival ministers of Habsburg Spain and France, seized the opportunity to claim these lands. Imperial troops serving the Austrian Habsburgs and a French army now threatened to invade the northern Italian states.

In the summer of 1630 both armies and their allies occupied and devastated Savoy, Casale Monferrato, and Mantua, with the ultimate objective of the two rival powers being the Valtellina and the Genoese Alps. The troop encampments and the battles between Imperial and French forces left behind an annihilated territory that extended from the Ligurian coast to Mantua.

On 21 September 1629, General Aldringher, one of the two chief commanders of the Imperial army, ordered two hundred select soldiers and five hundred horses to cross the Oglio River. They conquered the city of Ostiano and made it their new headquarters. This battle marked the beginning of a campaign that was to last for the entire winter, ending in the sack of Mantua on 18 July 1630. Counting on aid promised by the Republic of Venice, the new duke, Carlo di

Nevers, of the French branch of the Gonzaga family, opposed Aldringher. After much hesitation, however, Venice failed to keep its
word, causing the defeat of Gonzaga's army and the occupation of the
duchy by Imperial troops.

In December 1629 speculation spread through Italy that Richelieu's
forces, having just captured La Rochelle, were about to intervene on
behalf of the duke of Gonzaga-Nevers. From December to March,
Mantuan troops repeatedly defeated the Imperial army, forcing it to
retreat to Castiglion Mantovano, Ostiglia, and Goito. In March the
French finally crossed Savoy and occupied Pinerolo.

During the same period, Spanish troops led by Ambrogio Spinola
captured Casale Monferrato. The Po valley thus became one of the
most important diplomatic theaters in the Habsburg move for pri-
macy in Europe.

Contemporary chroniclers and historians were certainly aware of
the magnitude of the deployed forces in northern Italy and the complexity of the various goals and alliances. They carefully followed
both the battles and the developments of diplomatic meetings with a
sense of impending catastrophe. For all concerned, whether pro-
French or pro-Spanish, the sack of Mantua in July 1630 (often compared to the sack of Rome one century earlier) marked the end of
an era.[14]

It must have been a very risky business to cross the Po valley. The
region had been sacked, burned, and thoroughly destroyed by the
war, and it was now being devastated by the plague. Yet even during
the worst month of the war, two of the Marquis Ferrante de' Rossi's
servants, Filippo and Antonio, traveled across the Po valley twice,
eluding guards, quarantines, and armies.[15]

The Florentine Public Health Magistracy arrested the two on 12
July 1630 at the lazaret of San Marco Vecchio. The chancellor questioned Filippo first. Five months earlier, in the middle of winter, Filippo and a group of servants had left Florence with their master. They
traveled to Bologna, where they spent two days, and then continued
on to Ferrara. From Ferrara they journeyed to Mantua, arriving during Lent. Two weeks later they again departed, this time for Bozzolo,
the estate of "the prince, my master's uncle." The group spent a good
part of the season there with the marquis's family. In May they began
their trek back to Mantua. According to Filippo, "there were no signs
of mortality or plague" in the city. The chancellor grew angry and

accused the servant of lying, "because it is well known that there was plague in Mantua." In actuality, he insisted, the marquis and his retinue had left in March, not because of any desire to join his family, but rather to "escape the contagion."

Why did de' Rossi send his men back to Florence while he remained behind? Where did he hide? How did Filippo and Antonio manage to traverse the grand duchy and reenter the city?

According to Filippo, the two had no other task but to bring "two bags of miscellaneous objects" to the palace near Santa Croce in Florence. "The customs officers confiscated" these sacks on their return. Unlike the cases we have already examined, it is relatively easy to trace Filippo and Antonio's itinerary, because they went by horse "from Ferrara to Faenza" and then by donkey from Marradi through Borgo San Lorenzo to Florence. The plebeian mules befitted the humble origins of the men, who had to dismount at the Gate of San Gallo in order to carry the bags through customs.

The second servant, Antonio, added some significant details to his companion's testimony. Whereas Filippo was a native of Tuscany and had worked only three months for the marquis, Antonio came from Lake Maggiore and had worked in the marquis's household for three years. Perhaps Antonio's seniority granted him access to information to which Filippo was not privy.

During the family's stay at Bozzolo, Antonio fell ill with a pain in his chest. Confined to his bed for a few days, he was told that the Marquis Ferrante had gone to Castiglion Mantovano, "the location of the duke's cavalry." During their trip from Florence they had been compelled to stop for a quarantine twenty miles from town, in Massa di Ferrara in the monastery of the friars of San Martino. The marquis was there informed of his brother's death. Since his brother had served under the duke of Mantua, the marquis later went to the military headquarters to acquire more information. Antonio reiterated that although they had passed through Mantua twice, they had not seen even the smallest sign of the plague. He did note, however, that many people had "died of fatigue and starvation."

The servants' report suggests that this story revolved around a domestic environment: the marquis's trip back to his family's estate, his affection for his mother, and the objects in the bags taken back to Florence. The people, places, and dates of the journeys, however, point to a different scenario, one surrounded by war.

First let us examine the territory of Bozzolo and its prince, Carlo

Scipione Gonzaga, the uncle of the Marquis Ferrante.[16] Comprising Reggiolo, Novellara, Guastalla, and Castiglione delle Stiviere, Bozzolo extended west of the duchy of Mantua. It was one of the smaller Gonzaga courts, reconstructed at the turn of the sixteenth century. Contemporary chroniclers and historians agreed that the prince of Bozzolo played an important role during the Imperial invasion. He supported Aldringher's contingents as they attacked Mantua. Duke Carlo di Nevers had asked Carlo Scipione Gonzaga for permission to encamp with his troops at Ostiano, within the borders of the Bozzolo estate. In return, Nevers promised that he would ward off any attack made by the Imperial troops, now entrenched beyond the Oglio River. Yet Scipione "recalled how Duke Vincentio had charged his mother with being a witch. Thus, he now directed his hatred toward Duke Carlo, Vicentio's heir and successor. He pledged to defend Ostiano without Carlo's aid and honestly admitted that he was considering opening his borders to the Imperial forces in order to gain their good will."[17]

Thus, on 21 September 1629 Commander Aldringher succeeded in crossing the Oglio River with two hundred soldiers and five hundred horses and began the military campaign in the area around Mantua, thanks to the support of Scipione Gonzaga. Later the castle of Bozzolo, still the headquarters of the Imperial army, witnessed the great celebrations of the weddings of Commanders Aldringher and Galasso to the Countesses d'Arco. "These splendid and unrivaled festivities" took place in the midst of a land devastated by war and plague.[18] It was during this period of time that the Marquis Ferrante de' Rossi and his servants arrived at the Gonzaga estate and prepared to spend the winter. What the servants took to be a quarantine in a family's embrace, chroniclers and historians believed to be complete participation in political events.

That December, bolstered by the news that some forty thousand French troops were preparing an assault on the Italian peninsula, the duke of Nevers launched a successful attack. He captured Castiglion Mantovano on 31 December and defeated the Imperial troops at Goito on 4 February.[19] Before their final defeat, the Imperial troops scored an important victory at Ostiglia, which ended with most of the population being massacred. Here we encounter the second of the characters cited in Antonio's testimony: Carlo, the governor general of Montferrat and brother of the Marquis de' Rossi.[20]

Carlo de' Rossi fought alongside the Marquis Alfonso Guerriero at the fortress of Ostiglia when the inhabitants revolted against the occupying Imperial troops. Betrayed by the Venetians, the battle ended tragically—Carlo de' Rossi wounded, the town sacked, and the population decimated. Although nineteenth-century historians portrayed de' Rossi as a heroic warrior, contemporary Spanish chroniclers depicted him as a coward.[21]

To escape the enemy and to be wounded while fleeing are infamous acts. Carlo de' Rossi was thus described in two very different manners, as hero and as "villain." The chronicles of the campaign in Mantua note his presence only in Ostiglia. We have no further information on the vicissitudes of his life after he was wounded.[22] Antonio's testimony alone mentions the date of his death.

In contrast, chroniclers described Carlo and Ferrante's uncle, Carlo Scipione Gonzaga, in detail. A staunch supporter of the Empire, Gonzaga played a leading role in the fall of the duchy of Mantua, for both personal and familial reasons.

The pro-Spanish historian Capriata attempted to minimize the significance of the final tragic debacle. But he painfully agreed that "pride, cruelty, stinginess, and military lust ran rampant" as a curtain of mourning fell over the scene of the devastated city.[23]

In the final analysis, the support, both of friendship and of aid, provided by Carlo Scipione Gonzaga to Aldringher failed to protect his lands. Imperial troops remained in Bozzolo until 2 March 1631. The estate ultimately paid twenty thousand *thalers* in currency to the Imperial forces, as well as giving wine, bread, meat, and anything else the soldiers needed.[24]

Displaced against the backdrop of his two relatives' choices and respective fates, the itinerary of Ferrante de' Rossi—his travels throughout Mantua, his sojourn at Bozzolo, and his journey to Castiglion Mantovano—follows a route that was politically difficult and perhaps even contradictory. By comparing the dates and the events, one might reasonably surmise that he actively participated in the war on the side of his infamous brother.

These considerations very likely influenced the Florentine magistrates as they decided the fate of the servants after their arrest in the lazaret of San Marco Vecchio. The sentence was promulgated on 15 July, just three days before the final Imperial assault on Mantua and the subsequent fall of the city. Filippo and Antonio were expelled from Florence "and ordered not to return without the explicit permission of the magistrates."[25]

Paralleling the events of the war and dynastic decisions, the two servants' experiences serve on a lesser scale to highlight the rigorous ability of the Magistracy to exercise power over the privileged classes. Filippo and Antonio's arrest provided the authorities, who wanted to trap the Marquis de' Rossi, with information about his possible movements. On the same day as the servants' expulsion, 15 July, Public Health officials learned that Marquis Ferrante "was staying at the baron's villa near Prato."[26] The imminent sack of Mantua had probably convinced him to find refuge with friends across the frontier.

The magistrates ordered an official, a member of the Otto di Guardia or a corporal, "to lead a squad of twelve or fifteen soldiers at night to infiltrate and search the palace. Once [the marquis was] found and arrested, the guards should call for the magistrate."[27] Captured while asleep, the marquis would certainly be forced to confess "his whereabouts from the beginning of April to his last trip" to Prato, "as well as to inventory his Public Health documents and tell where they had been issued." The documents were to be sent to Florence with the utmost haste, addressed "to the hand of the chancellor of the Public Health Magistracy."[28] In the meantime, guards were instructed to keep the villa and its noble hosts under surveillance.

The criminal documents do not record the marquis's testimony. His version of events, then, remains for our purposes inevitably linked to the testimony of his servants. For once the words of the humble illustrate the life of the powerful. Obviously their testimony contained elements that aroused the alarm of the Florentine magistrates. The sentence promulgated on 15 July, for example, declared that "the officials of the Public Health Magistracy of the city of Florence banish the Marquis Ferrante de' Rossi, along with his servants and belongings, from the state under penalty of death and confiscation of goods."[29]

"TO RETURN HOME AND GET MY WIFE AND SON"

The episode of the young soldier Michele di Paolo paradigmatically confirms the terror and speed with which information and reaction chased those returning from war. His story springs out of the other front of war, around Genoa, where geography delineated the struggle for Montferrat by the duke of Savoy, the French forces, and the Imperial army.

As in the case of the Marquis de' Rossi's two servants, the solitary route of the traveling Michele di Paolo traces an itinerary of conflicts, treaties, and truces, held together by a heretofore anonymous individual destiny. The relationship between these two dimensions appears intricate and unresolved; the personal vicissitudes seem to avoid the weight of the events decided by others.

A quick exchange of letters between Florentine officials and the commissioner of Pistoia, Giovanni Lappi, signaled Michele di Paolo's passage through the grand duchy.[30] Lappi sent the first message on 12 July, writing, "I have heard that a soldier has just arrived from the battlefield; he used to be one of Captain Bruni's men. That particular company has passed through restricted areas." These rumors impelled the commissioner to take immediate action: "I rushed to Pescia to check out the validity of the story."

Beginning his investigation in Pescia, Lappi questioned the priest of Borgo a Buggiano, who confirmed nothing more than the arrival and "good health" of the soldier. Others interrogated by the commissioner refused to answer. "No one wanted to tell me where he lived," Lappi complained, adding that even Michele di Paolo's uncle denied having seen him.

Through intermediaries Lappi explained to the soldier's wife that his intentions were well meaning. He merely wanted to quarantine the young man; he was not interested in pressing criminal charges against Michele for having left a restricted area. An anonymous note told Lappi that the soldier was hiding "in a field of lupines," and, despite his assurances to Michele's family, the commissioner tried to capture him. Lappi later recalled: "I called the corporal and a few guards. We encircled him very quietly in the field to prevent his escape, and I went ahead to try talking to him. Feeling unsafe, he did not fulfill his promise." The stalker was as clever as his prey. In the foreground, a network of informers, relatives, and tricks surrounded both men. In the background, the stubborn hostility of the villagers led them to find, advise, and hide Michele.

The young man vanished. Lappi searched for him everywhere and immediately notified the local authorities: the vicar of Pescia, the castellan of Montecarlo, and Marquis Vittore. In the meantime, he placed Michele's wife and son under house arrest, "as they had dealings with him."

Michele appeared in the village from out of the blue. Although his behavior seemed normal, the commissioner viewed it as a provocation. Lappi reported, "I know that he arrived in the village on Tuesday and spoke to a woman." Then Michele suddenly disappeared and, according to the rumors, went to Massa. Placing Michele's wife and son under strict house arrest, however, eventually turned the tables in favor of the commissioner. On 17 July the magistrate of Pescia and the notary Tedeschi were finally able to question the fugitive after he had returned to his home in Selvapiana di Buggiano. Fearing contagion, information was exchanged at a distance. Michele stood at the window, while the two officials remained in the sunny yard.

Michele described his trip. He left "Bagno alla Porretta and arrived at Pavana, in the territory of His Most Serene Highness. The small village of Pavana comprised eight to ten houses." The magistrate asked about the routes, hoping that the fugitive would provide information on gaps and errors in the network of control. Was this the main road? "Yes, it was the main road leaving Pistoia."

This route crossed the Apennines at the pass of Porretta and descended to Bologna. As it was the primary artery, Michele must have avoided many guards. The magistrate became increasingly interested and asked for further details. He discovered that Michele had stayed on the main route only for short distances. Michele recalled, "I entered Pavana on Friday night. After passing through both Pavana and Legha, I slept under an oak. On Saturday morning I arrived at a forest near the border of Pistoia, where I stayed until evening."

The forest concealing Michele on that Saturday overlooked Cutigliano. The soldier, hiding in the mountains of Abetone, moved along the ridge of the range. When he reached Porretta, he found himself in a place that is still called Grande Faggio. By taking the higher path, he managed to avoid the Public Health guards he would undoubtedly have encountered had he decided to travel toward Pistoia through Pontelungo.

The soldier finally did arrive at Pontelungo by following the Ombrone River. He then took the main road to Florence. He recalled, "I went to Madonna di Monsummano and stayed there until Sunday night." On Sunday Michele walked some twenty kilometers, much of which went through the mountains. "I spent Monday in a field of lupines. That evening I returned home, but my wife immediately sent me away. I then went back to the field of lupines in Massa, where I stayed until Friday." Thus, hidden in a field of lupines, Michele survived for five days. In that particular field, he met Lappi and adeptly escaped arrest.

The magistrate asked how he had been able to survive. "I ate nature's food, especially grain. Sometimes, because nobody wanted me around, I went hungry." Obviously, after traveling, starving, and sleeping under the open sky for many nights, his appearance was not reassuring, especially not during those calamitous times. Yet the distrust between travelers and those who remained behind was reciprocal. "I didn't return home because I couldn't trust anyone": Michele thought that the peasants would have denounced him to the guards, just as they had denounced Antognone and his son Francesco, who had been in hiding in the mountains of Pistoia.

Michele began his journey by traveling to Genoa by sea. His final destination, though, was Milan. His description of these new peregrinations captured the magistrate's attention. Why Milan? The magistrate asked Michele to outline his serpentine itinerary accurately.

"I was one of Captain Francesco Bruni of Pistoia's soldiers. After landing at Otri, we were quartered at Campo. Then we moved on to Novara, encamping there for six days. Next, we went to Nove to join our battalion. I left on 13 June, five weeks ago, and traveled to the Genoese mountains. I couldn't finish my journey because they sent me back, leaving me no other choice but to return to Milan. I then went through Gavi and Tortona to Parma. From Parma I traveled through a countryside hitherto unknown to me, to Modena. I left Modena and entered Bologna at the border town of Crocetta. From Crocetta I went to Pollano, and from Pollano to Bagno della Porretta."

The road from Voltri to Novara passes through Alessandria, where somewhat before Michele's arrival Giulio Mazzarino, Spinola, Panciroli, and Collalto had held a delicate diplomatic meeting to try to resolve the conflict over Montferrat. Casale, besieged and under Spanish attack, lay a few miles to the north.[31]

Michele di Paolo embarked at Leghorn on 13 June. He was one of many infantrymen who went to Voltri in Liguria to aid the Spanish troops defending Genoa from the French and Venetian attack.[32] Along with the other Tuscan infantrymen, he was transferred to Campo to help Count Giovanni Serbelloni "keep the enemy far away from those fortifications which extended in the direction of the Valtellina on the left side." Serbelloni now "was in control of the entire strip of territory from the Valtellina to Novi."[33]

Chroniclers carefully described the harsh territory, the insurmountable peaks, and the passes that were familiar only to natives of the region. To avenge their suffering fellow countrymen, the Ligurians, who were reputedly "strong men used to climbing steep rocks," would suddenly attack entire armed encampments, stealing from and killing the enemy soldiers.[34] Therefore, the French and Spanish armies had to struggle over positions; the ability to climb mountains and to scale the jagged rims safely, even in icy conditions, was essential. The territorial dimension paralleled and enhanced the human condition: "With ropes attached to one another, they jumped over the mountain edges." Frequent Ligurian attacks, in combination with hunger, disease, and desertion, "emptied the fields more and more."[35]

Other soldiers who fled through the Alps must have felt the same terror and misery as Michele di Paolo. Starting out toward Milan, he passed through Tortona, Novi, and Gavi, then through the Po valley to Parma, Modena, and Bologna. Finally, he climbed the Apennines and reached Porretta.

How long had it taken him to reach Bologna from Modena? "I left Modena on the evening of the day of Saint Peter. Since they wouldn't let me in at Crocetta, I returned by a different route. In the evening, however, the soldiers arrested me, threw me in a cell, and interrogated me. They didn't release me until four days later." His travel documents, then, remained in the hands of the soldiers who had arrested him. Although the young man asserted that the documents were valid, he was unable to convince the magistrate. Furthermore, the magistrate's suspicions were confirmed when, after additional investigation, he discovered that the defendant did not have a passport and had not even asked his captain for leave papers.

Was he a deserter? Why had he left his regiment without asking for a permit? "I came home to get my wife and son, who were evicted on 3 August. I was afraid that I would find them in the streets."

A motive suddenly materialized for this long and exhausting journey, fraught with so much danger. A man's intimate need to defend his most valued possessions overshadowed the solemnity of war and diplomatic relations among states. Thus, the tenor of the story shifted to the realm of private sentiments. Compared to the imperative of caring for home and family, even the plague mattered little to Michele. "Only two of our soldiers had died," Michele reported. Anyway, it did not matter whether the plague had reached Parma because, he argued, "I went around the town. I cannot even tell you whether anyone had died because I traveled only at night and never asked anyone anything."

Why had he chosen to come to the grand duchy when he knew that its borders were carefully patrolled? He explained, "Any other state would have denied me permission to travel anywhere." Michele stressed the rationality of his personal goal, thereby contrasting the public world of official decrees to the private exigencies of his journey.

While standing in the sunny yard, the magistrate and his notary gathered the necessary information about this soldier, who had even traversed battlegrounds to reach his family. They could now send the investigative report to Florence. In the meantime, however, they ordered the soldier arrested, taking the precautionary measure of "tying him so that he could not escape" and demanding that "his family not interfere." Finally, they ordered the "guards to handcuff and, at the end of a long rope, lead him to jail. He was to be interred in a solitary cell, his feet chained." The family members who helped the magistrate in the arrest were "to be kept in isolation, so that they would not have contact with anyone else until the magistrate's further order."[36]

THE GOOD SOLDIER PIER FRANCESCO

War testimonies continued to underscore the relationship between plague and battlefield. We will need to examine military developments again, because the Thirty Years' War served as an antecedent and background to the Florentine epidemic. The war, erupting into the personal lives of these travelers, allows us to read history from different perspectives and see how it opens undulatingly and then oscillates between the private realm and collective events.

The following events occurred some months after the ones we have already discussed. In the winter after that July, on 21 January, one of the vicar's guards captured a young traveler on the route to Firenzuola.[37] Like all other travelers, this man was very fatigued by the long journey. He wore "a black hat, a woolen coat, cotton trousers, linen socks, and black shoes. Everything was torn." In addition, he was very young—"his beard and sideburns were newly grown." The vicar asked how old he was. "I cannot tell you because I don't know," the boy answered. Could he be around twenty years old? "I don't know."

"My name is Pier Francesco, and I'm the son of Marchionne Farsetti da Talla di Casentino." Perhaps the fact that he had been raised in the mountains, far from towns and villages, explains his complete lack of knowledge about biographical data. Like many other unemployed young men, Pier Francesco had decided to enlist in the army. "I was recruited in Arezzo by Cavalier Gondi; under his command, I went first to Leghorn, then by ship to Otri, and then on land to Novara, where we stayed for five or six months."

His itinerary virtually paralleled Michele di Paolo's. They both had disembarked at Voltri and gone to Novarra with the rest of the infantry from the grand duchy. Pier Francesco, however, having neither family nor domestic obligations, could leave the army at any time by following the proper procedures and making sure that all his travel documents were in good order. In October at Valenza, "once peace was made, they were granting leave to all foreigners for one or two months, so I applied for a permit to go home, which my superiors granted."

After these words, Pier Francesco produced the documents and, on the vicar's request, unfolded them on the table. They were dated 2 November 1630 and were signed by Annibale Filangieri, a famous commander who had fought at Casale, Alessandria, and Valenza.[38] He commanded a *terzo* of four thousand infantrymen in Novara for the grand duchy of Tuscany. Listed among those soldiers was one "Pier Francesco di Marchionne Farsetti da Talla nel Casentino, who served in our *terzo* for seven months, fulfilling his duties with the utmost diligence and honor and always proving to be competent in the art of war."

For two months and nineteen days, the good soldier Pier Francesco traveled. Unlike other infantrymen who were fugitives, Pier Francesco could travel relatively easily along the major arteries without worrying about being arrested for the lack of documents. Protected by the papers signed by Commander Filangieri, this soldier went from Valenze to Reggio Emilia in only five days. He stayed there for one month "to work with a spade in the vineyards."

No longer in uniform, the young man returned to civilian life, earning his living as a laborer and manual worker. After leaving Reggio he went to Castelfranco, where he worked for eight days transporting bricks and debris "to the new fortress that the pope is building." Pier Francesco kept a safe distance from the "enclosed territories" for fear of contagion. Because he was penniless, he slept in abandoned houses and open fields before finally entering the grand duchy.

Although he was the first soldier to cross the border calmly, neither taking precautions nor cheating, he was not stopped. The vicar asked how this was possible.³⁹ While walking on the same road, Pier Francesco reported, "I saw five or six soldiers who were playing games near the roadblock. I walked past a peasant who was going through the checkpoint at the same time. The soldiers did not see either one of us."

The all-pervasive network of checkpoints failed because of one moment of distraction and enjoyment. Even during the plague and war there was time to rest and play. Perhaps the cold of a winter night made Pier Francesco's passage through the second block easier. At Pietramala, he said, "I went through without being seen," and in the evening there was not a single soul outside, although he heard voices from the guard box.

Ironically, the only traveler with all the necessary legal documents went past roadblocks and borders unchecked, begging along the way for "one thing or another." Pier Francesco was not only respectful of the law but also pious. "After he emptied his pockets, he had nothing but a medallion. He did not even have a single coin and was dressed miserably."

While waiting for the inspection, he was put in jail with a Roman.

A ROMAN DESERTER

Pier Francesco's cellmate was also a soldier, who had arrived at Firenzuola a few hours earlier. Detained and waiting for clearance, he had already been questioned by the vicar, who described him as an "unknown person, almost like a vagabond . . . since he had no papers."⁴⁰ As usual, the criminal records describe his physical appearance and clothes in detail: "a young man of normal height whose beard is cut so as to hide all, save a part of the sideburns. He has blond hair, wears a grey cotton coat, turquoise socks, black shoes, and a grey hat." Although he was without proper travel documents, this man, the same age as Pier Francesco, was in much better condition.

"My name is Giuseppe. I'm Antonio Gallo's son and come from Rome. My father comes from Milan. I was a carder, but now I'm a soldier." Thus, he was an unemployed carder who, like many other unemployed men, found a job in the army. In September he had enlisted in Naples in the infantry of the prince of Satriano, who headed a *terzo* and was currently fighting on behalf of the Republic of Genoa in its war against Savoy.⁴¹

In the prince's army, Giuseppe was "under the command of Captain Don Tomaso Stinca. In his *terzo,* we traveled by boat and landed near the coast of Genoa. We marched to Milan, to a neighborhood called Casano, where we remained for approximately one month."

Giuseppe served as a soldier until 2 January, but then the relationship between the soldiers and Captain Stinca became increasingly tense. A confrontational relationship of black deeds and revenge had developed between them, making life in the camp intolerable. "Six comrades quit because that captain mistreated us. He hated us because, unlike most of the soldiers in the battalion, we weren't Neapolitans." The vicar asked them what kind of abuse they were talking about.

> Our landlord gave us six *parpagliole* every day, the kind of money that comes in big pieces. The captain was supposed to take two each day to buy shoes and wood, but he never bought any wood, and I had to pay eleven *giuli* for my shoes. Once I told the captain that he should give me all six *parpagliole* and that I couldn't go on like this.[42] He answered, "You know what? Just hand in your uniform, and I'll give you a leave of absence so that you can go." So I took my papers and left with some of my comrades.

According to Giuseppe, life in the military was pretty much like everyday life, characterized by abuse and petty rivalries. In the *terzo* of the prince of Satriano, Captain Stinca exploited his power and took advantage of his soldiers, trafficking in uniforms and shoes. "That soldier, Captain Stinca," a local chronicle of some years before had said, "is like a dog," penniless and "despised." Even when salaries were paid on time, they were "very little" and "not enough."[43] Generally, after being dismissed, mutilated and wounded soldiers were forced to beg. Why should it surprise us that a soldier who had enlisted to avoid starvation was later driven to leave the army when he was not fed enough? Desertion was like a hemorrhage: it weakened all armies. Throughout the 1600s, army officers had to accept the fact that many of their soldiers were going to vanish.

Giuseppe escaped with five companions. He remembered something about almost all of them, particularly those who were also Roman. "One was named Giovanni di Fiore, and I think that he was from Parma. Another was called Giovanbatista Cristallino, and he was from Rome. The third one's name was Mario di Nicola, who was also from Rome. The fourth was Piero Boccane, and I don't know where he came from. And the last one was Jacopo Greco; I don't know where he came from either." Together, they left in the evening, after "the captain ordered us to remain on guard in the courtyard so that we could go somewhere in the morning. When we were all assembled in the courtyard—there must have been forty of us—he said, 'My soldiers, although we have been like brothers, things have got to change now.'" Given all the abuse of the previous month, the future seemed ominous, "and we started to look into each other's eyes. We found a hole in the wall behind the wine presses, and that night at about four o'clock six of us left. We crossed the river by boat and reached Bergamo, fourteen miles away. Our objective was to join the Venetian army."

Thus, the six soldiers had escaped at night through a hole in the wall and traveled by boat from Casano to Bergamo along the Adda River. The vicar asked if they had enlisted in the Venetian army.

> No, sir, because when we arrived and asked to enlist, they told us they didn't need any more soldiers. So three of us left Bergamo—that is, I and the two other Romans. We obtained travel documents from the Public Health Magistracy and went to Brescia, some thirty miles from Bergamo. We were looking for a job, but they wouldn't even let us enter the city, saying that if we had been soldiers of Venice they would have hired us but that they didn't want anybody else.

The living conditions of Venetian soldiers were probably relatively good. Perhaps their salaries were paid so much more regularly that soldiers of other armies were tempted to enlist. Certainly the fact that these men were Romans had created a series of obstacles for them; they had first been mistreated by a Neapolitan captain and then ignored by the Venetian army.

"The three of us left for Mantua, passing for two days through lands whose names I don't remember. But we never arrived at Mantua, because when we arrived in Castelfra' a *terzo* of German soldiers stole our clothes, which were made of good cotton. The soldier who undressed me gave me the clothes he was wearing." Giuseppe's clothes were probably the same ones he had stolen from Captain Stinca, who would not approve Giuseppe's travel documents unless the soldier forfeited his clothes. Giuseppe decided to keep his clothes and escape at night; it was those clothes that the German soldier later stole.

A fugitive wearing the uniform of a *lanzo* and wandering the Po valley corresponds to the stereotypic plague victim of that time. Indeed, in Como, a little to the north, the clothes of German *lanzi* were what brought the plague to Milan. Tadino, a physician who chronicled the Milanese plague, carefully followed the trafficking in clothes, materials, and goods. "On 22 October 1629," he recorded, "Pietro Antonio Lovato entered the city carrying many clothes that he had bought or stolen from German soldiers."[44] A bubo appeared on his left elbow, and he died a few days later. The German soldiers would trade almost anything, and an epidemic started in Lecco because its inhabitants so desired the Germans' furs. Disease and death were thus spread by these exchanges, which involved, of course, theft, barter, and the spoliation of dead bodies. Tadino's chronicle grows ever denser as it tells these stories about clothes and materials. A "buffalo robe" purchased by a peasant, for example, becomes the protagonist of a compelling vignette of life and death.

In this manner the two infantrymen described the Thirty Years' War in Lombardy. These poor picaroons, exhausted by days spent in military camps and by officers' abuse, were both attracted to a life of ravaging and profiteering.

The fugitive Giuseppe's story—about how he tried to join the enemy's army and how a German soldier robbed him on the road from Brescia to Mantua—does not end there. After they had met a band of Imperial soldiers, the three comrades turned toward Cremona. "We got there in two more days and then traveled to Parma, where nobody was allowed to enter, with or without papers. So we decided to go to Modena, but we couldn't enter that city either. Then we went to Castelfranco di Bologna, a castle similar to this one, where papal soldiers are stationed."

Giuseppe's cellmate, Pier Francesco, the soldier from Casentino, passed through Castelfranco as well. He stayed there and worked as an unskilled construction laborer building the pope's fortress. Whereas Giuseppe's two companions also decided to stay, "hoping to receive some help from those papal soldiers," Giuseppe chose to continue his journey.

> I asked myself what I was doing there. I didn't have the means to survive, and until now I have lived by begging, and those soldiers couldn't help me. Deciding that it was better for me to return to Rome, I left Castelfranco. One day later, I arrived at a tavern two miles from Bologna and spent the night on some hay in a stable. The following day I got as far as a tavern eleven miles from Scarica l'Asino. Last night I made it to Pietra Mala, where I was found by two young men and brought here.

Once again, it was crossing the border of the grand duchy that caught the magistrate's eye. Giuseppe was asked to explain precisely how he had traversed the passes to arrive in Tuscany. His story takes us back to the mountains: "In Scarica l'Asino I asked two men in the central square if I could pass through there. They told me that the normal pass was guarded but that if I gave six *quattrini* to a child, he would take me along a different route where I could cross the border and avoid guards. I would be able to get in easily. Since I had one *gazzetta,* I gave it to a boy of fifteen or sixteen."

The Venetian coin in Giuseppe's pocket was worth four Tuscan *quattrini.* He wanted to make sure that he could begin his journey by paying less than the amount requested. After some bargaining, Giuseppe and the boy began the hike. The boy took Giuseppe "up into the snowy mountains where there was no path. When we reached some houses at the foot of a mountain, he said that they belonged to Florence and were guarded. Then he led me far away from them and pointed out a way that would lead to other guarded houses. He warned 'That is a roadblock. Don't go there. Keep walking straight. After you pass those houses, you can go anywhere you like.'"

Walking on the newly fallen snow off the usual path, the two could avoid any checkpoints. Before the descent, they separated. Giuseppe followed the boy's advice and continued on by himself: "I saw the houses . . . and once it got dark I walked in the snow far from them until I saw the road nearby. After I had walked along it for about half a mile I ran into two young men who arrested me and brought me here."

The vicar asked if he had the official papers signed by the captain. "No, sir, because we escaped, and, as I told you, we didn't ask for a passport or for a leave of absence." When was the last time he had been paid? "We haven't received any money since we left Naples. We got only enough to eat day to day." He was talking about the six *parpagliole,* the equivalent of about three Tuscan *soldi,* which Captain Stinca always reduced, supposedly to pay for wood and shoes, thereby taking advantage of his soldiers.

Did he owe the captain anything for the clothes he was wearing? "I don't know." Did he think "that he had paid for his clothes?" "Sir, I have served for three months, and the king of Spain's captains gave me nothing except these clothes. Whenever the salary came, they took everything and gave us nothing."[45] Moreover, his uniform had been stolen by someone who, like himself, was searching for clothes and money.

"Was there any plague in Cassiano, where their *terzo* was, or anywhere nearby?" the magistrate asked, changing the subject. "No sir, because there was no longer any contagion in the duchy of Milan. Only in the city of Milan itself was there still some plague, but they said that they had ended the quarantines on the twenty-first of this month. Outside of Milan all frontiers are open and there is no disease."

The facts supported his assertions. Florence had also established a quarantine during the month of January; however, the winter witnessed the lessening of the epidemic. Even in Bergamo, Brescia, and Venice there was no mention of the plague, and quarantine everywhere was about to be ended. The Po valley was free as well, and "nobody was dying any longer" in Mantua, Cremona, Parma, and Reggio.

Was there plague among the king of Spain's soldiers? I do not know, Giuseppe answered, but certainly not in my *terzo*. "Had he ever fought in a battle?" No, because as soon as he arrived in Naples in September with the three other Romans Giuseppe was taken to the Arsenale for twenty-four days. Then they were divided into ten groups and put on ships, where "we spent a long time at sea." They spent another ten days "in a land not far from Genoa, where we were unable to cross the river." It took another ten days to reach Cassano, where they stayed for one month and where "nothing happened."

The Roman Giuseppe's testimony ends here. He was undressed and "examined carefully. No written document or money was found in his clothes, and he looked like a healthy young man." He did not even have a medallion like the one the pious soldier Pier Francesco carried in his pocket.

Waiting for the decision of the Florentine magistrates, the vicar Carnesecchi of Firenzuola kept the two young men in jail, providing them with eight *soldi*'s worth of bread "at the expense of the Public Health Magistracy."

BELISARIO'S ESCAPE

War chronicles and soldiers' testimonies end here. Yet one last episode concerned a journey, in particular the movements of a livestock trader and his shepherding family from the Apennines. It is a peculiar story, because for the first time the traveler avoided arrest and managed to escape. Not the protagonist but his family offered the details on his journey. Belisario's family never left their home, their herd, or their village, but they talked about him after they made his escape possible.[46]

The story began in the summer—on 12 July 1630, to be precise— in the village of Pieve di San Stefano. The soldiers of the Bargello guard went to the house of Belisario, a livestock trader and one of the grand duke's mounted soldiers. Reputedly a black marketeer, he was engaged in criminal activities that carried the death penalty.

The armed soldiers arrived with the order for his arrest. In the yard facing the house, the soldiers of the Bargello guard were confronted by Belisario himself, carrying an arquebus and shouting, "Who's there?" A guard reported that Belisario then "ran back into his house. My soldiers and I followed him. When I saw him going into the house, I yelled, 'Comrades, go watch the windows,' and followed them."

While trying to enter the house, the Bargello guards realized that the door was being held shut from the inside. Some women were trying with all their strength to prevent them from opening the door. "The mother resisted. Hearing all the noise, the sister-in-law arrived, . . . and she helped keep me out. . . . But with my soldiers' help I finally got in. Belisario hit my dog in the face and then escaped up a ladder. He reached the door on the second floor. . . . Opening it, he saw a guard stationed outside. So he shot at the guard, who threw himself on the ground for protection. That is how Belisario managed to escape."

Belisario was a dangerous man, a skilled soldier and armed. As the quick battle with the soldiers demonstrated, he was also prepared to kill. The entire family was duly arrested, and a gun found in their house was confiscated.

From his relatives' testimonies, from the wall of diffidence and hostility which dragged the questioning into repetitions and silences, emerged the affection and admiration that everyone felt for this eldest son of the family. Always mounted, with an arquebus over his shoulder, Belisario was like a hero to his family. He went to the market of Maremma and the May fair of Montalcino to sell animals. His very absence, the fact that he had actually escaped, made him even more charismatic, as if surrounded by a halo of invulnerability.

Moreover, the local populace greatly respected the mounted soldiers who maintained order in the rocky Apennines. In Pieve San Stefano, the mounted guards had been established in 1629, and Belisario had been working for them for a year. His family's admiration for him mirrored the admiration the villagers had for these soldiers who protected them from the bandits and criminals that infested the region.[47]

Belisario's brother Agnolo testified first. He said, "I'm nine or ten years old. Our family consists of my father, mother, seven brothers, one sister, one sister-in-law, and grandmother." Each member of the peasant family had a precise function within the unit: the younger brothers took care of the cows and sheep, and Belisario and his father, Mariano, bought animals in Siena and sold them at Montalcino and Bologna in May.

Whereas animals and markets belonged to the male domain, the women worked in the house. When the soldiers arrived, Belisario's mother said that she was making cheese. The sister-in-law claimed that she could not move because her hands were busy in the flour where she had poured the yeast. They all lived in the same house, and according to the boy Agnolo, "Mariano's the boss." Besides the three brothers still residing at home, there were another two, one a "priest in Perugia" and the other a "friar with the Zocholi brothers." The family did not see Belisario very often; Agnolo had last seen him on the previous Wednesday. "I was with the herd at Can del Cerro, and it must have been sunset. . . . As I was watching over the animals I saw Belisario on his horse going toward the house, and I asked him, 'Belisario, how are you?' He responded, 'I'm fine, how are you?' Then he left and went home. I stayed with the animals."

Nobody discussed journeys in any detail at dinner, but Belisario told them that he had just come back from Florence. He showed them his travel documents from the Public Health Magistracy. Because the testimonies were extorted from unwilling witnesses, the family's behavior sounded artificial. The mother, for example, claimed that she did not know where her son went to buy animals, stating, "They don't tell me, because I'm a woman." She explained, though, that she made sure that Belisario's papers were in order in case he wanted to go to Pieve. "As things are so difficult now, a man has to have all his papers. Only peasants never think about this, so they get in trouble all the time." Soon after, she contradicted herself by admitting that those who lived in the vicarage of Pieve did not really need travel documents, since the personal knowledge of neighbors and villagers guaranteed the good health of everyone in the community. In addition, her testimony was inconsistent with the answers of her children. Hers highlighted her affection for her eldest son. When Belisario came home on the Wednesday evening he dined alone with his mother, "because peasants eat as soon as they get home. Belisario was so tired that he ate by himself. Then he waited for the others to spend some time with them."

When the soldiers arrived, "I got up from making cheese and said, 'Who are these people,' and they replied, 'We are officers of the court.' I asked, 'What do you want?' and they answered, 'We want to know who ran into your house.' I responded, 'It was my son.' Then they demanded, 'Where is he?' I answered, 'Look for him yourselves!' We went upstairs, but he had already vanished."

Belisario was not a traveler. So far as his family was concerned, he had either returned or escaped. Nobody knew that he had ever gone to Bologna, and nobody admitted to knowing about his affairs. They just waited for him, seeing him only when he came back.

The testimonies delineate the hierarchical and sexual organization of the family. The sister-in-law, Lisabetta, confirmed what her mother-in-law had said. This lack of knowledge stemmed from their being women: "and I don't pay attention to men's business" or to their talk. The children of the house, Santino, Cristofano, and Agnolo, looked after the animals and shared the same bed. Camillo, Lisabetta's husband, spent his days cutting trees in the woods and shared his wife's bed. The family kept the gun in the house because Belisario "was a mounted soldier."

The attempted arrest of Belisario ends here with his silent and hostile family locked up in jail.

Unexpectedly, on 30 July, a dispatch from Florence offered some news of the fugitive. His father, Mariano, spontaneously went to see the vicar of Pieve di San Stefano and said that his son Belisario, while hiding near Sasso Corbara in the duchy of Urbino, had been killed when he fell asleep on a road. The assassin had approached, hitting him with a stone and crushing his skull. The killer, a man from Meldola, had been arrested, and Mariano "was on his way to make sure that he was punished."[48]

In Florence this group of travel testimonies opened the chronicle of the plague as if to suggest coincidentally the persistence of an ancient theme, the medieval *pestifera vagationis*.[49] Those who journeyed, the restless and the searchers, were the ones who endangered the health of city dwellers. It is no coincidence that before the city closed its gates and isolated its ill it paid attention to threatening individuals, examining the value of the old equation connecting disease to vagabonds, and vagabondage to a maleficent torment.

The ten testimonies we have here examined refer only to those itineraries that the Florentine Public Health Magistracy believed dangerous: those descending through the Apennines from Milan, converging predominantly on Pistoia. There is not a single case, for example, of a traveler newly arrived from the state's southern borders being put in jail. We can therefore conclude that the number of arrested individuals constituted only a small fraction of the total number of people who attempted to enter the grand duchy. By the time their stories reach our hands, they have already been culled. These people are, in fact, only part of a larger anonymous crowd, most of it lost because the magistrate considered it insignificant. In this sense, a precise logic emerges from the voices of prisoners in the texts that the chancellor transcribed: the reports, details, and dates attempt to single out the exact moment when the chronicle of the trip intersects the history of the plague. In which place, path, encounter, or object is the germ of contagion? These travel records are thus somehow impure, filtered through the record keepers' attention.

Taken as a whole, however, the testimony allows us to perceive common elements. From the web of interrogations emerge categories of types, the same types that crowd the pages of the contemporary novels and treatises describing charlatans and vagabonds. Beggars, soldiers, and pilgrims, and the infinite other subcategories celebrated by the literature of the late Middle Ages, reemerge, as Piero Camporesi notes, "in the heart of the picaresque."[50] In the mid–seventeenth century the Dominican brother Giacinto Nobili, alias Rafaele Frianoro, translated the now forgotten *Speculum cerretanorum* of the late 1400s. His work marks clearly the passage of the vagabond from the popular literature of the late Middle Ages to the baroque.[51] In his important text *Il vagabondo*, we can trace some of the interconnections between vagabonds in popular literature and those actually interrogated by the Florentine Public Health Magistracy in 1630.

The portrait of the "fake *bordone*," the begging imposter who pretended to be a pilgrim returning from the most celebrated sanctuaries, reminds us of Jacopo Terracini of Palermo, who posed as a poet. He claimed to have avoided the plague in his native city and then to have gone on a pilgrimage to Loreto.[52] This character type in Giacinto Nobili's *Il vagabondo* is very similar to that described by the author of *Speculum cerretanorum* in the story of Rotondo.[53] If we consider that the deeply entrenched typology that was transmitted by a genre of literature unique to Italy remained almost identical for two centuries, we can assume that the fake pilgrim and fake vagabond were familiar characters to seventeenth-century magistrates used to the widespread pauperism of that era.

Another case suggesting the paradigmatic character of bandit literature is the story of the father and son, Antognone and Francesco, who hid in the Pistoian mountains. You will remember how the poor laborer's young son, bitten by a dog, was questioned by the magistrate whose suspicions were aroused when he saw the boy's wounded knee. One character in Pini's and Nobili's texts is a "tarantulated" man who pretends to have been bitten by a tarantula.[54] This character was a variation of the French subspecies of *Hubins* whose beggary was based on the claim of having been bitten by a rabid dog. In contrast, the very presence of a child indicated a specific kind of criminal begging, where the young boy made "the shoe" for the adult—in other words, the father directed the evil action from a distance.[55]

Deserters constitute one of the largest categories of bandit literature. Dirty and ragged, they wandered the countryside and cities, pretending to be wounded and mutilated. They also begged and, by relating stories of battles and prisons, encouraged people to pity them. In seventeenth-century jargon they were called *formigotti*. The servants Antonio and Francesco, Michele di Paolo who deserted for family reasons, the good soldier Pier Francesco Farsetti, and the Roman Giuseppe Gallo can easily be assimilated into this *formigotti* category. These defendants, veterans of the war raging in Mantua and Genoa, were beggars and dirty, ragged fugitives. They admitted that they lived off charity. They probably told stories of war and simulated wounds to make money, just as the *formigotti* of the novels, the likes of which one was wise to avoid, did.

Finally, there is the case of the charlatan Bastiano Giannelli who, arrested at Volterra in the middle of a screaming crowd, was charged with plague spreading. He was a prototypical plague spreader, one who marked the passage of the semantic shift from the many-sided charlatan of the late Middle Ages to the vagabond and quack physician of the early modern period.[56] He confessed to the magistrate that he wandered throughout the countryside selling not only insignificant items but also the roots of Saint Apollonia, sealed soil, pilaster, and grain oil, all of which were remedies against the most common illnesses: toothaches, eye infections, and fevers. In this sense it is not merely coincidence that the only other case involving a charge of plague spreading was pressed against a foreign doctor, Ciminelli, who was reported to have poisoned. Once again the accusation slid toward an identical semantic convergence, charlatanism, which, although posing as a science, in fact spread death. During epidemics guardians of bodies courted danger and ran the risk of stepping beyond the law. Bastiano, who sold medicines in the countryside, and Doctor Leandro, who worked at the hospital of Bonifazio in Florence, were regarded as false healers and, therefore, as charlatans. Only a small leap of the imagination was required, therefore, for them to be suspected of spreading the plague.

Just as the defendants' profiles paralleled those described by novelists, so did the locations and other minor details mirror those of the picaresque tales. Thus taverns, sanctuaries, haystacks, and people who, in giving directions, tricked travelers emerged in both archival documents and literature: *formigotti,* fake *bordoni,* and charlatans rest, drink, play, and cheat at every opportunity, and in the same spaces where the individuals we have studied began their journeys.

The convergence of texts is strong, and the events recounted by the imprisoned characters extend into the modules of genre with apparent ease. Compared with the novels, however, one element was missing in their testimonies: the swindle and spectacle. The defendants suspected of carrying the plague are viewed, so to speak, backstage, devoid of the constructed role described by the authors of bandit literature. In front of the magistrates there were no open wounds, no card games, no magic tricks—only poor travelers who had been hit by war, misery, and fatigue.

There is something in the testimonies, then, that is not in literature. While we are tempted to imagine that the soldier Michele di Paolo, in order to escape from Milan to Pistoia, took advantage of his vicissitudes as an erstwhile soldier to beg for food and money, we know for sure that his family was evicted on 3 August and that this action was what led him to desert. Thus, we know why Michele di Paolo became a *formigotto,* even if in his testimony he did not explain how this passage took place. The same holds true for the others. We are told how the lack of work, pressuring creditors, or the desire to hide an illegitimate child influenced family events and led to deserted houses, enlistments, and travels: unique individual cases whose impulses and desires are not mentioned in novels.

In other words, through a judicial apparatus the sentences passed by the Florentine Public Health Magistracy opened new perspectives. After a short time in jail, the defendants were all released. Assumptions deduced from a fixed typology broke down in the face of the trial, which required verifications and confirmations. Whereas literature evoked through clothes and gestures a countersociety of immutable characters, the criminal trials, by attending to details, differences, and circumstances, penetrated beyond generalized masks and reconstructed, albeit fragmentarily, the actors' profiles.

First of all the magistrates, compelling the defendants to talk, asked questions that delineated the itinerary of responses. Subsequently the replies moved freely, focusing on detailed descriptions which the trial recorder transcribed accurately, even to the point of reporting improper speech and dialects. The use of the third person was limited only to the prosecution and was therefore reduced to the barest essentials. Actually, it was usually the accent and the contents of the defendants' testimonies that led the magistrates to respond in astonishment. Any time they suspected a lie, contradiction, or trap, the magistrates got angry, started threatening, and asked increasingly pointed questions. Unlike the literary texts, criminal documents recorded an intense game of language. Moreover, these relationships were, so to speak, face to face, where roles could switch and the defendant could drag the judge along the jagged ridges of silence, challenge, and astuteness.

Perhaps this is the element of spectacle, of *performance,* that literature depicts in the exterior forms of masks and types. It was in the encounter between defendant and judge that the missing link of the relationship with authority became embodied. Only this oral theatricality could, in time, produce biographical profiles for these travelers.

Dealing directly with the magistrate, the defendant talked about himself in the first person (as no character of bandit literature would ever have done) and even reported his dialogues with others in the direct form. These dialogues were concise; they served as a sort of humoristic intermezzo within the testimonies. Recall, for example, the Roman soldier Giuseppe Gallo and his arguments with the detestable Captain Stinca. Together with the verbal exchange, there were also the self-reflections of Giuseppe ("I asked myself") and the thoughts he shared with other companions ("We started to look into each other's eyes and think about our self-interest"). Thus the testimonies provide us with a stratified text, one articulated on many linguistic levels. In another case Belisario's mother, after her merchant-soldier son managed to avoid arrest, reported her exchange with the soldiers who came to arrest him. The furious velocity of the account with its angry "Look for him yourselves" conclusion allows us to measure the degree of hostility that animated the woman's resistance, both verbal and physical, to the "court."

The direct form of address renders the dialogue and exclamations of these texts theatrical. The defendants did not dilute their own significance in these events. They organized their experiences around a precise hierarchy of private and domestic values, an economy of essential relationships, and the constraints of time. Thus, for example, the magnitude of the events disintegrates as the Thirty Years' War is projected onto the background of Michele's family worries or the imminent sack of Mantua competes with the two servants' concern for their master's bags and their pack animal.

In a certain sense, what emerges from the testimonies is a society of people who have power despite all their hardship. Through the protagonists' perceptions appears a distant gallery of sharply drawn portraits. Moreover, the testimonies reveal the defendants' miming, amplifying the oral tension of texts that correspond to the gestures and movement of bodies. That the phrase "keeping him at a distance of eight armlengths" began Antognone's interrogation symbolized the magistrate's fear of cantagion. The scene was described in a precise visual context; before the interrogation Francesco was "taken out near a walnut tree," and we picture a small silhouette hiding behind the tree, bending to avoid the branches. Then the phrases "he showed his bandaged leg" and "after he removed the bandages a wound was seen" reveal that the magistrate had been forced to come closer than the safe distance of eight armlengths to observe the wounded limb. Before he answered the chancellor's questions, the deserter Michele di Paolo accurately examined the window and secured the shutter with a rock; while engaged in this simple act he was described by the notary, who was watching him from the sunny courtyard below. These are the flashes, the miniatures that stick in recorded memory and decompose the fixed stereotypes perpetrated by novels. Unlike the language of the ruling classes and professional groups, dialogues in these testimonies are direct, devoid of adjectives and abstract terms. As thirst was measured by the number of bottles drunk in taverns, so too was hunger represented by eating too many figs, too much bread and cheese, or a few fish and an onion, and fatigue portrayed by dusty shoes and a sudden weariness.

The magistrates focused their attention on the present. They attempted to find the epidemic wherever it was hiding. The testimonies, in contrast, looked to the past, delineating more than one reversed trajectory. The particular point at which a travel report intersects a story of plague is lost within a path ramified in various directions: family, war, work, and street. These are the common sites of communication and exchange, shaken by unpredicted events and fragmented by the minute details of everyday life. Thus the epidemic appeared to those witnessing it as an obstacle along the path, forcing everyone to make detours, to cheat, to delay, to slide toward a stubborn resistance against authority. Even in the first testimonies, private space works like a dam against the proliferation of regulations. If one were not going to investigate all its ramifications, the plague would remain, like a cruel exception, suspended in time, while the widespread social perception of those who witnessed it was wrapped in the density of affection and common relationships. The opaque weight of normality burdens even the moments of emergency, the extreme and exceptional dangers.

It is on the disruptions of the coherent character of official explanations that I focus in the pages that follow.

pure soil and hills that face east is better than springwater from rocky beds and hills that face north. Springwater from valleys is also bad. Well water belongs to a third category. In some places, such as Florence, where wells run as deep as the Arno River, water is acceptable and does not pose any dangers. . . . Water from lakes and swamps is useless and should always be avoided, particularly if aqueducts are new and made of lead. By seawater we mean water from calm oceans, consequently fresh and uncorrupted.[6]

The omen of the plague explicates that deterioration, that ever-present sliding of each quality toward its opposite, which is mentioned only briefly in the *Farmacopoeia,* almost as if it were a shadow. "The air becomes heavy and humid, while the fog, dust, and heavy warm winds increase. . . . The waters and fields smoke, producing a stench. Fish do not taste or smell good any longer, and animals are born out of the putrefaction everywhere."[7]

The moon and the humid asteroids exacerbate the mutation of bodies par excellence. When the moon reaches its full phase, it combines heat and humidity to generate a "perfect putridity," that is, the plague.[8] The soil becomes unproductive because it is affected by the imbalance; famine is the most direct cause of the epidemic, predisposing human bodies to devastation through a slow and constant erosion of living conditions. An impoverished diet and intense suffering allows evil humors to grow, subsequently condensing in the bodies of the poor, because they are weaker, or of women and children, because they are "made of tender elements and full of humidity" and live "in disorder."[9] The nature of these people is, as it were, overwhelmed by the "extraordinary putridity" which developed

spoiled, acute, and unabating fevers, . . . accompanied by malignant symptoms such as bubos and cysts. . . . Bubos grow especially between the leg and the body, some under the arm, and occasionally behind the ear. Cysts, however, can grow all over the body. Some people are hit by a delirium after the fever. Others become very thirsty, suffering from a completely dry mouth and a headache, . . . as well as from vomiting and an unsteady, irregular, weak heartbeat.[10]

According to the treatises, these symptoms were followed by sudden death, usually within seven days. Those who took immediate measures to arrest the disease, however, were usually cured.

These texts, containing diagnoses and *exempla,* were written a posteriori, that is, after the epidemic had already ravaged the poor neighborhoods of the city. Therefore, the concise arguments appearing in these pages do not reflect the confusion that generally precedes and accompanies the actual manifestation of the disease. Denunciations, suspicions, and medical reports follow one other, becoming confused in a normality that continuously obfuscated the terror, attenuated the perception of danger, and consequently postponed the alarm. From the middle of summer to October, when the plague was officially recorded in Florence, chronicles, scientific treatises, and criminal documents recorded the unstoppable slide toward calamity. Only the edicts promulgated by the Public Health Magistracy, which had long been in contact with its Milanese counterpart, provide us with the sense of breathless anxiety on the part of those who, foreseeing an inevitable struggle, gathered all their strength.

On 6 August, when it was first rumored that the contagion had entered the city, the leaders decided

> to call on the doctors that the magistrate will choose. For the time being, the following physicians are appointed: Zerbinelli, Cervieri, Pellicini, Napoletano, and Punta. They are requested to compile a list of treatments for the plague and of the necessary medicines. They should gather tomorrow, Wednesday, 7 August, to execute these orders . . . so that the herbalists can do whatever is necessary. To cope with the growing crisis, herbalists are asked to send experienced people to the Magistracy so that, accompanied by two doctors, they can inspect herbalist shops and, shop by shop, inventory all of the city's medical supplies. . . . This team should then make a report to the Magistracy, so that, in the event of a shortage of supplies, action can be taken.[11]

Doctor Zerbinelli was requested to determine the "available quantity of medicines and antidotes, particularly oil-based poison remedies." In addition, he was "to renew the prohibition to extract them and to list these medicines publicly, so that any individual could know of them."[12]

The regulation of the quantity and quality of medicines in herbalist shops was part of a broader policy of administrative and environmental surveillance, one aspect of which was the prohibition of the export of elements essential to traditional remedies against the plague (such as theriaca, a mixture of various drugs and honey used as an antidote to poison). Good food supplies were guaranteed by complex verification procedures at the source, and roadblocks were set up to prevent the black-marketing of raw materials through the Apennine Mountains. Careful attention was paid to the numerous anonymous denunciations made by citizens: digging by the Compagnia di San Giorgio produced bad smells, exposing the nearby homes to stinking miasmas; a castrated pig of the worst quality was hung in a butcher shop on the Piazza San Lorenzo; and the butchers at the Arch of San Piero stored innards that were spoiling.[13]

The combination of rumors from below and state ordinances from above provides us with a feeling for the oppressiveness of the streets of Florence. The magistrates' lucid, concise prose, together with the common prose of denunciations and supplications, allows the daily colors, odors, and voices of the Mercato Vecchio to come alive. Yet this daily routine only appeared reassuring; in fact, it had begun to disintegrate, leading to suspicions, alarm, and denunciations.

The ordinances of the Public Health Magistracy were the first to break taboos, openly pronouncing the word doctors still avoided: *plague*. In the official reports forwarded to the Magistracy, the Galenic prose insisted on calling the disease the evil that "gets sticky." On 28 August, the college of doctors reiterated that the sudden, numerous deaths were caused not by the plague but by a putrid fever combined with tumors and bubos.[14] Antonio Medici, a court physician, maintained that the disease was a "simplicem epidemium." Other doctors, including Stefano Rodriguez de Castro, the Magistracy's Portuguese adviser, and Niccolò Zerbinelli, agreed. Doctor Zerbinelli went even further, basing his diagnosis on the presence of the French (venereal) disease beginning to spread in the city. As this illness was contagious, he discounted ipso facto the possibility that the plague could be spreading as well, for the medical authorities believed that two similar diseases could not coexist.[15] In short, deaths should be attributed to a contagious fever that arises from a combination of causes, internal and external, and that may result in a variety of symptoms. The symptoms may affect all or only part of the body. The disease may or may not be lethal.[16]

Among common people, however, the reassuring horizon delineated by the official reports had little effect. By the beginning of August, an anonymous denunciation indicated the presence of a sick person in Santa Maria del Fiore. There, a candlemaker had died in three days, and "when he died, it was said that a bubo was found between his legs. His father, Valentino, is a textile worker and lives on Via Tedesca. It is said that another of his sons is sick and will not be alive tomorrow."[17]

Bubblelike symptoms could also suggest skin rashes and therefore indicate ordinary diseases, which were not suspect. The common appearance and routine course of familiar diseases obfuscated the visibility of the plague. One feels this clearly when looking at records of the earliest arrests of individuals charged with hiding their relatives. Their interrogations reveal common episodes of dysentery, fevers, seasonal disturbances, overeating, or female disorders. They also reveal simple problems, such as that of Domenico Guidi: "The man was in the garden, picking some pears, but fell when a branch of the tree broke." His bubo was obviously not the result of a contagious disease but of his fall from the pear tree.[18] Worms in children and women's pregnancies constantly aroused fears of the "bad disease," which, particularly in the homes of the poor, was confused with the symptoms of these ordinary conditions. Even the presence of the French illness, mentioned by Doctor Righi, contributed to the confusion. Consequently, symptoms were treated with analogous remedies: unguents for wounds and bubos, and opiates for insomnia.

The contemporary Milanese trials against plague spreaders also reveal a context in which ordinary diseases were confused with the plague. These testimonies show that syphilis spread to neighbors and relatives, and its symptoms suggested the use of various remedies.[19] Pimples and bubos could have various causes: perhaps the bite of a scorpion or a mad dog, or even carnal relations.

Behind this discussion of particular symptoms and their individual causes, an etiological background on which a consensus slowly focused began to take shape. The plague was the product of a deterioration, of a comprehensive ecological alteration. Within this perspective, the disease belonged to the vast universe of poisons generally produced by air. This meant that the plague possessed "invisible properties"; in short, the substance remained inactive until it encountered a human body. Once in a body, the poison "could be activated by the natural warmth" and thereby release the infected liquids.[20] As the sickness was caused by poisoning, it is not surprising that the reaction moved from the plane of environmental etiology, which involved erratic seasonal sequences, temperatures, and air qualities, to a causal chain of events determined by human actions both voluntary and involuntary.

This duality also appeared in the Florentine treatises on the contagion. Like most epidemics of the modern period, the plague chose its victims selectively; it spread throughout the poor districts, attacking those who already suffered from hunger and famine. According to most doctors, this pattern corresponded to a sort of proper ecological and social balance in which political categories were used to justify exclusive class divisions. According to Alessandro Righi, the human body consisted of both noble and less noble organs. Noble organs, including the heart, brain, arms, and legs, were able to expel dangerous substances toward the periphery. The less noble organs, such as the skin and the various glands, did not possess such abilities and consequently became the depository of poisons expelled by the noble organs. The city poor were likened to the less noble organs, "nec possunt ad alios transmittere, ideo necessario, si quid mali in Civitate est, ipsi recipiunt et retinent cum sint glandulae Civitatis."[21] Functioning as the city's gland, poor people attracted contagion and vice, serving as a sort of putrifying pimple where all sorts of diseases coagulated. Thus, Doctor Righi concluded, "Florentiae quoque aliqui contagiosi morbi exorti sunt"; the contagion did not come from far away or outside but rather germinated in the streets and homes of Florence. Only "ill-advised" rich people, who voluntarily ran the risk of contracting the disease, got sick.[22] According to the theologian Filiberto Marchini, the plague, following a long-established tradition, could be spread "humana arte," by powders, hidden in clothes or soap, made with the liquids expelled by infected bodies.[23] Finally, Francesco Rondinelli's chronicle, based on these same assumptions about the means of contagion, discussed the human chains responsible for spreading the disease.

The plague consolidated hierarchies and differences: the unconscious deaths of the poor were opposed in Righi's text to the deaths of some nobles who contracted the disease, thus breaking down social barriers. In this manner the emergency sanctioned the codes of belonging and of isolating and targeting improper contacts and unusual encounters. It emphasized the borders between the licit and the illicit, between disease and good health, between normalcy and transgression. To understand how the disease progressed, to be able to spot it in a living body, meant being able to distinguish the ill-defined territory of poisonous miasmas from the well-defined perimeter of fevers, wounds—even a knife wound—and uterine infections. Having recognized the disease, one then had to trace its origins, singling out the event that triggered the contagion.

Only the manifestation of the disease could dispel the opacity of

the other symptoms. In his *Consiglio contro la pestilenza,* Marsilio Ficino wrote about this problem at length. His book, widely read in
Florence, was in the sixteenth century the most commonly cited
source on this topic, particularly by writers dealing with therapies.
Visible symptoms appeared on bodies at the last and culminating moment of a process of total disorder: "Unbelievably strong and continuous fevers, increasing chest pains, uneven heartbeats, cloudy urine,
bubos, wounds, miscarriages, violence, cruel wars, and natural and
divine miracles."[24] The people prone to contract the disease easily are
those with tempers; in contrast, the melancholic are protected by a
cold and dry constitution. Melancholy people also have "narrow passages" that limit the circulation of the poison between the heart and
the peripheral organs. The warmth and humidity of the body favor
the inflammation, and the disease first manifests itself by the boiling,
putrid liquids around the heart.[25]

At this stage, as the contagion appears to besiege the central organs
of the body, Ficino suggests intervention "right on the spot" so that
the symptom will appear clearly. Thus, unguent and crystals of arsenic should be applied to the wrists, back of the neck, temples, chest,
nostrils, throat, heart, stomach, and underarms.[26] The poisonous
miasmas penetrate the body mostly through the skin (which is particularly open in angry people). Thus, the best defense is a therapy based
on steamed air: "If you asked me through what passages does the
poison penetrate, I would respond through all the pores of the skin;
when it enters through the mouth, nose, and the wrists, it has an
immediate effect."[27]

According to Ficino and the authors who followed his view, the
infected body, displaying implicit symptoms, was an open organism.
Its openings were in danger because they were an integral part of the
osmotic relationship of exchanges between the elements and the rest
of the body. Therefore, the unguents, fumigations, massages, and
small sacks and precious stones placed over the heart were designed to
restore the balance between external and internal spaces without ob-
structing the passages between inside and outside and their filtering
mechanisms. The key was to keep the malignant liquids captured by
the bubo from moving toward the heart, as they naturally tended to
do, until they were ready to be expelled. The growth of the bubo
actually confirmed that the organism was fighting the disease by sending all the poison to that one spot.

Throughout, Ficino paid great attention to passages and holes, to the relationship between top and bottom, inside and out. It was in passages that the contagion insinuated itself, and it was from there that the disease had to be extracted. The symptoms appeared in those areas to which organs tended to expel the poison: behind the ears, from the brain; under the arms, from the heart; and between the legs, from the liver. Bubos were of four different colors, depending on their internal composition: black, yellow, green, or red. At their appearance they ought to be isolated from the heart by tourniquets, and the bubos themselves ought to be treated with unguents to speed their growth. In official medical language, these unguents were called *rottori* ("breakers"), and it was suggested that the following items be used in their preparation: animal excrement, mustard, poison ivy, rock salt, cantharide powder, crushed glass, turpentine, pork fat, and an onion cooked in the fireplace and applied while still hot. The Florentine *Farmacopoeia,* which was legally required to be in every herbalist shop, itself prescribed the use of animal substances to warm the bodies of the sick.[28]

Ficino suggested that delicate individuals take either almond oil or lily oil. For local applications, one should "boil oil and water together until they become one substance and cook bran flakes and dry, fat figs together and then crush them."[29] Waiting for the disease to develop, one should start purging the body, first by administering bloodlettings. Rondinelli agreed that for those with strong constitutions bloodletting could lead to recovery, provided the phlebotomist "do it carefully—taking much less than people usually do, in consideration of not only the present forces but also the future ones, thereby avoiding those dangers which weakness can produce. One hopes for the poison to withdraw toward the interior parts of the body."[30] In medical treatises this matter was at the center of numerous debates concerning such matters as how much blood should be let; where and when the operation should take place; and whether this should be done to everybody, regardless of age or sex. Some debates questioned whether pregnancy or complexion influenced the success of bloodletting. Moreover, these treatises discussed phlebotomists' techniques, particularly the belief that blood should always be taken from the ankle, even when, as in the case of the Florentine epidemic, bubos typically appeared "between the legs."

Ficino's prescriptions, which were adopted by barber-surgeons,

forced sufferers into a series of bloody interventions, the many variations of which were discussed. These authors rarely mention the
physical pain, which must have been overwhelming for their patients.
Even Rondinelli, who did not belong to the doctors' guild, suggested
exercising caution when cauterizing, "so that the pain is not exacerbated, and patients do not die of desperation."[31] In contrast, doctors
avoided such emotion in their professional language. They were probably more interested in the classic origin of pain, in the failure of the
body to suppress deadly humors: *dolor dolorem trahit*.

After the bloodletting, doctors prescribed sour drinks—cedar
syrup, vinegar water, and other such liquids—to be taken before
meals. Occasionally the purification was intensified by "scratching
bitter things and onion juice on the [hemorrhoid] with glasses and
leeches."[32] Right under the bubos, wounds were to be cut. While the
cuts remained open, the poisonous liquid would flow, as "nature sends
the poison to disgusting places, like sewers, far from the noble organs
and the heart."[33] The practice was therefore like the "fountain," a very
common treatment for infections of all sorts and one of the easiest
techniques available for purifying the organism of all poison. With the
"fountain," a cut was made and kept open—in cases of plague, for at
least three months. This type of treatment was sometimes used as
preventive medicine, and Doctor Fabrizi d'Acquapendente reported
that it was common in Florence to burn children's necks to protect
them from infantile infections. Mothers would take their children to
the barber, who would "administer fire to the infants."[34] All of these
therapies were based on a conception of physical pain that was shared
by barbers, barber-surgeons, phlebotomists, and doctors, even
though the treatments referred back to classical traditions.

To recover from the plague, then, involved treatments that had already been tried for other diseases. Convinced by its success in the
epidemic of Pesaro, Gerolamo Mercuriale, a distinguished academi-
cian in Padua and later in Pisa, had been one of the earliest supporters
of administering the "fountain" between the legs.[35] When it was necessary to make the cut below the bubo, however, the cutting glass had
to be inserted above: "Insert a large cutting glass, then make the cut
with a razor blade. Next, remove the cutting glass and suck the blood.
When there is no more blood, apply three leeches and cover the
wound with a pigeon whose chest has been cut open. . . . Some

people prefer to use a plucked rooster and its soapy, grey extracts, applying all of it to the wound."[36]

The use of quartered animals to heal infections appeared in both official medical texts and compilations of popular remedies and the plethora of secret recipes. Stefano Rodriguez de Castro, an academic in Pisa and a consultant for the Florentine Public Health Magistracy, suggested that the poison would be attracted by applying a "shot" rooster, pigeon, and dog, one after the other, over the bubo. The practice, he noted, was an ancient one. Dioscorides recommended the application of a "chicken" over bites or wounds caused by poisoned weapons.[37] Later, in his *Historia Vitae et Mortis,* de Castro's contemporary Francis Bacon made fun of therapies such as these, based on the principles of the analogic correspondence between substances. In particular, he accused Ficino of being one of the many unenlightened healers who prescribed "dirty and loathsome" remedies. Although calling them mistakes and superstitions, Bacon still considered these remedies "useful," if "disgusting." Thus, he implicitly confirmed the density of the mental universe on which such therapies were based, the prestige of the ancient and modern authors who continued to prescribe them, and the complexity of the cultural (not only medical) processes necessary to construct different theoretical paradigms.[38]

Attracted and "boiled," the humor was finally to be expelled. "The bubo should be burned gently . . . with incandescent gold, silver, or iron. The instrument should be round at the top and should be shaped like a not too acute diamond at the bottom. After making the incision, cover the wound with cabbage leaves." These methods are very useful to "turn off" the poison.[39]

The plague was therefore a form of pollution, a general poisoning. It is no coincidence that the most common remedies against the infection were the same as those used for weapon wounds and snake and scorpion bites. Arsenic crystals, recommended "ex occulta qualitate, vel similitudine et affinitate eiusdem cum interiori veneno," were also useful for rabid dog and tarantula bites.[40] Theriaca, the most common antidote against the plague, was made mostly of snake meat, which, according to Galen, had to come from an eggless female. Since ancient times, this remedy had been used against toxins of equal strength.[41]

There were also, however, more potent modern remedies, which people of ancient times did not know about. Some had come from the

New World, for example the *contraierba* or *antiherba,* recommended by Marchini and de Castro, but unknown to Ficino. The root was native to the Caribbean, whose savage cave, mountain, and forest dwellers ("agrestes, pilosi, ferino monte antra, montes, sylvas incolentes") had diets consisting largely of human flesh. To catch their ideal prey, these cannibals used arrows made poisonous by local herbs. In addition, the antidote to these poisonous herbs grew locally. This *contraierba,* which induced warmth and sweating, was an aromatic diuretic to be drunk with orange juice.[42] This American plant, which sold for six *soldi* an ounce in Florence, like the powder the Milanese plague spreaders used to save themselves from the contagion, was a modern medicine. This latter powder, distributed by the Public Health Magistracy of Milan, was made of sulphur, arsenic, Palestinian incense, carnations, nutmeg, myrrh, radish leaves, ginger root, orange peel, peony leaves, mastic, and rue seeds. All these ingredients were to be crushed and put in a small sack made "of red damask," which was to be hung from the neck and worn over the heart. In winter, it was to be worn outside of the shirt so that "sweat not damage it."[43] If the Milanese plague spreaders and those who dealt with the rotten substances of dead bodies were protected by this powder, what better remedy could there be to ward off the poisonous miasmas? The Florentine magistrates who acquitted those accused of spreading the plague paid some attention to these rumors. Consequently, they permitted the Milanese powder to be sold locally.

The toxic universe of bites by rabid dogs, snakes, tarantulas, and scorpions, of venereal disease, and of bodily wounds was amplified into one of "violent illnesses." In Archduchess Mary Magdalen's seventeenth-century prescription book, the plague was solidly inscribed in a multifaceted poisonous complex: wounds caused by arms; melancholia, "the children's disease," including night fears and sadness; and saturnine diseases, which hit children and women especially.[44] Against these diseases popular texts also prescribed disturbing and symbolically significant remedies: blood, including human blood; bones, including human bones; and lion's meat, recommended for epilepsy.[45] Universal balsams, such as iperic oil and the oil of red dogs, were used against poisons, wounds, and common diseases. Thus, the symptoms of the plague hid among the symptoms of ordinary illnesses and fantastic diseases. It is here that we have to look in order to identify the practices and behaviors surrounding infected bodies.

THE EARLIEST SUSPICIONS

The first suspected case of plague appeared at the beginning of August a few miles from Florence, in Trespiano on the road to Bologna. After crossing a mountain pass, a poulterer encountered on his arrival an acquaintance, Viviano. Although the poulterer's poor appearance and painful walk made Viviano wary, the sight of gold offered in exchange for hospitality convinced him to take his friend home. After a few days, everyone in the house died. The contagion began to spread from there. By sunset, the news spread to the city, and the magistrates ordered the first precautions to be taken. That night, hidden from the other villagers, the bodies were removed and their belongings and bedding burned.[46] On 6 August other cases of sudden death were reported in Cianfo, a small village near Trespiano on the road leading to Florence. The senatorial families of the Albizi and the Carnesecchi and Doctors Cervieri and Zerbinelli oversaw the transformation of the hospital into a lazaret. They also posted forty guards around Cianfo to prevent anyone from entering or leaving the village. Rumors about the deadly contagion became more and more insistent; "they were even heard in Florence, but only faintly, in the ear of a friend, with the usual warning not to spread it. No one believed it, and no precautions were taken."[47]

Meanwhile, the Florentine deputies located the origin of the contagion and dispatched Antonio Manni to investigate the health of the family of the poulterer who had died in Trespiano. This functionary filed his report on 7 August. He went as far as Doccia, where the victim's brother, Matteo Citi, lived, but was able to speak only to Bartola, Matteo's seventeen-year-old daughter. She told him that the family members had dispersed to different residences. Simone, thirteen or fourteen years old, had gone to San Donato in Poggio "to be safe." Maria, the youngest, six years old, went to Trespiano. Maddalena, ten or twelve years old, was in Cianfo.[48] Could it have been Maddalena who, having been infected by her father, had spread the disease? Manni continued to question Bartola, who, fortunately, was "in good health." Had they hidden any sheets or other valuables before leaving? Yes, Bartola answered, taking Manni to the place where, in the night, they had buried some sacks of grain. Bartola then opened a door, behind which "two dresses, a sheet, a cloak, belts, hats, and other clothes for a young woman" were stored. Manni ordered it all to be disinfected. He locked it all in one room, placing the seal of the Public Health Magistracy on the front door.

No one in Florence, just a few miles away, knew what was happening. There were some rumors; however, even doctors maintained that it was a disease which "attacked" but did not kill. But there were some who, reflecting on those rumors, tried to retrieve from their memory the experiences of the past. Francesco Rondinelli reported on this underground flow of information, which dated the outbreak of the epidemic at the beginning of the summer. On 15 June, a forty-five-year-old native of Castel San Casciano and resident of Via del Cocomero, Tommaso Ciucci, was buried in Santa Maria del Fiore. He hired a young man from Bologna, who was probably already contagious, to work in his shop selling Bolognese veils. The young man, after running a high fever, died in the hospital, where Tommaso had immediately taken him. "Two or three days later, on the evening of Thursday, 12 June 1630, Tommaso was attacked by a fierce fever and went home early." Although a doctor came to see him, the shopkeeper, with two bubos on his neck, died before he could receive even extreme unction. The doctor advised the family to bury him outside of the duomo near the canonica. There, two gravediggers of the Compagnia della Misericordia stole his hat.[49]

Nobody paid any attention to the sudden deaths of the veil maker and his apprentice. The episode at Trespiano, the quarantine of Cianfo, and some other events, however, allowed the chronicler to tie together apparently irrelevant and unconnected incidents. On 3 August, the Public Health Magistracy was notified of the illness of one of Cavaliere Megalotti's servants. The maid had a strange bubo on her knee, which looked like a scorpion bite. The doctors, sent to Via della Stufa to investigate, reported that

> this morning we visited a servant . . . of Cavalier Megalotti. Doctor Cervieri and the barber-surgeon Giovanni discovered that the trouble was slightly over the knee. We concluded that it could not be a carbuncle, as she did not have the symptoms that usually occur: the itching bubbles, like grains of wheat, which produce a scab after they break; the deterioration of the skin that sometimes occurs even without the bubbles; and the ulcers that always accompany the scabs. This scab has a black, ashen color. The bottom is so strongly attached that it is like a nail. Moreover, it is corroding and inflaming the nearby tissues to an extraordinary degree. The ulcer we saw is deep and concave; in fact, it is almost round. The ulcer is neither black nor large, and the inflammation is not very big. It is very dry and does not expel any liquid.

Thus, the ulcer seems to be a bubo in bad shape . . . but not deadly. Also, the woman did not feel itchy and thought that she had been bitten by an animal.[50]

The lack of fever and the color of the wound, combined with the absence of the liquid substance, made the doctors more confident. Yet a few days later the woman was taken from Florence and confined in Compiobbi. This case was reported because the servant might have spread the contagion to her master's family—an apparently irrelevant episode that became visible because of its proximity to the rich.

In much the same way, the news of what happened at Garbo spread. When Signora del Garbo died, one of her tenants, the tailor Domenico Castelli, denounced the case to the Public Health Magistracy. Knocking at the door, the guards got no answer but could see through the keyhole the signora's dead body on the floor.

To understand the cause of the two deaths meant to shift the axis of the narrative toward the circumstances that preceded them. The pen of the chronicler therefore began to reconstruct the chain of events. A widow with four children lived in a "large old house" along the same road. On 6 August, the birthday of Grand Duchess Christine, the widow bought some flour with the gift she received in honor of the festivity. "Having made dough, she and her children ate it," after which all suddenly seemed to lose their minds and died the following day. What could have caused this sudden chain of death?

"In the corner toward the square," the draper Sisto, who had just replenished his storage area with merchandise bought at Trespiano, and his fellow workers died. A little window in his shop opened onto a courtyard where the widow and her children came and went regularly.[51] With similar explorative persistence, the chronicler followed the itinerary of the contagion to the quarter of Santa Maria Novella in Briga, welding one ring in the narrative chain to another. Here, too, it was the closeness, the proximity of houses and shops, and the communication between them that originated and spread the contagion: the bakery, the convent, and the house where a tired nobleman, for his distraction, spent the night in the bed of the infected servant.[52] Not only improper contacts but also everyday life occurred in neighborhood spaces, such as the courtyard that connected the draper to the widow. Some exchanges—of linens and food, for example—took place out of a sense of solidarity, habit, and compassion. The contagion insinuated itself into a daily life that ignored the danger and disregarded the apparent threat. For the rest, everyone recognized that the plague was by nature an obscure disease, whose immediate origins were for the most part incomprehensible. Not everything was clear about the contagion, as the barber-surgeon Corsi of the lazaret of San Marco Vecchio rightly pointed out to the Public Health magistrates who questioned his professional skills: "In a case of fevers, I think that a good doctor should intervene. He should also be a good philosopher and astrologer so that he can understand what he cannot see. I'm only a barber-surgeon and can't do that." [53]

HIDING THE SICK

During epidemics, the Public Health Magistracy prohibited physicians and barber-surgeons from "working around the city" and treating illnesses other than the plague, and it requested that they treat only those plague victims whose cases had been reported. "As soon as they hear that someone is sick, they shall go visit him, not from the window, but from the bedside. Then they shall refer the matter to the Magistracy, describing the nature of the illness so that a hospitalization order can be issued. . . . They shall not be paid by the sick person but by those who remain in the house." The punishments for breaking these ordinances were "physical" and monetary: violators were to pay the sum of ten *scudi,* half of which was to be distributed among the poor. [54] Salaries were quite good: of the personnel in charge of visiting those who stayed at home to care for the sick, the doctor was to be paid seven *scudi,* the barber-surgeon five *lire,* and the herbalist three *lire.* [55] The doctor responsible for a neighborhood earned a monthly salary of thirty *scudi,* although as the epidemic waned, the salary was lowered. [56] Because employees tended to avoid posts in lazarets, either refusing or leaving them, the Public Health Magistracy offered "very high wages": eighty *scudi* to doctors and forty to barber-surgeons. [57]

Still, an anonymous denunciation indicated that the magistrate's orders were often disregarded. It complained, predictably, about inequalities in the treatment of patients and about clandestine earnings:

> The poor are assassinated by the treatment of barber-surgeons, who, when they call on a poor person, ask him to turn the lights on and undress. Then they order him to the lazaret without even considering whether the man was healthy the day before or whether his disease might actually be an ordinary infection. . . . When they have to call on

a nobleman, however, they sit by the side of the bed, touch him, and treat him, without filling out the proper reports for the authorities. This is how they profit, damaging the Public Health Magistracy, the masters, and the poor people.[58]

The relationship between official healers and ordinary people was thrown off course by the ambiguous symptomatology of common illness and viewed as dangerous because it inevitably led to the lazaret. In addition, the involvement with money that this relationship entailed betrayed the egalitarian aspects of the state Public Health administration. In the aforementioned quote, in fact, the respectfully treated "nobleman" became a "master," thus illustrating how the democratic nature of Public Health policies could be corrupted.[59]

It is easy to find examples of bribery, of gifts secretly given by individuals who could afford them, but cases are rare of an artisan or shopkeeper paying off a barber-surgeon for an advantageous diagnosis. We have found only one such example, the denunciation prepared by Captain Ottavio Diligenti against the crucifix maker Innocenzo Battista Faccetti, whose mother had a bubo on her right arm. Diligenti sent a guard to investigate the suspected case. The guard, arriving at Innocenzo's shop to find the man working behind the counter, was told that a "barber-surgeon with blond hair" had just been there to check on the woman. In between questions the guard had time to look around; he saw several objects, such as carvings of the Virgin, that were quite valuable. He asked what one figure was worth, and Innocenzo naively confessed that he had made it to give to the barber-surgeon. Innocenzo was a young man who lacked caution; according to the report, this admission led to his arrest, the locking of his house, and the charge of hiding a woman suspected of having the plague.[60]

Doctors and barber-surgeons moved quickly between the homes and streets in their jurisdictions. They adeptly avoided the traps set by the Magistracy, always ready to justify themselves by an involuntary mistake, the ambiguity of symptoms, or the patient's unpredictable reaction. Also, they were able to escape legal charges because of the scarcity of sanitary employees and the Magistracy's high attrition rate. Those suspected of accepting bribes, though, were confined to the lazarets and forced to work in public institutions for a set period of time. Thus, denunciations and legal procedures follow one another, then suddenly vanish; like a promising path, they attract, then drop us. Occasionally, an individual profile was sketched, as in the cases of the barber-surgeon Cesarino Coveri and the guild brother Vittorio Greco and of the neighborhoods where they worked, around San Ambrogio and the Church of San Lorenzo. Voices rose, delineating complicities and fears, but neither defendant was punished. Unlike other crimes, those committed by physicians and barber-surgeons leave us with a sense of incompleteness and vagueness; despite all rumors, the doctors and barber-surgeons under investigation, unlike their patients, managed to escape unscathed.

The first suspicions of Cesare Coveri, whom everyone called Cesarino, started at Titolotto, a boarding house in the quarter of Croce. Eight to ten people lived there, most of them artisans, textile workers and glove makers, who worked in nearby shops. In early November the owner of the boarding house died. A barber-surgeon was called to prepare his death certificate so he could be buried at the Church of San Lorenzo. A few days later the chain of sick people grew. The deceased's wife and daughter, who had taken care of him, were again visited by Cesarino. He said that they did not have a contagious disease but ordered them hospitalized for observation at Santa Maria Nuova. At the hospital, however, bubos were found on the disrobed women's bodies. The two were immediately placed in isolation and taken to the lazaret of San Miniato. Meanwhile, the guests at Titolotto continued to work, meet people on the street and in the shops, and keep busy with their ordinary activities. The magistrate ordered all seven arrested, charging them with concealing the facts. The witnesses mentioned Cesarino's name, and it was presumably on the reports filed with the authorities, yet, for the time being, the magistrate decided not to arrest him.[61]

The delay, however, was short lived because, three days later, after the conclusion of this episode, a new denunciation was made, converging all suspicions once again on Cesarino. A secret informer reported the deaths of the tavernkeeper Antonio di Goro, his wife, and their three children. They lived on the Via Zanobi with Antonio's nephew, Guido, who was also a tavernkeeper and, miraculously, was still in good health. Like the boardinghouse owner, the Goro family had also been treated by Cesarino and buried in the Church of San Lorenzo. Because his uncle's family had been diagnosed as having a noncontagious disease, Guido could continue to work in his tavern, and the barber-surgeon continued to go from one infected house to another. A little later, at the home of Donna Costanza on Via della

Scala, two women, Nannina and Benedetta, died. Cesarino sent other residents of that house to Santa Maria Nuova, where people afflicted with ordinary diseases were treated. Once again, it was the hospital doctors who discovered the signs of the plague and who immediately sent the new patients to the lazaret of San Miniato.

At this point, the chancellor had a considerable amount of evidence against Cesarino: the anonymous denunciation and the news of the burials at the church, an illegal action for which the Public Health Magistracy vigorously prosecuted people. Most damaging, perhaps, were the barber-surgeon's reports, which contradicted those prepared by the physician of Santa Maria Nuova. Significantly, the barber-surgeon's violations substantiated the popular image of a poisoning doctor and help us to understand how Cesarino was actually responsible for spreading the disease—ordering people to the hospital when they should have gone to the lazaret and burying corpses at the church, contravening the law requiring that they be buried in the fields. After the magistrate had found the source of the deaths, he ordered the arrest of Cesarino and the tavernkeeper Guido Pubbi, who, to keep his customers, circumvented Public Health ordinances.

"I lived with my uncle Antonio di Goro, a tavernkeeper, near Macine. My uncle lived in my house, upstairs with eight of his children. One of his children, Antonio, died about a month ago. Next his daughter Marta died, then Lazzera, and finally Goro. His wife . . . died a few days after Antonio himself."

What did they die of?

"Antonio had a drop on his tongue. Four days later he could hardly breathe, and he died after ten days. His wife ran fevers and died after ten days. The children had worms that got worse after their parents died, . . . and they, too, finally died."

Were they visited?

"Yes, sir, they were visited by a Cesarino of the Public Health Magistracy. He never said that there was a chance of contagion and said that they could be buried at San Lorenzo."

Was this barber-surgeon sent by the Public Health Magistracy or was he called by the family?

"I went to call him, . . . and I never gave him anything. He came back several times and told me that there was no possibility of the bad disease. I lived in a room downstairs with my wife and three of my children, two girls and a boy. My son is now in Leghorn."

From Guido's story it would seem that, despite common interests, the uncle's and nephew's families led separate lives; the relatives downstairs were indifferent to the destiny of those upstairs. The defendant accentuated the tragic banality of the deaths, the result of apoplexy (dropsy) and worms, and the church burials. Only one cousin was still living at Guido's home, and another had been hospitalized at Santa Maria Nuova on Coveri's orders. The other two had died, however, and had been buried "in the usual field." Guido, claiming that he did not know the reason for such a burial, did not fool the chancellor. It sounded like an admission of guilt. Obviously, the tavernkeeper could not keep all the cases of contagion secret. Perhaps he decided, therefore, to hide only those in his own family, abandoning his cousin to the destiny of other infected people. In fact, Guido's wife had fallen ill a short time before. She, too, was visited by the accommodating barber-surgeon, and the husband did not report the case to the authorities. The long series of deaths and burials at San Lorenzo, however, attracted the attention of a neighbor, who made the denunciation on 11 November, thereby suddenly cutting short the relationship based on profit and tutelage between Guido and Cesarino. While in jail, a fellow inmate informed the tavernkeeper that his house on Via Zanobi had been locked: "A guard called Barbino told me the news last night when he came here to pick up a mattress."[62]

The sentence was promulgated on 20 November, and the tavernkeeper Guido di Goro was condemned to be attached to the rope twice in a public street.[63] The sentence made no mention of the barber-surgeon Cesarino. Later we will find him working again in country villages,[64] where it was rumored that he was one of those barber-surgeons who examined patients "with the glasses of Galileo."[65] Ordering Cesarino's expulsion from San Lorenzo and Florence, the magistrate opted for a solution that would not deprive the Public Health Magistracy of an employee, given the already scarce number of workers. Actually, the man's job became more strenuous, because he had to travel the countryside in the middle of winter with little chance of making illegal profits from a population exhausted by famine and decimated by the epidemic.

In the quarters assigned to them, barber-surgeons were under a double control. First, they were directed by noblemen, who, assigned to the same neighborhood, kept track of the sick, the suspect, and the healthy and made sure that the sanitary personnel performed their duties. Second, they were supervised by medics and herbalists, who were legally required to accompany them on visits to patients.

Vittorio Geri, a barber-surgeon in the quarter of San Ambrogio, however, often visited patients by himself. He especially liked to call on women who were left at home alone. On 17 November, for example, Vittorio went to a house on Via Maria. He usually paid a very brief visit there, keeping, of course, a safe distance. "I told her to stay at the top of the stairs and undress," stated the report ordering the woman's hospitalization at San Miniato. After doing his duty there, the barber-surgeon went to attend to the wife of Paolantonio the launderer. She, too, was alone in the house. According to her denunciation, Vittorio apparently "put his hands on her breasts. Then he embraced her, asking, 'Do you want to have sex?' The woman resisted, saying, 'I'm going to tell my husband' and then managed to escape his advances."[66]

The chancellor made assurances that measures would be taken against the barber-surgeon. Yet once again the story comes to no conclusion. The charge was too unimportant to bother firing one of the Magistracy's necessary employees.

On 29 November a much more serious charge was leveled against Vittorio Geri. He had helped Alessandro Manzuoli, a goldsmith of the Ponte Vecchio, hide his sick son, Girolamo. This time, the relationship between father and barber-surgeon was not merely suggested but openly stated in the denunciation: "Vittorio Geri, barber-surgeon of the Public Health Magistracy, treated Girolamo without filling out the proper report. We can only conclude that this was because Francesco paid him a hefty bribe, as no one runs risks without proper recompense."[67] The investigation began to illuminate a number of other friendships and transferences from one house to another. Girolamo Manzuoli had left his father's home to "retire" to the house of Piero Billi, an acquaintance who lived on the Via Gualfonda. At that time, however, he began to feel the first symptoms of the disease. Then one day, on Billi's request, Alessandro came to pick his son up, only to watch him die in bed. No one had reported the sick man "for fear of being locked in the house." The barber-surgeon Geri visited Girolamo and did not say a word to anyone until the twenty-seventh, when he decided to fill out the report. The authorities discovered the violation because, right before his death, the man was treated and "some blood was let."

The Manzuolis were arrested on the same day, 29 November. The father, Alessandro, characterized his dead son as a young rebel who had left home "for some crazy ideas," only to come back sick just in time to die. Alessandro and his other son, Francesco, reputedly never saw Girolamo during the three days of his escape because, like many other artisans, they had moved into their goldsmith shop, carrying only a few things with them and setting up a sort of domestic organization. Still, they knew that the young man had been visited by Vittorio Geri, a barber-surgeon of their quarter, who ordered that some "dirty wool and oil of white lilies" be placed over the patient's bubos. These remedies were classic. The fat of sheep wool was efficacious, according to the famous *Oysipum* of Dioscorides, and the Florentine *Farmacopoeia* explained how to prepare and apply the remedy, later to become famous under the name of lanolin.[68] The oil of white lilies was also officially advocated by physicians and magistrates. This liquid could be prepared by a variety of methods, including the ones used by Niccolao and Mesue.[69]

Obviously Girolamo's father denied the charges of bribery and carefully explained their dealings with the barber-surgeon. Alessandro and Francesco Manzuoli both tended to underscore Geri's responsibility in the episode. Although they admitted that they did buy the oil and wool, they maintained that they did not know that the barber-surgeon was going to apply them directly to the bubo. Moreover, they did not mention the bloodletting.[70] Finally, the story of Girolamo's running away from his father's house because of his "crazy ideas" seemed designed to cover up the timely decision to isolate the sick from the healthy, thus permitting the shop to remain operative.

We can deduce from Piero Billi's testimony as well that Alessandro Manzuoli's behavior was actually motivated by these considerations. Billi was arrested a few days later and charged with hiding Girolamo in his house. On 3 December he was interrogated by the chancellor. "His father begged me to take care of him." Then he explained how he was locked in the Manzuolis' house because he had taken the young man there shortly before his death. He reported, "The barber-surgeon Vittorio, who lives in the Borgo Albizzi, came to see Girolamo and put a compound of white lilies and dirty wool on his bubo. On Wednesday, Vittorio let blood from Girolamo's feet" (medical and surgical treatises said that when a bubo appeared between the legs, the bloodletting should be administered at the ankle).[71] What the Man-

zuolis did not admit, Piero immediately confessed. He did not, however, know who had sent the barber-surgeon to the young man's bedside.

It is not clear what relationship existed between the woolworker
Piero Billi and the goldsmith's family. It sometimes appears that Piero
Billi was only a trusted handyman on whom the father called when
his son got sick. At other times Billi, apparently resentful of his
friend's family, looks like Girolamo's accomplice. After all, Girolamo
had been forced to seek refuge in Billi's house because Alessandro had
delivered his son to the guards. There, in the woolworker's house,
"Girolamo got very sick and had to go to bed"; he asked that someone
call his parents. Drained of energy, the young man was taken home
on the shoulders of Piero and Lorenzo, an apprentice "of the Pittis."[72]

Perhaps Piero was a "bad companion" for Girolamo, the black
sheep of the family. Certainly he was a little questionable; one report,
thrown in with some of the Magistracy's other documents, says that
on the night of 16 August, Billi, "with the help of somebody else,"
removed the body of his dead servant from his house "with the intention of taking it to Santa Maria Novella and leaving it there, thereby
hiding the major crime of not reporting the death of an infectious
person." Billi was caught with the body on his shoulder, just as he was
about to drop it on the corner of Via Gualfonda. This action was not
only criminal, but also sacrilegious.[73] Despite this earlier episode, the
two trials remained separate, and on 4 December Alessandro and
Francesco Manzuoli were released,[74] along with Piero Billi.

Girolamo Manzuoli's disease was quite different from the ordinary
illnesses that afflicted the Goro family. In Girolamo's case, although
the symptoms were unclear, the remedies employed indicated that it
was certainly the plague. Still, Vittorio Gori was neither arrested nor
prosecuted, and the Magistracy's documents do not mention any sentence against him. The fact that he hurriedly reported the case just
before the burial was to take place at the church probably discouraged
legal charges, especially given that doctors were allowed to visit patients only once unless they had been reported hit by the epidemic.
We are therefore led to believe that either the goldsmith did not offer
a bribe large enough to ensure his son's burial at the church or else the
family thought it more expedient to separate the infectious person
from the others. By not paying too much attention to Girolamo after
his death, the continuation of work in the shop would thereby have

been guaranteed. Finally, the young man's rebelliousness and his bitter relationship with his father circumscribed the borders of their illegal attempt to keep him alive and allowed them to forget about him after he died.

A report filed at the chancellor's office a few days later mentions Vittorio Geri's name once again. On 12 December, the Magistracy conducted an investigation of the silk weaver Giovan Francesco Lorini, who, aided by his cousin Zanobi, an herbalist at the Piazza della Madonna, supposedly did not report the disease of his mother, Antonia. Intimidated by the guards, Giovan Francesco admitted that Zanobi "applied medicine and performed several operations" on Antonia, in violation of the guild regulations that prohibited herbalists from administering any "medicinal solutions," that is, laxatives.[75]

Zanobi's transgression, like his aunt's illness, was ordinary. Giovan Francesco diagnosed her illness as being the "mother's sickness." Maybe because of the proximity of the genitals to the urinary tract, women attributed the early symptoms of plague to a uterine pain, a delivery, or a pregnancy. As always when a threat was characterized by familiar symptoms, this diagnosis reassured the family. In fact, Giovan Francesco remarked that Antonia had suffered the "mother's sickness" several times before. "I did report the case to the Public Health Magistracy," he recalled. Thus, the barber-surgeon Geri came and, after three or four visits, concluded that it was the "bad disease" and ordered Antonia to be locked in her room. The son claimed that a woman had assisted his mother without any medicine; Antonia had had only "two bloodlettings, one performed by Zanobi, and the other by said woman who assisted her." His cousin also sent a young apprentice who brought "an orgeat prescribed by Porcellini, who, however, did not receive permission to visit her."

From the young silk worker's testimony emerged a comprehensive knowledge of laws and regulations. The care he took to point out that the two bloodlettings were performed by the apprentice and the woman and that the herbalist had nothing to do with them indicated that an agreement had been reached with the cousin, who subsequently admitted the truth after his capture. Even the detail of Doctor Porcellini's prescription of orgeat brought to mind the article in Code 1560 that regulated the relationship between physicians, barber-surgeons, and herbalists and the proper way to prepare prescriptions.

The story was constructed with remarkable coherence. While protecting his cousin, Giovan Francesco tried to defend himself as well. Zanobi was interrogated after his cousin. He especially tried to defend his own conduct vis-à-vis the guild's regulations; he explained that he went very near the woman's bed and that the medicine was brought by "Antonio, my apprentice." He denied that he applied the medicine to the woman's body. In addition, he claimed that the apprentice had probably not performed the bloodlettings, as there was in the house "a woman who knew how to do them," whom all witnesses held responsible. The chancellor was not entirely convinced and sentenced Giovan Francesco Lorini to be tied to the rope twice; the sentence was later commuted to a fine of twenty *scudi*. Zanobi, in contrast, was acquitted, although he had to pay half the cost of "his arrest." [76]

Giovan Battista di Jacopo Bramanti, apprentice of the herbalist of San Sisto, did not get away so easily after he secretly aided a victim. A young man of nineteen or twenty years, he was sentenced to be led around the city on the back of a donkey, followed by five years in jail, "for helping administer medicine to his sister, who was contagious." [77] Giovan Battista would run from the herbalist's shop to 13 Borgo San Lorenzo to treat the pregnant Baccia and her sick husband.

At the chancellor's office he presented a story that was not very convincing. Baccia, he claimed, had been visited by a Public Health barber-surgeon who "could find nothing but fevers." The barber-surgeon filed a report, indicating that the disease was noncontagious. Baccia's fever, however, "produced a pain on her right side between her legs." Giovan Battista applied some pork fat "to see whether any sign of contagion appeared." This test, simple and available to everyone, had been suggested by Marsilio Ficino, among others, to ascertain the nature of an illness. The barber-surgeon was alarmed, however, when he returned to visit Baccia and discovered the substance in her groin. He immediately ordered her hospitalized at the lazaret. According to a petition from her sister, Caterina, Bacci's "skin turned inside out"—that is, she miscarried—in the lazaret. Later, Bacci and her husband both recovered completely from the disease. So why did the grand duke not order Giovan Battista released? The story did not have a happy conclusion. The boy, who earned three *scudi* a month, lost his job and was imprisoned at his family's expense for many months. Even the officers said that he was an "excellent artisan and a very quiet young man who did everything, not for compensation, but for brotherly love." Yet, for those who practiced medicine illegally, the sentence was tough. Giovan Battista was ordered to spend the rest of his sentence in exile, as soon as "the passes open."[78]

In cases such as the two we have just examined, sick women repeatedly confused common female pains with the symptoms of the plague. Many women, pregnant or having just delivered, died with bubos under their clothes, in pain and usually while working. This was the case, for example, with the veil maker Paolo Bosi's wife. Bosi told the chancellor that until two days earlier, his six-months-pregnant wife "was always in the shop, working and eating." She also went to church. Her husband did not pay too much attention to his wife's pains because she always suffered a lot when pregnant, and "her skin turned inside out often."

Paolo and Polita lived with their five small children in a house. With another baby on the way, one wonders how many others had died before birth. For those who, like Polita, spent many years surrounded by the fears and pains of pregnancy, perhaps the burning between her legs could be confused with other symptoms. Certainly her husband, who "was always out selling merchandise," minimized its importance.[79] Paolo Bosi did not even try to find a drug or advice on how to lessen his wife's pain. The charge of hiding the infected woman, then, coincided more with a resigned indifference than with the strategies of secretive complicity which oriented the behavior of many others.

"One of the pregnant women in Alessandro Benvenuti's house," also alone and comfortless, died. According to the rumors, she died after having suffered uterine pain for four or five days. Her body was taken to the front door, where Doctor Francesco Bartolini and the barber-surgeon Agnolo Dotti discovered "a bubo that people in the house say was caused by fire, as though she had burned herself there," on her left thigh. It was probably a cauterization she performed herself to purge the bubo of its poisonous liquids, as doctors and books prescribed. The wound, in fact, was "perfectly round and surrounded by a purple color," such as those left by the iron bars used to light the kitchen fire.[80]

The sense of isolation and indifference that characterized the deaths of these sick women, who may have been poorer and more lonely than others, was not evident in the following episode. Here the picture is one of familial cohesiveness around the suffering women. It is probably no coincidence that the help orchestrated by the relatives, who were determined to guarantee Maria's and Lisabetta's recoveries, finally had positive results. The plague could be beaten by the solidarity of those who, recognizing the symptoms, hid the sick by bribing barber-surgeons or doctors. From the trial testimonies there emerges a very lively and typically female perception of the contagion, the body, and the treatment. Once again, full of details and narrative force, the same words are used to describe both the plague and pregnancy. To the standard series of symptoms the disease added one more bubo, thereby doubling the pain of more ordinary and more ancient sufferings: the uterine pains, the monthly "purges," and the threat of miscarriage.

On 14 October, an anonymous denunciation reached the chancellor's office. The denunciation was filled with invective against

> Maria, the daughter of Bartolino, a shopkeeper on Via dell'Agnolo, and Lisabetta, her sister. Because three bubos grew on Maria, and one on Lisabetta, in about four days, they were locked in the house. They called for a doctor, asking especially for Franzesino, a Public Health doctor, and Jacopo da Massa, a Public Health barber-surgeon, who lived in their neighborhood. These men had already stated that Lisabetta's two sons, who had died in that house, had died of the contagious disease. Thus the house had been locked. When the two men arrived they entered the house without being seen by the neighbors. When they saw that there were some valuable items around, they decided to treat the two women in exchange for money. They prescribed a good purge, which the herbalist from San Piero prepared. Another half purge was prepared by Franzesino with some powder. He gave it to Donna Maria, and four days later the bubos between her legs were healed. They lanced them, and within ten days the two women were in perfectly good health, although Donna Lisabetta was pregnant and miscarried after taking the medicine.[81]

According to the denunciation, the two men made thirty-four *scudi* a day for treating the two women, and they failed to report the sicknesses to the authorities. In fact, they declared that there was no plague in the house and that it could be reopened. The shop where Maria and Lisabetta worked was also opened, and the two women resumed work as soon as they had passed through the worst stages of their illness. But the miscarriage, apparently caused by the powder that Doctor Franzesino had given Lisabetta, complicated everything. The precision with which the secret informer, presumably a neighbor, described the episode made his report into a little manual of practical surgery.

The two sisters were interrogated by the chancellor on the same day as the denunciation. Lisabetta testified first:

> About five weeks ago, I was running a fever. Eight days later I miscarried. After a few more days, a bubo appeared on my thigh. . . . After I had miscarried and before the bubo appeared, I called for Doctor Franzesino and the barber-surgeon to come see me. He prescribed a salve and chicory water for me. He didn't give me any medicine or anything else. When we called for the doctor, the door was open. Earlier it had been locked because two boys had died of petechiae and the bad disease. So Franzesino ordered that the boys be buried in the fields. My mother treated the bubo with pork fat, but I never told the doctor about that. I never took any powders or medicine. The doctor and the barber-surgeon came ten days ago to let some blood. Franzesino gave the order, and Massa performed the operation. My husband paid him. But I don't know if he paid him, I don't think he gave him anything. My widowed sister Maria, my mother, and my husband were at home. . . . The first time, my husband called the doctor.

It is immediately obvious that Lisabetta's testimony was meant to exculpate Franzesino from the accusations of inducing a miscarriage and of treating her secretly for a contagious infection. She repeated over and over that the doctor actually went to visit her only long after the baby had died of a violent fever. As in other testimonies, Lisabetta also tried to minimize the role of the doctor by claiming that he administered only simple medicines ("some salves"). She denied that any real hard medicine was prescribed, mentioning only remedies available in any herbalist's shop. She claimed that the bubo was treated by her mother, who applied a common remedy. The barber-surgeon only lanced the bubo and performed the bloodletting, according to his competencies.

After Lisabetta, her sister Maria testified. Maria was a widow who returned to the family after her husband's death.

> My husband died five weeks ago. That very evening, I went back home. Two weeks later the two boys died. At that time I was running fevers and had three bubos, two between my legs and the other under my right arm. Doctor Franzesino came to see me, and he gave me a laxative and a bloodletting. Then he gave me some powders. Upon taking them, I started to sweat. The bubos began to disappear the next day. A bloodletting was also administered to my sister, and, although she had not taken any of the powder, she miscarried the following day. She had a bubo between her legs, which was cut out by the barber-surgeon Jacopo. Jacopo said that it was a bubo and that she had not yet recovered because she still had a bandage there. I remember that she had the miscarriage the night after blood had been let.

Obviously the two sisters had not agreed on a common strategy. Only Lisabetta tried to prove Franzesino's innocence. She must have been surprised when her sister confirmed all the charges. In order to get well, Lisabetta had accepted the bloodletting and the purge, even though she knew that the treatment might induce a miscarriage. Maria was explicit: the barber-surgeon performed the bloodletting, and then Lisabetta miscarried. Lisabetta was called on once again and forced to tell the truth. Thinking about that night, she was overwhelmed by her emotions, which she had controlled so carefully during her previous attestation. "Jacopo da Massa cut the bubo, but I don't remember who did the bloodletting because I was out of my mind and crazy."[82]

The arrests and the trials examined up to this point demonstrate that the hiding of sick people, made possible by bribing a barber-surgeon, stemmed from the desire to continue working—to keep open a tavern or shop and deal with customers and clients. The tavern-keeper Guido di Goro, the goldsmith Manzuoli, the silk throwster Giovan Francesco Lorini, and the apprentice Giovan Battista Bramanti tried to conceal the plague just to be able to keep working. Maria and Lisabetta, secretly aided by the complicity of their family, served their father's customers while the wounds of their cauterizations were still open.

These strategies for hiding sick and dead people require some consideration. First, there was substantial consensus on the part of the Florentine citizenry on treatments and the personnel who should administer them. None of the trials here examined unveiled the existence of healers who used illegal cures or who were outside of the guild of doctors and barber-surgeons. Even those who tried to confront the fury of the plague by themselves did so by using methods prescribed in medical manuals and substances listed in the official Florentine *Farmacopoeia*. Domestic medicine involved only one variation, the use of simple medicines that were easy to store at home or to prepare in the kitchen. As long as they were simple, such potions, oils, preservatives, powders, and juleps, as well as every type of salve, were not subject to the control of the guild. They could be sold and kept on the shelves of any kitchen.

In addition, the consensus expressed for treatments reflects a widespread use of current medical terminology. Witnesses described their experiences by speaking of categories and concepts that were, more or less, of scientific origin. When they perceived the sudden and violent occurrence of the plague, they described how it erupted, attacked, and "took hold." Moreover, they described the symptoms in the same way that treatises and physicians did: the fever, the bubos, the sense of burning and choking, and finally the various stages of treatment, of the therapy and medicine applied. In contrast, ordinary illnesses were called by their popular names (no such name even existed for the plague): dropsy (apoplexy), the holy sickness (epilepsy), and the matrix (pain in the uterus). The terms used in the medical literature were meant for specialists—midwives, country priests, herbalists, and, in general, a literate public—but they also circulated by word of mouth. It is precisely this double level of expressive codification which leads us to believe that the chancellor did not modify linguistic expressions but rather left them in their original form. These two aspects, linguistic and behavioral, are welded into the same circuit: to bribe a barber-surgeon or to call on a friend who owns an herbalist's shop means, at a minimum, to share their language. The consensus is thus expressed in social practices, which presupposes some sharing of the forms of verbal communication.

We must also look at the dilation of the tasks of sanitary personnel. In two trials, witnesses relied on treatments of herbalists who were prohibited by law from performing those treatments. Perhaps, in the eyes of those who committed the crime, the fact that they were related to the victims lessened the responsibility of their act. Here crimes assume the character of acts committed under familial and neighborhood pressure, rather than from a conscious desire to set oneself outside of the state system of assistance. It is difficult to know whether people who did not receive medical assistance died in greater numbers than those who did. Certainly the cases of Paolo Bosi's wife and the unknown woman who tried to cauterize the bubo by herself, both of which ended in death, lead us to believe that the first category was indeed larger. Yet Girolamo Manzuoli, whom the barber-surgeon Geri treated with the oil of lilies and dirty wool, also died, while Baccia, the herbalist Bramanti's sister, and Maria and Lisabetta, treated by Franzesino, all recovered.

Cases, divided equally, do not prove any correlation between those who made diagnoses, offered treatment, and prescribed remedies on the one hand and recovery rates on the other. A contemporary report, *A Note Concerning All Sick People,* dealing with those who had been hospitalized in the lazarets of San Miniato and San Francesco between

1 September and 20 December 1630, came to similar conclusions. Governor Donato Bisogni, who forwarded the document to the Public Health authorities, calculated that the total number of people in the lazarets was 5,860—2,503 men and 3,383 women. The deaths number 2,886 (1,333 men and 1,553 women), and 2,220 individuals (924 men and 1,296 women) were still being treated.[83]

Finally, from those trials concerning women, another important element emerges which sheds light on these considerations. From the evidence gathered, particularly the testimonies of the sisters Maria and Lisabetta, recovery from the plague also demanded choosing between the epidemic disease and pregnancy, between a difficult and uncertain survival and the sure death of an unborn child. This element, never made explicit in the chronicles and completely ignored in the historiography, embodies an absolutely feminine aspect in the reading of the contagion. For a great number of women, the bubo was a prelude to a stillbirth or miscarriage; the bubo's fantastic projection made it resemble a monstrous pregnancy from which one could, perhaps, be saved only by sacrificing the other pregnancy, the one that gives life.[84]

Compared to the long-lasting ordinary illnesses and the long subsistence crises examined by medical historians, the additional suffering of women vis-à-vis men interrupts the undifferentiated sequel linking epidemics.[85] To introduce the gender differential into otherwise neutral statistics opens a narrow space of unpredicted transparency that cannot be mechanically deduced or linked to graphs of prices, agricultural output, or demographic trends. The history of disease and death is the history of perceptions, individual options, decisions, and desires in which one can locate and follow the different threads of female and male sensibilities.

WOMEN AT HOME, MEN IN THE SHOP

Part of the strategy of hiding the sick involved a second type of behavior: fathers and sons leaving home and setting up cohabitation in the shop. We already saw this in the trial of the goldsmith Manzuoli, who, during the illness of his son Girolamo, moved into his shop with his healthy son, Francesco. In such cases, bribing a barber-surgeon enabled the family to divide into the sick and the healthy, the home and the shop, and, generally, the female (mothers and daughters) and the male (fathers and sons).

The gold beater Lessandro Conti, nicknamed "Contino," was arrested on 19 December for "moving" his son from his home, where his daughter lay ill. Contino had taken his son to his sister's house in San Frediano. After two days, though, when symptoms of the plague appeared there, the father, "lowering his son from the window down into a garden" at night, took him back home.[86]

Matteo Saccardi, an herbalist who owned a shop near the Carraia Bridge, was also involved in this story. On his arrest and interrogation, his predictable first reaction was to exculpate himself. Pointing out his knowledge of his duties and rights, he claimed:

> I never applied any forbidden medicines, such as blood lettings, salves, and theriaca. . . . I know the gold beater Alessandro Conti, and I gave him some medicine for his daughter. . . . She had been running a fever and said that she had not had a bowel movement for three days. I prescribed a mild laxative, which I sent to her on Saturday. I never saw her again because she died Sunday night. I know that Doctor Salustio Fabri of the Public Health Magistracy saw her Sunday, before she died, because he asked me to send her some medicine. The pots and everything else sent to her were left in the house. Alessandro wasn't home at the time.

Like the herbalist we encountered earlier, Matteo Saccardi specified that he had only sent, not applied, the laxative, making it clear that he had not violated guild regulations. He even called it a "mild laxative" to diminish, not without some sense of humor, his role in the episode. As for the rest of the story, the general picture is quite clear: the child displayed the symptoms of an ordinary disease. No one ever mentioned the plague. The only allusion to a different kind of disease was his reference to the professional prudence his apprentices took by not entering the house and asking for the return of the pots.

Contino testifed on the same day as Saccardi, 19 December. In his testimony, he tried to hide the real reason that he had left home and moved into his shop. With a reassuringly casual, domestic air, he said:

> I own a shop where I sometimes eat, drink, and sleep. I stayed there Wednesday night because I was going through my accounts, and it got late. I slept on some linens. . . . On Thursday, the eve of the day of Santa Lucia, my daughter Vettoria played with some of her friends. That evening she became ill. At midnight, a young man I don't know who lives in my neighborhood came with a message from my wife saying that I should send for some eggs because Vettoria was sick. I called on Bordone, who told me that the priest who had attended Vettoria said that it was not the bad disease. I went to the priest myself,

and he told me that, although it wasn't the bad disease, I should keep away from my home. So I went to sleep at my sister-in-law's instead, where I ate, drank, and slept from that evening on. I didn't eat at home Thursday morning; I had breakfast at the Greek tavern in the Mercato Nuovo. On Wednesday night, as I said, I slept in the shop. . . . I have five children and a grandchild but am left with only one son, who is nine years old. He is at home now and, as far as I know, is not sick.

Obviously, Alessandro denied that he took the son to keep him away from his sick daughter. So, the chancellor repeated what the herbalist Matteo Saccardi had said, underlining the gaps in Contino's testimony. The herbalist was brought in from another room, and the two were put side by side. "After formally recognizing all the witnesses," the magistrate repeated the same questions. Matteo confirmed his testimony: Yes, sir, the boy got sick at Alessandro's sister-in-law's house. "I know this because I visited him in that house."

Contino insisted on his line, but another version of the episode slowly began to emerge. "My daughter was buried in the fields" after the visit of the Public Health doctor, he admitted. There was no doubt about it: she had died of the plague. On 23 December, Alessandro Conti once again faced the chancellor, who warned him that he would be taken to the torture chamber if he did not tell the truth. The threat produced new testimony.

Thursday morning, my son Silvestro came to the shop as he did every morning after school. My wife let me know that, since I wasn't coming home on account of the child's sickness, I had better take the boy with me. So I brought him with me to my sister-in-law's house. On Monday night, he told me that he hurt all over. The next morning I went to Master Matteo Saccardi and asked him to come examine him. He came and told me that the boy didn't have the bad disease but that, in any case, it would be better if I took him back to his mother. Following his advice, I took him back home, passing through the house of the gold beater Domenico and a garden. I've heard that he didn't get sick and is still fine.

What Alessandro had not immediately confessed was that he had promised Matteo Saccardi to keep quiet. "As he appeared to have told the truth," he was released. In fact, it would have been difficult to prosecute Contino. His daughter had been buried in the fields, with the required medical attestation of the Public Health Magistracy. The recovery of Silvestro, his beloved son, also kept Contino from being prosecuted for removing a sick person from an infected house and then returning him at the first signs of contagion.

In early November, an informer told the chancellor's office that a violation of Public Health regulations had taken place in the house "above the butcher's slaughterhouse" in the neighborhood of San Jacopo. The family living there had been quarantined. One son, Domenico, the informer charged, had escaped in order to return to his shop. Domenico di Bastiano Picchi, another gold beater, was the "master of three looms." Captain Ottavio Diligenti immediately arrested him, and the interrogation began on 8 November. The crux of the matter lay, once again, in the socially differentiated behavior that was exhibited in the face of the epidemic. In particular, the reaction to the plague had two aspects: first, a man abandoned his house at the earliest signs of the contagion, moving to his shop; and second, solidarity and cohabitation with fellow workers emerged. This experience is typical of male socialization in times of danger and pain.

"I didn't ask the master if they wanted me to go back home," Domenico said. "It's been twelve days since I left home. The only reason I didn't go home was that I had other important work to finish. There's no one at home other than my father and mother." Then, almost incidentally, he remembered that his brother also lived at home and that his brother was ill. Of course, Domenico said, no one knew what illness his brother had.[87] Domenico was taken back to jail, pending the arrival of new evidence from the investigation.

At the same time, five of his friends, who may or may not have been gold beaters, went spontaneously to the chancellor to present a petition on Domenico's behalf. In the petition, "We, the undersigned," told the magistrate that one day, while "having lunch" with Domenico in the shop, they noticed a mattress. They asked Domenico what in the world he would use that for. He answered that he had to eat and sleep in the shop in order to meet the big rush of orders, showing them the golden cloth he was putting on the loom. That was the reason, they stated, for the temporary living arrangement. And, one after the other, they signed their statement.[88]

The chancellor, however, was not convinced. Such behavior was so common among shopkeepers that they could not possibly have been confused by it. On 23 November, after another thirteen days in prison, Domenico Picchi was taken directly to the torture chamber. There, the chancellor asked him if he insisted on refusing to reveal what disease his brother had. The court in fact knew that he was aware of the nature of his brother's disease and that this was why he had left home so quickly. After all, he had abandoned his family after, not before, the disease struck. Domenico remained quiet. "He was undressed and tied to the rope. . . . Then he was lifted so high that he began to scream, 'Poor me, my arms are broken!' He kept repeating, 'I can't say anything more.' After hanging there for the time it takes to recite a Miserere, he was lowered, as it did not appear that he deserved more punishment, and then he was dressed and returned to his place." Domenico's story ended here. No sentence appears in the court's records, but we can assume, based on similar episodes, that because he resisted the torture he was freed.

For masters and workers, the shop was not only a place to escape infected family members and continue working but also the focal point of friendship, solidarity, affections, and routines. Friends as well as relatives were central to people's choices and behavior. Domenico Picchi, for instance, the textile worker prosecuted for not reporting his brother's disease, was arrested three years later on a charge concerning a fellow worker. In this case, unique in the entire criminal documentation of the Public Health Magistracy, Domenico proves to be a recidivist. On 8 June 1633, during a resurgence of the plague in Florence, our textile worker was "prosecuted" for not reporting the death of Giovanni di Vergilio, whom the barber-surgeons found dead in the house of the sick at 72 Via San Stefano.[89]

Domenico reputedly fed Giovanni di Vergilio, another textile worker in the same shop, and "sent him some boys every morning and evening to serve him and make his bed, until he died." On Saturday, when they realized he was about to die, "they abandoned him and did not report him to the authorities, as the law required." The body was accidentally found by barber-surgeons who, while visiting a nearby apartment, smelled a suspicious odor from under a closed door. Despite the tender and loving care he gave Giovanni, Domenico was able to maintain his normal daily routine. On Sunday he went to church at San Romo, afterwards going to drink some wine at the Greek Tavern. Later he went on a stroll with his friends. On Monday he went to church again at Santa Trinità, and then he joined the procession of the Compagnia di San Stefano. It was an ordered and sociable life, made up of playing, praying, working, and drinking. Even when he transgressed the edicts that prescribed the death penalty for those who hid bodies in their *own* houses, he was careful. When Domenico realized that his friend was getting worse, he "took him to the house of said Giovanni and *there fed him.*"[90]

Arrested on 8 June, Domenico managed to avoid capital punishment because, in violation of regulations, he had been able to get Giovanni's body to Giovanni's house. He was condemned to be led around the city on a donkey and then to a life sentence. On 28 September he presented a petition requesting that his sentence be postponed for three months because his "looms were full of work" and he had to satisfy his customers. On 8 October he was granted a one-month postponement.

Domenico's punishment corresponded exactly to the edict's provisions. We believe that, in comparison to the similar case of Niccolò di Lodovico Villani and Batista Matteo, called "Morino," a "master of manufactures," Domenico's punishment was extreme. The charges against Niccolò and Batista involved their failure to report the illness of their apprentice Luca, nicknamed "Lupo." In this case, however, there was evidence that the omission led to the infection of "two other apprentices and that, because of their actions and sloppiness, twelve other people were sent to convalescent homes."[91]

The importance of the shop and its function of orienting the social reorganization of families confronted by the plague was also at the center of another trial. Here, as in the previous cases, the nucleus of parents and children is divided along vertical axes: male and female, and home and work. Yet in this case additional details shed light on male cohabitation, making the picture increasingly vivid.

Three linen workers, the brothers Giuseppe, Giovanni, and Clemente Baragliuoli, who lived on Via de' Cimatori, were arrested on 2 November. They were charged with violating the edict of 24 October, that no sick individual was permitted to walk on the street.[92] Giovanni began:

Our family consists of a father, four brothers, and four sisters, and one of my sisters died first. She was running a fever before she died and is buried in San Romolo. Eight days ago, our mother died and was buried in the countryside. Then one of my brothers, still a child, died, and we buried him in the fields too. Our father told us that we should leave the house for the sake of our work, because if we got sick we wouldn't be able to work.

These last words were tragically ironic—as if the last two burials in the fields were not clear signals in and of themselves. The disease had already devastated the Baragliuoli family, having hit the women repeatedly, but the alarm was sounded only after the death of one of the boys. When the son Giuliano died, the surviving males gathered to decide what to do; they decided to follow their father's advice, "for the sake of work."

"From then on," Giovanni continued, "we have been living in the shop. We brought a mattress from home on which Clemente and I slept. We put the mattress over some hay, and Giuseppe Zuccherini, our apprentice, gave a bench to us." In addition, neighbors helped organize their cohabitation. For example, Clemente would give money to a woolworker from a nearby shop, who went shopping for them. This friend then gave the groceries to Giuseppe, who was entrusted with cooking in a kitchen set up in the back courtyard, far from curious eyes in the street. The community's solidarity continued even after the three were arrested. In fact, they were released because the silkworker Lorenzo di Francesco Pistelli came on his own to the chancellor's office to pay the bail of fifty *scudi* each.[93]

The outbreak of the epidemic, as we have seen, crystalized around differences in social status as well as sex. It lowered and insinuated itself, like a cruel sieve, to divide and then recompose various human and social configurations. The nuclei of artisans' families were split apart, leaving women at home alone to care for the ill and the husbands and sons in the shop, often alone but for their fellow workers, masters, and apprentices. It must have been difficult to move from home, to relocate mattresses and other necessities—in the case of the Baragliuolis, "a pair of benches, a boxspring, and mattress" so they could sleep on a real bed. These were very visible activities, especially for those, like all the people we have examined so far, whose shop was far from home. Nocturnal relocations were difficult because edicts strictly prohibited circulating in the street after the ringing of the bell and before the sunrise Ave Maria.

To get news about the sick at home would require counting on, as in the case of the gold beater Alessandro Conti, a chain of apprentices, friendly herbalists, relatives, priests, and neighbors, who would report snatches of information or go to the house to exchange news directly. The division of the domestic nucleus therefore required solidarity, a network of complicities, a system of silences, and preorganized actions in the event that somebody was caught. Nothing was ever left to fate or the spontaneous impulse of terror or escape. Moreover, from the testimonies there emerged a compact texture of choices and priorities, characterized by a proliferation of mediators between home and shop, healthy and sick, and families and Public Health authorities. In the detailed stories recounted by defendants and witnesses, one is struck by the absence of panic, by the ability to control the fear of contagion and death within the borders of a well-thought-out transgression that took advantage of the ambiguities of the law.[94]

To move into the shop meant also to occupy a daily and public space, one characterized by the everyday habits of traffic and normality. It was an implicit strategy to regain control over a territory larger than the fearfully small area allowed by the Public Health Magistracy. Yet the controls of guards and magistrates moved in ever smaller concentric circles: from arrests made in shops only a few blocks from home, other arrests involved artisans who lived and worked in just one room or on two different floors of the same house. There, going down a staircase, opening a door onto the street, or opening a back window for some light constituted a crime.

On 31 January 1630, twenty workers were arrested: woolworkers, plumbers, lantern makers, barrel makers, and shoemakers, all charged with working despite orders to stay at home in quarantine.[95] The fast-paced interrogations revealed very minor violations, indicating that the spaces for work and living coincided; the house door and the shop door were one and the same, just as the window that shed light on the workbench was the same that provided light for the dining table. Jacopo di Antonio Scali, a blacksmith of Via de' Guicciardini, speaks for his fellow citizens whose living and working conditions were quite similar to his: "I live and work there with my son. We live in the shop where we sleep and eat and do everything else. . . . The only light comes in from the door. . . . I was actually eating when, in order to see, I opened the door to let some light in. I then moved the table near the workbench."[96] Again, transgression became confused with ordinary behavior; opening the door and pushing the table to the side so as to see one's plate, getting some wood for a fire, or cleaning a room was punishable in times of emergency. The possibilities of circumventing the edicts shrank; spaces granted to life, affection, and work were reduced to mere shadows.

And yet the plague itself could help resolve the constant worrying, and the zeal of some Florentines in abiding by the letter of the law obscured an almost comic utilitarianism. Michelangiolo di Vettorio Incontri, for instance, ran to the chancellor's office to report that his cousin, who lived with him, had fallen ill. He was so insistent that the doctor, just to get rid of him, signed the hospitalization order without even going to visit the patient to verify his condition. The bureaucratic process followed its course, and part of the house was closed— which was precisely what Michelangiolo wanted: to postpone, for who knows how long, the eviction that his landlord had ordered. "Now that the disease is with us, we don't want to violate the law. People can't be evicted from infectious houses," he answered the chancellor, who had become suspicious of such exemplary behavior. Thanks to the plague, the cousin ended up in the lazaret, while Michelangiolo stayed peacefully at his house in San Giorgio.[97]

USURPED COMPETENCIES

Besides the doctors and barber-surgeons of the Public Health Magistracy, herbalists, in roles more or less like those of advisers, relatives, or family friends, appeared in some of the trials we have already examined. In their testimonies we have seen how these tradesmen carefully avoided violating those articles of the guild's ordinances that prohibited them from "applying remedies." An infraction of these guild regulations would also have been a violation of Public Health edicts, a fact of which defendants and herbalists alike were conscious. These considerations oriented their testimonies; consequently, they tried to prove themselves innocent of breaking both Public Health laws and guild rules. Here, as in other cases, deep fissures broke through the surface of control, altering its cohesion and operational consistency and thereby guaranteeing normalcy and activity typical of daily life.

From the herbalists' testimonies, which presumably were consistent with those of the defendants, one can assume that the help requested of them had led to their administering a drug or otherwise attending to the sick person. In this manner the competencies of a doctor were replaced by those of the herbalist. What really concerns us here is the social request to a member of the minor echelons of the guild, to an herbalist who attempted to extend his professional capabilities and liberate them from the guild restrictions. In Florence, even street vendors and market workers would be inscribed in the membership lists of the guild of doctors and herbalists if they paid their dues. Vettorio di Agnolo Vallerani, for example, who sold "unguents for burns and scabies in the square," joined as a regular member on 5 March 1632. Also enrolled were Michele di Domenico Zanardi, a "distiller" from Ferrara, and Battista Oliva, a Turkish convert to Catholicism who sold unguents on the street and "wrestled a bear." [98]

Even during the epidemic, healers of all sorts addressed petitions to the grand duke in which they guaranteed that they had gained experience in previous epidemics and in which they submitted new prescriptions. A German, Volchemar Timan, a member of His Most Serene Highness's guardcorps, claimed, for instance, that he knew a secret cure that had already been used successfully during the epidemic in Genoa. [99] Frabrizio Ceci of Pesaro wrote that he had a drug that would work for all victims of poison, "whether dead or alive." He claimed that the head doctor of Urbino, after seeing the effects of the remedy, had given him permission to "spread the prescription throughout the state." [100] Antonio Pedoni of Milan asked for permission to put "a table on the street to sell simple curative roots and coral powder, which would be useful to both herbalists and the general public." [101]

The requests were carefully considered, and usually permission was granted. The remedies advocated in these petitions were not only publicized but also legally sold and administered, even at the peak of the epidemic. The knight Captain Cesare Sabatini praised the virtues of a "syrup" he had invented and suggested that the herbalist Francesco Lotti sell it on Via de' Guicciardini. The drug was designed to evacuate "most of the poisons that are in the unfortunate's body" by sweating and urinating. According to a certain Giovanni Paserina, the medicine's effect on his twelve-year-old daughter, Clarice, was beneficial. Having taken the drug, "the girl passed a worm through her lower parts, and, by the grace of God, she is now well." [102]

Under the control of the guild, which collected dues and issued licenses for all kinds of purposes, the number of professional healers substantially grew. If they obeyed the guild's rules and regulations, street vendors would enjoy the same right to prescribe particular antidotes to patients that doctors enjoyed, and they would be similarly regulated. For example, street vendors were not permitted to sell oil "as a fake remedy" or maltha, which was under the control of "watchers." Nor were they allowed to sell any prescription "that would be effective against a snake bite."[103] The numerous unknown country healers were requested to present themselves to the authorities to be enrolled in the guild as well, or else face a fine of twenty-five gold *scudi*.[104]

The "Orders, Provisions, and Statutes Concerning Doctors and Herbalists," copied in the official prescription book, separated legitimate from illegitimate practices. These orders cautioned those who "obtained a license" not to exceed their rights and competencies. In particular, the illegality of the widespread practices of "giving purges and bloodlettings" was noted. This document also condemned doctors who offered their name or help "to barber-surgeons or others, who accept bribes or prizes for agreements reached to the great detriment of all."[105] These infractions bring back to mind the trials we have already examined: the request to an herbalist to preparc a laxative, the agreement—more difficult to prove—between a doctor and a barber-surgeon to issue a prescription or write up an illness or death certificate. All these crimes tended to expand the prerogatives of sanitary personnel, while ignoring the actions of secret healers.

Contemporary medical treatises, in contrast, mentioned common treatments not controlled by the guild. Avoiding polemics, Stefano Rodriguez de Castro, the Magistracy's offical doctor-adviser, observed that "everyone, even those who do not practice the art of medicine, offers remedies he has heard about or read of in an old book."[106] Traditionally, widespread experimenting for secret cures by healers who did not belong to the guild was tolerated. Galen himself had used drugs prepared by street vendors, and even then, de Castro noted, nobody really knew what the "Orvietano," the famous antidote used widely in Europe against the plague, was.[107] In the infected city, many had been healed by powders that doctors had been given by people "who were not doctors."[108]

The circularity of medical knowledge and popular practices, such as those of street vendors and charlatans, was confirmed by de Castro. He believed that this circularity originated with the *auctores* and Greek doctors, who tended to expand and legitimate a wide variety of healers. In his view, the guild similarly granted licenses to anyone who would pay the dues and obey its rules and regulations. The boundaries between the various types of healers were overshadowed by the distinction between those who had professional educations, organized and controlled by the universities and the communities of doctors, and those who had had only nonacademic apprenticeships. All these roles, though, were regulated by the guild, by its membership, its hierarchy, and the licenses it granted for the purpose of administering specific treatments. In this sense, the high and the low did not oppose each other but rather coexisted; as we have already seen, they shared the same practices and prescriptions for the treatment of the ill. In addition, institutional specialization in roles and tasks was counterbalanced by a social demand for more generalized assistance, assistance less obedient to the professional categories set by the guild.[109]

Let us examine a few more stories that concern treatment and the tactics deployed to extend the competencies of both Public Health personnel and semiprofessional specialists.

The stablekeeper Giovan Maria Bardi was "prosecuted" for having secretly treated the wagon driver Antonio di Domenico. Having found Antonio sick, Giovan gave him some medicine, then asked the neighbors not to report the illness. The crime was discovered only after Antonio's death, when his body was found abandoned in his empty house. As in the case of the textile worker Domenico Picchi, this episode also reflects affection and solidarity between fellow workers: Giovan Maria was a stablekeeper who took care of His Highness's horses; Antonio was a coach driver. After the jail sentence was imposed, Giovan Maria petitioned for a pardon, saying that his transgression stemmed from the great friendship between the two men.[110]

Of more importance than the fact that the two men worked in similar jobs, however, was another peculiar element of the story. Stablekeepers were also veterinarians, and many of them wrote treatises on the anatomy, diseases, and proper care of horses. During an epidemiological emergency, a stablekeeper, given his knowledge about the bodies of animals traditionally considered to be similar to those of men, could offer a friend precious advice.[111] The grand duke's master of stables, Vincenzo Ferri, wrote a learned treatise on the various breeds of Tuscan horses in which he explained how "to distinguish between the many breeds of horses that we know about; and to diagnose easily and treat the various external and internal diseases that affect horses—their origins, symptoms, and treatments." He then wrote a shorter treatise, in which he "taught the manual operations to be used on tumors, wounds, dislocations, and other diseases," ending the discussion with a "general description of anatomy."[112] The prescription books advocated the same remedies for both men and horses. The "sympathetic unguent," for instance, cured wounds as well as scratches "on poorly shod horses."[113] Carlo Ruini's famous *Della anatomia e infermità del cavallo,* based on the more famous works of Andrea Cisalpino, described for the first time the restrictive circulation of blood.[114]

The last episode of disease and domestic assistance took shape on 22 October 1632. The plague had returned to Florence, and the tailor Niccolaio d'Adamo was accused of not reporting the disease that had killed his father-in-law, Piero, called "Pignone." Instead, Niccolaio had chosen to treat the sick man secretly at home on Via del Palazzuolo. The trial also involved some of the prosecuted family's neighbors, for Pignone's illness and death were evidently followed with the greatest attention by all the inhabitants of the street. The separation of sick and healthy as prescribed by law was thus lost, in the sense of the shared concern that appeared in the testimonies.[115]

Giovan Battista Giannetti, nicknamed "Barba," was interrogated first. Everyone on the street, especially the women and the barber Burichi, knew that Pignone "was sick with the bad disease." According to Barba, "Giovanni Fabbri came to my bakery this morning with the barber-surgeon Galletti to see the body of said Pignone. I went with them. After they had seen the cadaver, they noticed one of Niccolaio's daughters, a girl about nine-and-a-half years old. They undressed her and found a red furuncle between her legs. The barber-surgeon said that he didn't think it was a bubo."

When the child was undressed, the chancellor asked, had he seen any bandages, medicine, or unguents of any kind on the furuncle?

"There weren't any bandages, and I didn't notice any medicine there either."

The magistrate's insistence on this point was motivated by the fact that the child's father, Niccolaio, had worked for the Public Health Magistracy two years earlier as a barber-surgeon's aide. He had worked with surgical tools, knew how to make incisions and cauterizations, and had seen poisonous bubos opened. This acquired experience could have helped his family prevent Pignone and the young girl from being taken to the lazaret. In fact, Barba admitted, there were some rumors circulating in the neighborhood about Niccolaio's curative abilities, but they were only rumors, nothing more.

The chancellor called on another witness, the barber Burichi. Burichi's place was the hub of the street's social activity, and he enjoyed looking into other people's business. He testified, "I know Niccolaio very well, as he lives on my street. He's married and has four children. I see him quite often, maybe every day. I saw him this morning as well. Yesterday I saw his wife and one of his kids." For the past few days, though, none of Niccolaio's other relatives had gone out on the street or stopped at the barbershop to chat. "I didn't see them, and my wife said that Stella, a woman who lives on Via dell'Albero, said that it was because Niccolaio's daughter Geva was sick and at her grandpa Pignone's house."

Obviously the parents, made suspicious by the red furuncle on their daughter's leg, had taken her to the home of Pignone, who was already sick, in order to isolate her from the rest of the family. Burichi also knew of the barber-surgeon's visit to the cadaver. In addition, he maintained that everyone in the neighborhood had realized that Pignone had no hope of survival because his body was covered with bubos. But when the chancellor started probing, the witness suddenly became evasive, interrupting the flow of his testimony and denying any knowledge about clandestine treatments or medicine administered at home. Perhaps, he suggested, the magistrate ought to question the pastry cook Giovan Battista, who was close to the tailor's family. He and his wife would certainly know everything, including the length and nature of the sickness and the doctor's treatments.

But the chancellor decided to interrogate the defendant Niccolaio instead. On 23 October, Niccolaio was questioned from a distance: he made a sworn statement on a sheet of paper which was given to him at the end of a stick four arm-lengths long and was "thrown away" afterwards.

The story began with the illness of his father-in-law. The disease had started three days earlier with fevers, which later disappeared. Then a new crisis was followed by death. The bubos, according to the tailor, appeared on the body only after death. "I cleaned him, touching the body, but I didn't apply any medicine."

Did he ever see his father-in-law naked during the illness? "I saw him once; I looked under his arms and all over his body but saw nothing. I would've noticed something if it had been there, because I was an aide to a barber-surgeon at the lazaret during the epidemic. My wife, Caterina, saw him too, and she gave him some food. My children also visited him."

What caused the father-in-law's disease? Perhaps Pignone knew how he had gotten sick and had told someone. "He was sick because his woman had given an inheritance to someone else for nothing." We have seen similar answers in which an attempt is made to confuse the story of a disease and death with ordinary events and arguments, thereby suddenly revealing the human side of domestic life. For a moment, attention was captured by these secondary elements and invariably diverted from the primary discourse. In this case, however, the chancellor did not let himself be led astray and kept asking questions.

"My daughter Ginevra felt sick on the nineteenth or twentieth of this month because her mother beat her on the kidneys. Since then she has been getting better. Yesterday morning a little inflammation was discovered on her upper leg, so she was taken to the lazaret." Because the marks on her body were only from her mother's beating, no one had given Ginevra any medication at home. The story of the daughter's disease was constructed on a new basis: the bubo disappeared and was replaced by the wound caused by her mother's beating. Thus the plague disappeared, its place taken by an episode of family arguments.

Caterina, Niccolaio's wife, followed the same strategy. "Pignone had some stomach pains but no obvious symptoms or bubos. Ginevra got sick because, three or four days ago, I slapped her face and then threw a pot at her, which hit her hard on the leg. When the Public Health officials came to see my father, they saw that my daughter had something on her leg and took her to the lazaret."

Did the daughter feel sick before she was hit?

"She was perfectly healthy."

The trial of Niccolaio ended here. The pressing questions of the magistrate were answered with these narrative strategies, a barrier of resistance put up by Niccolaio's relatives and neighbors. It was better to be considered a bit violent than guilty of treating someone illegally.

The meaning of this episode becomes clear when we consider the lazaret not only as an institution designed to isolate and control but also as a training center for those nonprofessional healers who operated legally throughout the city. In some cases, this hated institution provided intensive training to men and women in various jobs, projecting new competencies external to the guild but formed under its direct supervision. The experience of the epidemic broadened horizons and expanded capabilities, thereby transforming individuals and their interpersonal relations with friends and neighbors. No doubt the tailor Niccolaio was not the only one who used techniques learned from barber-surgeons to treat family members and fellow workers and who returned home with new abilities and hence new relations with others.

A later denunciation of the staff of the convalescent home of Rusciano reveals an analogous tension in which a public institution was recast as a profit-making operation. This evidence suggests that the response to the epidemic arose in an inexhaustible ability to construct new configurations of social relations within legal or institutional bounds that appear fixed. In a legal culture that did not rigorously oppose public and private spheres, groups and individuals, as they acted and reacted, systematically transgressed these bounds.[116] Thus, a convalescent home became a linen and clothing factory, and a lazaret a center for the training of clandestine domestic healers. The event, its official reading, and the offensive strategy of the authorities were constantly confronted by this collective reformulation and violation of regulations. The potential of individual interpretation always threatened to decompose both the discipline and the goals of the authorities.

THE SHAMEFUL DEATH

With respect to stricken individuals, social practices confirmed the tones of reprobation found in the chronicles; relatives, friends, and fellow workers hid the ill, failing to denounce their contagion to the Public Health authorities. All the variations in this pattern, from the appeal to an herbalist or stablekeeper for aid to the division of the family group, moved within this same horizon in which the ill and dead were concealed. The motivations that oriented this behavior were, as we heard from the defendants, the desire to keep a shop open, to continue to work, and to prevent the other family members from being locked in the house in compliance with the magistrate's orders. From the transcriptions of testimonies, however, another reason for this behavior emerged, one that surfaced in the trials we have already examined and which will become clearer in the four episodes we will now discuss.

The effort to hide the cause of a relative's death was sometimes discovered when a certificate signed by a neighborhood barber-surgeon aroused the magistrate's suspicions. We saw this in the case of the denunciation of the tavernkeeper Guido di Goro, who managed to bury three of his relatives in the chapel of San Lorenzo thanks to the attestation given him by the barber-surgeon Cesarino Coveri. This document, absolutely necessary for anyone who wanted a church burial, was passed to the priest, who, only after receiving it, could grant permission for burial in consecrated ground. In short, the trials involving investigation of a corrupt barber-surgeon or an unclear death certificate linked the hiding of bodies and the performance of honorable burials.

Death by plague was thought to be fundamentally dishonorable because all the ritual traditions linked to the differentiated stages of death were deviated and denied. First, the state of detachment: "It was a horrible and terrifying fear. One saw, day and night, . . . people taken quietly to their burial without singing. And there was that little bell in front, which scared people away because everyone knew what it meant."[117] Second, the burial: "They buried them naked in holes three arm-lengths deep. They covered them with lime and dirt. . . . The graveyard was surrounded by fences so that dogs would not come and eat the cadavers."[118] Even the stage of ritual reintegration of the survivors—codified by the funeral, the meal, the mourning, and periodic commemorations—was suspended by the prohibitions against all forms of social intercourse. The conditions of psychological and group marginality were, so to speak, assimilated to those of collective liminality opened by the epidemic; the suspension of the normality inherent in mourning was doubled by the general interruption of everyday life brought about by the emergency measures.[119]

The story of Ginevra degli Almieri, reported in Rondinelli's official chronicle and much like a recurrent dream, may render, at least in part, the sense of astonishment and loss of self caused by the modification of funeral rituals. Ginevra was rumored to have been mistakenly buried alive. When she revived a few hours later, she climbed out of the grave and went home. There, however, her husband thought "she was a shadow"; not only did he not recognize her, he even drove her away. So the woman went to Antonio's house, and Antonio welcomed her because "when she was a young lady, he had ardently loved her." [120]

After being buried hastily and disrespectfully, Ginevra refused to love those who had forgotten her. Perhaps those who survived, at least at a latent level, feared the consequences of their forgetting and not caring for the dead. These concerns were exacerbated by the brutality of mass graves in unconsecrated soil, the nudity of the bodies, and their defenseless exposure to wild dogs. We should not forget, however, that the transformation of the fundamental rituals of social life was imposed by the authorities in charge of the emergency; as a result, disorder and barbarism could be attributed to those who claimed the right to intensify institutional formality: the Public Health Magistracy.

Even canon law legitimated these choices of secular policy and justified the exclusion of plague victims from church burials because of the terror this would have caused the faithful gathered in prayer. The Barnabite theologian Filiberto Marchini, in the juridical section of his broad treatise, stated this question in clear terms. There he examined one by one all the theoretical problems inherent in funeral rites during epidemics: "Quaestio autem gravissima in hac Urbe non semel exhorta fuit, an Magistratus secularis posset impedire, ne aliqui Viri Ecclesiastici, et alii seculares Illustres intra Ecclesiam, vel prope illam in loco sacro humarentur." [121] The issue therefore concerned the highest echelons of the lay and ecclesiastical hierarchy. Was it legitimate for the chancellor to mandate burial outside of consecrated land? Was it legitimate to impose a dishonorable death on illustrious men? It was a "mixed case," in Marchini's opinion, because it concerned not only the spiritual salvation but also the common good, "bonum commune totius populi," of all those over whom the magistrate enjoyed legitimate jurisdiction in times of calamity. In fact, some high church officials—including the rector of the Portigian Jesuits and the canon Rondinelli—were buried with all due honors, thereby encouraging those who wanted to accompany their relatives to a proper burial to cite these cases as examples. Yet no church or lay official worried about the effects of deritualization on the populace at large. Marchini seemed willing to defend the open field burials, citing the opinions of Livy, Ovid, Lucretius, and Thucydides that carnivorous animals were disgusted by plague-stricken bodies. [122] Thus, common people could let Public Health gravediggers do their work and then let lay functionaries carry out the appropriate rituals.[123] All anxieties related to the rites of mourning in the populace were of secondary importance in the eyes of those in power.

An anonymous clerical writer transcribed the echo of terror arising from the loss of ritual in the obscure language of a prophecy screamed by a crazy man:

> At the beginning of the summer, there was in our city of Florence a poor man of lower status, called by everyone "Masino." Everybody thought he was crazy. . . . [Masino] went around screaming and shouting, "The air, the air, I will pay you tomorrow, in the countryside looking at the melons," and he did not say anything but that. Everyone thought he was crazy because it was impossible to understand what he said or what those words meant."[124]

According to this account, the poor man's prophecy announced metaphorically the disintegration of all civil links protecting the city. "What he meant to say by 'the air, the air' was that people would be taken to the fields like beasts to be buried carelessly. 'I will pay you tomorrow' presages the coming punishment, because God 'does not pay on Saturday and . . . over you [Florence] a payment is due.'" Finally, the third part of the prophecy specified what kind of punishment was in store: "in the countryside looking at the melons" meant that

> like animals, we would be taken to bury our dead in the countryside in graves, throwing them, some with their legs up, others with their hands up, others with their butts up, some in some ways, some in other ways, and there would be no respect for the rich or the poor, the noble or the ignoble, and all would be thrown in the graves one on top of the other, as though we were hay or pieces of wood. But no, that is not true, not even like hay or wood, because in that case we would be careful. The bodies would simply be left there, some covered, some uncovered, some with their arms out, some with the head or the foot out, as meals for dogs and beasts.[125]

The scandalous punishment therefore consisted of the dishonor of a savage death, no longer civilized by rituals, weeping, and prayer. The description recalls the late-medieval imagery of the Triumph of Death, in which piled bodies of agonizing men gave way to the passage of a winged or sickle-carrying skeleton.[126] In the seventeenth-century text, however, the baroque sense of the representation altered the iconographic style, following the Counter-Reformation theory, which stressed with obsessive insistence the centrality of mourning.

Giovan Paolo Lomazzo, in his *Trattato dell'arte della pittura, scultura e architettura,* printed at the time of the Council of Trent, devoted an entire chapter to the paintings to be put in "chapels, graveyards, underground churches, and other melancholic places."[127] The predominant theme was burial and the solemn escort of the body to the consecrated grave. The accent was on tears and the rituals of detachment, exemplified by Jesus taken down from the cross and embraced by Mary "and the Marys who weep"; "Sarah who buried herself in the sepulcher prepared by her husband"; Jacob on his deathbed surrounded by his sons; and Ebron taken to his burial.[128]

The Florentine text contemporary with the epidemic turned the notion of honorable death upside down.[129] Nothing could be worse, more despicable, or more unhappy than to die badly, just as nothing could be happier, more familiar, or more human than to be buried in a church in one's own tomb with one's own relatives, after a funeral and traditional ceremonies. Nothing was more senseless (*insentius*), uncommon, and cruel than to be buried in the fields outside of the city.[130] Stressing these values, Righi opposed them to those (Socrates, the Cynic philosophers) who separated the idea of death from that of the territorial destination of the body confined to the tomb.[131]

Honorable death was particularly linked, in social memory and in practice, to the sepulcher, which was enclosed in the sacred perimeter of the church. In the goldsmith Orazio Vanni's will, mentioned above, existential and financial worries seemed to fade away only after the purchase of a family vault in Santa Maria Novella, "in front of the Ricasoli Chapel." The spatial coordinates with which Orazio defined his vault were identical to those he used to describe his shop, so that the house, the shop, and the vault assumed in the will of this rich bourgeois a similar sense of rootedness within a series of connected and defined spaces.[132] As a result, danger assumed the character of nomadism, of wandering, of what came from the outside. It was therefore no coincidence that the earliest trials of the summer, when the first rumors of the contagion began to spread, involved travelers and deserters.

To be buried outside the city walls, far from the family vault or one's own church, meant exclusion from the texture of family and neighborhood life. As opposed to the family vault or the engraved tombstone, which exalted and arrested the flow of genealogical succession, burial in the fields dispersed all visible elements internal to the process by which a group established itself in a city like Florence, where this process was sedimented in privately written family memoirs and *prioristi* (lists of the positions one's own ancestors had held in the city magistracy).[133] In an urban culture deeply attentive to expressions of individualism, dishonorable death threatened the very possibility of deciphering bodies physically. Naked, mutilated by animals, victims of the elements, cast among thousands of other bodies piled up at random, the dead became unrecognizable, even for their future resurrection.

On 6 July 1631, "rumors began to spread that some infected cadavers, poorly buried, had been eaten by dogs. . . . A dog that had been in a place where bodies had been buried brought the plague to a house, the name of which we do not know. However, the villa is called Campigna, five miles past Marradi."[134] This denunciation sent to Florence by the Public Health officials of Marradi synthesized the whole horror of dishonorable death: the dead came back in pieces, left at front doors by the dogs who had devoured them.

On 5 November 1630, Captain Ottavio Diligenti forwarded to the chancellor's office a report against the noblewoman Adriana Giusti. She lived near the Pitti Palace, and her windows opened onto the garden of His Highness. Diligenti accused her of keeping in her home a sick servant who had caught the plague from Adriana's son, Camillo. Presumably the woman was a wet nurse. What really concerned the captain was how the young child had been buried. The barber-surgeons, he suggested, did not report the nature of the illness, and consequently none of the relatives was locked in the house.[135] The death of the child, little more than a baby, provides us for the first time with a glimpse into a well-to-do person's home. The indiscreet eyes of neighbors could not peer through the windows opening onto His Highness's garden; these people could, however, penetrate the crowded rooms of the poorer quarters of the city. The burial in the church, therefore, can be easily explained by the nobility's sense of honor and propriety, as well as by Adriana's love for her infant son. Unfortunately, no document reveals whether the child was baptized; if he was not, the burial would have served the additional purpose of preserving the young creature within the consecrated perimeter of the tomb, thereby pacifying his restless soul, which may have come back among the living in one of the many shapes described in folkloric literature.[136]

On 16 January a denunciation was made against Domenico Becatti, a servant of the Florentine Magistracy of the Nove.[137] Everyone in the neighborhood of San Lorenzo was talking about the death of his son, who was buried in the basilica. The captain of the guards, Piero da Ponte a Sieve, went to gather some testimonies to shed light on the episode. Caterina, called "Ricciarda," presumably a neighbor of the Becattis, spoke first: "Throughout the quarter, everyone says that the boy died of the bad disease." She even mentioned that she had seen the boy clearly when he was still alive: he had walked with his arm outstretched, a clear sign that "he had the disease." She also claimed to know that before the sacristan of the basilica could permit the burial, he had asked the gravediggers for the death certificate. They had one, which had been properly countersigned by Vittorio Geri. We have met this barber-surgeon; he was involved, albeit indirectly, in the trial of the goldsmith Manzuoli, whose son Girolamo he secretly treated.

Captain Piero was not convinced by the information received and continued his investigation. He went to interrogate the gravediggers who had taken the boy's body to the burial site. They worked at the convalescent home of San Gallo and, one after another, confirmed what Ricciarda had revealed. They had never seen the boy before, and performed their duty properly. On the paper given to the sacristan was written, "dead by ordinary causes." Vittorio, the first gravedigger to be interrogated, formulated a hypothesis: perhaps the boy died of the "Benedict disease," because he "had dark spots on his face." The second gravedigger, however, remembered that Domenico Becatti, the boy's father, had said that the boy had died of a chest disease. Since everything was legally done, with all the proper documents, "we put him in the church." Yet on the evening of the following day, the sacristan of San Lorenzo came looking for the gravedigger Vittorio, asking him to get "some lime to cover the body. When I refused to go, he threatened to have me fired." In the end, after renewed threats, the gravedigger did bring some lime and, with the aid of the priest, spread it on the grave.

Like many of the very short trials concerning episodes in which a body was hidden, the testimonies in this trial provide few details, almost as if the delicacy of the subject prevented its translation into words. We therefore have to proceed through fragments, allusions, and clues. First, the prosecuted father, a minor bureaucrat who had no commercial interests or shop to take care of, did not leave home when his son got sick. Furthermore, the rumors in the neighborhood contradicted the gravediggers' report on the nature of the disease that killed the boy. Also, the paper was signed by the questionable barber-surgeon Geri. Finally, and most importantly, the sacristan hurried that night to ask for some lime to cover the grave. This procedure was very rare when dead notables were buried in churches.[138] We can also picture the network of complicity: the father who obtained the paper from the barber-surgeon stating that his son had died of "ordinary causes," the gravediggers who upon receipt of a little money were told what the official cause of death was, and, lastly, the accommodating sacristan.

Later we will meet Ottavio Amoni, a central figure and a relevant witness at the canonization hearings for Domenica da Paradiso. Ottavio, too, hid his wife, Lisabetta, for fear of the consequences to his family; he, like Domenico Becatti, was a functionary of the Magistracy of the Nove. The powers of this Magistracy were growing at that time; a post in the Nove provided a valuable opportunity to ambitious men from the provinces who had migrated recently to Florence. Even Andrea Cioli, the grand duke's powerful secretary, had worked for this Magistracy for a while. Perhaps owing in part to this bureaucratic profession, Domenico Becatti developed a sense of social status and the hope of one day occupying an important public administrative position. These aspirations deserved to be anchored in some form of genealogic visibility, by Domenico's bribing a barber-surgeon and two gravediggers to ensure that the body of his son killed by the plague was not thrown into a common grave.

Up to this point, the honorable burials in the church, and the game of complicity that had prepared the way for them, remain within horizons of domestic tenderness and family prestige. Possibly Domenico Becatti and Adriana Giusti had the bodies of their sons buried in the consecrated ground of the church so that, when the epidemic was over, they could return and pray for their dead children, peacefully at rest surrounded by other family members.

The next trial, although similar in type, differs in many respects from the trials we have examined thus far. It portrays a socially confused and animated scene in which the network of intrigue is more striking than any conventional ideal of the "good death."

In early December, Margherita, a shoemaker's wife and a young seminarian's mother, died near the Convent of Sant'Ambrogio. Despite the rumors that she had died of the plague, she was buried in the convent church, and her house was not locked. As she was the mother of a future priest, she was probably a pious woman, and we can easily find the link between the ecclesiastical burial and the nuns of Sant'Ambrogio: in her will, Margherita left her belongings, "both furniture and otherwise," to the nuns. To thank her, the sisters granted permission for her body to be buried in the church.[139] The pious Margherita had just been buried when a number of people arrived on the scene: first came Pier Francesco Gelati, a shoemaker called "Ninci," and Andrea, a stablekeeper, who, "following the nuns' instructions," began to execute Margherita's dying wishes and load her belongings for removal. The job was difficult for only two men, so the sacristan Zanobi came to lend a hand. Others came as well, until finally the entire community had become involved in the operation, with men carrying pieces of furniture and women the kitchen tools. Even a priest and his father, Taddeo, "a servant in the Compagnia dei Bianchi," volunteered. After emptying the rooms, the movers took everything to Raffaello's barbershop, behind the Church of Sant'Ambrogio.

Margherita's last wishes revived a neighborhood sociability that had probably been withdrawn during the epidemic, and it was precisely this unusual traffic of people and goods up and down the stairs that attracted the guards' attention. The stablekeeper Andrea and Ninci were duly arrested. The two men's story repeated all the familiar passages. "Jacopo da Massa, barber-surgeon of the Public Health Magistracy, gave permission to the prior of Sant'Ambrogio to bury the woman in the church there," said Andrea. Then, Andrea continued, on the eve of Santa Lucia, Giovan Battista, the altar boy of Sant'Ambrogio, and someone nicknamed "Lacchezzino" said that "the prior would like me to help in the relocation of the stuff from that woman's house. . . . So both of us went and took everything to Raffaello's barbershop. He is no longer at his shop but is with the nuns." Now we see the possible sense of that temporary storage: did Raffaello die of the plague also, leaving the shop to the nuns of Sant'Ambrogio in exchange for a promise to be buried in the church? In any case, the objects from the dead woman's house, located "near the convent," and from the barbershop, located right behind the church, became the property of the church as the convent area increased.[140] Thus pity and the funereal culture surrounding Margherita, who was certainly not poor, become entangled in deeper structural modifications of far-reaching social impact.

The last trial involving a process of cultural modification around death that was in direct conflict with Public Health regulations took place somewhat later, in the spring of 1633, when the disease was spreading again. This complicated story revolved around the socially unacceptable love between Michele di Francesco Ticci and his servant Caterina Burchielli.[141] As usual, the violation was well orchestrated, demonstrating a mixture of intelligence and ability to utilize the ambiguities of the law and the mercenary complicity of two barber-surgeons in the usual community of neighbors, servants, and relatives. Michele Ticci, "a citizen of Florence," lived on Via Larga with Caterina, one of his servants. At the beginning of May, Caterina fell ill and was visited by two barber-surgeons, Giuliano di Cosimo Rosi and Annibale Galletti. The barber-surgeons signed a report stating that she did not have a contagious disease. Some days later, Caterina, in agony, was taken to a relative's house on Via Zanobi, not far from her master's house. She had just been put to bed when she died. Thanks to the certificate of the two barber-surgeons, Caterina was buried in the basilica of San Lorenzo.

The episode would have gone unnoticed had not a chain of deaths on Via Zanobi come to the attention of the chancellor. Until then, the street had not been hit by the plague. Jacopo Burchielli, Caterina's brother, having fallen asleep on the same bed where Caterina died, got sick and died. Next a young girl, the daughter of Piero Cappelli, a tenant in the same house, and Perugina, Caterina's sister-in-law, died. Finally, another woman, a tenant in the house, died. Her three children were immediately hospitalized "for the usual purges and quarantines." It was as if Caterina had come back to her relatives to kill them. Moreover, one of her relatives denounced the episode to the magistrate.

It was not often that a citizen of the residential neighborhoods of Florence took the time and trouble to bury a servant in San Lorenzo. Generally servants, both men and women, were either abandoned to their fate or else given to someone, paid for by the master, to care for them far from the house.[142] We recall the case of Piero Billi here, whom the guards arrested when about to abandon the infected body of his servant on Via Gualfonda. This fact suggests that the difference between a dishonorable death and an honorable death was also an emotional difference, a transposition of physical attachment onto the funereal ideology, articulated differently according to social class and status. People were scared of the fate of those to whom they were attached. They protected themselves from that fear through a series of precise guarantees, smoothing the absolute brutality of the loss and taming it within socially acceptable forms of ritual.

Thus, Michele Ticci took care to bury Caterina in the church, but he simulated formal obedience to the regulations by having her moved to her relative's house on Via Zanobi before she actually died. The law, which prohibited the removal of an infected body from one's *own* house, was therefore observed. But it was a trick that many, many people used, and the chancellor was not fooled. When he interrogated Michele, he was able to put him immediately on the spot because all the witnesses were against him. It was a cross fire in which everyone referred to previous testimonies, to what others had seen, observed, said, and touched, thereby delineating a sort of underworld of relatives and servants who were in constant communication and contact. Between Via Zanobi and Via Larga, the flow of communication on Caterina's health was intense. Moreover, it was amplified by the gossip of the neighbors, who added their side of the story.

The first witness against Michele was Giovannino, another of the servants, who said that he helped Caterina for at least eight days. During that time he was in contact with Caterina's brother, Jacopino, with whom he discussed the illness and described the symptoms, which were getting more and more alarming: "a bubo on her left breast, another one between her legs, and her body was covered with furuncles." Giovannino also confided to Jacopino that his master had called two barber-surgeons of the Public Health Magistracy, with whom he planned the fake death certificate. The news traveled from person to person to Via Zanobi—even the "two young men" who were then hospitalized had been aware of it.

After Giovannino's testimony, Caterina's sister-in-law, Perugina, arrived at the chancellor's office. She was upset because her husband Jacopino had died. Under oath, she admitted that she brought the two barber-surgeons to Caterina's bed and, removing the sheet, showed them, "by candlelight, a bubo on the left breast, another between the legs," and the furuncles. The scene was extraordinarily vivid, the black spots in the dark background of the room illuminated by Caravaggio-esque lighting. Perugina returned twice to repeat the story of the visit, finally making a defense of the two barber-surgeons virtually impossible.

Next, the woman who washed the corpse testified. She confirmed that she saw "a bubo on the breast and blood in the skin, all over the black cadaver." Then the porters carried the body from the master's house to Via Zanobi. One of them caught her final whisper, in which she complained of "a great pain in her breast and between her legs." Finally, when the body was taken from the house for burial at San Lorenzo, a curious neighbor who watched the activity from her window ran to report that she "saw her face and it was black, as if she had been painted."

Michele's position was then completely undermined; he was forced to confess that he had bribed the two barber-surgeons, Rosi and Galletti, and said that he gave them three *scudi* to prepare false reports, one certifying that it was not a contagious disease, the other a death certificate to be given to the priest before the burial. The documents were drawn up in his presence, as soon as he paid the agreed-upon sum. This time, after such an explicit confession, the two barber-surgeons were charged with the crimes as well.

"It is demonstrated *ex officio* that the crime that ravaged the whole neighborhood began only with the arrival of the servant. She was taken from the house of Ticci on Via Larga on 3 May and died the following morning at nine o'clock." Considering the very grave consequences of their acts, Michele was sentenced to two years' exile in Pisa, and the two barber-surgeons to four years' exile in Leghorn.

The four episodes of infraction stemming from the will to bury one's dearest in a church delineate social itineraries for acculturating death that were directly opposed to the ritualization imposed by the Magistracy. These modes stress another way of handling individual crises triggered by loss, and in this sense they render inapplicable the theoretical paradigms linked to the rites of passage outlined by some anthropologists. That is, the liminal environment induced by the crisis did not here produce the sense of ritual *communitas* frequently described by Victor Turner. On the contrary, the conflict was intimately connected to a central stage of biological passage: the Magistracy's rules were perceived as upsetting and disaggregating all traditional behaviors belonging to strategies of "civilization." In this sense, the suspension of normality was expressed, for individuals as well as for families, as the moment of highest risk; it followed the need to break the previous social code as prescribed by law, the moral economy on which class identity rested. The passage therefore fueled the conflict itself, not the *communitas*. Thus, the administration of liminality underlined differentiated modes of ritual vindications.

The main defendants in the trials we have just examined belonged, for the most part, to nonproductive enclaves: the noblewoman Adriana Giusti; the bureaucrat Domenico Becatti; Margherita, the seminarian's mother; and Michele Ticci, "citizen of Florence," who had at least two servants and no trade. Their sense of honor and genealogy, concretely circumscribable within the perimeter of parish and tomb, placed them in the documents of criminal trials because they were accused of trying at all cost to ensure an honorable death for their loved ones. This behavior contrasts with what we have already seen among artisans, who at the first rumor of contagion fled to their shops with their sons, leaving the women behind to care for the sick. Sometimes this strenuous defense of life and work impelled them to abandon the bodies of relatives and apprentices and leave them to Public Health personnel to discover and bury in the field. This division probably corresponded to a somatic culture oriented by priorities and values and differentiated according to social status.[143]

Until the contemporary age, the lower classes traditionally identified the body with physical strength. Thus disease, conceived as a sudden and violent event, was perceived as a sign of weakness. Often our witnesses described the symptoms of contagion as an "accident of pain of the body," thereby underlining the immediate ability of the disease to break physical resistance and erupt into an unpredictable otherness. Even popular hagiography pivoted on a similar binary code of strength and weakness, in which the ability to withstand the assaults and attacks of the disease in all its configurations was praised as a heroic virtue.[144]

As they did not possess family vaults and were instead used to the humble burials mentioned by Boccaccio, the city's working classes were preoccupied with the lives of those who, through labor and pain, earned bread for all. Resistance to the epidemic was therefore particularly rooted in being at the shop with fellow workers and neighbors. What counted in the body was physical strength, the ability to withstand the fatigue of the loom, the hammer, and the lathe. Generally, the negligible attention paid to the needs and feelings of the body was paralleled by its being used to the highest limit of work and fatigue. Now all the cases of women whose plague symptoms were hidden by other symptoms and duties—the sequence of pregnancies and work in the house and shop—spring back to mind.

Paying greater attention to one's body, being more conscious of its needs, was related to a sort of inversion of the body's economic functions; as reliance on physical strength in the productive sphere decreased, other forms of consumption (medical, alimentary, aesthetic) increased. While violating the regulations to preserve the honor of death, members of the upper classes defended an aesthetic sense of the body as well—its function of harmonious decorum internal to genealogically ordered rhythms. The bodies of relatives were also symbolic of the spiritual sense of lineage.

Domenica da Paradiso's canonization hearings, which began in December 1630 in the midst of the epidemic, marked the highest point of development of this funereal ideology as a genealogic and political administration of death and an aesthetic consumption of the body. This zenith ideally completed that process of civilizing the collective passage through the biological absolute, and the making of a cult and the universe of symbols surrounding that cult operated to create the baroque ideal of an honorable death.

3

Property

Theft, Relocation, Exchange

On 28 September 1630, the officials of the Florentine Public Health Magistracy submitted a proposal to the grand duke for the improvement of the Bargello guard. Until then, the personnel of both the Otto di Guardia and the Balia, the ordinary criminal magistracies, had carried out most of the regulations, arrests, and punishments against those who disobeyed Public Health ordinances. These two administrative organs, however, proved to be inadequate as the disease continued to spread.

The Florentine officials nominated a former member of the Otto Magistracy, Francesco di Filippo, or "Luna," for the position of corporal "of public health." He was to have "six men under his command to execute all orders . . . and [each was to] receive a salary of six *scudi* per month," whereas his other officers earned only three.

As they centralized public health legislation, Florentine officials attempted to attenuate the apparent conflict between the two magistracies over certain domains. Which magistracy should enforce punishment? Where should punishment be publicly carried out? The personnel of the Otto Magistracy claimed a monopoly over executions, exacting seven *lire* from each prisoner. The Public Health Magistracy also demanded the right to regulate executions; it did not, however, demand any money from the prisoners.[1]

The grand duke approved Luna's appointment a few days after the request was made. Still, on 31 October the officials insisted that they needed a further expansion of the Bargello guard. They asked that Ottavio Diligenti, a member of the Otto Magistracy since 11 September, be appointed captain of the Public Health Magistracy, to earn a monthly salary of 15 *scudi*. He was to command one lieutenant, Luna, as well as fifteen corporals.[2] On 1 November, Ottavio Diligenti, known as "Cappellaio," was thus commissioned, and later that month the city chancellor published the names of the members comprising the new administrative organ. After Ottavio, the following were listed according to their rank and salary: Francesco di Filippo, "Luna," fifteen *scudi* per month; and corporals Bastiano, "Faccia," and Sanino, "Quattro Fiorini," the same salary. In addition, the remaining officers were appointed with a monthly salary of three *scudi:* Marco di Angiolo Verani; Bastiano "the Red"; Giovanni Battista, "Cianca"; Giuseppe, "Cornacchino"; Oratio, "Baccellone"; Lessandro, "Battilano"; Santo di Domenico, "Barbino"; Agostino di Antonio Zeri; Lessandro, "Bellegote"; Innocentio di Guido Gherardi; Giovanni di Vincenzo Vettore; Ferdinando di Vetorio, "Tessitore"; Domenico di Matteo, "Bolognese"; Tommaso di Michele Lippi; and Domenico di Piero, "Ammazzacani."[3]

This group of men that made up the Bargello guard were linked from then on to the people they constantly pursued. Hunters and prey alike found themselves on the same roads and constantly surprised one another, making arrests and escapes respectively. In the denunciations, reports, and testimonies at the Magistracy, the investigative style of the captain or corporal delineated the profile of his prisoner. The clear social picture that the Bargello officials painted through gestures, objects, places, and colors configured a rationality that differentiated one guard from another. The career of Cappellaio, Ottavio Diligenti, for instance, was very short. Appointed on 1 November, he died of the plague just two weeks later. By 14 November the Florentine officials had already proposed a replacement for him to the grand duke.[4] A constant and rapid turnover thus characterized the new public structure, which only a few individuals managed to survive. Others, like Luna, were expelled for malfeasance.

During Ottavio's term, from the first to the thirteenth of November, forty individuals were captured. Cappellaio was a zealous guard. Well informed, he controlled, monitored, and even anticipated the outlaws' moves each time their merchandise was sold by black marketeers. In fact, it was Cappellaio who arrested the only thief to be executed in the public square—a punishment surely meant as a vivid example to the townspeople. This episode marked Cappellaio's glorious, albeit brief, service in the ranks of the Public Health Magistracy.[5]

A GARDEN PLOT AND A MEDIUM-SIZED BAG

Ottavio's first important arrest was of a young printer, Niccolò Galeotti, on 3 November 1630. The trial documents begin with Diligenti's presentation of the case to the Public Health officials: "Here comes Captain Ottavio Diligenti. He [reports] that a secret informer told him that two individuals had climbed over the wall surrounding Signor Guadagni's garden plot. They could not be identified, yet they were clearly seen by a female neighbor and by Signor Guadagni's gardener."[6]

Having gathered the neighbors' testimonies, Cappellaio went to the site of the crime with Lieutenant Luna. Cappellaio recounted:

> I thought that the thieves might have tried to enter the empty house, as the owners had been taken to the Badia. So I decided to go check the place out with Captain Luna. We went to the house, which is on Via de' Pilastri, across the street from Il Fiasco d'Oro. After we passed behind the garden plots, we asked the witness precisely where she had seen the two men. We then took a ladder and climbed the wall. In that wall, we saw a hole with some dirt, as if scraped from a shoe. There were no footprints in the garden, so we called the gardener and asked him whether he had seen anyone climbing the wall.

The man answered:

> I saw two young men this morning, around the time I was going to have breakfast. One was about twenty years old . . . and the other eighteen. They wore dark clothes and came from the direction of the walls of the Pinti Gate. When they approached me I asked them, "What are you doing around these plots?" and one answered, "We're going home, since the front door's locked and we can't open it." They climbed over the wall at exactly this spot.

A naive yet sincere answer, reflecting a common practice. Many people returned to homes that had been closed after the death of a relative or simply out of fear of contagion. They would climb walls or go around gardens to get into their houses. They would enter not through the front door, which had been locked by Public Health officials, but by the back door. In this manner they would not leave any sign of their clandestine passage—no nail extracted, no iron bar forced beneath the door—and thus would run little risk of being caught by the security forces. Yet they always left traces to be uncovered by neighbors, those who saw but remained unseen. Some dirt on a rock or a hole in a wall might be suspicious enough for a neighbor to file a report.

After some time, the gardener said that he saw the two men descending the dividing wall between two gardens and "returning to the same plot. One of them carried a medium-sized bag. They left through my doorway." If he saw them again, he concluded, he would certainly recognize them.

After listening to the gardener's testimony, Cappellaio and Luna followed the two men's path. "We went to the door of the barred house. Seeing that it had been tampered with, we asked a nearby young man if he knew who lived in that house."

The boy told Cappellaio that "an old woman lived in the room downstairs, but that she had gone to San Miniato. Her two grandchildren used to visit frequently. The elder is a printer named Niccolò di Giovanni Galeotti; the boy did not remember the name of the younger." The picture slowly became clearer and clearer. An old woman who lived alone had just been taken to the lazaret of San Miniato. She had only two relatives, usually sloppily dressed, who sometimes went to visit her.

Now we can see, Captain Ottavio argued, how two young men were able to walk safely through the garden, over the wall, and to the very door of the house. "We thought that only the old woman's relatives would know the way to the back door; therefore, we carefully attempted to capture them to recover the stolen goods." The search for Niccolò Galeotti began.

It was easier to begin the search at sunrise. "On the morning of the third, I arrived at Niccolò Galeotti's home with my lieutenant and guards. We found him lying with his father and younger brother on a bare mattress. We asked him whether he worked and what kind of job he had. He replied, 'Although I'm a printer, I've been unemployed for the past two weeks because my master just lost his four sons.'"

Everyone knows that unemployment is dangerous. It encourages bad qualities, and some of these, most notably laziness, lead to illegal trade and theft. The officials asked Niccolò to get dressed, carefully searching his clothes before he put them on. "As we went through his pockets, we found a *lira,* that is, a silver *giulio* and four *cratie.*" Sensing danger, Niccolò found an excuse to leave the room. As he exited, barefoot and half-naked, "he dropped another coin. He tried to hide the silver coin beneath the bed so that we would not find it."

The search for the young man's coin led them into the bathroom. "We lit a lantern and found a coin attached to some excrement. Then we went back into the room and finally found the silver coin under the bed. Because we knew that neither the young man nor his father was employed, and we had just seen how he tried to hide the money, we believed that we had the man we were looking for. So we arrested him and sent him to Sant'Onofrio Prison."

Before he took Niccolò away, Captain Ottavio asked the younger boy if his brother had visited a young fellow worker who "always dressed in black." The guards then went to this young man's house and asked to see the father. The mother explained that her husband had left and that they had temporarily closed the shop after their sons had died.

The plague occasionally interrupted the course of an investigation. The deaths of the printer's sons made it difficult to find and interrogate the young apprentice. On 19 November, all four shop workers were finally brought to the magistrate. The gardener who had testified in the case saw the individuals from "near the door" but failed to recognize any of them. Not surprisingly, they denied all accusations. Even Niccolò, although admitting that his grandmother, Angela Germini, lived on Via de' Pilastri, asserted that he knew absolutely nothing about the theft. Moreover, the guards had been unable to find the, as the gardener put it, "medium-sized" bag.

While waiting for an opportunity to arrest all four print shop workers, Cappellaio found out that the shop's owner, Simone di Pietro Ciotti, had, despite his sons' deaths, indeed been working. Since the beginning of the month he had been in the shop "and worked." "A great number of people" were always in and out of the shop, obviously running a risk of contracting the disease. Cappellaio therefore arrested Ciotti and took him to the lazaret of Sant'Onofrio for interrogation.

"I live on the street across from the monks of Badia. Our rooms are over the print shop, which has been there for the past three years." He and his wife still had a son and daughter; out of their six children, four had died. His eldest son had died two months earlier, after an illness of about ten days. Another one fell ill some two weeks later. A traveling doctor's aide diagnosed him as having the dreaded disease and ordered him immediately to San Miniato. He died within two weeks. When one of Ciotti's daughters was subsequently struck, the father recounted, "the same doctor's aide said that she smelled wormy, so I notified the Public Health authorities. Covered with worms, she lasted only one hour. Approximately one week later, my six-year-old daughter got sick. The aide claimed that she wasn't in any danger. She died in only two days." The doctor's aide, "a small man with a black beard," did not administer any medicine to them, Ciotti pointed out in an attempt to explain that he had not planned to treat them clandestinely at home. The dead children had been buried at the Church of Santa Margherita, and Ciotti was able to provide the burial documents, signed by the priest, to prove it. Since plague victims were to be buried in fields, not in churchyards, these papers served to exonerate Ciotti from the charge of spreading the plague.

From the sobering account of this tragic sequence of events emerges the care with which the father observed the prescribed rules and regulations. He always reported his children's deaths to the authorities. In addition, he arranged for medical attention and carefully obtained the proper certificates. In only one case did the doctor's aide diagnose the plague, and this son died in the lazaret. The others died of ordinary illnesses, succumbing to the high child mortality rate caused by worms and fevers.

The last element of this story of death, the church burial records, ended the long legal chain. In the father's testimony, the plague was nothing more than one of various possible causes of death, a detail that seemed to be of little importance. What the father thought to be the almost daily recurrence of death was, to the authorities, a catastrophic situation. As for Niccolò, the magistrate released him because of insufficient evidence. Thereafter, no trace of either him or his master printer remained.[7]

The investigation of Niccolò Galeotti ended in three days. The denunciation was filed on 2 November, the investigation conducted by Cappellaio and his guards led to his arrest on the third, and the printer Ciotti was taken to court on the fourth. For the four apprentices to be released and the case concluded, one of them, the one dressed in black and probably Galeotti's accomplice, had to return to Florence with his father. On 24 November, Niccolò and his friends were released from jail.

"A CRIME OF THE GREATEST IMPORTANCE"

On 5 November, Cappellaio decided to put an end to all trafficking in stolen goods. Thieves would often steal from houses closed by the

Public Health Magistracy. Because he "believed that much of the illegal trading, especially of linens and clothes, took place in the ghetto," Cappellaio decided that he and his guards, "in disguise," would begin their investigation there at night.[8]

A young man standing at a well aroused their suspicions. Andrea di Domenico Passignani, a gardener at the Arch of San Piero, was busily hiding some linens wrapped in a tablecloth. In particular, he had "two sheets, a towel, three good square-patterned pillowcases, four *scudi,* and an image of the Virgin Mary that bore the engraved name of Francesca Betti, the wife of Simone. . . . Continuing the search," the officer reported, "we found a knife with a narrow iron handle in his pockets." The weapon made Cappellaio even more suspicious; he believed it was probably linked to a theft.

"I used the knife to open the door where I got this stuff," the boy admitted. "Tell us the location of this door," Cappellaio demanded threateningly. "I stole these things at Santa Maria Nuova. The door was painted and locked with iron screws."

Thus, the door, bearing the sign of a white cross, had been closed by the authorities. "We thought that it would be better for him to show us the exact location of the house. We went with him, and he pointed the door out to us. We all recognized the house because it had already been broken into once before. Although it had been closed for forty days and stank terribly, we decided to see whether the knife could really open the door."

The house had not been locked for fear of contagion; rather, it was being disinfected with herbs and sulfurous fumigations. There was therefore no danger of spreading the dreaded disease, and the only crime committed was theft.

The guards recounted:

> We ordered Andrea to open the door. Because we had tied him up he asserted, "I can't do it." We then took the knife and broke in ourselves. . . . We went upstairs and asked the boy where he had found the linens. He replied that they had been in the second wooden chest, which he could barely see in the dark. We verified that some things were in fact missing from the chest. Because we had discovered these items in the young man's possession, we left the house and took him to Sant'Onofrio Prison.

Cappellaio was still not sure whether this incident was the only crime Andrea had committed. He warned the boy that if any other crime was uncovered, his situation would become much worse. In fact, even in this case the guards were unable to find the *regolo,* the tool officials used to seal front doors. Cappellaio knew that Fagni the "perfumer" had been in that particular house. According to Public Health regulations, the *regolo* ought to be in its proper place, nailed to the door of the disinfected house.

As he left the house and walked along Via Rosa toward Briga, the captain noticed that another door had been forcibly opened. Moreover, the wood merchant's house, which had been closed as well, was open. A librarian, whose name was not noted, rented this house. From his window the librarian had caught a glimpse of the thief, who had "closed the door" behind him and "escaped very fast," thereby preventing the librarian from recognizing him.

Streets, however, were never deserted, even during epidemics. A coachman had noticed the man. "The thief," he reported, "was a small man. He was dirty and wore a shabby cloak."

"The librarian had said the same thing about the man who was near the door," Diligenti recalled. "We concluded that the thief had robbed more than one house. We hoped to discover during the course of the interrogation whether he had used a knife to break into the houses and where he had sold the stolen goods." The testimonies of both the librarian and the coachman, therefore, depicted a professional thief. Cappellaio wondered whether this man had been caught before. He remembered that "a thief carrying a knife like Andrea's had been arrested by the Otto guards around the twenty-fourth of the previous month." Diligenti recollected the episode clearly because he had then been a corporal and in charge of the area where the arrest had taken place. Although the thief had managed to escape imprisonment that time, it was becoming increasingly clear that this man was "a professional thief, who carried a knife to force open doors." The moment to act with determination had arrived, Diligenti concluded, and punishment "was deserved by this thief who went into homes he knew to be shut."

On 6 November, the interrogation of Andrea Passignani began. He was twenty years old, "as seen by his smooth face." The chancellor asked him what he had been doing in the ghetto that night.

> I had some things that a man had given me. I was waiting for him when the guards arrived. . . . I didn't know the man; he had seen me at San Piero and asked if I had a job. I replied, "No," and then he asked me to

carry some of his stuff for him. I told him that I would, so he took me to a house in Santa Maria Nuova and entered with a key. He then gave me the things and took me back to the ghetto. He asked me to wait there for him while he went upstairs at the house of some Jews. Just then the guards came and arrested me.

Was he, Andrea, carrying anything when the guards found him?

"I didn't have anything except for a small knife, one of those which can be closed. It was very small, but the guards took it away from me anyway. It was this small," Andrea said, pointing at his finger. "The soldiers asked me where I had found the things, and I told them about the house and the guy who had given me the stuff. I then took them to the house."

How was the door opened?

"They opened it. They used a long knife, one of those knives which cannot be closed." He drew a halfmoon, about as long as a forearm, to indicate the shape of the blade.

In that case, there were two knives. Who owned the large knife?

"I did."

Where did the guards find it?

"They found it on me, in the ghetto."

Did he own any other knives? Why until now had he claimed to own only one knife?

"I owned two knives."

Why had he neglected to mention the large knife when he had talked about the smaller one? Andrea remained quiet. The magistrate insistently asked further questions to put more pressure on the young man. Who told the guards to open the door with the knife?

"I didn't say anything."

Then why did the guards use the knife to open the door?

"I don't know."

Letting the tension ease up, the magistrate pursued another line of questioning. Had he ever returned to the house?

No, I never went back. . . . When I went the first time, at the bidding of that guy, I'd been unemployed in San Piero for two weeks and didn't have any more vegetables. . . . It was one o'clock in the morning when I went to the house, . . . and I opened the door with the same knife that I later gave to the guards. The stuff that the guards found on me had come from a chest. I left the house, closed the door behind me, and went to the ghetto where the guards found me. I told them that I wanted to sell the things, even though I hadn't spoken yet with the Jews.

The role of the other man now diminished, because Andrea admitted that he had indeed suggested to the guards that they open the door with the knife, just as he had opened it the night before. He claimed that although he had taken the things from the chest, he had been unable to identify them because it was so dark.

The magistrate again changed the course of the interrogation. He wanted to know more about Andrea. Why had he lost his job, for example? "My boss fired me because he found me at a barbershop one day." Hence, this dissolute young man had not lost his job because of the plague and the resultant crisis in commerce but rather because of his passion for gambling.

The magistrate resumed his attack. The court knew that the same house had been robbed once before, and evidence suggested that Andrea Passignani was responsible in both cases. Nevertheless, it was not plausible that he would be able to find his way through the house in the dark, go upstairs, and open the chest. There must have been some previous reconnaissance as part of a larger plan. Andrea vehemently denied these charges and was sent back to his cell. He remained there until 21 November, when the second interrogation took place. This time the scene became more threatening—he was introduced to the torture chamber.

The record notes, "The court warned Andrea to tell the truth. The court knew very well that he had stolen some things from the house and may indeed have stolen even more. Therefore, unless he told the truth, he would be tortured by the rope."

The young man insisted, "I can't say anything else."

In that case, considering that he had stolen items later found on his person and that evidence strongly suggested that he had committed other crimes, the court decided to ascertain whether he was indeed telling the truth. To gain more information without prejudicing the evidence already acquired, he was ordered to take off his shirt and was tied to a rope. . . . As he was lifted higher and higher, he began to scream, "Oh, Jesus!" and then, "Take me down, I want to tell the whole truth!" They lowered him down and sat him on a bench. . . . He admitted, "I had been in that house with a blacksmith four or five days before my arrest. I opened the door with my knife and took five or six little towels and six or seven handkerchiefs. I sold them at the old market to somebody I did not know for four or five *giuli*."

The list of stolen goods became longer. "I took two necklaces and the ring that I am now wearing. . . . I stole them by myself. Nobody else helped me."

That was sufficient for the time being. They left Andrea hanging from the rope long enough for him to recite a Credo. The interrogation was to resume in a few days, so the man was taken back to his cell.

On 22 November, the court recalled Andrea to the bar. On 3 December, Corporal Luna and the guard Vincenzo Vettori accompanied him to the torture chamber, where he was undressed and bound. The questioners asked him to list all his robberies and the names of his accomplices. This time the mere sight of the rope forced him to scream, "No! Don't tie me up. I want to tell the truth."

Thus the second part of the confession began.

> Last Saint John's Day I found at my house a chest belonging to Signora Caterina, a widow who rented a room there. When I opened it I found six *lire,* which I took. Although Signora Caterina missed her money, she never said anything about it to me. She died a few days later. . . . Marco's wife, Lisabetta di Marco Porta, who now lives in Borg' Allegri, and Santa, who lives where I do, heard Caterina complain about the theft. . . . I stole a little money here and there, including occasionally from my boss.

Perhaps the boss never figured it out. In any case, it does not matter now. "When I lived in Rovezzano, I took a cloak from the house of Pietro, a tailor. It was lying on the table, and I think it belonged to his son, Vincenzo. The cloak was made of twill, and I sold it to a second-hand dealer in Florence for seven *lire.* . . . It must have been six or seven years ago now."

So he had begun to steal at the age of thirteen or fourteen. He was not originally from Florence; he came to the city to traffic in stolen goods. He even remembered how much he had made. What happened to the tailor Pietro? Although he had died, his son, Vincenzo, was "still alive." Someone would have to find him to question him about the stolen cloak.

Had he committed any other crimes?

"I didn't do anything else," he replied. No one believed him, and the guards approached to tie him to the rope again. He yelled, "I don't want the rope. I want to tell the truth!"

The third confession began. "I've lived in Florence for three years.

I've only committed two other criminal offenses here, no more. I stole a cloak from a house on Via Santa Maria and a *celone* [a cloth used to decorate a table or bed] from the Piazza d'Arno." Once again he had stolen a cloak, an expensive and desirable piece of clothing, a symbol of one's position in the social and cultural hierarchy.[9] One witness had already described Andrea's cloak as "shabby and dirty." For those who could afford nothing better, a valuable cloak became, not surprisingly, an object of envy.

He must be more precise, the magistrate insisted. Andrea obeyed: "I took the cloak from a man named Cavalleggeri, I think. He lives in a newly painted house. Cavalleggeri asked me to go get some hay about two months ago. The cloak was hanging on the banister. I sold it to a Jew, whom I don't know, that very evening for six *lire*."

To a young apprentice trying to get by as best he could, sometimes working for a blacksmith, sometimes carrying things here and there, temptations abounded. Especially for someone like Andrea, whose eyes were quick to spot what was attainable, who capitalized on the confusion or carelessness of the wealthy. It was not every day that a cloak was left unattended "on the stairs." It was better to take advantage of the situation immediately.

"I found the *celone*," Andrea continued, "at a house on the Piazza d'Arno. It was about midnight, and the house had been left open. Unfortunately, I sold the cloak for only four *crazie*. No, I don't know who lived there."

The interrogation ended, and Andrea was sent back to jail. Six days later, on 9 December, Corporal Luna began an investigation to see if the confession was true. He went to the houses Andrea had mentioned. First he visited Cavalleggeri, who lived with his brother, Raffaello Ferroni. Suddenly a new problem arose. The owner of the *celone* was "imprisoned at the Bargello. Ferroni had escaped and was now a fugitive." Andrea Passignani thus seemed no worse than his victims. Some women who lived in the house, however, answered Luna's questions and verified that there had indeed been a robbery.

Luna continued his investigation. He went to Andrea's house, where Madonna Caterina, the woman from whom Andrea had stolen six *lire*, had lived. The plague had created a vacuum there. The house was empty, as Caterina, Lisabetta, and Santa, who had been hospitalized at San Miniato, had all died. "The house was locked, and I could only question Andrea's father, who confirmed the robbery."

The sudden appearance of death in an account of life is perhaps the key that best explains how the epidemic was sensed and perceived. The uneventful passing of days, the chatter of neighbors, the movement of people and goods, and the skill of a thief are the benign signs of a period of good health. Luna's visits, on the contrary, in which he met only emptiness and silence, speak with great effect of this cruel break in time. While disease reduces those spaces that life generally provides, namely play, leisure, and intimacy, an epidemic denies time itself. Only survivors—in this case, the women and Andrea's father—are able to talk.

On 9 December, Andrea Passignani confirmed his last confession. The documents, witnessed by Vincenzo Vettori and a Bargello corporal called "Scattino," specify that he did so "far from the threat of torture." Removed from the torture chamber, Andrea could have changed his testimony. Instead, he ratified it.

The sentence was promulgated and transcribed on 13 December. It established that Andrea had confessed to his first crime "without the use of torture" and to the second "with torture. Both crimes were confirmed and verified." In addition, Andrea had "confessed to stealing six *scudi* from a woman's house." It continued: "Because the victims have died and Ferroni has escaped, these crimes have not been verified. However, Andrea has himself confessed to and confirmed the robbery." Stealing from a house closed by the authorities was regarded as "a theft of the greatest importance." Accordingly, the sentence was "death by hanging in the usual place, after the approval of His Majesty." The young man's age was not regarded as an attenuating factor.

The grand duke approved the sentence three days later. The authorities "arranged for the execution to take place on the Piazza al Bargello della Sanità" on the following day. A postscript notes that the execution occurred on 18 December.[10]

On 13 December, the very day that the Public Health Magistracy promulgated Andrea Passignani's death sentence, Ottavio "Cappellaio" Diligenti died of the plague.

A LIT LANTERN

Both the stories of the printer Niccolò Galeotti and the gardener Andrea Passignani recount the vicissitudes of young men. Elements in the latter case stress and underline themes present in the former—in particular, poverty, a small family, and the sense of uncertainty and risk. Although the characters in the following testimony are similar to Niccolò and Andrea both psychologically and socially, these protagonists are women, Antonia la Baccellona and Margherita di Giovanni Fortini.

On 21 October, Margherita, who was already incarcerated, was brought before the magistrate "for the Bargello examination." She lived alone near the Lupica tavern.

"I was taken to jail the day before Santa Luca," she began. "My husband lives in Rome. I earn my living as a seamstress and do cleaning on the side as well."

With whom did she live?

"I live with a woman named Antonia, whom we call Baccellona. Her son is a guard."[11]

Antonia's son, called Baccellone, a law-enforcement officer in the Bargello guard of the Public Health Magistracy, worked under the command of Ottavio Diligenti. Margherita did not like sharing rooms with the mother of this man. A few days earlier, she explained, Corporal Luna of the Bargello guard had arrested a certain pimp from Rome, Giovan Maria. This man "manages three prostitutes," Luna reported to the chancellor, "but does not make much money off them."[12]

Giovan Maria was arrested for violating the curfew laws when he went to Margherita's house at ten o'clock one night. The light of a lantern inside the house had convinced him that someone was indeed at home, so he knocked vigorously at the door and yelled to be let in.

The following day, Antonia Baccellona told her son about the confusion surrounding Giovan Maria's nocturnal visit. Margherita, his lover, was also arrested. At the court, Margherita explained to the magistrate how the lantern had caused the incident. She made it clear that she and Antonia did not get along: "Antonia keeps bringing up a lantern, but she ought to be more careful in sticking to the same story. I wasn't there, and each time she tells the story, she tells it differently." Trying to defend herself, Margherita added, "Sometimes people come to my house to pick up clothes I've mended for them; however, nobody ever enters my bedroom. I always stay at my friend's house on Via Maffia."[13]

Did she know a Roman named Giovan Maria?

"Yes, I clean and mend his clothes. . . . He comes to my house occasionally, when he needs something."

When had she last seen him?

"He came over about fifteen days ago because his cloak needed to be fixed. . . . No, I don't sleep with him. I only mend his clothes, just as I do for everyone else."

Where did Giovan Maria live?

"He came from Arezzo some six months ago and now lives here in Florence with some Spaniard or Neapolitan."

Did she know that "there had been some burglaries in her neighborhood?"

"Antonia once told me that somebody had robbed Madonna Caterina's house, just across the street. But I don't know the details, since I was not home at the time."

Did Giovan Maria know anything about the burglary at Madonna Caterina's?

"How should I know? He's at Santa Trinità."

This marked the conclusion of Margherita's questioning. Two days later, on 23 October, Orazio di Bernardo Baccelloni, a Florentine and a staff member of the Public Health Magistracy, was interrogated.

> My mother and our housemate, Maddona Margherita, told me that the house across the street, which had been closed by the authorities, was robbed. My mother also told me that Giovan Maria had knocked at the door that night. When she opened the door he told her that he had seen the lights on. This man does not usually venture out at night; typically he returns to his girlfriend's house at midnight. A friend, though, told me that the Marquis del Bufalo had caught Giovan Maria stealing. . . . I don't believe that Margherita had anything to do with the burglary. But I do think that Giovan Maria was involved, especially considering that he has changed jobs twenty times since arriving in Florence.

On 1 November, the magistrate called on Giovan Maria himself to testify.

> I was arrested at the corner of Lupica and have now been in prison for twenty-one days. I have most recently been employed by Signor Sarcinelli. In Florence I have also worked for Marquis Guicciardini, the Marquis del Bufalo, Captain Girolamo Gualtieri, Father Zacchia, and Andrea di Ruota. . . . I moved to the city nine years ago. Before that I lived on ships and in all sorts of other disgusting places. During the two to three months prior to my arrest I was living at Balì Sarcinelli's palace.

He was not involved with "any women."

Did he know Margherita Fortini?

"Yes, I know her. She sews my clothes. I go to her place whenever I need my clothes mended, even at night." He denied all the charges, however, claiming that although he knew Antonia, he had never discussed any lantern with her.

The story of Margherita, Antonia, Baccellone, and Giovan Maria ends here. The stolen goods were never recovered, and no case of pandering was ever proved. Furthermore, no one confessed to the crimes. At any rate, a twenty-one-day jail sentence seemed to be a reasonable punishment in such a weak case. The similarities between Giovan Maria and Andrea Passignani are evident: both were foreigners, neither had held a steady job, and both had simultaneously worked for more than one employer. These factors sufficed to arouse suspicion. A visit to the house of a Public Health guard triggered the events that culminated in the arrest of Giovan Maria.

Finally, it is worth noting that these women who lived together were typical of women who lived in houses closed by the authorities.

Since September, Deputy Jacopo Jacopi of the *sesto* (quarter) of San Ambrogio reported, "while distributing charity, I found only thirty-one people" in the administrative district surrounding Santa Croce. He continued, "This really surprised me because that neighborhood is usually very crowded. The group consisted of only one man, who was twenty-two years old, with the rest women and children." There were only five men in eight houses:

> One works for the Public Health Magistracy, another at San Miniato, and the other three claimed to have left their homes before the lock-up order was issued. . . . This confirms what I had heretofore believed, that is, that any man who can earn more than one *giulio,* the amount we give for support, does not want to stay home. I am afraid that if we fail to find a solution to this confusion and protect only women and children we will be wasting our money.[14]

This sketch reminds us of the episode we have just examined, in which the only man on the scene was a Public Health officer. During periods of epidemics, those who work for the authorities do not engage in business of any kind. Instead they stay at home with the women and servants. This cadre constitutes a separate chapter in the history of the Florentine plague. Careful control, which was especially necessary for quarantines, illuminates a world of widows, young women, mothers, and workers. These women managed to survive the emergency with their great imagination and flexibility, by establishing links of solidarity, inventing solutions, and playing tricks. First prostitution insinuated itself like a shadow into the lives of women who lived alone. This accusation, always implicit, was like an inclined surface, on which the inquisitor rolled or pushed many episodes. Whether they were "listed" in the registers of the Onestà, the magistracy of public decorum, made almost no difference. Yet the crisis in manufacturing, in conjunction with the widespread poverty of the popular classes, forced many women, particularly in the textile industry, to become prostitutes.[15]

Selling bodies represented the female counterpart of male disreputable activities; only women, despite Public Health regulations, were thereby able to realize a profit.

Caterina d'Agostino, for example, the daughter of a Florentine textile worker, was sentenced to a whipping. Although "too young to be listed in the register [of prostitutes]" and ignorant of the regulations, she had gone out with a man in the middle of the night. When, somewhat later, "she discovered that she was five months pregnant, a strong pain almost induced a miscarriage." Thereafter, the punishment was commuted to a fine of twenty *scudi*.[16]

There is also the case of Brigida di Francesco, like Caterina the daughter of a textile worker. She was listed in the register but was caught with a man at night. After spending four months in prison, she was fined twenty *scudi*.[17]

"I WANT MY THINGS BACK"

During the epidemic, the removal of goods by women often followed a gendered network of characteristics and points of contact. On 27 October, Corporal Luna arrested Felice Cipolli, a married woman, who during the curfew had gone to see her sister Baccia to get some of her belongings: a shirt, a handkerchief, and a receipt from the Monte dei Pegni, a bank that operated as a pawnbroker. Her sister "watched over" her things so that Felice's "husband wouldn't do anything bad with them." According to Felice, her husband, a marble cutter at the Galleria of the Medici Palace, was an untrustworthy man. She suspected that he might prefer her stepdaughter, and Felice defended herself by putting her own family's interests ahead of his.[18] Felice's suspicions were what pushed her to violate the edicts, resulting in her arrest by Luna. Likewise, Dorotea's anxiety for her hospitalized daughter, Ortensia, led to the arrest of Dorotea, a widow, who hid jewelry, linens, and her daughter's coat dresses at Agata's home.[19]

At the same time, Luna arrested an entire family for the "chaotic" removal of a sheet. He seized Simona, a widow thirty-six years old, her children, and her mother after one was caught throwing a sheet from the window of a closed house to another below. The children testified at the trial. One, Diamante, recounted, "I saw Grandma throw a sheet to a child, who then took it home." She corroborated the confession of her younger sister Francesca, who was thirteen years old. The sentence, issued six days later, prescribed an exceptionally rigorous ceremonial punishment. "The court has examined Corporal Luna's denunciation of Simona, wife of Marco. The court has heard the confessions of her daughters, Diamante and Francesca, about how they helped throw items out of their grandmother Marta's window. The court duly condemns Simona to be publicly bound to a rope in the air, lowered, and then freed."[20]

Affection or solidarity, born out of habit and time, did not always characterize women who lived together. This particularly proved to be the case when a woman who had been presumed dead returned home, only to find, after a thorough examination of her belongings, that some of her things were missing—whereupon she made a denunciation to the authorities.

The case of the wet nurse Maria, who worked for the Public Health Magistracy, typifies this process. When she came home from the lazaret, she made a list of all stolen items: an old sheet, two old shirts, a bottle of oil, a bottle of vinegar, a pound of salt, two small towels, one apron, and two pairs of scissors, one small and the other large.[21] The theft occurred while her husband and her daughter, also named Maria, were under quarantine restrictions; they later died. At that time Maria the mother and her sister Costanza were recovering in the lazaret; finally they were able to leave in good health. She suspected two of her female boarders. "Three or four women live at my house. They are Caterina, who is married, another Caterina, a widow, and two young women, Maria and Barbara." She suspected them because Maria had found a cooking pot at Caterina's, and one of them had returned a sheet to the house.

The small value of the objects and the familiarity that emerged through the rediscovery and return of the stolen goods mitigated the initial charges. The magistrate asked Maria "whether she wanted to press charges against any of the women." She responded, "I don't want anything bad to happen to them, but I would like my things back."

Costanza's words best described this group of women who lived alone. First she said that the widow Caterina was an honest woman. Then she reported, "I have heard bad things about the other one." The younger Maria worked in the silk industry. She had once tried to steal from her landlady but had given up when caught by her neighbors. Women who constantly entered and left houses, who were always looking out windows and standing near cracked doors, knew and reported everything.

The objects stolen from the wet nurse Maria were domestic items: pots, sheets, shirts, and scissors. Their disappearance constituted more of a long-term loan than a crime. Well hidden, they improved furnishings and enhanced shabby wardrobes. To be sure, these items would have met the same end as those confiscated by the Magistracy: they would have been divided into two groups, good objects and bad, with the good to be fumigated and the bad to be burned. What harm came, then, from the women dividing these items among themselves? Although they knew that Maria had been taken to the lazaret and, indeed, that the entire family had caught the disease, these women seized her linens without worrying about the contagion. Such a theft of clothes generally implied a risk of death; yet fear never stopped anyone, even if it was necessary to undress a dead man to take his cloak.

SPIRITS OF THE DEAD AND EXCHANGES

Memories and the attachment to domestic spaces and objects that people attempted to save from the fury of Public Health officials continued beyond life. They extended to the lazarets, to wills, and to priests.

The movement of goods, linens, and clothes primarily concerned women and servants. It almost seemed as if domestic habits, spaces, and work converted the people who cared for those objects into the objects themselves.

On 28 October, Margherita Rinieri made out her will in the lazaret of San Miniato. Residing "near Santa Romanina" in the Tribolo district, she left "five *scudi* and seven *soldi,* to be found in a little bag in a box over her armored chest, to Sister Maria Grazia, a nun of Santa Agata in Florence." She also left the sister "three pieces of linen, which are in said chest." To turn one's thoughts to those places and recollections sedimented by everyday life must have been a relief to people facing death. The little bag, the box, and the armored chest were reminders of the familiar gestures of opening and closing that preserved one's most valued treasures. Perhaps even the objects themselves, their size, weight, and appearance, calmed the thoughts of those who lay confined in a place of disease and death.

"To Alessandro Salviati," Margherita wrote, "[I leave] the bunch of lace in the green box, . . . two buttoned towels, and two plain towels." To her sister Lucrezia she left "the locked chest, . . . the coral necklace, . . . three good sheets, the red towel, a shirt, the bed, mattress, and bedding, two white towels, handkerchiefs, shirts, aprons, and sheets."[22]

On 12 July, Geva, a servant of Giulia Guelfi Gherardi, dictated her will. She left to Caterina, another of Gherardi's maids, "a good shirt, an apron, a pair of socks, and a handkerchief" as a token of her appreciation for the help given during her illness.[23]

On 19 August, Clemente di Alessandro Mannini, a Florentine nobleman who lived on Via dei Pilastri, wrote his will "from bed." He left "his black suit, cloak, hat, and shoes, as well as four *scudi,* about the normal wage, to his tailor Bastiano in gratitude for help during his infirmity."[24]

Sometimes servants sold the inherited clothes to junk dealers, or *rigattieri.* During epidemics these *rigattieri* were kept under tight control. For example, a black dress left in one of Pietro Galiani's storerooms caused a plethora of testimonies to converge in an effort to trace its origins and establish whether it carried the contagion.[25]

These trials introduce us to the complex world of property, the stratified planes of memory, and the ramifications of family, neighborhood, and employment. Each object, whether stolen, removed, or relocated, obscured the precise links and motivations that the defendants permitted to emerge in their testimonies. Moreover, these intersections negated the importance of the charge of theft: it is as if the single act of stealing would suffice to explain the sense of privation caused by the loss of an object to someone who managed to escape death during the epidemic. An unbreachable gulf grew between thieves and their victims, between those who were healthy and could steal and those who were hospitalized. A trail of belongings and memories was kept alive by such an exchange of objects between the dead and the living.

A close analysis indicates that thieves were usually related to their victims. Whether co-workers, guild brothers, or neighbors, the boundary between outright theft and the protection of property became hazy. Stealing from the Public Health authorities and reclaiming the belongings of brothers and sisters for the family unit translated into the preservation of the patrimony. The removal of these defined and specified objects kept the community of dead and living viable. This act completed a circle, within which operated wills, gifts, donations, and prayer offerings made in memoria.

According to Marcel Mauss, "Among the first groups of beings with whom men must have made contracts were the spirits of the dead. . . . They in fact are the real owners of the world's wealth. With them it was particularly necessary to exchange and particularly dangerous not to."[26] Confronted with this chain linking dead and living, the sanitary measures of disinfection, although respectful and circumspect, provided a screen of aesthetic judgments concerned solely with the quality and value of goods. The Public Health Magistracy charged the cleaners with separating the "bad things," destined to be "burned at the distance of a gunshot from the Gate of San Gallo," from the good, to be catalogued according to owner and household. "These items were accompanied at all times by a guard who would ensure that no one approached them. The guard was not permitted to take anything for himself either." The belongings were then taken back to San Marco Vecchio, where another guard received, "inventoried, and appraised" them.[27]

Therefore, two different channels of communication developed: the first within the "community of the suffering," the second within the power structure.[28] Whereas the former evolved within a circulation perimeter based on the value of use, the latter remained inscribed in a marketplace that separated "good things" from "bad" ones. Only when the value of textiles, wood, or gold spared belongings from the purifying fire, thereby assuring their eventual return to their owners, did the two qualities, use and exchange, coincide. Mourning for someone who owned "good things" thus unfolded within the confines of a familial memory codified by the presence of objects that survived individuals. Conversely, for all others the private circuit of memory and mourning broke down when the "bad things" were burned. The Public Health authorities regarded as criminals those relatives, neighbors, and fellow workers who moved linen, opened chests, and relocated objects to prevent their destruction by the state. Only constant reintegration of the threads of memory between the dead and the living healed the wounds that the epidemic caused.

In this sense, the theme of property is rooted in the defense of individual and familial rights of mourning. Fundamental values are therefore at stake in the struggle between an ideology that translated objects into money and the jealous protection of objects per se. Different goals and behaviors developed around objects. Some bore witness to the complexity and tenacity of family ties, while others belonged to the mercenary complicity of profit above all else.

FAMILY STRATEGIES: THE EXCLUDED BROTHER-IN-LAW

On 11 January 1630, Salvatore di Vincenzo Tortorelli, a baker from the Porte Vecchie, was arrested in front of the Pagoni tavern. He was charged with entering the house of Giovanni di Iacopo Dolci, his deceased brother-in-law, and stealing "a gold seal carved by Matteo Bracciolini that Giovanni had worn as a ring, the gold wedding ring of Giovanni's wife, a gold coin, two necklaces valued at twenty-five *scudi,* and a suit that was similar to the one Salvatore now wears." The baker later gave the ring and the coin to "his mistress," who was also arrested.[29]

Brought from his cell to testify, Salvatore immediately explained his relationship to Giovanni Dolci: "He was my brother-in-law, Lucrezia's husband." Lucrezia, Salvatore's sister, had died in the lazaret. Subsequently, he recounted a story of inheritance, of rights and priorities that in this particular case had been orally transmitted by those involved rather than codified in a will. "Lucrezia's heir—she was the last to die—is young Caterina, my other sister." The jewels found on Salvatore by the guards were, as such, family property. "The gold seal once belonged to my father, and the wedding ring to my mother." Giovanni had bought the coin for Lessandra Pavoni, his lover.

Interrogated again on 13 January, Salvatore elaborated on the episode. He had entered his brother-in-law's house through his own house, so he was not obliged to force open the door, which the Public

Health officials had locked. Yet the chancellor was not convinced and ordered Salvatore undressed and tied to the rope. When tortured, the baker confessed that in fact he had broken into Dolci's house and taken some gold that he found in a box. His sister Caterina helped him "take some necklaces and rings" he claimed belonged to them. This confession extracted under duress tended to legitimize his action of violating a closed house with the aid of his sister. According to the magistrate, it was still a crime and must be punished. On 27 January, he sentenced Salvatore Tortorelli to be tied to the rope and publicly flogged twice.[30]

A considerable amount of relocating and stealing took place in the houses of brothers-in-law. All of a family group's hostility and diffidence seemed to focus there, on the acquired family member. The brother-in-law was actually a foreign element that interrupted the cohesion of parents and children, and brothers and sisters. In the case we have just described, the siblings opposed the rights of their brother-in-law, claiming a vertical transmission of inheritance that excluded him. He could, however, legally fight the claim through his position as the deceased wife's husband.

In the following episode the tables are turned, when the husband of a dead sister is charged with stealing various objects from his wife's family. While the baker Salvatore went into his relative's house, thereby delineating a horizontal opposition, the barber Lorenzo entered the house of his father-in-law, a shoemaker commonly called "Napoli." Even in this case, though, a conflict between the two brothers-in-law followed the initial vertical clash. Lorenzo was arrested on 3 January and charged with stealing from his father-in-law's house. Napoli and his daughter, Lorenzo's wife, had been hospitalized at San Miniato. Taking advantage of the shoemaker's absence, Lorenzo apparently entered the house and stole a great number of linens.[31]

After his sister died at San Miniato, Bernardino, Napoli's son, was the first to testify before the chancellor. The evil disease had carried his sister away, and nobody knew where she had been buried. Bernardino, too, had been hospitalized, but he had recovered. When he returned home, he realized that a theft had occurred: twenty-five pairs of sheets, "most of them beautiful and finely embroidered," and other clothes and towels had been taken. He was the first person to report the loss and had no doubt that his brother-in-law was responsible. Napoli's entire family lived in the same house, and Lorenzo occupied the first floor. "He's adept at opening locked doors, and he knew where all the stuff was."

The defendant, Lorenzo, testified immediately thereafter and charged the other in-law, "Giovanni, nicknamed 'Gonfiolino,' a tavernkeeper in Vinegia," with the crime. The stolen goods, he added, were in the house of Laura, "who lives in Parione." The opposition between the family and its newest member, the barber Lorenzo, openly surfaced during Bernardino's cross-examination. Lorenzo declared that Laura was in fact Bernardino's sister, Napoli's daughter, and Lorenzo's sister-in-law. Lorenzo reported that she also took care of the belongings of another brother, "who is now in Germany."

In sum, brothers and brothers-in-law alike had violated Napoli's home, each attempting to preserve his own inheritance rights. All the thefts involved a complex mechanism of exchange, compensation, and exclusion within a family group already threatened and torn apart by the epidemic. The initial phase of the case, focusing on the axis of the vertical relationship between father-in-law and son-in-law, gave way to the contestation of brothers, who directed their hostility toward the marginal figure of their brother-in-law. The sister's marriage had legitimized her husband's position within her family. When she died, her brothers allied against her husband and threatened his role and prerogatives. The criminal proceedings indicate that the couple was childless; nevertheless, Florentine law protected the rights of a widower. In cases where there were no surviving heirs from previous marriages, the husband was to keep the dowry as well as inherit one-third of his wife's personal belongings.[32] Perhaps here the general confusion and rapid progression of events, which even preceded the official news of the sister's/wife's demise in the lazaret, interrupted the legitimate transfer of property.

Once again, the event (of plague or death) becomes relevant because it triggered socially organized actions and procedures. The division of linens and sheets among relatives provided the biological event with a foundation of values that bound the family together.[33]

Up to this point, the most surprising theme is how little fear contagion caused. In overcrowded houses, stinking alleys, and rooms that still held the dead, both actually and in memory, neighbors, relatives, and friends came and went—entering, stealing, taking things at random, and getting caught. They passed items from hand to hand, through windows and doors, wells and gratings; they knocked down house walls, climbed garden walls, and even lowered goods by rope from rooftops. The epidemic appeared to generate every emotion save fear of death. The family, the shop—those factors which, established during a life, could persist through time—occupied the thoughts and actions of those remaining in the city.

This was not the case for Antonio and Bastiano, the brothers of the tavernkeeper Lorenzo del Piccino, whom Commissioner dell'Antella charged with burglarizing the house of their deceased brother-in-law. The two defended themselves by claiming that they were afraid of contracting the disease. Yet it is interesting to note the extent to which fear of the plague appears in those cases where long-standing jealousies threatened affectionate family relationships. "The wife of my brother Lorenzo is in Arezzo," Antonio testified. "In his home," he continued, "he now keeps a prostitute and an illegitimate daughter." Such unfaithfulness, highlighted by the presence of an illegitimate child, isolated the husband from his own family, which preferred to side with the abandoned woman. This relationship went from bad to worse when the family learned that "the illegitimate daughter was to be the recipient of the entire estate." Antonio concluded, "She was his sole heir. We lived two miles from each other, so I don't know how he died. I've heard, however, that he died of the plague."

An examination of the testimonies reveals that the brothers were preoccupied with giving Lorenzo a proper burial, contrary to the commissioner's orders. "We explained to him that we wanted to bury our brother in a particular place. He refused our request. We told him that dogs had uncovered and eaten other people's bodies. He agreed that we could dig the grave ourselves but prohibited us from approaching the priest or the house." The warning, they asserted, was unnecessary. The fear of contagion would keep them from the victim's house because, they claimed, "we don't want to take death home."[34]

Therefore, people feared catching the disease from those whom they did not love, from relatives with whom only formal relations, codified by "papers" establishing rights of inheritance, existed. Could the act of violating a dead person's house constitute, in and of itself, a revenge for having contracted the plague?

NEIGHBORHOOD RELATIONSHIPS

Even community relationships, developed over the years by people sharing the same street, parish, or shop, continued to thrive during the epidemic crises and to affect reciprocal behavior. The continuous presence of neighbors always emerges in the testimonies, as a sort of pause or comment in the story, a function generally attributed to the chorus in classical drama. Archival sources provide a great number of attestations, declarations, and testimonies from those who watched furtive actions from their windows, who noted a death or a person taking things covertly into a house by the back door. Common formulaic statements such as "To the best of my knowledge," "We, the neighbors," "As his neighbor, I have to say," and "As we saw from our window" suggest the attentive presence of others in one's daily life. An involuntary offense, a minor quarrel, or jealousy might render a neighbor a secret informer to the authorities.

In the following episode the tight sequence of testimonies in which people who lived next door or across the street are named and referred to clearly reflects the great amount of gossip, lies, suspicions, and information that circulated through one quarter of the city. The protagonist, Domenica Grassilli, was denounced by her neighbor Benedetto Benvenuti, a woodseller.

According to the report, Domenica had stolen a gold necklace with the intention of dismantling it and selling it piece by piece. Noting that the necklace was the work of a professional, the woodseller suggested that the defendant's husband "had guided his wife's hand and helped her get rid of the stolen goods."[35] The necklace was sold to a goldsmith on the Ponte Vecchio, Pietr'Antonio Artini. Questioned by the authorities, he admitted that Tommaso Grassilli, Domenica's husband, had given him a piece of the necklace but claimed that the rest of the necklace had come from a man who boarded at their house. "When Domenica was discovered, she poked a hole in the floor and threw the necklace to the downstairs apartment, where a construction worker lived. He found the gold and brought it to me." Thus, the fear of being caught red-handed with the stolen necklace ultimately betrayed Domenica. She got rid of the necklace as soon as possible, flinging part of it into the apartment downstairs. The goldsmith, a relative of the woodseller, showed the necklace to Benedetto. "When I did so, he recognized that it belonged with the piece he had bought." Domenica and her husband, Tommaso, were immediately arrested.

Domenica testified before the magistrate on 18 January. "My husband, Tommaso, is a textile worker, and I work with gold threads. I have a daughter whom I am still nursing. I found the pieces of the necklace when I was on my way back from Nunziata on Tuesday, eight days ago, near the Misericordia Vecchia at the Piazza del

Duomo. No one was around at the time, and I did not show them to anyone except my husband, that very evening." It was therefore a casual discovery, made on leaving a church. Certainly this woman, her eyes used to gold, could immediately recognize the thirty pieces from a distance. Domenica admitted that she knew Benedetto, the woodseller, who lived next door at the Borgo San Niccolò. She also confessed that she had heard that his wife had lost a gold necklace and that he blamed Domenica's brothers for the theft. Yet Domenica reiterated that she had had nothing to do with the necklace's disappearance. She explained that the day after the discovery, her husband put the gold into "three pieces of paper" and took them to a goldsmith on the Ponte Vecchio. He sold the gold for one *pilastra*.

The magistrate inquired into Domenica's life and personality. She told him that she had two brothers, Bartolomeo, nineteen, a textile worker, and Giovanni, seventeen, a turner. They lived with two boys, "her nephews," and their mother. Could one enter the woodseller's house directly from her brothers' house? Domenica claimed no. Continuing her description of life on that street, she proved to be an attentive observer. "The woodseller's wife goes out more often than I," Domenica said, and she wears her necklace "when she goes out." Two different lives: one comfortable, able to leave the house frequently, adorned with a gold necklace; the other more difficult, restricted by work and a nursing baby. The necklace must have been the object of numerous fantasies: "the woodseller's necklace was ordinary, well turned and polished, while the one Domenica found was "in very bad shape, and nobody could recognize it."

Tommaso Grassilli, Domenica's husband, was interrogated the same day. He confirmed his wife's testimony about her discovery. He added, however, that the goldsmith on the Ponte Vecchio had told him that he and Benedetto, the woodseller, were friends. He claimed to recognize the necklace immediately. Tommaso must have felt extremely embarrassed by the situation. Nevertheless, the Grassillis could not simply keep the necklace since—as the magistrate reminded them severely—they owed huge debts.

The woodseller Benedetto Benvenuti testified after Tommaso, offering the magistrate his own version of the story. When his household left town for Epiphany Tuesday, someone broke into his house and stole a necklace that he kept in a drawer. It was worth at least fourteen or fifteen *scudi*. The Benvenuti family, the newest to the

Borgo San Niccolò, had moved there one year earlier. Their only friend in the neighborhood, "Giovanni Battista, sells cooking pots and lives next door"; they traded with him some. Their relationships with other people in the community were superficial. Benedetto believed that two boys, Cecchino and Meo, "who live next door," were the culprits. "From the roof of their house you can easily come into my room through a window that I always leave open." The woodseller seemed disappointed, saying, "I always thought that they were good people."

The mystery remained unsolved once again. The fast-paced game of theft and accusation did not lead to a confession, and nobody was charged with the crime. Moreover, the Public Health Magistracy declared that as its officials had never locked the house under question, the case lay outside its jurisdiction, and so passed it to another court.[36] This episode in daily life thus signaled the occurrence of normal arguments in the middle of the epidemic. Domenica cared more about her neighbor's gold necklace than she did about the dying or quarantined people on her alley or even across the street. The story developed between the two women. Domenica, weighed down by the imperatives of work, baby, and her husband's debts, watched and sighed, tremendously curious about the new family in the Borgo San Niccolò.

This presumed theft offers us an insight into the continuation of ordinary crimes even during the crisis of the plague. It confirms how daily life, complete with sentiments and grudges, went on despite edicts, sanitary precautions, and death. The story of Domenica Grassilli occupies an intermediate position between the case of Andrea Passignani, who randomly stole at every opportunity, and that of the brothers who allied against their brother-in-law. Here, the transgression was carried out by only one individual, although supported by neighbors in her courtyard and on her street.

WORK AND SHOPS

Besides the family and the community, an individual's occupation could also provide the basis for criminal activity. Combined with a sense of belonging to a family or to a street, work continued through and extended expectations beyond the crisis of epidemic. Anachronisms and future-oriented actions constantly characterized social perception of the disease. Individuals violated edicts in the expectation of a better time to come, when a life of normal commerce and relationships with friends, relatives, and fellow workers would resume.

This was the case, for example, of Federigo Tergozzi, the "former keeper of bedding supplies at the lazaret of San Miniato." He and Filippo di Piero Lippi, a mattress maker, were accused of "pilfering a number of unpurified mattresses, blankets, and pillows and taking them home to sell afterwards."[37] Taking care of the linens at the lazaret, a rather ordinary job, provided Federigo with an opportunity to steal with an eye to future gains.

The story of Niccolò Durante Vannozzi is similar. A blacksmith at Ripoli, he was arrested for bribing lazaret officials to obtain three hundred pounds of iron and some linens for domestic use.[38] This episode is pertinent because privileged dealers controlled the commerce of raw iron. No one in the blacksmith guild was entitled to trade iron outside the district of Florence.[39] Thus, Niccolò violated two laws: first, by bribing lazaret officials to obtain three hundred pounds of iron; and second, by breaking the regulations of his professional guild.

During the same period, Cesare di Michele Fantasti and his son, Francesco, were arrested. Both men worked as chimney sweeps and were accused of stealing "a few things" from the infected house of Giovanni di Andrea Landini.[40] The victim was in fact Francesco's brother-in-law. Francesco and his father forced open the door of the house and took a few metal objects that would be useful for their business: "a pot, two brass candlesticks, a metal image of the Virgin Mary, and three rings."

In such cases, criminal actions were divided into three categories. Some people, like Ludovico Puccetti, only facilitated another person's crime without actually participating in it. Ludovico's action stemmed from his sense of solidarity with other textile workers. He supervised the purification of linens and clothing. He made exceptions, however, for silk materials, returning them to their owners "before the end of the quarantine and purification process."[41] Regulations imposed a severe punishment on those public servants who favored private individuals. Ludovico Puccetti was sentenced to death and given only one month to appeal the court's decision. On 31 March, his sentence was commuted to exile to Pescia. Although he was not permitted to work in the textile industry there, one of his relatives, the captain of the fortress of San Giovanni, helped him obtain an exemption on 23 September 1633. Meanwhile, after paying a fine of thirty-five *scudi,* his death sentence was commuted on 7 February. Finally, the Florentine government abrogated his exile order on 3 October 1633.

Work not only contributed to the practice of stealing objects useful to one's business, but it also encouraged the preservation of guild brothers' belongings, especially tools. The tailor Paolo Francesco di Varnesi and a group of his friends forced open the door of the shop of Bartolomeo Bruschi, a fellow tailor who had recently died of the plague. Paolo Francesco inventoried "all of the cloth and fabric in the store," located at "21 Via dell'Anguillara," before the Public Health officers arrived to carry out the disinfection.[42] Such an inventory by a guild brother could prove to be a well-considered measure, since guilds stipulated that their members must come to the aid of a fellow's family in times of sickness, death, or poverty. In this particular case, however, the action directly conflicted with Public Health ordinances and was therefore criminal. Although Paolo Varnesi admitted that he had known that the house had not yet been disinfected, the court judged him to be merely "a meek and simple man, in short, an idiot." He was sentenced to four months' exile from Florence.

GRAVEDIGGERS' SALARIES

This final example, highlighting the contrast between social group ethics and Public Health measures, introduces one last subdivision within the category of theft. Here, forms of circular exchange intersect with the behavioral codes enshrined in guild statutes; work delineates a cohesive and coherent horizon, one openly opposed to the measures required by the emergency. The protagonists here are gravediggers or other people charged with the task of removing and burying the dead. In periods of epidemic, this group diversified and grew in number. Like all other echelons of the Public Health structure, gravediggers became objects of fear and were replaced at an astonishing rate.

Two groups in particular were charged with removing bodies. First, there were the gravediggers themselves, forming an improvised low social class. Second, there were the members of the Compagnia della Misericordia, a hierarchical neighborhood organization aided by the porters of Bonifazio Hospital. This latter group was singled out

for a specific crime, removing clothes from dead bodies, a "crime"
that was closely linked to their everyday routine.

On 24 November 1630, the Florentine Public Health administrators
reported to the grand duke that

> Andrea di Stefano Boccini of Legnaia, a gravedigger of the Compagnia
> della Misericordia, has confessed to removing the shirt from a cadaver
> before its burial in an open field. He transported the shirt to Florence
> by hiding it in a coffin. When caught, however, he claimed to have
> buried the shirt with another body. He also said that the victim's wife
> had given him the shirt. This is a major crime, and the Magistracy
> recommends that the gravedigger be sentenced to prison.[43]

From this gruesome story of a man who took a shirt off of a corpse,
put the shirt on himself, and then put it back on another dead body
emerges a striking familiarity with cadavers and an indifference to the
revolting signs of contagion, which, according to popular wisdom,
spared only those who stubbornly ignored them. "Desperation made
them self-confident. They believed that those who lived in fear would
die. They chose to remain dauntless among the stricken by day and
then go out, drink, and gamble by night."[44]

That the crime was reported to the grand duke testifies to the gravity of the situation. The interrogation was held just a few hours earlier
and offers, in contrast to the consistency of the official records, only a
confused and entangled picture. Andrea Boccini, twenty-two years
old, had worked in the wool industry in Volta a Legnaia before enlist-
ing in the Misericordia. Maybe this risky job provided him with a
sorely needed opportunity to make money, by trafficking in goods
stolen from the dead.

"He said that his mother is still living and that he has three sisters,
two married and the third only thirteen years old," the magistrate
wrote. Andrea recounted:

> I'm a gravedigger in the Misericordia. We went to someone's house
> who had just died and took his body to the fields outside the Gate of
> San Frediano. The wife of the deceased offered me and my co-worker
> Fracassino (I don't remember his real name or where he comes from)
> the shirt on her husband's body. So, before placing the body in the
> grave, we took the shirt off—it was new—and put it in the wagon and
> brought it back to Florence. . . . When we reached the gate, the guards
> asked us, "And whose shirt is this?" I answered, "It used to belong to
> the man in the wagon." Then we went to get another corpse in Prato.
> When we passed through the gate, we showed the shirt to the guards

again. Afterwards, we put it on the body of this other man and buried him.

The guards broke the clear agreement between the two gravediggers: "I wanted to keep the shirt for myself and give something else in return to Fracassino. . . . He agreed to that deal."[45]

Therefore, the shirt given by the victim's wife to Andrea and Fracassino had not been stolen; rather, it was compensation for the services of removing and burying the body. Each defendant charged with a similar crime insisted on this detail, which transformed the action, believed by the magistrate to be a crime, into a trade, a gratuity paid in kind. The agreement between Andrea and the dead man's wife antedated another agreement between Andrea and his partner: Andrea could keep the shirt if he promised to offer his co-worker something in exchange as soon as possible.

The large number of similar episodes attests to the common practice of giving away the clothes of the dead. Doctor Cesarino Coveri, for example, when taken out of Florence to prepare a death certificate, watched in astonishment and anger as the victim's wife gave the clothes of the corpse to the wagon driver, who immediately put them on.[46] This lack of caution and disregard for the danger represented by the clothes of the plague-ridden body exasperated the relationship between doctors and the riotous proletarian gravediggers and body removers. In fact it was more the fear of spreading the contagion than the suspected thefts that alarmed the magistrates as well.

Clothes aroused possessive instincts whether or not they were offered by the victim's relatives. Once, for example, six Misericordia workers, while burning the clothes of the stricken Benedetto del Maestro, picked out a few for themselves: "a piece of black velvet, a collar, a cotton cloak, and a pair of red pants with gold tails." They divided most of the clothes among themselves, selling the remainder to the first and second of the six defendants. The former had "left the Compagnia della Misericordia under the pretext of returning home to close a window"; the latter also "bought from the third defendant a cotton cloth, which had been stolen from a house on Via Buia." Matteo, the fourth defendant, paid eight *lire* to the fifth, Pietro, an officer of the Misericordia, who had secretly stolen the clothes. The sixth defendant, Bastiano, "a friend and relative of the said Matteo, . . . took the clothes from the Compagnia as they had agreed, hiding them in a villa in San Miniato alla Palma, four miles from Florence, where they were later found by the Public Health Magistracy."[47] In this example, the salient point is the commerce among the six men; they distributed the clothes and took them out of the city, thereby threatening the countryside.

The relationship between gravediggers and cadavers' clothes had a long history, which helps to explain why these practices survived. Traditionally the gravediggers' work, which was considered easy, was paid not in currency but with clothes from the bodies they buried. Moreover, since gravediggers had to share their allowance with the officiating priests, selling these clothes provided them with an income. Ever since the black death of 1348, the importance of gravediggers had grown, and even herbalists participated in selling clothes, herbs, and perfumes to bathe dead bodies and coffins. The decimation wrought by the plague, however, compelled the guild consuls to change some of the organization's statutes, especially in order to end the commerce in clothes. Thus, they outlawed buying clothes from gravediggers, priests, or other workers who buried plague victims.[48] The reform of 1349 clearly proved to be ineffective, for the new code of 1375 reported "numerous denunciations to the consuls regarding the enormous profits of gravediggers."[49] Most of the time, these workers were not even listed on the membership roles of the guild, "something which is most unfortunate for the city of Florence and shameful for the guild."[50] Consequently, the state issued an order mandating that "all those commonly called gravediggers" must submit to the rules and regulations of the guild.

Along with the new guild controls, a salary increase was approved. In the item "Gravedigger Salary Regulations," new rules demanded that they should "clean the streets," "prepare the wood tables for the placement of corpses," "remove carpets and mattresses," and "shave and dress cadavers." Each gravedigger was required to carry on his person an official publication detailing his duties. This list, however, left some room for traditional private bargains, as when, for example, it declared that it was "impossible to measure the effort that each individual procedure requires."[51] This was especially true for illustrious deeds ("Foremost considering the deaths of famous statesmen, as well as knights and doctors").[52]

Gravediggers were not only required to dispose of cadavers, but they also had to be adept at handling, dressing, and burying them.

Their solicitude must have assuaged the survivors' pain. From this perspective, there was always some opportunity for private bargaining to guarantee a less brusque, more delicate removal. This tradition remained alive for centuries, accepted by both sides, as women continued to offer shirts or cloaks to gravediggers in exchange for a quick burial, especially during epidemics.

Indifference to contagion and death, as we have noticed, characterized this work, based as it was on risk and good luck. The magistrates themselves, in contrast, dealt carefully with those gravediggers who, despite trafficking in infected clothes, had served for a long time. It always helped a defendant's case if he could claim to be a gravedigger; this attenuating circumstance almost granted him an aura of immortality.

During the plague, the figure of the *monatto,* the body remover, was also complicated by disturbing elements. All sanitary personnel, including body removers, wore a bell around one ankle. They had a monopoly over the bodies of the dead, as well as over the ill. Taken from their families, the sick and dead were crowded into the common spaces of lazarets and graves. In addition, they were exposed as objects of study, to be prodded, cut, and burned by doctors, surgeons, and barbers. During the plague, the state exercised the right to regulate the body, not only its exterior (in behavior or dress), but also its interior. Surviving relatives frequently accused doctors and sanitary personnel of poisoning and robbing patients, a reflection of the conflict that affected the entire history of contagion: the rivalry over possession and administration of bodies. In this vein, the gravedigger was the last link in a chain that began with the mandatory denunciation of the disease, then led to the hospital and the physician's scalpel and fire, and culminated in death. This essential element within the centralized administration of bodies often fell on those who had been sentenced to death and, given the absence of volunteers, were subsequently required to perform the tasks of body removing and gravedigging.

In the complex juxtaposition of archetypal symbologies in the trials of the Milanese body removers, the images of gravedigger and body remover, masters of bodies, were imbued with fear and suspicion. "I got this foam from a *monatto,*" Piazza, a Milanese Public Health commissioner explained to the magistrate, "and he gave it to me after I promised to pay him ten *scudi.*"[53] The foam, which the *monatto* had taken from the mouths of dying men, was allegedly used to prepare the "maleficent oil" that had killed half the population of Milan. The chaotic commerce of exchanges, hence, enabled gravediggers to sell substances expelled by the bodies that were subject to state regulation throughout the emergency. Like a specter, this infernal commerce encircled and threatened the other form of trade, the old and long-established practice of bargaining with families. Far better to compensate their services with a shirt or nice cloak than to allow the gravedigger to appear with his filthy substances.

The discourse on property and clandestine relocations of goods from infected houses was entirely confined within the city walls, in quick passages between delineated spaces (alleys, gardens, backdoors, holes in walls) and infected and forbidden spaces (houses, rooms). Social behavior, therefore, was displayed within a clearly defined spatial opposition: on one side, under normal circumstances, people could move freely in open spaces; on the other side, people fell ill and died in enclosed spaces. Within the city, this spatial opposition alluded to the opposition of social classes. The rich and the noble, as well as the medical personnel administering charity and medicine, operated in the open spaces. The working classes, the poor, and suspected victims of the plague remained in the closed spaces. Within this social grammar, simplified and articulated in a binary structure, infractions were instantaneously evident. One step taken past a forbidden door, a hand penetrating a locked window, constituted crimes in and of themselves.

Social constellations were increasingly constructed and deconstructed around minute contours: doors, windowsills, and passageways between first and second floors—in short, increasingly narrow delineations of space and movement. Some reports appear to indicate that the defendants' stubborn, comic, and clumsy efforts to open a locked door embodied for them the whole meaning of the plague in some symbolic manner. Perhaps this was the case for Giulia, a prostitute with great initiative and imagination, who claimed that the lock placed on her front door by the Public Health authorities did not work. She reported, "I asked a boy who lives off charity for some bread. As I pulled the basket up, it hit the lock, knocking it off; so I left and went to the house of my friend Francesca."[54] If not for the lock, we would never have known about Giulia, her street, and her neighbor with whom she enjoyably spent the evening in the company of three men. Their testimonies revolve around those spaces, an arbitrary border measuring just a few inches.

The evidence on removed and relocated goods is thus inscribed within a discourse of topological transgression: in order to steal or recover one's rightful belongings, it was necessary to transgress that border between the "inside" and the "permitted." In spatial terms, the behavioral models imposed by the sanitary edicts expressed alien categories. The content of this language is ethical as well as juridical: inside/outside corresponds to legal/illegal, healthy/unhealthy, yours/not yours, good/bad, friend/enemy, and so forth. From the record of actual behavior, however, we can deduce that the semantic distinctions officially applied to the epidemic were opposed by long-established collective interests. If, for example, edicts prohibiting the removal of objects made the spatial category "inside" coincide with the juridical category "yours," social practice would differ and would propose alternative priorities; "inside" could be amplified until it included the familiar group of the living as well as the dead. Not even the fear of contagion prevented relatives from organizing a complex game of roles to ensure the unity of family and property. As we have seen, only in the story of the Del Piccino brothers did the sanitary prescriptions fail to encounter opposition in the imposed separation between space and property.

Nevertheless, some trials illustrate the delineation of autonomous ethical-spacial frontiers around the original nucleus of parents and children. In these cases, the threshold of inside/outside, and therefore of mine/yours, defined a system of inclusion and exclusion that damaged the acquired, and excluded, family members. Those brothers who at the (real or reputed) death of their sister allied against their brother-in-law to preserve their family's property serve as the best example. Here, violating sanitary edicts also implied violating ordinary legislation.

Outside of the family, a dual transgressive dynamic stems from the workplace. First, the desire to acquire useful objects for the shop encouraged their removal, thereby opening a circuit of accumulation/transformation that avoided waste but at the same time damaged public assistance structures by creating public commerce. Second, guild regulation merged with the commerce of specific goods in a perspective of permanent traditional behaviors (the gravedigger). It is perhaps no coincidence that the only episode involving looting was alien to the complex moral economies that inspired most people's actions. Andrea Passignani, like a Defoe character, operated beyond the limits of the consolidated cultural system.

Beneath the surface of the law we have found a stratification of different ethical and behavioral models appropriate to different social groups. And beyond the orientation to the past we have seen how the discourse of property opened a narrative projection oriented toward the future. Testimonies describing thefts and relocations pushed the story ahead, toward expectations, links, and work yet to come. Time, blocked by the edicts, was perforated and decomposed by this stubborn social movement which clandestinely prepared, preserved, and ensured the regeneration of life.

4

Serving
the Public Health Magistracy
Officials, Fumigators, Plague Spreaders,
and Doctors

Many people wanted to work for the Public Health Magistracy. They could not hope, of course, to work in the upper echelons of the administration. Most important bureaucratic posts were reserved for nobles, and the prime positions in the lazarets were filled by clerics. Commoners could, however, try to secure jobs on the lower and intermediate levels, especially as commissioners, as bailiffs who locked infected houses, and as Bargello guards. The magistrates continuously received requests "to replace those who had died." Naturally, many people wanted to take advantage of the inevitable turnover caused by the epidemic.

Most often, the background of the petitioner largely coincided with the sought-after position. Thus, most of the men and women applying from the popular classes were artisans, textile workers, and porters. Moreover, the requests themselves often highlighted this similarity between background and position, perhaps indicating the petitioners' hopes of gaining temporary employment. Domenico di Andrea, "a fisherman nicknamed 'Loto,'" petitioned to become a guard "near the fish market of San Niccolò, where he would like to work."[1] When his request was granted, Domenico became a guard on the Arno River. Not too long after his appointment, however, his conduct proved questionable. He was arrested for selling fish on the black market with his fishermen friends.

Disgraced and destitute noblemen, unable to support themselves, applied for intermediate positions in the Magistracy. "Signor Giovanni Soli, citizen of Florence," for example, "always faithful to His Venerable Highness, requests an office in the Public Health Magistracy, because of his penury," which was exacerbated by the fact that "his properties have become absolutely unproductive in these times of misery."[2]

Commoners despised guards, fumigators, cleaners, and people who locked the doors of infected houses. These officers were violent and corrupt; furthermore, they used their uniforms to appease their stubborn desire for revenge or to take advantage of those whom they were supposed to protect and serve. Florentines called them *nibi,* meaning "kites," which symbolized the feeling of being surrounded by rapacious birds.[3] Still, in spite of all the denunciations and the hatred, there was in fact an established system of bargaining and mutual pressuring between sanitary personnel and civilians that was designed to circumvent Public Health regulations. As a result, Public Health officials would sometimes, on request, lock a room on the second floor rather than on the first or issue a special permit for a secret wedding.

Although these acts seem irrelevant, in times of contagion even a small divergence between institutional control and daily practice made social communication possible. In addition, everyone knew and recognized the *nibi,* unlike the magistrates or the officers of the lazarets. People called these workers by their first names or nicknames, and everyone knew where and with whom they lived. Indeed, often the *nibi* lived in the same quarter in which they worked. Wearing the uniform of the Public Health Magistracy, they played, for a short period of time, the role of mediator. Members of the body social appeared to understand this role well and responded with weapons based on either a common past or a known weakness. Thus began a long process of bargaining, verbal onslaughts, and, ultimately, denunciation to the authorities.

A GOOD-HEARTED OFFICIAL,
A POULTERER, AND TWO FIANCÉS

On 11 October 1630, Public Health guards arrested Ulisse di Bartolomeo Dolci, an official who locked infected houses. Three days later a formal charge was pressed against him. The magistrate had heard that many houses that ought to have been closed because of contagion had in fact been left open, and "people were let out of them despite their possible infection." Because Ulisse Dolci had been in charge of closing those houses, "he was to be investigated for committing said crimes."[4]

On 14 October, Ulisse went to court. After taking the oath, he explained what tasks he was supposed to perform:

> I have been working for the Public Health Magistracy for two and one-half months. About two weeks ago, Commissioner Nobili ordered me to go with a guard to lock houses, rooms, or apartments according to the situation. . . . Lunetti, the chancellor's auditor, gave me a list of the houses or apartments I was to lock. . . . He said that the chancellor wanted me to confine the people only in those apartments which had been hit by the disease.

Had he followed his orders? Had he locked only the infected houses? Had he really locked in all people who had been in rooms where the disease had been?

"Yes, sir, I locked all of them—the houses and the people. I also wrote down in my notebook the names of those I quarantined. I sent the guard to lock the other houses and to check if there were people who had come into contact with the stricken. I ordered them to Sant'Onofrio, as Lunetti and the commissioner had told me to do."

The procedure was simple and the execution of the orders seemed easy. Escorted by a guard, Ulisse had recorded the names of those he locked in the house. Then he filled out a report for his superiors, Lunetti and Nobili. Was it possible that some of the houses he was supposed to lock had actually been left open?

"If that happened, I told the guard to go back and lock it, because I had too much to do."

How many times did this happen?

> I remember four cases. Once in Borgo Ognissanti, at the house of a gardener of the Palazzo del Lanzi, we couldn't lock the house because the guard had used all his locks. Anyway, everyone was not at home at the time: four young people were missing. This happened about six days ago, and I told the guard to come back later. The second time, it was at a textile worker's house on Via dell'Oriuolo. We didn't lock it because the body was still in the house. The third case was at a house in Cella di Ciardo. Because there were two dead bodies in that house when I arrived, Luna told me that he had sent someone else to lock it. The last house was at San Jacopo. There were two bodies there as well. That evening I found out that Father Giulio Ricardi had locked it. In addition, we left open Barbera Tornaquinci's house because the corpse was also still there, and I told the guard that we would come back the following day.

Had he gone back to check if the guard had actually locked the houses?

"No, sir, I had too many other things to do."

Had he ever been offered money to leave a house open?

"I've been asked many times, but I never accepted and I never promised anything." Then he added in a soft voice, "I know where this rumor comes from."

The magistrate heard this comment and immediately asked, "Where does it come from?"

"I received an order from Lunetti to lock a room on Via Federighi, and I did. However, I was reproved because I had locked only the room, not the whole house. Yet I had been told to close only the room." To avoid being blamed, he tried to pass the responsibility on to somebody else, this time to Lunetti.

Did he know a certain Lorenzo, the magistrate asked, a poulterer from the Mercato Vecchio?

"Yes, sir."

Did he know whether this man had sick people living with him in his house?

"He lives with Jacopo in Campo Corbolini, near Marche. I know because I locked his house."

Was Lorenzo inside when the house was locked?

"No, sir, he had been away for four or five days, according to a paper he sent me. So I didn't look for him inside the house."

Where was he?

"I don't know. He sent the paper through Luna, an Otto guard, two or three days after I locked the house."

What kind of paper was it, and what had he done with it?

"I didn't bother to read it. [Luna] told me that it said that the man was not at home, so I just put it in my pocket. I still had it when I was arrested."

Had he shown that paper to his superior or to any other official of the Magistracy?

"I didn't have the chance to show it to anybody, sir. I locked that house on Sunday, only eight days ago."

Something was still unclear to the magistrate. Why had Ulisse waited two days for the poulterer's attestation? Why hadn't he waited for everyone to be home before locking the door? Why had he run the risk of letting the poulterer get away without justification?

"The women told me that he hadn't come home yet, so I said, 'If he hasn't come back, we'll see.'"

Then Luna brought the attestation to Ulisse, and the guard Matteo went to lock the house. The magistrate became more and more suspicious: How much had the poulterer paid for such an allowance?

"He didn't give me any money, sir." Whether the other guards were bribed, he claimed not to know. Ulisse "was warned to tell the truth, because the magistrate had heard from numerous sources that he had left many houses open and had let many people go." The chancellor insisted that he wanted to know the entire story: how many houses, which houses, "the reasons [Ulisse] had done so, and how much he had been paid."

"By the grace of God, I haven't done any of these things. As to the guard's actions, I just don't know, because all I did was send him to lock the houses. I don't know anything else."

Did he know whether the guard had stolen anything from the infected houses?

"No, sir, I don't know. . . . I don't have anything else to say. . . . I did my work right."

Ulisse Dolci was sent back to his cell, and three days later, on 17 October, Lorenzo de Francesco Ferruzzi, the poulterer at the Mercato Vecchio, was interrogated.

Had he ever kept sick people in his house?

"One child, whom they sent to me eight or nine days ago at the Monte. . . . Yes, sir, they locked my house while I was in it."

Was he ordered not to leave?

"The order was at home, but I didn't see it because I was out for five days."

What explanation did he write, and to whom did he give it?

"I gave the attestation to Luna."

The poulterer's absence from home can probably be best explained by the common behavior of most artisans and traders. When a family member fell ill, the father/husband left the house and moved to the shop in order to continue working. He would borrow a mattress and a few pots from the neighbors to begin a new cohabitation with his fellow workers. He would go home from time to time to find out how his family was doing. In these social groups, then, an immediate separation occurred between the males, who went to live at the shop, and the females, the mother and daughters, who stayed home. Because the practice was quite common, the magistrates knew very well that an official's complicity could prove invaluable for anyone who wanted to leave his locked home freely.

More evidence accumulated against Ulisse Dolci. After the poulterer's testimony, which contained many holes, Antonia di Giovanni di Cristofano, a textile worker, was interrogated at the office of the hospital of Sant'Onofrio.

> I was locked in my house with my father, mother, sister, and younger brother. My older brother had died. On my father's suggestion, my younger brother had arranged for me to get married and to go get the ring. We asked for a license from the Public Health officials, those who dressed in grey, and they gave it to us. On Monday we went to San Frediano, where I was given the ring even though my new husband wasn't home. . . . Then we returned home and were locked in. . . . The Public Health officer who gave us the license had wanted to lock us in, so my father gave him a little money. After I got the ring, he locked us in and told us never to go out. . . . There were two Public Health officials when I got the license; one was dressed in grey, and the other one, dressed in black, carried a dagger. . . . I don't know how much my father gave him. . . . My husband has never been at my house, nor have I ever spent the night at his place.

Antonia's testimony recounted the story of a wedding that could not take place; the groom was away from home, and the bride was not in his bed. The textile worker, the father of the young woman, was advised to support the two young people and to supervise an exchange of engagement rings. He thereby kept his word, even though it had been believed that the plague would prevent him from doing so.

For the first time, an eyewitness accused Ulisse Dolci of receiving some money. Her words were immediately confirmed by the testimony of her new husband, Domenico di Antonio Campestrini, a textile worker like his new father-in-law.

> Eight days ago, a man came to my shop with a message from my father-in-law. He said that my father-in-law had gotten a permit from the Public Health officials to leave the house so that I could give the ring to my bride. . . . I did it on that very day, and my father-in-law and wife left their home. Then, on Tuesday morning, they were locked in. . . . I haven't been to their house, but I've heard that the Public Health officials granted them this favor because my father-in-law gave them a little money, but I don't know how much. . . . I don't know

who the officials were who accepted the money because I didn't see them, but my father-in-law told me about it.

Money provided Giovanni's family with a day of rejoicing. As Antonia and Domenico had been locked in the house on Tuesday morning, perhaps they had enjoyed a night of passion.

The investigation continued on 18 October with the interrogation of Mattio di Antonio Lorini, the guard under Ulisse Dolci's command.

"Captain Luna ordered me to go with Ulisse to lock houses, . . . as that is what I always did. The day after Luna hired me I was paid twenty *soldi,* and I was always paid thereafter."

How did he lock houses?

"The guard reads some papers and tells me, 'Lock that house!' So I take a bar and nail it across the door. . . . Sometimes nobody is in the house, and we have to come back the following day."

Did they leave one house open at the Borgo Stella so that a wedding could take place?

"Ulisse gave the father of a bride in the Borgo Stella permission to stay out of the house so that her fiancé could give her the ring—but only for one morning."

What had induced Ulisse to grant that favor?

"While I was there, I didn't see anything."

As far as Lorenzo's house was concerned, "While he wasn't inside, it was locked from the front and the back." Warned that he had better tell the truth, Mattio remained silent. He was then sent back to his cell.

On 21 October, Lorenzo Ferruzzi was taken to the torture chamber. There the magistrate interrogated him for a second time, asking him whether "he had decided to explain how he had avoided being locked in the house, because it was not believable that while everyone else was in the house he was outside. The magistrate strongly suspected that he had bribed the Public Health officials."

Lorenzo insisted, "I have never seen or given anything to the man who locked me in the house." He denied it even when the magistrate threatened to use the rope. The fact that a public official was involved in the episode made the affair all the more serious ("in terms of both the punishment and the importance of the case"). Lorenzo was in real trouble. "That truth might be obtained from the defendant, the man was told to undress and was tied to the rope." After the magistrate had ordered the guards to hoist the man up on the rope, "he still remained silent." How much had he paid for the guard's complicity? "I have nothing else to say. I can't say any more. I have six children."

Lorenzo remained in that position "for the twelfth part of an hour" without saying a word. Then, when it appeared evident that under no circumstances would the man confess, "his body was lowered and dressed, and he was sent back to his cell for the time being. . . . [The magistrate said that] as soon as Lorenzo ensured that he would keep himself available for further questioning, he would be freed."

Lorenzo was released when his fellow worker at the Mercato Vecchio, Giovanni di Lorenzo Butini, paid the bail of fifty *scudi*. His release was witnessed by the torture officer Carli and the guard Domenico, called "Stoppone."

On 21 October, after hearing all the testimonies, the magistrate called on Ulisse Dolci once again.

Did he know a young woman named Antonia di Giovanni, the wife of the textile worker Domenico, who lived on Via Maffia?

"I don't know her."

So he did not remember the case of a newly married woman who needed to leave her house to get her ring from her husband?

"I don't recall it."

Think about it carefully.

"The father of a young bride in the Borgo Stella, whose house I had to lock, told me that he wanted her to get the ring in case one of them died. The husband hadn't been at home, so I told the father that I would come back later to lock the house. Actually, I returned the next morning."

Did he know whether the bride had gotten the ring?

"They told me that she had and that they had wanted it given to her in church."

What motivated him to grant the favor? Did he not realize that his orders prohibited granting such favors?

"I don't know. Perhaps just to be nice."

Who had paid him?

"No one gave me anything." Ulisse denied having received any bribe, and the magistrate granted him ten days to prepare his defense.

On 7 November the official was taken to the torture chamber "so that he would confess how much money he had received and how many houses he had left open."

"I didn't take anything from anyone" were the last words that Ulisse pronounced. He was undressed and raised on the rope, where he remained for fifteen minutes. Then he was lowered and taken back to his cell.

Only silence and physical fortitude enabled Ulisse to escape with a mild sentence. Given the fact that he had remained silent for "fifteen minutes on the rope," he was sentenced to be "led around the city along the usual path on a donkey, the punishment for embezzlers holding public offices. . . . His Highness was notified of the sentence."[5]

A mediator of orders from above, the public official Ulisse Dolci performed his duties between two different social configurations: Lorenzo's relations to his family and his shop on the one hand, and Domenico and Antonia's wedding on the other. He served as the inevitable interlocutor, almost as if to narrow the flow of communication between the two groups. His willingness to accept a tip to ignore a bar that had been improperly installed across the door allowed the two young people to get married, despite the danger of contagion, and enabled Lorenzo to provide his family with food and money. His readiness to be bribed permitted the two interpretive processes—of the urgency of the wedding and the separation from the family—to be made explicit. Thus two strategies, two distinct social practices that oriented the experience of the plague for Antonia, Domenico, and Lorenzo, converged on Ulisse's figure and role. According to these reports, the epidemic *was* a clandestine wedding for the two young people. For the poulterer, the epidemic *was* escaping to his shop. Through Ulisse Dolci, these choices, sentiments, and hopes became realities.

THE GAME OF ROLES

The story of Cice, a Florentine corporal of the Bargello guard, and Benedetto, a guard at the Gate of San Niccolò, was quite different. With one of their friends, nicknamed "Vedovino," they found themselves at the center of a complicated plot, which converged on a round of cheese that played the same role as Antonia's ring.

On 22 November, Corporal Luna prepared a report against three men: "Piero di Francesco, called 'Vedovino,' who used to be a tavern-keeper; Felice, 'Cice,' a corporal of the Bargello guard in Florence; and Benedetto, a guard at the Gate of San Niccolò." According to a secret informer, they had gone together to a grocery store owned by Giuliano di Andrea Poggi, a shopkeeper in San Niccolò, and, "upon arrival, they claimed to be Public Health officials. Vedovino acted as the boss and ordered the guards to search the store. They obeyed. When they did not find anything that violated the edicts, they . . . decided to tie up a young man there with a rope." Pretending to be an important Public Health official, Vedovino gave the order to immobilize the young man, saying, "In the name of His Highness, I order you not to leave these rooms." Then the bound man gave a *tallero* to the guards, who later spent it in a tavern.

Still not satisfied, the men went to the bakery of Domenico d'Antonio. There Vedovino said to the owner, "I know that you have a piece of rotten cheese here." The man responded that it had already been thrown into the Arno. Vedovino responded, "Arrest this man, and take this woman to the lazaret!" Then he began to search the shop, saying, "Give these men a bottle of wine, and I don't want to hear any more about it." The baker gave Vedovino everything he demanded and, given the men's importance, gave them a *giulio* as well.

In the denunciation, Luna declared that it was extremely important to prosecute these three imposters because they "pretended to be Public Health officials, thereby denigrating and damaging the real organization of public servants who perform their duties correctly."[6]

Taking advantage of the exactitude with which the Magistracy controlled the food supply of the diseased city, the three men were able to scare the baker and other shopkeepers by accusing them of selling rotten food. During this same period, denunciations were often filed against butchers who left the bridges and banks of the Arno dirty. In addition, edicts were passed to ensure that new wine was sold only after a certain degree of fermentation had been reached and at a fixed price. Thus, for the inhabitants of the quarter of San Niccolò the increased state control of the food supply provided the opportunity for the tavernkeeper to terrorize his neighbors who sold cheese and bread.

On 22 November, Pietro di Bastiano Macinai, an apprentice from the Borgo San Niccolò, testified at the Magistracy.

> Last night, at around three o'clock, Vedovino came to my shop with two other guys. One was Benedetto, a guard who is stationed at the Gate of San Niccolò, and although I don't know the name of the other,

he is a corporal of the Bargello guard. I've heard, however, that he is called Corporal Cice. Vedovino said that he had been sent by order of the grand duke and the provisioner—he didn't say which provisioner. He asked me to light a lantern so that he could search for spoiled food. He started looking, while the other men found two or three pounds of caviar that had not yet gone bad. They broke up the caviar into many bits and asked me to put it in a bag. Vedovino told me that he might tie my master and me to a rope. Then they went upstairs. All this time I was alone, but about half an hour later Antonio Battinzecca and Father Bastian Paolini returned, and Vedovino ordered them to give him some money. So Antonio Battinzecca gave them a *tallero,* since the shop-keeper was not there and I didn't have any money. They took the money and left.

Vedovino seemed to move with confidence throughout the neighborhood. He was able to extort money from Battinzecca. The next person visited by Vedovino and the guards, "Madonna Cosa," the sister of the baker in San Niccolò, testified after the young apprentice.

I work in the bakery of my brother Domenico. . . . Last night, at about three o'clock, three people I don't know came in. People said that they were guards. One wore a cloak and hat. Another said that he wanted to see if we had any rotten food. They didn't find anything, and I asked them, "Why are you looking?" They answered, "We'll take you to the lazaret and your brother to jail." One of my children went crying to my brother. Domenico came and told them to search the shop. They answered, "Don't waste our time, because we're going to arrest you." Then they left, and nothing else happened. I didn't give them anything, and I don't know if my brother gave them anything. When they came in, our next-door neighbor, Maria, was there.

Madonna Cosa added that she would indeed recognize the three men if she saw them again.

The baker Domenico Tognetti was called as a witness after his sister. He recounted, "Last night, at around 1:30 in the morning, three men came into the shop [at the entrance], near the stove where my sister stays. One of them was called Vedovino and said that he was a corporal." Domenico confirmed the two guards' testimonies and his sister's report of the search. While Vedovino was arrogantly proclaiming, "We are important officials of the Public Health Magistracy," Domenico said, "I arrived, and they asked me if I had any storage rooms. I told them no and said that they could search the whole shop because there wasn't anything there. Vedovino said, 'Arrest this baker, and take him to jail. And send this woman to the lazaret.'" Cice answered that he would execute the order whenever Vedovino wanted.

Vedovino then took me to one side and said, "I'll be happy to do you a favor. Just give us some money so we can buy some wine." After taking the money, they stopped searching because they knew there wasn't anything but bread, cheese, apples, and other fruit. The shop is small, and it only takes a few minutes to search the whole place. And so they left, and nothing happened after that.

Did he remember if anyone else was present at the scene?

"I came in because I heard noises coming from the shop. As far as I can remember, there was nobody else there but me," Domenico concluded, barely able to control himself when he thought of Vedovino's arrogance and of the *giulio* that he had paid the guards and the fake Public Health official.

Finally, on 27 November Piero di Francesco, nicknamed "Vedovino," was called to testify. Standing in front of the magistrate, he began,

> About one and a half months ago I spoke to the provisioner, Signor Giovanni Nobili, and asked him if he wanted me to look for spoiled food and dirty storage areas. I worked for three or four days for someone called "Cappellaio," an official at that time of the Otto Magistracy, bringing back to him a lot of rotten food that had been thrown into the Arno. . . . I wasn't salaried, but the provisioner gave me a *scudo,* and Cappellaio once gave me four *lire.* . . . The last time I went looking for rotten food was last Thursday, when I visited two or three shops in San Niccolò. I got Cice and two other guards, who were drinking at the tavern, and we went to three little shops. One was named Sano, and I've forgotten the names of the other two. When I found rotten caviar in one of the shops, I put it aside and told them "Leave it alone." The shopkeeper started complaining. I left the guards and went outside. I don't know if the guards got any money. I sure didn't.

Vedovino continued to deny the charge ("I didn't receive any money, and I didn't see anybody giving any"), even after the magistrate said that he had proof that the man had received a *tallero* and a *giulio* from the shopkeepers.

This testimony draws a picture of occasional and voluntary work. The job of inspecting with Cappellaio stemmed from Vedovino's proposal to the provisioner. Nobili did not even bother to pay the man a salary but rather gave him a tip from time to time. This temporary work fit well with Vedovino's regular job as a tavernkeeper, actually allowing him to take advantage of his knowledge of the community and the locations of food supplies, which personally interested him. This choice confirms what we have previously noticed about the social origins of the middle and lower echelons of the Public Health Magistracy. Because of quick employee turnover, none of the witnesses were surprised or suspicious of Vedovino. Used to seeing different individuals wearing the uniform of the Public Health Magistracy, they all regarded him as a real Public Health official.

After Vedovino had testified, Corporal Felice di Vangelista Ascinelli of the Bargello guard appeared in court to recount his version of the episode.

> I went to the tavern of San Niccolò on Thursday night. Vedovino came to get me, and we left together. Vedovino entered a shop and, in the name of the grand duke, asked me and another guard, Benedetto, to go in as well. We didn't want to, but he repeated the request. Seeing that he had some rotten caviar, we came near. I told him to get rid of it, but he just left it there. Then he went into another shop, looking around with a lantern; I didn't notice if he found anything. After that he went into another shop, where he didn't find anything either. I didn't receive anything, . . . nor do I think that anyone else did. . . . Vedovino claimed to have the authorization of the Public Health Magistracy to search any place he wanted.

Obviously, Cice's testimony was incomplete, since he was implicated in the case as Vedovino's accomplice. Still, the nature of the deception that had been planned at the tavern table became ever clearer. Vedovino, who knew the neighborhood well, dragged the two men along. Because his tavern used to be in the same quarter, he knew everything about everyone. His accomplices therefore trusted him. He obviously knew how to find rotten food at the bakery or grocery. The bribe given for their sealed lips would later be spent on wine at the tavern by the three men together.

Benedetto di Giovanni, a guard at the Gate of San Niccolò, testified after Corporal Cice.

"Thursday evening, I was with Corporal Cice at the tavern of San Niccolò. Vedovino came, and we drank together. Afterwards, Vedovino went into a shop and said that we represented the grand duke." In short, the responsibility for the whole episode was all Vedovino's. Benedetto confirmed the previous testimony, adding that after the search "a man named Battinzecca and a priest named De Paolini came in. They had some discussion, but I don't know what they talked about. We then went into two other shops. The corporal told me he had gotten something that would buy us a bottle of wine. He didn't tell me how much he had gotten. That's all I can tell you." Thus Be-

nedetto naively broke the silence that still united Vedovino to his accomplices. The witnesses' testimony was finally confirmed.

The last person called to testify was the goldsmith Antonio Artini,
nicknamed "Battinzecca," who had paid the money on behalf of his
friend the shopkeeper.

> A couple of evenings ago—I don't remember when exactly—Bastiano
> Paolini and I went to the store of Guiliano the grocer. His apprentice
> was there as well. I heard Vedovino blaspheme against God and the
> Virgin Mary, and the priest gave him a *giulio* to make him leave and
> stop such bad talk. He gave the coin to the corporal and told them, "Go
> away," which they did. I don't know what they wanted at the shop, but
> I do know that they made a lot of noise and cursed.

This statement provided the finishing touches to the picture: the
agreement made at the tavern, the imposters' sacrilegious and arrogant behavior, and the money paid to get rid of Vedovino.

It should be noted that no other witness brought up the fake Public
Health official's blasphemy against God and the Virgin Mary. Perhaps
people expected that type of language from him; or maybe the other
witnesses were not as sensitive to cursing as the priest. In any case, it
is certain that the priest, unconcerned with the reasons for the swearing, gave Vedovino a *tallero* to make him stop, at the same time saving
the shopkeeper from the thug's threats.

Ulisse Dolci and Vedovino received different punishments for
crimes that were, in fact, quite similar: accepting bribes. The consequences of their infractions, however, were not of the same gravity.
Ulisse allowed suspected carriers of the plague to circulate freely in
the city, delaying locking the houses for his own financial interest.
Vedovino, posing as a Public Health official, made a little extra money
to spend in a tavern. Because the social consequences of the two actions were different, the Magistracy imposed a lighter sentence on
Vedovino.[7]

Both the real and the fake Public Health officials acted at the center
of interpretive social schemes constructed by the epidemic: a secret
wedding, separation of home and shop, deception at the expense of
shopkeepers. Whereas the character of Ulisse dissolves in the background, becoming a neutral element in a broader picture of exchanges
and wills that were external and probably alien to him, the profile of
Vedovino becomes clearer. The threatening words, the oaths, the arrogant gestures, the plan discussed in the tavern amid laughter and

bottles of wine, and the fake uniform—even the details of his old profession as tavernkeeper and of his active confrontation of the plague—tend to delineate a sort of stage character. Vedovino, his sarcasm directed against the two shopkeepers, was actually at the center of the story: he was the protagonist. This fake Public Health official circumvented the Magistracy's rules, creating, with the help of Cice and Benedetto, a new personal code in the game of roles. At San Niccolò on Thursday, 21 November 1630, the plague assumed the character of a parody and the quick rhythm of a pantomime.

A FUMIGATOR'S OPPORTUNITIES

The third trial of a Public Health official moved along a different path. Bartolomeo Fagni, a fumigator, was accused of stealing a long list of objects from locked houses left under his control. The fumigators, also called "sulphur workers" or "perfumers," were assigned the tasks of disinfecting closed houses and emptying them of their furniture, which was later burned. These employees were easily identified by the red cross on the front of their white uniforms and by their wagon, popularly called "the wagon of disease." There were sixteen perfumers in the city, four assigned to each quarter, and, like gravediggers, they lived together, segregated from the rest of the population, on Via del Giardino. Before the outbreak of the epidemic, prostitutes, also considered to be socially infected and hence contagious, had lived on that very street.

The Fagni case reopened the universe of those lost, stolen, and destroyed belongings searched for and chased after with a desperation typical of the entire story of the epidemic. The structure of the trial followed a layered pattern: denunciations and inventories were piled on top of one another until they formed a complicated web surrounding the suspect. Once again, thanks to those officials who were immersed in the lives and deaths of their fellow citizens, we can see what would otherwise be opaque: the list of items that Fagni reputedly stole opens a door into the interiors of many poor houses, into the daily life of those who were inevitably becoming poorer and poorer. Importantly, denunciations signaled an angry rebirth of life; those who transcribed, verified, and calculated the losses were, in fact, those who had survived and returned home after the devastating passage of the epidemic and a stay in a lazaret.

The long sequence of charges pressed against the fumigator Bartolomeo Fagni was opened by a very well documented denunciation prepared by Angelica di Giovanni Bandini, who went to the chancellor's office in person and listed all her losses. The social picture she represents leads us to the familiar scene of women who, left alone, share a common solidarity.

"Some two months ago, I went to Badia, where people with sick relatives are sent, and left my house empty. Because my neighbors knew that I had left my white linens in some water, they went to the magistrate to ask permission to get the sheets. The magistrate sent two employees to go get them. My neighbors, however, told me that the two men remained in the house the whole day."[8] Always keeping an eye on everything, the neighbors knew that Angelica had been taken to the lazaret quickly and that she had left her linens wet. As they could not enter her house themselves, they went to the magistrate and asked him to save the sheets somehow. Perhaps only such a small detail, such an insignificant fact, can explain these women's familiarity with the justice system; in any case, the magistrate responded quickly to their request and sent the appropriate officials. Yet the neighbors' trust in the Magistracy appeared to be tempered by their desire to supervise its actions. The long stay of the two men in Angelica's two rooms (an entire day just to take the linens out) aroused their suspicions.

"About one month ago," Angelica continued, "I returned home. A man with a grey-and-red-striped cloak opened the door, and we went inside at the same time. . . . I discovered that twenty-one receipts of belongings that I had pawned were missing from my white box." Angelica did not know who had taken the receipts, but she heard about the two officials who had been in her house. One was the son of a cleaner and lived in the Borgo San Pier Gattolini, two doors past the Gatta tavern. The person in question was Fagni; everyone in the neighborhood knew his father and the house.

In the course of her narration, Angelica listed the receipts of the objects pawned two years earlier at the bank.[9] Because she had difficulty remembering the items, the money she had made from each transaction, and the dates, Angelica's list vacillates between different dates. In any case, she had to go to the Monte bank almost every month and had been unable, two years later, to recover any of her belongings. One is struck by the movement of the inventory toward objects of lesser value. After she had given up her jewels, Angelica had had to renounce her linens, then her towels, and finally her aprons. In contrast with 1629, the year 1630 was given over entirely to the pawning of sheets and linens. In June, a pot was even added to the list of other objects pawned earlier the same month. Given this list, it is no longer surprising that the neighbors asked the magistrate to save those linens Angelica had left out in the water when she was taken to the lazaret.

A new denunciation, presented by Barbera di Giuseppe Soggi, arrived on 13 December. On the seventh, Barbera had been sent to the lazaret of San Miniato on the orders of Doctor "Vittorio, who lives in the Borgo degli Albizi," and "a certain Fagni, a Public Health official." They suggested that she not "take any of her belongings with her because they would be confiscated and destroyed." Barbera, worried by the doctor and Fagni's warnings, "gave them all her things, not even having the time to write an inventory." After she was released from the lazaret of San Miniato she asked that the two men give her back her belongings, but in vain.

Like Angelica, Barbera prepared a list from memory: "One hundred eight *giuli,* eight *piastre,* countless *cratie* and *quatrini,* two silver spoons and a fork, two moon-shaped pairs of earrings, two golden earrings, two pearl necklaces, four rings, two gems—one enamel, the other turquoise—and an enamel ring."[10]

Meanwhile, the charges against Bartolomeo Fagni continued to grow. On 12 December a veritable chorus of accusations seemed to rise from all directions. Michele Capaccini, a tailor from Pistoia who lived in Cella di Ciardo, reported the loss of "a vase with a curative oil" and five or six *ducati.* Lessandra di Paolo, who lived "in Maramau's house" in Boffi, reported the theft of a knife and cutting stone, four new *pilastre,* and an old *pilastro* dating from the era of the grand duke.

Bartolomeo was searched and two keys were found in his possession. Some guards went to his house and found that one of the keys might have fitted a drawer which was, however, without a lock. They therefore assumed that the stolen goods were hidden in it.

To make the defendant's position even more difficult, Fabbri, his accomplice, surrendered two stolen mattresses to the authorities.[11]

On 16 December, Bartolomeo Fagni, "extracted from jail," was interrogated by the chancellor.[12]

No one lives at my home except my mother. Sometimes the priest from Lucca stays with us. I stay from time to time at the Guicciardinis. I began working for the Public Health Magistracy at the end of August, right before Saint Bartholomew's Day. At first I was asked to live with the others on Via del Giardino. Then they told me to take care of the beds in the districts of Bonifacio and Sant'Onofrio and the quarter near Via del Giardino. The accountant Romoli arranged for all compensation. Next they appointed me provisioner at the hospital of Zalani, where I also had to take care of the beds.

Thus, Fagni's first jobs concerned the beds of the hospitals where adults and young orphans lived on Via del Giardino. Everything was done according to the orders received, and all accounts were handled by Romoli.

"After all this, they asked Durazzini and me to open houses. When Durazzini was appointed provisioner in Legnaia and Settignano, I was left to do the work alone." As in other cases, the fast turnover provided the lone worker with his opportunity.

What did he do when he came to open a house?

"I first had three men working for me but soon took on a fourth, Lorenzo Fabbri, who worked in the lazaret's linen services. I provided him with two men to help get the linens and the laundry. The others helped me open houses and burn what had to be burned, according to my instructions."

In this way, intermediate officials like Fagni and Fabbri divided laborers among themselves and reorganized their subordinates' work. In essence, they destined the lower officials to other tasks or possibly death by the disease. Being a fumigator in fact turned out to be rather dangerous, and "sulphur miners" died at a shocking rate, sometimes reaching "even seven" per day. It was precisely for this reason that, fifteen days before his arrest, Bartolomeo had asked his superior for a "leave of absence." Cucchi was chosen as his substitute.

The magistrate, however, was suspicious at the leave request. Could it stem from an illegal activity?

"Signor Romoli told me," Fagni explained, "that I ought to ask for the leave. So I talked to Signor Luca, who told me that he thought it was a good idea."

Why did they suggest his leaving? After several questions, Bartolomeo admitted that some people had complained about him to his superiors. "Signor Luca told me that someone had complained about a little bottle of poison antidote that I had confiscated."

This complaint came from the tailor Michele Capaccini, who was stubbornly trying to recover his medicine. Earlier he had attempted to talk directly to Fagni, but the result was a terrible argument filled with insults. Afterwards, when the poor tailor continued to try to retrieve his potion, he became the butt of fumigators' jokes. The previous Saturday, in front of the Church of San Pietro Martire, Fagni suddenly saw the tailor coming toward him. "Here is your potion," Fagni said sarcastically to the man, while smiling at the guards. This time the tailor got mad and yelled, "Are you making fun of me? You're the one who stole it, and now you're laughing at me?"

"What is stealing or not stealing?" Fagni argued, beginning to taunt the man once again. "Fuck me in the ass!"

The two began to fight. The tailor screamed when Fagni "hit" him with the handle of his dagger. The tailor finally managed to escape, shouting insults at Fagni and the "home of the Fagnis."

The hatred of the official, whose family and address were known to all, was characterized by swearing and familiar language. After this fight it was obvious that the tailor would denounce Fagni to the authorities.

Bartolomeo denied that there were any stolen goods in the box. He claimed that it contained only eight *scudi,* "a pair of silk socks, some pieces of paper, and the receipts of the beds that were taken to the hospitals." To substantiate his correct behavior, he reminded the magistrate that the guards had found only a religious "necklace" when they had searched him.

From 19 December on, after Bartolomeo's interrogation, a number of other witnesses were quickly examined by the magistrates. Piero di Lorenzo Maiani was asked to report on a theft that had occurred in the house of "the weigher Iacopo, in the Piazza del Grano." He said that the stolen goods were golden objects and seven *lire.* "Someone called 'Sergente' put them in his pockets. He accompanied the guy" who was entrusted with opening infected houses. The fumigator made Sergente "put them [the stolen goods] in his pockets."

Maddalena, former wife of Pietro Forini and daughter of Antonio Lombardi, testified that after the death of her parents and the hospitalization of her brother, Fagni's men had closed and later reopened her house on Via San Gallo after they sprayed it with sulphur. Here, too, silver and gold were missing "and some little crosses made of silver with *reliquie.*"

On 21 December, Baccio d'Agnolo Bassini, one of Bartolomeo's assistants, was called forth to testify. It was he who sent the belongings of Jacopo, the weigher of the Piazza del Grano, to San Marco Vecchio for disinfection. He admitted that, on that occasion, "a ring, seven and a half *lire,* a golden bell for a necklace, and some other things remained in the hands of one of Fagni's men, someone called 'Capitano.' I don't know whether the ring was made of silver or gold." Apparently Fagni confiscated these objects for himself.

A gap seemed to open in the testimonies, and the magistrate immediately called on the defendant's assistants. On 23 December the court listened to the fumigator Domenico Bacci's confession; contradicting his fellow worker's testimony, he denied any wrongdoings. The magistrate ordered the man to the torture chamber. When tied and lifted on the rope, Bernardo began to scream, "Oh! Poor me, I'm going to die," but he admitted nothing.

The same procedure was followed with Battista di Vangelista Rondinelli, another fumigator under Fagni's command, who was interrogated the same day. Although he had worked for the Public Health Magistracy for only one month, he remained loyal to his superior, denying all charges. Under torture, he screamed "for the eighth part of an hour" but did not confess or confirm anything.

The situation did not change, despite a final denunciation by the baker Rosso, who, immediately on leaving the lazaret, reported that one of his tenants had seen Fagni's team steal a cloak and a white linen sheet from his house.

These charges and reports failed to build a strong enough case against Fagni. His knowledge of the correct procedures in opening houses, combined with his ability to accuse his fellow workers with the thefts, finally set him free. The sentence, promulgated on 8 January 1630, stated: "Charged with the crime of letting the men who worked for him disinfecting houses . . . steal several goods," Bartolomeo Fagni "improperly claimed to have the authority of a higher Public Health official for reasons that have not yet been explained. . . . As no evidence has been brought to us, despite the torture of two of his assistants, . . . and as no stolen good has been found in Fagni's possession, . . . we order that the man be set free from jail." [13]

Lack of evidence, then, put an end to the case of Bartolomeo, fumigator of the Public Health Magistracy. All the reports, charges, testimonies, and investigations offer themselves to us as readings characterized by lists: lists of goods that were lost, stolen, or unsuccessfully reclaimed. More than the plot, these lists give some sense to the process surrounding the trial. Unlike Vedovino and Ulisse Dolci, Bartolomeo Fagni broke the link between owners and their objects. In this way he was not at the heart of social ramifications, but a part of the fundamental binary relationship between individuals and their belongings. The cumulative properties of this language thereby appeared to submerge the defendant in the memory of those objects that had disappeared. Neither complicities nor transactions characterized the relationship between Bartolomeo and the witnesses; rather, it was one merely of abuse.

GROUP VIOLENCE

Violence, a permanent characteristic of social inequality and one of the most predictable behavioral outcomes of people who give orders, came to symbolize the authority figure. One aspect of that representation—intimidation—was so pervasive that the action almost lost significance. Consequently, trial records, such as those we have already examined, offer less in the way of authority character descriptions than do the recorded denunciations made against violent and arrogant officials. In these reports, the paths of social communication suffered a precipitous drop, thickening into motives for abuse. Officials and citizens—soldiers and lonely women, for example—confronted each other outside the usual web of intermediaries that worked to ease the direct struggle against Public Health administrators. Overburdened by this head-on opposition, these reports constitute a monotonous litany.

Elisabetta Ponti, the first to file a report, described one violent episode. Alone in her house except for her young daughters, she fearfully watched as Marcantonio Veriani, a corporal of the Public Health Magistracy, and two of his guards, Barbaccia and Battilano, approached her house. After brutally entering, they made advances: "Be quiet, we are not here to harm you"; and, more explicitly, "I'd like your good graces." Although it was primarily the corporal who wanted to sleep with her, his subordinates tried to convince Elisabetta to accept his proposition. "Go talk to the corporal. He wants to exchange a few words with you," Barbaccia said, pushing her into a small room. There, after the door had been closed, Elisabetta was offered money for sexual favors. Sensing danger, she began to scream, "Leave me alone!" The corporal, however, angered by her resistance, kicked her and forced her to "have carnal relations." On leaving the house, Corporal Marcantonio actually bragged to his men about his violent actions against the woman, revealing that moment of intimacy and solidarity among men after a rape. Surprisingly, however, the two guards testified in Elisabetta's favor.[14]

The textile worker Giovanni di Giorgio Uberti experienced a violent episode of a very different kind, which he immediately reported to the chancellor. He described how the door of his locked house had been forced open on 19 October. Two guards suddenly appeared before the tailor, his daughter-in-law, and her children. Giovanni recounted, "One of the guards was quite young and dressed in brown. The other was also young but dark. . . . He wore a hat and had very long hair that hung in his face." The two men began to scream at me to get ready to go to the lazaret, yelling, "Get dressed! We will come back to get you after we go to the nearby house of a family of ten people." Somewhat later they returned and made a proposal. Approaching the subject indirectly, they asked for some wine. The daughter-in-law instantly realized what they had in mind. "Wait!" she said, and ran upstairs. According to the tailor, she came down with seven *testoni* "and counted them into their hands and in my presence." After they had gotten their money, the guards left "in such a hurry that they forgot to lock the house."[15]

In both these cases, the side that was superior in number and better armed won. Because neither the widow Elisabetta, alone in her house, nor the textile worker Giovanni, an old man living with his daughter-in-law and her children, had anything with which to bargain, they were left open to exploitation. They had no other choice but to report the events to the authorities and denounce the abuses without delay.

In a similar chain of events, some gravediggers in the Compagnia della Misericordia—better known as the "priests of Public Health"—were the protagonists. This story is about priorities and prestige. Headed by Simone di Francesco Galli, called "Ventitre," the group was on its way back after burying a plague victim when they ran into Piero di Antonio Pauletti, a soldier just arriving in the city at the

Croce Gate. Anyone wearing His Highness's colors had to be a person of quality, and the arrogant gravediggers quickly began arguing among themselves. Whereas they ought to have allowed him to go ahead, they instead walked more closely together, making it impossible for him to walk down the middle of the road.

The soldier, knowing how to defend his honor, "took his dagger in his hand" and hit one of the aggressive gravediggers "on the hand, although not very badly." The other gravediggers quickly reacted and "turned against him, hitting him with sticks and with even the cross." The principal defendant, Simone Galli, and the soldier fell to the ground. Galli succeeded in grabbing the dagger and struck the soldier "on the left breast" and "on the face, causing a large bloody wound." The gravediggers then covered the soldier's body with a cloak and took it to their quarters, where, seven days later, Piero Pauletti "lost his life miserably."[16]

This brawl, which broke out through lack of courtesy, reminds us of the fight between Lodovico, who later became Father Cristoforo, and "the Signore, an arrogant and professional troublemaker."[17] The gravedigger Simone, like Father Cristoforo, made peace with the victim's relatives. He thus avoided capital punishment, being sentenced instead to a term in jail followed by exile in Pisa with his comrades.

Violence is stingy with respect to details. Breaking into the text, it cuts the links between characters and between those characters and their past. A brutal and opaque device, it does not let anything come through to the surface. Only one element in the story we have just recounted suggests a different reconstruction. Both the victim, the soldier Pauletti, and his assassin, the gravedigger Galli, came from Madonna del Sasso. Perhaps old arguments lurked behind the violence? This trace was not examined in the trial; it remains merely a clue, suspended in air.

In open contrast with these stories of abuse, the following episode reads like an exemplary play. Centered on a terrible joke, it introduces us to those mechanisms that direct the actors behind the curtain. Like a mask, a Public Health Magistracy uniform hid and gave a different character to fundamental and persistent conflicts. This episode occurred in the little village of Galiano. Surprisingly, the village authorities refused to resolve the case, so the victim of the crime brought his suit to Florence.

The facts are easily recounted. One October morning, Bartolomeo di Berna Cammelli, a hospital guardian, noticed on his way out that his front door had been covered with excrement. His wife, Anastasia, and their eighteen-year-old daughter came out of the house when they heard the man's shouts and swearing. The three were met by the taunting laughter of some Public Health officials. Furious, Bartolomeo denounced the act.[18]

All of the people involved were interrogated, and a picture of rural social conflicts was reproduced, with as much care as an *in vitro* experiment. Bartolomeo had served for many years as a guardian of the local hospital, which was owned by the Florentine hospital of Santa Maria Nuova. Thus, he was unfamiliar with farmwork. His aggressors, in contrast, although they wore Public Health uniforms, were all peasants: the first defendant, Giacomo di Marchionne Elmi, worked on the estate of Signora Cerini; the second, Stefano di Domenico del Rosso, worked for the nuns of Boldrona; the third, Pierino di Nello, a day laborer ("I worked wherever I happened to be"), was so poor that he probably could not afford a wife; the fourth, Antonio di Serra Serrani, worked the land of Prince Don Lorenzo; and the last, Sandro di Giovanni Nelli, was a wagon driver ("When I go to Florence with one of Signor Marchese del Monte's animals, I also take along one of mine"). Moreover, the rector of Galiano was himself a peasant, which explains his refusal to denounce the action to Florence. He rented his house and his farm from Signor Ubaldino Ubaldini. It was therefore no wonder that the rector decided to cover up his fellow villagers' prank on the guardian Bartolomeo.

The action, carefully described in all its crude details, highlights the consequences of inequalities of wealth. The despicable Cammelli was envied because the hospital had for years provided him with his own house. He was also married and had a young and desirable daughter. Whereas he worked in a dry, clean environment year-round, the peasants and the wagon driver had only now escaped the cold, muck, and fatigue because the village rector had appointed them as guards during the epidemic, providing them also with uniforms and shelter near the village gates. Why not dirty one who had always kept his hands clean? The excrement thrown at the front door of the despised Cammelli is a bodily metaphor for the life of the fields. Like mud, it dirties; like manure, it stinks. This old image of the land and the intestines provokes amusement.

EXCESSES AND PECULIARITIES

Most sanitary personnel worked in hospitals, lazarets, and convalescent homes, not only taking care of patients but also staffing these institutions. They worked in supply rooms, kitchens, laundries, and disinfection rooms. These men and women were suspected of wrongdoing by the hospitalized, who so charged them.

In a web of violence and reciprocal abuse, conflicts abounded within the walls of these institutions: employees and guards against provisioners; buyers and cooks against nuns and priors. Most of these denunciations concerned thefts. Hospitals, lazarets, and clinics became magical theaters in which linens, clothes, blankets, and mattresses disappeared. Then, after they had been wrapped and passed from hand to hand along corridors and halls and through windows, bars, and doors, they would suddenly reappear in the house of some corrupt woman. Internal and external mediation and complicity were manifold. Furtive eyes watched and gossip and hearsay traced this endless movement of goods, this unquenchable thirst for material possessions.

A long account, "The Memory of the Excesses Committed by the Officials of the Convalescent Home of Ruciano," clearly delineates this web of complicities. In this document, the mail carrier Jacopo confessed to having participated in crimes, asserting that stolen blankets had been transformed in the hospital itself into clothes that could be traded in the city marketplace.[19] In the middle of the action was a storeroom worker, Paolo Landi, who seduced and organized the nurses. The first co-conspirator was Domenica; she stole food and linens, resewing the material into other forms. Next Lucrezia, "the Pistoian servant who worked for Doctor Tedeschini," aided in the operation. Her naïveté enabled Landi to seduce her "with a promise to marry her."

Landi's prime helper was Aurelia, the Ruciano hospital "superindendent"; she also engaged in "carnal relations" with him. Together they ran a lucrative business based on trafficking in stolen goods. They took apart linens and made them into aprons and other clothes; once they even secretly made a talisman out of some bedsheets. Unflaggingly, Paolo and Aurelia used "new sheets to make aprons, socks and other things." They often went to the storerooms for a "secret meal." Thus they transformed the hospital into a small factory where stolen materials were diligently taken apart and sewn up again, turning out all kinds of garments. "A sheet tied up with an apron" was lowered "from Aurelia's window" to be taken to Lucrezia, an accomplice on Via Gora. From the same window, bread was thrown to the mail carrier below "with the words that he should leave it in the hole behind the palace, which had been specially prepared to hide the objects that were stolen each day."

A chain of accomplices stretched from Ruciano to Florence. As in a rigmarole, senseless and endless, we read that Corporal Antonio gave a sack to the peasant Domenico. Domenico took it to the city on a mule, where, at the Piazza d'Arno, he gave it to a laundryman, who was "short with a brown beard." This laundryman left the sack in the storage closet of a shoemaker "from Ricoboli," where it remained. The intertwining of the texts into a spiral of lists, the endless repetition of the same charges, and the chasing after identical goods confirm the same impression of a never-ending social capacity to react.

Although the epidemic put an end to some commerce, it opened other avenues. By granting those normally excluded from more traditional forms of exchange the right to take part in new forms, this turnover was accelerated. In these confined spaces, where communication was dense, the scene of a macabre party was played out, a sort of ritualized, somewhat predictable staging of the turning upside down of all things—of waste and of license. The speed of the circulation and stealing was proportional to the risk involved: thefts of clothing, secret meals, deflowerings and other sexual relations were played on the chessboard of death. It was a fantastic game that, for those who understood it, had its own rules.

Obviously, the patients were the losers. Many had been hospitalized for no reason: "I have seen people who, having fallen from a horse, were wounded in the head and the arm. Then they were taken to the lazaret."[20] In addition, the hospitalized were generally forced to share a bed with three or maybe even four other patients, thereby passively assisting in the widespread stealing. Still, the patients, men and women who were suspected plague carriers, did not lose their morale. Rather, they reactivated the mechanisms of protest and denunciation.

The correspondence between the lazaret superintendents and Public Health officials echoed constantly the complaints, protests, and insults of those who, forced into the institutions, kept the Public Health

Magistracy employees under surveillance. One said, "A certain Margherita di Vincenzo Cappelli, a nurse at San Miniato, and her friend, a nurse's aide, have come to me. They reported that they have seen a number of poor young women raped and that a number of other excesses have been committed."[21] They also said that the barber-surgeon Coveri "examines his patients with the glasses of Galileo."[22] In addition, they surmised, "As far as Lisabetta is concerned, she claims to have been poisoned with fruits and wine, but I believe that she filed the report in anger."[23] They voiced many general irritations: "Many complain that the food has been malignantly administered," and so forth.[24]

The reactions of patients rarely reached the extreme. Raffaello di Giovanni Bacci, though, imprisoned at the lazaret of San Miniato because he was caught writing a denunciation against a Public Health employee, escaped and ran back to the city. There he was arrested and returned to the hospital. Then "he pretended to be very sick, so he was extracted from the jail and brought to the ward. From the ward, he managed to escape again, naked." Arrested a second time, he was brought before the chancellor, to whom he confessed that he had run away "because of the strange things that were done to him in jail and in the ward by those officials."[25] Maria di Matteo Porta was also unwilling to accept enforced hospitalization. She escaped only eight days after being admitted. Her reasons, however, were different: she was three months pregnant and had two daughters, eleven and sixteen years old. Maria escaped through a door that had been left open. "Jesus helped me for the sake of those two children," Maria said, "and besides, I couldn't stand the stench."[26]

NECROMANCY BOOKS, A STICK, AND BAGS OF SUSPICIOUS POWDERS

Besides the protests against abuses and the quantity and quality of food, there were also accusations with ramifications that crossed into complex semantic universes. Hospitals were the epicenters for charges of poisoning; although a specific mode of social interaction should have led to patients' recovery, hospitals were instead turned into institutions of death. In this way, the epidemic took on the guise of a lethal poisonous pollution that was spread deliberately.

The image of a doctor who administered poison rather than medicine has long-established anthropological roots.[27] Generally, this image originated in people's diffidence toward healing practices that claimed to be exclusively scientific yet whose validity was questioned. In Florence, the small group of highly specialized physicians aroused great hostility in the population. The epidemic underlined the clash between two systems meant to deal with the crisis. The sanitary system was highly centralized, controlled from above, and structured in a series of exact hierarchies; but medical knowledge, as a body of ideas, traditions, and practices, did not necessarily coincide with administrative procedure. In short, a hospital's organization, the hierarchy of its personnel, its administration of care, and its scrutiny by the Public Health Magistracy resulted from a political decision, selected from among a plethora of possible avenues, to impose a series of measures which some defined as "the dictatorship of the Public Health Magistracy."[28]

Hospitalization forced patients to acknowledge that being inside the sanitary system did not alleviate the anxiety of being actually treated; nor did the professionalism claimed by the guild of doctors compensate for the exclusion of traditional healers and remedies based on oral lore. Patients realized too that they were at the mercy of a system based on inequality, in which Public Health employees grew rich at their expense, capitalizing on the horrible situation.[29] The hostilities, grudges, and envy that enshrouded the relationship between patients and Public Health personnel moved along an inclined plane, slipping from denunciations of abuse to the disturbing and unpredictable denunciation of poisoning.

At the beginning of the epidemic, Bonifazio Hospital, one of the oldest in the city, was involved in a complex legal struggle. Specifically, two trials highlighted the unstable symbiosis between denunciations of common illicit behavior and the more rare accusations of plague spreading. The first trial, against the buyer Benedetto Bettoni, started with the suspicion of profiteering. The second, against Doctor Leandro Ciminelli, stemmed from a charge of sorcery.

The first episode constituted the more rational, predictable side of the emergency. It was an astute crime, consistent with the position of the man involved. The events revolved around a reassuring daily routine. Bettoni pocketed the overhead that was arbitrarily imposed on the food supplies he delivered to the hospital. The accusing witnesses were tradespeople in the Mercato Vecchio: butchers, apprentices, and fishermen, who were careful about the quantity, quality, and price of the merchandise they sold. The voices from the market tables communicated an illusion of good health, inscribing the dialogue on a set of dietetic and, consequently, daily habits.

As often happens in a discussion of food commerce, the intrigue in this case surfaced within the family unit. Bettoni's relatives were peasants who traded their livestock with the very butchers who testified in his favor at the Magistracy. Having been a middleman for a long time between his relatives and the tradespeople, Bettoni could have cheated the hospital's accountant at any time. In this picture, the plague was superfluous, an irrelevant background event. Benedetto was an old employee; he had been working as a buyer for more than fifteen years. Thus, intrigue and profit motivated not only those who had worn the official uniform of the Public Health Magistracy for only a few weeks, but also those who had spent their entire lives in the service of the institution. This first trial, which opens Bonifazio's doors for us, ended with the firing of the buyer and a long jail sentence.[30]

The trial against the Neapolitan, Doctor Leandro Ciminelli, was completely different. Charged with having poisoned his patients and with having exhibited violent behavior, he was inseparable from the epidemiological context.

Doctor Leandro was the first defendant who did not belong to the common people. In social status, he was far from the crowds of textile workers, day laborers, and artisans we have examined thus far. In his letters he reveals shades of grief and anger, as well as a sense of humor; in other words, he offers us a full character. Perhaps coincidentally, the trial documents did not record his testimony before the court, only the words of his accusers. By a curious stylistic coincidence, this vacuum becomes an integral part of his character, providing him with an essential detail: that is, the Neapolitan physician left behind a written report, put together and written either in his room at Bonifazio or in the cell to which he was later taken. Its mediated and reflective prose, characterized by a baroque style, showed clearly that it belonged to a *higher* language, the language of those who ruled. Because the trial documents lack the doctor's own words, they inadvertently miss those rapid discussions that would have made Leandro's testimony similar to those of other defendants, whose vivid imaginations were so like those of novelistic characters. Ciminelli had nothing in common with the world of artisans and the picaresque; rather, his story revolved around the artificial world of correspondence.

The plague had not yet been officially declared in Florence when the Neapolitan doctor wrote a nervous letter, full of criticism and fear, from Bonifazio Hospital to the magistrates. He attentively followed the spread of the disease among servants and nuns and immediately denounced the opportunistic thefts of clothes by assistants and barber-surgeons. "The other day they all gathered together to take a cloak from the body of a man who was about to be buried. If not for my threats, they would have done it." [31] There was no medicine, and the hospital was "a miserable, impractical home. . . . The blessed nuns and the prior are so outraged, one would think I had brought the disease. . . . I sweat blood, all in the service of God." Perhaps he had a premonition of the suspicions that were to arise. Still, he devotedly pointed out problems, including how inadequate the supplies of the medicine needed to fight the spreading infection were.

> I should be the one to carry out all the mechanical tasks because these people are new to the plague. This hospital used to take care of only two or three patients at a time, and the herbalist's storeroom is empty. When medicine does come, it comes in only small amounts and is distributed according to the prior's orders. . . . In spite of the large garden, I cannot have a place to grow oranges, grapes, lettuce, and other vegetables. . . . I urge Your Honors to send me a person who knows how to write and who can help me with these burdens. [32]

Instead, the magistrate merely sent a visitor, Giovanni Fabbri, to the hospital at the end of August. He said that there was no reason to worry; the few reported deaths were caused by the "same sickness" of little importance and by a "disease" that could not be identified. [33]

Somewhat later, the chancellor received a note entitled "The Opinion of His Excellency Doctor Signor Leandro, Physician at Bonifazio." [34] Its tone was dramatic.

> Crowds of plague-stricken people are coming here, and it is impossible to stem the tide of pestilence with inexpert people who are not used to witnessing death, and it will grow all the more as the doctors' own fear grows; I am amazed that I myself, continually assailed by the poison of fevers and the bitter fumes of the plague, be it by the grace of God or by my own defenses, remain well and have caught nothing. Yet others of my profession keep so far away from me that I can scarcely hear their words; they are so laden with herbs, sponges, vinegar, and balls that one might think this the age of Pallas rather than of Mercury. That is

why the epidemic spread in Palermo. . . . Doctors ran away, and thus fear and contagion grew. But when, either because of penalties imposed or for mercenary gain, they turned all their efforts to overcoming this evil and grew more confident that they could treat it, the disease lost its strength and its fire went out. There was no other cure, although someone attributed the end of the plague to Santa Rosalia. . . . Now we have to follow that example, ensuring that all hospital doctors know how to deal with this disease and to assist patients. . . . The grave-diggers, . . . going around uncontrolled in the city day and night, spread the disease throughout the city. They should always be accompanied by a guard when they are called for their work. . . . Last night, twenty-one people were released as healed. I was proud . . . to have my lost reputation, won by my sweat and blood, somewhat vindicated.

Leandro's unsolicited advice, his belief that he was different, and his professional arrogance were to be rewarded by isolation. Proud of his Galenic education, he referred to distant examples and thought of his Florentine colleagues and the ecclesiastical personnel with disdain. He also dictated instructions to His Highness's magistrates, thereby cutting the threads of potential support one by one.

On 10 September, a letter from the chaplain of Bonifazio announced Ciminelli's arrest and provided particulars. The doctor had been found with foreign currency in his possession. Furthermore, some "mysterious powders" were discovered in his bag.[35] A few days earlier, strange rumors had reached the chancellor's office concerning the "peculiarities of the doctor at Bonifazio." These rumors had convinced the authorities that Ciminelli should be fired and thrown in jail or, better, given his familiarity with patients, a lazaret. The final decision was a compromise between the two alternatives. The doctor was taken to the jail of San Marco Vecchio, where people and their belongings were waiting to be purged of possible contamination.

The following days were filled with yelling: "He screams like a dog"; "for God's sake, . . . I'm afraid he won't leave this place alive unless he is taken somewhere handcuffed and bound"; "if Your Highness so desires, I will be happy to keep him in my rooms."[36] Eventually, Cosimo Ramazzotti, the commissioner of San Marco Vecchio, was moved by the fate of the poor Neapolitan doctor, who remained ignored and desperate in solitude. The commissioner was even willing to share his own rooms with the prisoner, as the doctor seemed so different from all of the others.

In the meantime, at Bonifazio Hospital, Ciminelli's successors were replaced one after another. On 3 September Ludovico Aggiunti was appointed to the post, but on the sixteenth a letter signed by Niccolò Giovagnuoli, a former doctor of the lazaret of San Miniato, hinted at Aggiunti's sudden surprising departure. Doctor Giovagnuoli's description of Bonifazio Hospital concurred with Leandro's: patients were dying, the staff was untrained, the large "family" of gravediggers, barber-surgeons, and servants who served the new doctor were in poor health. Even the worried, melancholic doctor himself did not feel very well, reporting,

> I have been yawning for the past two evenings. I have also had shivers and have felt very hot, to the extent that once I almost fainted. I usually suffer from this sickness in the fall. Because I suffer heart obstructions and palpitations, my doctors told me before I came here to drink Tettuccio water with some iron. Your Excellencies should decide whether I can properly take care of this hospital,

where, despite burning aromatic herbs, "the air stank."[37] By removing the proud and arrogant Ciminelli, the magistrate had precipitated a crisis at Bonifazio; its command was being passed from hand to hand. The portrait of the fearful hypochondriac Doctor Giovagnuoli coincided with all the Neapolitan physician's satirical observations, his mockery of the precautions of his Florentine colleagues, who protected themselves with a variety of "herbs, sponges, vinegar," and perfumed balls.

In spite of Commissioner Ramazzotti's petitions on Leandro Ciminelli's behalf, the doctor remained in jail. The magistrates were preparing the trial, and no decision was to be made before the end of this legal procedure.

On 17 October 1630, Corporal Ottavio Diligenti of the Otto Magistracy submitted a detailed report. He wrote:

> In Florence there is a certain Doctor Leandro Ciminelli, a Neapolitan or a Sicilian, who works at Bonifazio. A man of bad spirit and thought, he has been seen possibly spreading the plague. Also, perhaps because he has so many patients, he has administered some powders and liquids . . . that resulted in some twelve to fifteen deaths per day. Since Ciminelli's removal, only fifteen people have died. In Leandro Ciminelli's bag we found some strange powders, a stick, and necromancy books. He was mean to people and a few days earlier hit Domenico Vaselli, the herbalist at Bonifazio, twice with a knife. . . . He also hit the servant Iachopo Bastieri with a stick for no apparent reason. . . . He released the monied patients the day before they died, almost as if he knew. . . . There is evidence that he is an impious man. Once, when he saw his servant Francesco kneeling before an altar, he screamed, "Get up or I'll

beat you!" Moreover, he gave a chicken to the barber-surgeons Marco and Cosimo and the herbalist Piero Landi two weeks ago. Aware of the danger, the two barber-surgeons ate the chicken and then immediately took the herbalist's cure. The herbalist did not take the remedy himself and died.[38]

The charges outline what could be called the career of a plague spreader. The medical profession was absolutely of secondary importance, for plague spreading stemmed primarily from the preexisting character of the poisoner. Leandro was reputed to have begun spreading the disease in order to become a doctor, attracting droves of potential new victims to Bonifazio Hospital. It was in such places of painful sociality that the healer/killer could best operate, carrying all the instruments he needed: the stick, the books, and the powders he used to kill patients and colleagues. The small detail mentioned in the vicar's letter announcing Ciminelli's arrest, the foreign currency, completed the portrait. This fact expanded the plague spreader's stereotype into a horizon of social opposition actually felt by those who launched the accusation. The plague spreader, like some types of witch, was an internal enemy, one who enjoyed links outside the community.[39] This agent established a dangerous connection between the inside and the outside. Besieged by the plague, the people of Florence identified the danger with people from elsewhere—those who traveled and those who crossed borders—so that the sanitary and political administration of the epidemic was characterized by the opposition between internal and external space, the one safe, the other threatening.

Leandro was a foreigner, his past unknown and suspect. In addition, his profession inevitably put him in contact with the inside of those bodies he threatened. The charge specified that poison was administered by water, that is, administered from the outside to the inside, and repeated the presence of both dimensions—inside and outside—in the duel fought on the hospital bed between life and death. Plague spreaders were therefore individuals who altered the normal relationship between the inside (the city, the body) and the outside. This image expressed, in a symbolic form, the latent fears that were linked to the passage of the disease, a threatening confusion of limits.

The chancellor decided to deliver Doctor Leandro's bag to a commission of experts. After examining its contents, they were to report their findings to the Magistracy. This very delicate operation was thus separated from the rest of the investigation, which centered on the episodes of violence and conflict at Bonifazio Hospital.

On 18 September, the chancellor himself went to the hospital to make the interrogations.[40] The first witness was Jacopo di Bastiano. "He called me once, about twenty days ago, and asked me to call the herbalist Piero Landi. Because I didn't do so immediately, he almost hit me with a stick. Then he didn't. I don't know what kinds of medicine he prescribed, and I don't know whether he took bribes from people."

This sober and perhaps fearful testimony was followed by the attestation of the linen supplier Martino Antonio.

"One evening many days ago, all of us were in bed, and the Neapolitan doctor came to see us. I got up, and he made me carry a lantern while he went to call Domenico Vaselli. He had a stick in his hand and wanted to beat us, but I ran away and so didn't see what happened afterwards." Martino's testimony did not verify the charges against Leandro. The violence of which he was accused was all in the stick and in the desire ("he wanted to beat"), but the action itself remained suspended, unfinished.

A third witness came forward to testify, Francesco di Giovanni Bongianni, "the Neapolitan physician's servant."

> A few days ago, in the evening, my master called me. He gave me a torch and took me to the room of the herbalist Vaselli. Since Vaselli hadn't gone to see the patients and hadn't written his report, the doctor wanted to beat him with a stick. But he did not, after the herbalist asked for forgiveness. The nuns have the doctor's money, and his bag is in Giovan Batista's rooms. . . . Whenever the doctor called on his patients, I noticed that he gave them water and some dairy products, but I'm not an expert on these things. . . . I don't know whether he ever hurt anybody because I've only been in the hospital for six days.

According to this witness, Doctor Ciminelli's anger seemed justified. The herbalist Vaselli, who chose to remain in his room rather than visiting patients and prescribing medicine, appeared to deserve Leandro's wrath. Up to this point, the testimonies traced the narrative with increasing intensity, and the details provided in the first testimony became more understandable in the second and the third.

The barber-surgeon Marco Parenti was called to testify after the servant.

> One evening, the Neapolitan doctor went to Domenico Vaselli's room with a stick. . . . From what I was told, he struck the herbalist on the

hand. I had to bandage it because he had been scratched. This happened because Vaselli failed to make his rounds because he had a hurt knee. I also know that Ciminelli went around at night, claiming that he had the authority of His Highness and that he could do whatever he wanted. The day after, when Vaselli was seeing a patient, the doctor called two gravediggers and asked them to put the herbalist in jail. At this point, Vaselli allowed himself to be locked up. Then, on the same day, Doctor Pesciolini took the key from the barber-surgeons so that he could go visit the sick nuns. When the Neapolitan doctor found out about this, he took some sticks and called some patients. Because people intervened, he didn't beat them, but a great noise grew in the hospital, and even Doctor Pesciolini arrived on the scene. The Neapolitan doctor threatened us all, as if he owned the hospital. The same morning, Vaselli was freed and moved in with the sacristan for safety. The Neapolitan doctor sent two people to arrest Vaselli and put him in jail again. . . . As far as medicine is concerned, I don't know if he did things he was not supposed to do. I don't even know what he did. I have seen his prescriptions, and they are empirical potions, since he probably knows little about physics. . . . I don't know if he wanted to steal money. I only know that when a priest died, he gave his one hundred *denari* to the Public Health Magistracy. All the money is now in the hands of the nuns, and I have nothing else to say about him, either good or bad.

Maybe Ciminelli was a violent man. The hostility around him began to coagulate, a fact that the barber-surgeons, the herbalist, and his assistants from the guild had made very clear to him. In his first letter to the magistrate, Leandro complained that his staff was so incompetent that he had to perform mechanical tasks himself. This leads us to assume that there had been arguments between the doctor and the barber-surgeons and suggests that the barber-surgeons refused to perform incisions and cauterizations of mature bubos. Perhaps the personnel preferred Doctor Pesciolini and talked to him about their problems with the hated doctor. Witnesses even denied Leandro the simple acknowledgment of identity, preferring to call him "the Neapolitan doctor."

The last witness, the barber-surgeon Cosimo, denied everything. "I have seen nothing, nor do I know anything, about the fight between the Neapolitan doctor and the herbalist. I don't know what the doctor did, because I only began to work there right before he left."

Of the six characters examined in Corporal Ottavio's investigation, two were dead (Domenico Vaselli and Piero Landi, the herbalists); Jacopo Bastiano denied having ever been beaten by the doctor; and the servant Francesco did not bring up the episode of the altar or his master's reputed irreligiosity. Finally, the two barber-surgeons, Marco and

Cosimo, did not even mention the episode of the poisoned chicken, in which they had been involved.

Whereas the deaths of the two herbalists can be explained, the contradictory, indirect reports on the doctor's violent fits, as well as the other witnesses' silence, appear to be unmotivated. The four witnesses most likely agreed to remain silent, and only one event, apparently unrelated to Ciminelli's story, can help explain this passivity.

On 14 September, just five days before the chancellor went to the hospital to take testimonies, a trial had commenced against the imprisoned buyer Bettoni, a former employee of the same hospital. Thus Bonifazio Hospital was already at the center of a large judicial investigation that threatened to involve other members of the staff. The Bettoni case was taking a bad turn, and the detailed accusations, the testimonies against him, and, most importantly, the defendant's own confession enabled everyone to predict a verdict of guilty. We should therefore not rule out the possibility that developments in this parallel trial influenced the witnesses in the Ciminelli case. They may have been afraid of an investigation of their own perhaps not quite perfect job performance. They wanted to keep the Magistracy out of the hospital altogether. In the meantime, the chancellor ordered that the "Neapolitan doctor's" bag be sent from Bonifazio to San Francesco, a lazaret for men only, "asking Doctor Giovagnuoli to open it with all the necessary disinfections and to make an inventory of its contents. After the powders are examined, . . . a report detailing the results should be sent to the Magistracy."[41]

On 6 November the magistrates received the results of the analysis, which they immediately forwarded to the grand duke.

> As far as the quality of the medicine is concerned, we could not come to a final conclusion, because the assisting herbalists are dead, and the others do not know anything about it. But, having examined the contents of the bag, we did find some powders containing traces of arsenic and antimony, as well as some other substances that we do not recognize. We think that all the substances found in the bag, together with the money, could have been used for preparing medicine.[42]

Thus, the mysterious powders were harmless and, when properly prepared, could be safely administered to patients.

Ciminelli remained in custody, although he was allowed to move from his enclosed cell to one with fresh air.[43] This satisfied Commissioner Ramazzotti very much: "The Neapolitan physician desires Your Excellencies' grace and wishes to receive his clothes so that he can change. Now that he is in a room with fresh air, his disposition is improving. Given his present sickness, he would like to have some of the powder from his bag so that he can keep taking it just as he was accustomed to do at the hospital."[44] This request looked like the perfect response to the charge of poisoning people: Ciminelli took the powder himself, claiming that it had saved him from the plague while working at Bonifazio.

In the second half of October, the news of Ciminelli's acquittal reached San Marco Vecchio. Leandro wrote to thank the magistrates, taking the opportunity to accuse those who were jealous of him of putting in his bag substances "of which I will tell Your Excellencies in due time." On that very day, 19 October, he sent another thank-you letter to the magistrates for the clothes he had received with Commissioner Ramazzotti's help: "I greatly thank Your Illustrious Excellencies for returning the clothes to me. . . . I beg that everything be returned to me as ordered, so that foreigners and prisoners are not freely killed under Your Excellencies' authority.[45]

Leandro hit his target. He accused the magistrates, proud of their efficiency and impartiality, of having almost condemned a foreigner. With irony and perspicacity, he understood his exclusion, the reason he had been deprived of his own name: he was not a citizen of Florence.

Doctor Ciminelli had always been a courageous man. He did not forget easily, and he wanted to be compensated for his suffering. Foremost, he wanted his belongings, still at the hospital, returned. He listed what was missing: "besides the money and the powders, nine pairs of black silk socks donated to me by the General of the Navy, a Neapolitan silk belt, two dozen silk laces, a new Milanese hat, a German knife with a sheath, a little knitted silk purse bearing a Maltese cross which belonged to my brother, a reliquary shaped like a silver cross, another beautiful reliquary, and other Agnus Deis."[46] How could a man be accused of irreligiosity when he kept among his most prized objects two reliquaries and various Agnus Deis?

On 5 November the magistrates published the doctor's writ of freedom, and on the twelfth they ordered that sixty *scudi* per month be paid to him in compensation "for all the time that he served at Bonifazio."[47] Doctor Leandro's integrity was therefore completely acknowledged, and he was repaid for the service offered with more zeal than others received. But for him it was still not enough.

On 17 November he personally went to the chancellor's office to denounce Giovan Battista Morandini, a priest at the hospital, for stealing his purse, goods, and money. Morandini refused to appear at the Magistracy, but he did write a few letters to clarify the incident. This rather unusual behavior "led one to think that he [Morandini] had taken improper care of said goods."[48] The magistrate, however, could not intervene because Morandini was a member of the church: the matter had to be examined by the archbishop. Thus, the magistrate returned to Leandro all the documents—his attestations and Morandini's letters—so that he could do whatever he felt appropriate with them.

For Leandro, though, the matter remained open. Later, in early December, the doctor wrote the magistrate a letter requesting compensation "for the time he served in San Marco Vecchio." The request led to a new exchange of letters, and the magistrates consulted with the grand duke. "Others were paid," the grand duke observed, "one *scudo* for each day that they served in the convalescent homes." The amount paid to the Neapolitan doctor, he asserted, should be the same. Being detained for suspicion of poisoning people was therefore to be treated as the equivalent of a simple convalescence. "After seeing all the documents produced, the magistrate compensated Doctor Leandro Ciminelli with that sum, which precluded any further request he may make."[49]

The trial of Leandro Ciminelli therefore ended with an acquittal; indeed, the doctor was even compensated for his detention. It was the only case in Florence that opened, and then soon closed, the possibility of a human cause for the epidemic, of an anthropological reading of the crisis attributed to the malicious intentions of an internal element.

Besides the Neapolitan doctor, we have found another possible plague spreader profile: Bastiano Giannelli, the charlatan who went all the way to Pistoia to sell his merchandise and then, in the Piazza del Duomo, was singled out and arrested. We have already discussed him, in our group of travelers, since his work as "traveling salesman" was characterized by continuous journeys (see Chapter 1).

Leandro and Bastiano, taken together, and despite their differences and social separation, complete the profile of the plague spreader. One was an urban healer, the other a country healer. Leandro, educated at the academy and a follower of Galen's theories, was listed among the doctors of the Public Health Magistracy and worked at Bonifazio Hospital. Bastiano, formerly Giuseppe Rosaccio's apprentice, was both a charlatan and shoemaker, who sold Saint Apollonia's herbs in the countryside near Volterra. Both were foreigners, the former from Naples and the latter from Burgo a Buggiano, and they combined distant origins with a similar practice of healing, although in different places and environments.

If mobility and the healing art were the characteristics that explained the perversion of poisoners/healers, the defendants' contexts and their accusers deserve some attention. Ciminelli was a high-ranking member of the guild of doctors and was denounced by the personnel directly under his command. Specifically, in the denunciation prepared by Ottavio Diligenti the accusers were two barber-surgeons and two servants of Bonifazio Hospital. Bastiano Gianelli, in contrast, a healer of the poor and of peasants (presumably without state sanction), was accused by the mob. In many respects the two characters were very different; but from the standpoint of the accusers, despite completely different environments, the common suspicion of "spreading the plague" could take shape and be openly pronounced: at the top, at the bottom; in the countryside, in the square, in the hospital; against a superior, a foreigner, an official healer, or a charlatan. The only common elements of the targets were their sex, their practice of healing, and their foreign origins.

In the letters sent by Doctor Leandro to the Florentine magistrate, hospital life had already been depicted as a competitive and argumentative environment. Besides having to compensate for the barber-surgeons' shortcomings, Ciminelli was also constantly opposed by the hospital's ecclesiastical personnel. Furthermore, the prior, without any medical competence, ordered medicine for the hospital in amounts that were totally insufficient. Before the outbreak of the plague, Bonifazio had had only "two or three patients." As a result, the herbalist's supply was absolutely inadequate to meet the new needs. The arrival of the foreign doctor—sent by the chancellor, whose own powers were limited in times of emergency—disrupted administrative procedures and the mechanisms for acquiring supplies. The voices and gossip, the violent episodes, the letters to the magistrate, the arrival of "visitors," not to mention the influx of patients, however hard to delineate in detail, confirmed that the hospital had lately become a place of "loosely defined and intensive social interaction."[50] In Bonifazio, as resentments grew the roles and functions of the staff suddenly revealed a margin of uncertainty and ambiguity. Ciminelli himself linked the nuns' proud and distrustful behavior to his own implicit responsibility in spreading the contagion ("thinking that I brought the disease"). Suspicion therefore belonged to the sphere of the predictable, of responses that had been formulated in analogous circumstances and contexts. The conflict, the uncertainty, the desire to redefine and establish new hierarchies, moved within a mental horizon that used the belief in plague spreaders as the ultimate weapon, as the final solution to existing tensions.

In the text presented to the chancellor's office, two parallel elements appeared: first, the character of the plague spreader; second, the "authoritarian" man. The link between the two was weakly suggested, but no causal relation between the intention to kill and an arrogant attitude was indicated; it merely put one after the other. The effect of these accounts is not explanatory but redundant and purely descriptive. The documents begin with a narrative introduction designed to introduce the protagonist and describe his negative rationality: "There is in Florence a certain Leandro Ciminelli. . . . Of bad spirit and thought, he has been seen possibly spreading the plague in the city." Leandro's crimes had therefore been committed *before* his arrival at Bonifazio Hospital, where he came not because of an order of the Public Health Magistracy but for his own precise purpose: "perhaps to have more patients and administer more powders by water."

The tensions apparent in the second part of the denunciatory letters to the magistrate seem, in contrast, to trace another profile, that of the "authoritarian" man. The situation at the hospital was now centered on poorly defined forms of interaction, which were constantly being changed and subverted. The chancellor's interrogations were meant to explore these rivalries. They tended to attribute greater importance to the contrasts between the doctor and other hospital personnel than to the image of the poisoner. The magistrate therefore separated the two parts of the denunciation, asking a team of experts to examine the doctor's bag while he heard the complaints against Doctor Leandro—which ultimately led to his arrest. The hospital employees were apparently satisfied with these measures, despite the fact that they precluded a charge of witchcraft.

In fact, the Florentine Magistracy relied on a long-established cultural and juridical tradition that tended to defuse accusations of witchcraft under the charge of "faking one's identity and abilities." Of course, this fact does not rule out the possibility that the image of the plague spreader—assimilated to that of the sorcerer, with his sticks, books on necromancy, and poisonous powders—was widespread. Such beliefs, if activated during periods of crisis and collective danger, would likely have become an "escape valve" for growing anxieties.[51] The fact that milder mechanisms actually worked efficiently in Florence (as opposed to the explosive social and political climate in which contemporary trials were conducted in Milan) suggests the degree of cohesion between citizens and institutions in Florence.

As time passed, however, the relationship between citizens and Public Health employees deteriorated. In spring 1633, during the third outbreak of the epidemic, the first signs of collective hostility against barber-surgeons, who were held responsible for the spread and persistence of the disease, emerged. Even as bargaining and application of pressure continued, family strategies, once straightforwardly corrupt and clandestinely in violation of regulations, were gradually replaced by open, direct confrontation with Public Health powers. The confrontations with barber-surgeons and other officials were often provoked by women, probably because, as we have already seen, it was the wives, widows, and young women who were locked in the quarantined houses with old people and children.

On the morning of 7 April 1633, the barber-surgeon Annibale Galletti filed a complaint with the chancellor. That day, at the sound of the Ave Maria, he went to 235 Via del Palazzuolo, where a patient awaited his visit. He remained in the house for some time (a fact he specified to stress his own professional care). On his way out he exchanged a few words with a shopkeeper and a tavernkeeper. The latter, "red in the face, told me, 'Get out of here soon or we'll give you the same treatment as was given the man in Camaldoli,'" referring to a barber-surgeon who had to be escorted by guards during his visits. The worried Annibale left quickly. As he was running away, he noticed that people "were quickly leaving their houses, and many women were at their windows screaming, 'We should hang these thieves who want to start all over again after the party is over.' Nothing else happened, because I left as soon as I could."[52]

Tension grew most extreme in another part of the city. In Via Porciaia, four hundred people, mostly women, confronted Jacopo Sassi, the man in charge of the distribution of daily aid to the poor locked in their houses. Large groups of people came out of their front doors, screaming that the barber-surgeons "wanted to fill their empty pockets and waited for the wagon's arrival so they could steal something." It would have been amusing to see what would follow, but Sassi was frightened enough to omit Via Tedesca and Santa Orsola from his rounds, "for fear of confrontations."[53] On the same street, Via Porciaia, in fact, about two hundred people, "whistling and screaming," escorted him to his home on Via Larga. After this episode, Sassi, feeling "great danger and fear," asked "to be relieved of his post."

That popular demonstration, which swept across Florence and arrived at Via Larga, not only threatened Annibale but also served as a warning to all the political powers of the city. Via Larga, which ran between the Convent and Church of San Marco al Duomo, was the street where processions were held, where the body of San Antonino, the protector of the city and representative of the reigning family's political destiny, was traditionally paraded. To the choruses, prayers, and hieratic silences of the procession the crowds from Via Porciaia opposed whistles and screams, breaking the circuit of rituals, both lay and religious.

Quickly realizing the danger, the deputies of the four quarters of the city energetically supported the populace's demand that all lazarets be closed and everyone be granted permission to be treated at home. In order to overcome the opposition of the Public Health Magistracy, which favored the old system of forced hospitalization, one deputy repeated to the city's administrators the charges formulated in the streets: "People will say . . . that in order to keep our power, we facilitate the spread of the disease, we try to make it stay longer to preserve our privileges, . . . and that we have found this new way to maintain our positions, as if it were a good thing to deal always with death."[54]

For a short time this popular demand, supported by the city deputies, was accepted and approved. With the spread of the contagion, however, the inadequate personnel and very high cost of this new decentralized domestic assistance program prevented its extension. The lazarets were reopened.

2

The Universe of Symbols

5

The Political Theater

At the *hora vigesima* on Friday, 15 November 1630, as the plague was mercilessly striking Florence, the rulers of the city, the apostolic vicar, the magistrates, and the public notary opened hearings on the canonization of Domenica da Paradiso, a tertiary Dominican nun and founder of the Convent of Santa Croce (popularly called "Crocetta"). Of all the memorable dead, only she deserved mention in the official remembrance.[1]

Seventy-seven years had passed since Domenica's death. Through a return to the past, the anxiety of the present crystalized. Domenica had not died during the plague; she lived to the ripe old age of eighty. Surrounded by candles and silver, her body now rested in the sacred sepulcher of the convent. During the proceedings, her tomb, far from the city, became a haven that contrasted with the barbarism of the mass burials. The sepulcher at Crocetta served as a precious nucleus around which gathered the court, the highest ecclesiastical officials, senators, and important guild members. Domenica's entombed body was clothed; not so the bodies of plague victims, lying scandalously naked in country graves, surrounded by fences that barely kept the threatening wild dogs at bay. Against the bestiality of the epidemic, the debasement of what was human, and the chaotic acceleration of life and death, the Florentine ruling class chose to focus on one of its own illustrious dead, representing it to the populace through a series of linked positive analogies: the enclosed city, confined by roadblocks, was like the cloistered seclusion of the Convent of Crocetta; likewise the convent, isolated by alleys and houses, was similar to the court. All these spaces stood for *good government,* and it was this myth that the court represented to the city through the memory of Domenica da Paradiso's life.

But this was not the only group involved in the canonization hearings. Doctors and notaries also testified. Unlike the court, which reiterated the legitimacy of its authority through the symbolic story of Domenica, the leaders of these liberal professions recalled the endless wonders attributed to her body. Doctors pointed out the body's miraculous state of preservation, and notaries discussed its thaumaturgical virtues, its ability to cure the disease-stricken. The testimonies of grand duchesses and dignitaries entwined with the lay registry, in which the power of the individual to triumph over evil was represented. Both threads diverged from a third reading, that of the nuns from the convent where Domenica had spent most of her life. Quite predictably, this group's memory ran along biographical lines of a different kind, far from the concreteness of the contemporary crisis.

One element, however, underlay all the testimonies: none of the speakers had ever personally known Domenica, nor had they directly observed any of the miracles attributed to her. In the absence of eye-witnesses, facts were verified by evidence found in biographies and manuscripts kept in the convent.[2] The only surviving oral tradition of any importance was recounted by the "ancient mothers," which the nuns jealously repeated in their testimonies. Moreover, each member of the convent community told an identical narrative; although part of a comprehensive context of written culture, this secluded group remembered a separate oral tradition.[3]

Through these multiple filters, the figure of Domenica da Paradiso emerged from a complex series of reconstructions wherein individual and collective memories were linked to the origins, roots, and gender of the witnesses. It is not completely a coincidence that the choice of this venerable woman for sainthood was linked to a period of time when, after the death of Grand Duke Cosimo II in 1628, two women shared the regency. One of the regents, Grand Duchess Christine of Lorraine, initiated the proposal to open the canonization hearings in Rome. These proceedings also expressed the claims of the female regency, now in transition to the male governance of young Grand Duke Ferdinand II.

DOMENICA NARDINI DA PARADISO

Domenica was born in 1473 in Paradiso, a village on the Ripoli plain, a fact that Annalena de' Pieri, the abbess of the Convent of Santa Brigida in Paradiso, learned from the ancient mothers. Although memory had to stretch far back in time—"fifty years ago"—the visual record seemed almost tactile. The places had hardly changed: Domenica was born "in this village, down toward the main road . . . to some peasants, honorable people, named Nardini." The abbess was unable to remember the exact year, but she believed that Domenica had been "baptized and confirmed in the Catholic faith."[4]

Even before her birth, the girl gave signs of an exceptional destiny, for she caused her mother no pain during the pregnancy. Already in childhood she adopted a frugal life: she never cried, ate only one meal a day, and preferred to pray in silence rather than play with the other children. The villagers of Paradiso said that the girl seemed to be the daughter of rich people: fair and rosy, with curly golden hair that fell to her shoulders.[5]

Like other contemporary figures who were made into saints, her adolescent years were marked by unsettled and complicated relationships with members of her family. After her father's death, her mother tried in vain to force her to marry. Her two sisters treated her with never-ending hostility, an expression of their envy. They appeared ready to accuse her of witchcraft, always a threatening charge to saintly individuals during their lifetime. The rivalry with her sisters knew no end. Filippa accused Domenica of having an affair with a young local priest and attributed her sister's "blood fluxes" to a voluntary abortion rather than to mystical ecstasy. Her other sister, Angela, even tried to poison her. Like characters in fairy tales, Domenica's two bad sisters met with their just deserts: Filippa, who had accused her sister unjustly, succumbed to cancer of the tongue, and Angela, who had attempted to poison her, died of stomach trouble.[6]

Meanwhile, Domenica's spiritual life developed through the rhythms of nature and her work in the fields. Her ecstatic visions elevated fragments of the rural landscape to celestial analogies. The garden, fruit trees, flaming red willows in the grey winter landscape, field chores of trimming and harvesting, the vintage, and wood burning suggested an infinite number of transpositions into mystical language, assimilating the various phases of the Passion into the cycle of the seasons.

After much insistence, Domenica finally left her family and went to the Augustinian Convent of Candeli. She was soon obliged to leave the cloister, however, for reasons of health. She then led a religious life at home in the habit of Santa Brigida until 1499, when she moved to Florence. She found a job there as a servant in the house of Giovanni Samminiati in the Pinti quarter. At the hearings, Albiera de' Guiducci, the wife of Giovanni's nephew, Filippo, reconstructed through the familial memory this particular stage of Domenica's life in Florence.

When she testified in November 1630, Albiera was forty-three years old. She had recently lost her husband, and one of her two sons had also died. She lived in the neighborhood of Sant'Ambrogio, one of the worst hit by the plague. She brought along her sister Maddalena to testify. Albiera told the magistrates that she lived off the interest of two hundred *scudi*. She began to tell her story under oath:

> My deceased husband, Signor Filippo Samminiati, said that his father, Giovanni—who was by then a grandfather, as Vincenzo was already born—had hired a servant from the village of Paradiso. Her name was Domenica, and she appeared to be a saint. In particular, he often said that Domenica, who later founded the Convent of Crocetta, took communion every morning very early, after which she returned to her room for prayer. No one ever saw her around the house.

Nobody could understand, then, how everything was cared for properly. Albiera's sources agreed that Domenica was aided "by a guardian angel," who "took care of the household duties" while she prayed. "Twenty-two people lived in the house, so there was a lot to do, particularly as there was no one else to do the work," Albiera observed with good common sense.

Domenica was eventually freed from a maidservant's destiny. "Because she desired to devote herself completely to God, she retired to the small house where I now live, which belongs to Signor Giovanni." Albiera continued, "She took in other women, including two of Signor Giovanni's sisters, and with nothing but a piece of cloth founded the convent today called Crocetta."[7]

A PIECE OF CLOTH

A piece of cloth marked the beginning of Domenica's practical vocation as a good administrator of the group. Through spinning, weaving, and selling fabrics, she saved enough money to purchase the convent. In Florence, wool- and silkworkers organized in guilds and shops; this group of working women without families therefore aroused the distrust of Cajetano, the head of the Dominicans, under whose rule they wanted to live. Domenica wore the clothes of the order even without ecclesiastical permission. Cajetano prohibited his brothers from having any relations with the group and demanded that the archbishop solve the problem.

In the popular tradition of fairy tales, stories often center on a scene in which a woman changes clothes, thus signifying a change of state. Domenica donned the Dominican robes because she had dreamed that Saint Catherine had given her the clothes of Saint Dominic to wear.[8] When she became an adult, however, she entered the world—including the extremely male-oriented world of the marketplace, as Virginia Malaspina, countess of Villafranca, carefully explained. Seventy-three years old and with a somewhat shaky memory, Virginia forgot some names and relied, unlike Albiera de' Guiducci, on a typically feminine oral tradition. She was, in fact, a pious woman. Fifty-nine years ago, at the Convent of Marta (where Virginia's sister Emilia had become a nun),

> outside, though near, Florence, . . . a certain woman from Camerino, Diamante Pagni or Vanni, if I remember correctly, met Mother Domenica da Paradiso. Diamante told me that Domenica was very virtuous and self-sacrificing. In particular, I recall that she said that Domenica began to think about how to build the convent with one or two pounds of linen. With an admirable constancy, she worked the linen slowly and gradually began to buy the necessary items for the convent. When she went to the market to buy ladles and other little things, people laughed at her and asked, "What do you plan to do with them, Domenica?" But she answered with great confidence, as if she already had the convent, "I am buying them for my convent."

The noblewoman added, "We know that she was never diverted from her holy goal, because she was able to buy the land, which now houses the large Convent of Crocetta, within seven years."[9]

A LARGE QUANTITY OF SEQUINS

By working, selling, and buying, Domenica saved 100 *scudi* in seven years, and on 29 January 1511 she bought the site of the convent for 190 *scudi*. The following day she purchased another piece of property for 240 *scudi,* arousing "great surprise" in the city during this "period of war and other evils."[10]

Sister Angelica del Macchia, prioress of the Convent of Santa Croce, specified in her testimony that the additional money had been given to Domenica by an angel sent from the Madonna. The other sisters, as well as the regents, repeated the story of the miracle of the money from heaven several times during the proceedings.[11] The quantity of gold varied in these recountings, its shining presence serving metaphorically to reiterate the values of a commercial culture that recompensed those who worked with fortitude and prudence.

On Tuesday, 3 December, Grand Duchess Christine of Lorraine, the former regent, testified that one hundred sequins had become fifty thousand *scudi,* which finally endowed the convent fully. The project to build the convent "in those years," she observed, "would have been difficult even for a prince," but Domenica, "of such lowly origins [being a peasant], had pursued her goal and founded the convent, providing it with many things, including approximately fifty thousand *scudi.* We were not surprised that she could spend so much, because we were told that she often received money from heaven."[12]

Perhaps not coincidentally, it was a young male witness, Michelangelo Buonarroti the younger, who detailed the fortune of the convent—that is, the terrestrial origins of part of it. "Giovanni degli Albizi, one of the first workers in the convent, quit to go back to work under Signor Banco da Barberino, his nephew. Barberino ultimately left all his possessions to the convent in his will."[13] In addition, the archbishop of Florence looked favorably on the project, making it possible for Domenica to purchase the land and continue work on the buildings. Moreover, he granted the female congregation the right to wear the Dominican habit, on one condition: Domenica was to place a red cross on the front of the robe.

On 28 April 1513, the group of sisters finally moved into the convent, after receiving ecclesiastical authorization to found it under the authority of the ordinary and the Dominican nuns. On 18 November the archbishop appointed Domenica convent vicar for a term of one year, and on 21 December 1516 Pope Leo X named her vicar for life, a decision later confirmed by another Medicean pope, Clement VII.[14] In fact, during the last years of the Florentine Republic, Domenica withdrew her support from the Savonarola faction and moved ever closer to a position favorable to the Medicis. Beginning in 1515 the prophetic voice emanating from the cloister of Crocetta differed openly from the Savonarolan faith still widespread in the city.[15]

Continuing her testimony, Christine of Lorraine linked this poor peasant's administration of the convent to her own role as regent of the grand duchy of Tuscany:

> We frequently admired the prudence of this good mother. We believed
> that it was something which exceeded the ordinary insofar as she was
> neither a noblewoman nor a woman of letters. . . . Yet she founded
> this convent and provided it with so many good rules and regulations
> that it seemed to us one of the most perfect unions of the spiritual and
> the temporal imaginable. It will certainly stand out for all those who,
> as we have often done, consider the rules and administration that she
> initiated.[16]

Yet at the same time, she considered it obvious—and her sister and
coregent, Mary Magdalen of Austria, concurred—that no "unlettered
citizen" could have ever "naturally" built "the administration and the
government that Domenica had instituted in the house" without
God's guidance "manifesting itself in these simple souls."[17]

The government of Tuscany was analogous to the administration
of the convent: both were gifts of God. Through Domenica, the regents reinforced the strength of the state, providing it with sacred
legitimacy.

POLITICS AND RELIGION

The court testimonies provide long lists of illustrious names of individuals who publicly wanted to support Domenica's status. The favor
she enjoyed in the grand duke's family made her a court saint. In addition, Countess Claudia d'Urbino was devoted to her; after having a
baby in Germany, the countess sent "a baby made of silver" as a votive
offering, "saying that she recognized the happiness of the delivery in
Domenica." Princess Anna, one of Christine of Lorraine's grandchildren, went "from the palace to the convent at three o'clock in the
morning" to venerate the sepulcher. Duke Ferdinand of Mantua and
his wife, Catherine, expressed a similar devotion.[18] Ferdinand I of
Tuscany's daughter, Maria Maddalena de' Medici, a nun at the Convent of Santa Croce, adored Domenica in the same manner. These
Medici women prayed on their knees in front of the tomb and sent
gifts of thanks for easy deliveries, just as a woman of the popular
classes would do. Some even became nuns in the convent founded by
Domenica da Paradiso.[19]

In a sense, the cult also belonged to the city, a fact that the Florentine aristocracy, notably Senators Camillo Rinuccini, Piero Capponi,
and Vincenzo Pitti, clearly acknowledged.[20] Not only were there ex-

ternal justifications, such as the delayed political recuperation of the saint–state relationship, but other, more specific elements also were associated with the model embodied by Domenica. Her biography indicated the presence of Saint Catherine of Siena, her dream of receiving the habit from the saint, and the correspondence sent to the Medicean popes on her behalf by her confessor, Francesco da Castiglione, canon of the Cathedral of San Lorenzo. Domenica's life, like those of Catherine and other contemporary tertiary Dominican "living saints," was characterized by the political encounters chronicled in her letters to the popes.

Like Domenica da Paradiso, Raffaella da Faenza, Domenica Tarugi, and Colomba da Rieti founded Dominican convents in Tuscan and Umbrian cities, assuming responsibility for female congregations during those terrible years of war. In such times of strong and widespread prophetic tension, the mystical escapes that marked the lives of these women were anchored in the quotidian concreteness of a female "regency." "Capable of predicting events, providing princes with good advice, and assuming the protection of a defenseless populace, . . . the imitators of Saint Catherine became the effective expression of a religiosity located within urban boundaries, toward which their activity was primarily directed. They could not be separated from the context in which they operated, the Renaissance court." [21]

Domenica's predictions were situated along two lines of periodization. First, in 1480, at the age of only eight, she predicted the Italian wars that lasted until 1560. Second, her longing for institutional reform foreshadowed the deserved "punishment of the clerics," which occurred in 1527 with the sack of Rome. The plague also hit Italy that same year. Within this broad period, her prophetic voice examined more specific events. Natural disasters and historic catastrophes were impartially listed one after another. Real men, not impersonal causes, were at the center of this periodization of the negative, and the natural and historical world was a bundle of sentiments deviating from a "just" end. An earthquake or a war made little difference: both were manifestations of a crisis occurring within a horizon of precise and identifiable design.

The link between guilt and punishment moved all the events of history and politics. In 1501, during Domenica's tenure at the Samminiatis in Florence, she had a vision in front of the Ognissanti Church. While hesitating over whether she should join the procession being held because of "fear of the plague," Domenica "saw groups of armed men, whose leader seemed to be a clergyman. A red hat was hanging around his shoulders." This detail, the misplaced hat, announced the threatening irregularity of the character in question: Cesare Borgia, Duke Valentino, cardinal of Valenza and general of the "Holy Church." He came to "trouble the peasants in the region of Florence . . . because their families did not fear God. Young men showed no respect, and young women no morality. Therefore, many of them were taken away by the soldiers." The city deserved a punishment—the invasion and the disease that threatened it. Yet it was not by the hand of Cesare Borgia, that opportunistic, politically motivated ecclesiastic and bloody man of arms, that Florence suffered its chastisement. Even Valentino himself was struck, destined to die.[22]

Domenica's vision ended here. The Madonna made clear only the identity of the invader; Domenica's biographer Borghigiani recounted the rest of the story, with numerous details and dates. Thus we know that Cesare Borgia left Bologna intent on occupying Florence. After arriving at Calenzano, "a castle seven miles away," and "sacking villages, taking many women prisoner" for reasons that "no one knew," he took the Signa road and went toward Siena. Therefore, Domenica's vision sheds light on what historians cannot explain: the unpredictable development of a catastrophe and the human actions that underlay it, in a deviation from the original plan. The punishment sufficed, and the city was, for the time being, spared.

For Domenica, political insight took the form of trances, and her language, the language of the senses.[23] Her access to writing, the medium by which a message might be arranged within an analytic semantic code, was a man, her confessor, Francesco da Castiglione. It was through the sudden speech released by a vision that Domenica, like other saints in the mold of Saint Catherine, understood politics and therefore became a self-asserting prophetess. Her biographer Benedetto Borghigiani explained how her predictions occurred, "through imaginary visions, ecstatic revelations or inspirations, and internal impulses, as well as through emotional pain, which martyrized her heart with a completely spiritual pain. . . . Similar afflictions were infallible signs of an impending punishment for those people or places for whom she felt sorry."[24] In this sense, the metaphors of the physical-individual body became situated in the realms of power and reintegrative salvation practices, and operated on both levels. A "voice" that announced the timing of history to the city, Domenica was also the city's body, a symbolic link through which the community reinforced its sense of belonging. At the dramatic climax of the crisis, as we shall see, Domenica managed to restore normality to Florence through a symbolic exchange between her own body and that of the city.

A MEDICEAN SAINT

In Domenica's prophetic activities, events progressed according to a providential, not a causal, order. God's plan became legible in the intricate network of visions and prophecies when in 1536, Cosimo de' Medici appeared and guaranteed Florence a long, lasting peace. The prophetic voice followed him while he crushed the last republican resistance at the Battle of Montemurlo.[25] With the defeat of those who had escaped from Florence and the suicide of Filippo Strozzi, the vicissitudes of decadence and guilt reached a turning point. The curve of history changed direction with Cosimo de' Medici.

The Medicean influence in Domenica's biography was confirmed once again in Bernardo Segni's *History of Florence*. Both Bernardo and his father, Lorenzo, worked as administrators of the Convent of Crocetta. According to Borghigiani, Bernardo was "a contemporary writer who knew the facts about Domenica well."[26] Bernardo witnessed all events from the Medicis' escape in 1527 to the siege of 1530. Moreover, he did not fail to stress in his *History* the "great influence" that Domenica exerted on the "soul of the Florentine people, urging them to reconcile their differences with Pope Clement VII and accept Medicean rule, which she predicted would return, in good faith."[27] In 1527 the Florentine aristocracy, on hearing the horrible news of the sack of Rome and the Medici pope's escape to Castel Sant'Angelo, believed that it could now assume full political authority and restore the first republic of 1494. Aristocratic and popular forces marched for a while along the same path; however, the "popular" side soon took over, overwhelming the "principal men." The political rupture divided the armed citizens. They were unable to unify, even in the face of the enemy that had arrived at the city's walls.

During this dramatic time, Lorenzo Segni, Bernardo's father and leader of the pro-Medici party, suggested sending high-ranking ambassadors to the pope in order to negotiate the return of Medicean rule. According to Bernardo,

> It was widely held that Lorenzo was a citizen who dearly loved liberty. In formulating the request favoring the restoration of the Medici family, he was influenced by the persuasive nun Domenica. She was born of a peasant family in Paradiso and gained fame as a devout person. Like others, he had great faith in her and followed her suggestions. I am well aware that she said that the Medicis would return to Florence, if not by peace then by force. I do not want to discuss her virtues and actions here, because they were extremely famous in the city at the time and, I believe, will continue to be so in the future.[28]

THE EXCHANGE

If Lorenzo Segni believed that there were reasons for the crisis of 1527 and its particular solution, Domenica viewed the plague and the social uprisings as part of a tormented universe of blood, which one could escape only through a ritual exchange. The nun asked God "to gather all of the Florentine *plague* into her body, and then to accept all of her *blood,* to be poured from her veins, offering all that she had in an *exchange*." The offer was accepted, and "her body, already consumed by fatigue, tears, and privations, was destroyed by a flow of blood from her nose and mouth. The doctors also let blood from her veins. Then a very hot humor spread all over her body, causing extensive pain."[29]

Sister Angelica del Macchia, the prioress of the convent, provided a more accurate description of that exchange and, in particular, of the apparently useless and redundant role of the doctors. Angelica, too, was convinced that Domenica had explicitly negotiated on behalf of the city: "She prayed to God and asked Him to punish her and take her blood, *not that of the citizens*." The heavenly response came quickly, and "the illness set in immediately," although it then lay "concealed" for some time (so that the pain would worsen). At that point, the doctors were called in. As was common practice, they "had to extract sixteen ounces of blood. Although they did not want to risk taking more, according to the doctors about twenty more ounces of blood burst out of her nose and mouth."[30]

The incubating disease preceded the exchange between the two bodies, Domenica's and the city's. Its occurrence confirmed the inadequacy of scientific reason and its forms of knowledge (the frantic doctors around the saint's body). In the midst of all that solemnity, the doctors' bumbling stupidity in deciding to take blood from the body of a saint who had made a deal with God almost makes us laugh. It also reminds us of the popular satires about Doctor Lava Titti or the peasant "called 'Grillo'" who prescribed infallible remedies that invariably produced the exact opposite of the effects desired.[31]

The cultural links between armed confrontation and blood date back to the biblical texts that prescribed the obligatory shedding of innocents' blood in case of war. The rationale was that contact with blood shed fortuitously or for someone else's violence incurred negative effects for the entire social group. Consequences were particularly grave (Lev. 17:14; Deut. 12:23) when the blood shed was between members of tribes descending from a common ancestor (as in a civil war). In that case, the entire group needed the punishment of blood, and the sacrifice became a collective ritual between the victim and the people. Thus, Domenica washed the blood shed by the citizens with her own blood, in a substitution of ancient origins. She demonstrated that she could save the city at its most critical moment, while simultaneously reintegrating a besieged group through her declaration of support for the Medicis' return to Florence, as we learned from Lorenzo Segni and other biographers. At the worst point of the crisis, then, Domenica not only exchanged her body and gave her own blood, but she also chose one political side over the other. Whereas Medici supporters were the just people, she said, republicans "fell victim to Satan's advice" and should be abandoned to their own destiny.[32]

For the Florentines of the following century, Domenica's physical fortitude (in withstanding such pain) and emotional strength (in predicting it) was intimately connected to the political destiny of peace and the dynasty that could restore it: the Medici. A horizon of consensus therefore existed, even more so because Domenica's example not only safeguarded the memory of the political conversion from Savonarola's dangerous prorepublican mysticism but also exhibited a slightly anti-institutional attitude toward the ecclesiastical hierarchy (she considered the sack of Rome to be the "punishment of the clerics"). In addition, her links to the grand duke's family, and therefore with the court, operated the symbolic reduction of all dissension within the Medicean field. The tradition of prophecy and Catholic reform was attenuated, finally fading away completely in a model of Counter-Reformation perfection.

The decision to place the memory and the body of Domenica once again at the center of the urban theater during a moment of collective danger was thus rooted in multiple links to the historical and symbolic past of Florence. Aided by her powerful patrons and reactivated by witnesses' memories, the little peasant, Domenica da Paradiso, reopened this great source of emotional energy for the body social.

6

The Anatomical Theater

On Saturday, 7 June 1630, the apostolic notaries and judges of the canonization hearings; the metropolitan canons, Paolo Poli and Vincenzo Baratta; and the prior of San Lorenzo, Alessandro Vasoli, all gathered at the Chapel of Santa Croce. Marquis Francesco Coppola and the lawyers Bartolomeo Sallio and Salvatore de' Taddei came with "aliquos doctores medicos" and other "graves personas" to prepare the visit to the sepulcher and the relics of Domenica da Paradiso.[1] On this solemn occasion they intended to certify the state of conservation of the venerable body. The canonical procedure prescribed that everything be conducted with the utmost secrecy to avoid popular "holy outrage" ("cum inibitione quod nullus audeat horam sive diem revelare, ad hoc, ut secrete fiat et omnis concursus et tumultus evitetur, et ita ut melius servetur forma literarum remissorialium debita cum instantia postulaverunt").[2]

The judges decided to go to the holy sepulcher at ten o'clock on Thursday, 12 June. The doctors and witnesses who were to assist in the examination of the body, the holy relics, and the documents in the convent's archive were also duly appointed. The judges selected six doctors, all members of the College of Physicians and advisers to the Public Health Magistracy, to sit on the panel: Antonio Medici, Niccolò Zerbinelli, Giovanni Ronconi, Benedetto Punta, Giovanni Nardi, and Mario Maccanti, the convent doctor. Along with this group of technicians, important Tuscan ecclesiastics were also to be present: Cardinal Carlo Medici; Alessandro Strozzi, bishop of Andria; Giovan Battista Malaspina, bishop of Massa and Populonia; Clemente da Montefalco, "Dominjis Florentinis generalem inquisitorem"; and Grand Duke Ferdinand II. All were sworn to secrecy and to respect anonymity. The notary, Tommaso Centenni, informed the witnesses of the time of the meeting and the "secret route" to take there.[3]

Four days later, on Thursday the twelfth, the judges and witnesses congregated at the Church of Crocetta around what had been Domenica's first sepulcher, "in dextero latere Cappellae majoris" (on the right side of the larger chapel). Following the judges' orders, the notary Centenni took minutes.

THE TWO SEPULCHERS

The tomb was raised, in Centenni's estimation, half an arm's length from the ground ("sive Monumentum sublevatum a terra tribus brachiis cum dimidio") and placed on two white marble pedestals bearing various inscriptions. It was supported by a marble plate under which lay a shield with a cross ("adest scutum cum cruce"). A still life of a skull and bones with an ornate inscription (at the time a popular motif) was suspended in the middle, and the engraved tombstone sat on a marble *tabula*.[4]

The empty sarcophagus lay over the inscription: the body of Domenica rested there no longer. On 7 June 1584, Cardinal Alessandro Marzi Medici, archbishop of Florence, had ordered the body examined; on verifying its identity, the decayed clothes were changed and the body itself was moved into an oratory of the convent. Significantly, next to the official, albeit empty, tomb hung a picture depicting the miraculous relationship between Domenica and the convent. In the center of the painting a building engulfed in flames was surrounded by a black cloud of smoke. Encircling the burning edifice were groups of nuns, some kneeling with arms outstretched to the heavens and others running in different directions. At the top of the picture the Virgin Mary, flanked by two nuns and surrounded by light, gazed down on the dramatic scene. A flock of black birds, symbolic of bad luck, flew away from them. The following lines were inscribed at the foot of the painting: "This is the convent of the venerable Domenica, spared from a great conflagration through wondrous miracles in the sign of the Holy Cross and through the intercession of the glorious Mother of God. MDXV."[5]

While the official sepulcher commemorated Domenica's good administration of the convent and of the women in her trust, a smaller one in the oratory was decorated with figures portraying the saint's spiritual itinerary and her promise of salvation for the faithful. It was a rite of initiation that culminated in the acquisition of knowledge.

The representation of collective events gave way gradually to that of the rhythm of an intimate biography and individual time.

Four nuns, the oldest and most important of the convent, guided the judges, witnesses, and doctors to the cells where Domenica had spent her life. Her body lay in a tomb in the oratory. The notary wrote down everything they found in the sepulcher. There were two pictures of Santa Maddalena and Santa Elena, a portrait of Domenica, and 168 ex-votos.[6] All these physical fragments of memory affirmed the body's effectiveness, making up a sort of anatomical museum full of arms, bones, hearts, eyes, men, women, and children. The great quantity of offerings pointed to the age of the image and the stratification of memory: the ensemble symbolized thaumaturgical potency and the powers of salvation. Pictures recounting the story of Domenica's life were mounted above the cell door. The first picture portrayed her childhood in a poor peasant family; shovel in hand, she talked with the Virgin Mary in a vineyard, and little red crosses hung from the vines. In the next she was threatened, like the Virgin Mary, by a snake. She soon tamed the snake, however, and, lowering her body, touched the serpent's tongue with her hand. In another painting, the adult woman lay sick in bed with Santa Maddalena by her side; Saint Catherine, holding a white woolen dress, gave the habit of the Dominican nuns to Domenica. In the last picture of the series, the two Medicean popes each rise to influence and fame.

Having examined the walls, the witnesses and the notary turned their gaze to the votive chapel, which was then opened: "pars interior sacelli apparet cooperta cortina sive velo sericeo riaurati coloris, quod Vulgo dicitur Cangio" (inside the chapel is a blanket made of silk of a golden color that the commoners call *cangio*). The judges ordered the silk blanket removed (*mandatu judicum*), and they saw an image decorated with a veil of silk embroidered in various colors ("mansiuncula ornata serico velo flammis diversorum colorum intexto") depicting the saint above golden stars on a blue background. Engulfed in a bright light and surrounded by angels ("nec non pluribus Angelis circumdatam"), a guardian angel offered Domenica a red cross.[7]

The notary measured the burial place in the judges' presence, as the procedure required. It was one arm-length wide, three-quarters of an arm-length deep, and four arm-lengths long. On the bottom were a green tapestry and flowers; the coffin was covered with a silk blanket. Centenni solemnly read the inscribed warning that anyone who dared

"aliquid in dicto sepulchro vel tumba ponere, vel ex eo autea subtra-
here, auferre, vel subripere etiam ex devotione" would be excommunicated without possibility of appeal to the pope. This grave admoni-
tion suggested a past of devotional practices, formerly prohibited by
Pope Urban VIII, in which there was close familiarity between venerated bodies and the communities that adored them.[8]

After reading letters authorizing her to proceed, the prioress, Angelica del Macchia, brought out the key to the sepulcher, "pendentem
a cordula serica rubea cum globulo lapideo eiusdem coloris." The detailed description of the key—hanging from a delicate red silk cord
(like Domenica's cross) attached to a sphere of red stone—appears to
have the function of slowing the narrative rhythm of the text, of sus-
pending for a moment the sense of growing expectation during the
various stages of the visit. Colors, images, fabrics, marble, two sep-
ulchers: we feel that we not only see and measure them, as the notary
Centelli did, but also touch them and feel the cold marble plates and
the sparkling softness of the silk. We are approaching the final revelation. The key serves as the essential prop preceding a revelation: now
the body appears on the scene.

Wrapped in a white cloth, Domenica rested under a crystal cover
bordered with gold. She wore a black mantle with a red cross. A
white veil and a wimple adorned her head. Holding the cross of a
rosary, her hands were folded on her chest. A crown of silver and gold
silk was gathered behind her shoulders, and she wore slippers made
of the same cloth as her dress. The body was covered with flowers—
lilies and roses—and a small cross of red paper and two angels lay
close to her head.

Two nuns recognized the body first. Benigna Carnesecchi specified
in her testimony that the saint's face still strongly resembled the cast
of her head in the next room, even though Domenica had been dead
for over seventy years.[9] Like the other nuns present, Benigna had witnessed the exhumation of 1584. She recalled how the similarities between the body's face and the cast impressed her at that time. Next,
Maria Vittoria Morelli remembered the same details. "I recognize it,"
she asserted as she examined the face beyond the crystal. "It looks
exactly like the cast, particularly the cheeks, the chin, and the forehead. It seems to me that she has not changed at all."[10]

This link, twice confirmed, between the venerated corpse and the
cast interrupted the proceedings. The judges requested that two artists

be questioned, "dominos peritos artis sculptoriae," to substantiate the resemblance "ad majorem rei claritatem et probationem."[11]

THE FACE AND THE CAST

The resemblance or appearance linking the body to its double introduces us to the complex and ambiguous domain of representation. In this particular culture, a system of complex connections juxtaposed nature, art, and anatomy, and thereby science and artistic depiction. The judges, facing the dilemma of the representation of truth, called for the testimony of two artists, Pietro Tacca, court Sculptor, and Michelangelo Buonarroti, namesake of the Renaissance painter, an influential art collector and man of letters. For the moment, the judges did not request the presence of the six doctors; the physicians would be called on to verify the physical condition of the body, not its identity—in other words, its quantitative proportions (skin, flesh, bones, weight) rather than its conceptual significance.

The baroque complexity of this identification was embodied in the fantastic comparison of a face, inevitably disfigured by time, to a cast that reproduced traits no longer in existence. The two artists were therefore not asked for a simple identification through direct perception of the face and its copy, but for an identification through "obscure and sentimental" perception, what we would call psychological perception. The problem of the portrait revolved around this psychological perception, the transformation of the reproduction into a transfiguration of the original model.[12] Tacca and Buonarroti were to restore the face's concrete identity to the barely existing profile. To appear and to be—image and model: this variance was the dilemma that the court artists were supposed to resolve.[13] According to Giorgio Vasari, images of the dead existed in every home in Florence, "over the fireplaces, windows, and cornices, . . . and are so realistic that they seem alive."[14] People did not place commemorative masks in those locations by chance; windows, doors, and chimneys needed protection from outside and, hence, from uncontrollable dangers. These images were like idols, full of strength and power; they also "facilitated the preservation in these houses of the memory of those who were revered."[15]

Counter-Reformation theory acknowledged the legitimacy of a portrait only if it was absolutely accurate. In his *Discorse intorno alle immagini* (1556), for example, Cardinal Paleotti upheld the need to abandon all the artifice of Renaissance portraiture, which was intended only to beautify models, and instead advocated a style of painting in which the highest possible anatomical resemblance was maintained, even if this meant representing bodily defects and imperfections. The baroque sensibility of the artists of the first quarter of the seventeenth century, deeply affected by anatomical knowledge and ever-present doctors, scientists, and barber-surgeons, produced likenesses that departed more and more from Renaissance canons of perfection. The macabre and the monstrous theatricality of anatomical investigation pervaded seventeenth-century body imagery. The open cadaver, a dualistic image of perfection and decay, became the most genuine *memento mori* of the time; the body symbolized semidivine humanity and its inevitable destiny of corruption.[16]

Casts and wax figures representing the life-size faces and bodies of the dead were very popular. Throughout the sixteenth century, the Benintendi family, of which Orsino was one of the most famous members, produced for churches wax votive images of illustrious dead individuals.[17] So many images were produced in the Benintendi shop that the local citizenry called them the "Fallimmagini," or Imagemakers. Throughout the seventeenth century, their shop had a major part in transforming the Church of the Annunciation into a kind of "wax museum." Warburg attributed the importance of these images to the "fetishistic magic" of a culture still anchored in pagan practices and superstitions, although we might rather think of the reverence Florentine citizens had for lineage and ancestry.[18]

It was the early Romantics who later incorporated the wax images into their hallucinatory "museum" collections. In the seventeenth century, mannequins and masks nourished the ambiguous fashion of the double and the living dead.[19]

TWO COURT ARTISTS

Like many of his fellow artists, Pietro Tacca, a sculptor and "court builder of statues," loved making wax figures of famous Florentines of cultural and political importance. Filippo Baldinucci remembered how the artist had created a "life-size" bust of Cosimo II: "The eyebrows, beard, real hair, and glass eyes were of such a color that they looked natural; the whole ensemble did not seem to be a fake but rather a living person. It was so lifelike that the great prince's mother, after his death, asked Tacca to remove the sculpture when she visited his house, because she could not bear to see her son alive in a statue." [20]

A protagonist of Florentine baroque art, Pietro Tacca acquired his skills while working in Giambologna's atelier, later replacing the noted artist as official court sculptor. When the master died, Grand Duke Cosimo gave Tacca Giambologna's big house in the Borgo Pinti. Pietro's salary as court sculptor was twenty-five *scudi* plus the amount to "maintain a horse." [21] With a group of his fellow artists, he worked on all the great court portraits of the time: Ferdinand I's funeral scene (1609) and the equestrian statues of Henry IV of France (1613) and Philip III of Spain (1616). Entrusted with designing the decorations for court festivities, he and Cigoli attended the wedding of Cosimo II and Mary Magdalen of Austria, as well as that of Ferdinand and Christine of Lorraine. His small world revolved around the grand duke's family, the Florentine court, and the Church of San Giovanni Battista in Rome. The street on which Pietro Tacca resided in the Borgo Pinti was the same one where Domenica da Paradiso had lived when she worked at the Samminiatis. It was also near the house of Michelangelo Buonarroti on Via Ghibellina.

Buonarroti came to the court at the same time that Tacca left the countryside to become Giambologna's apprentice. Buonarroti, however, was a man of letters, a successful poet who enjoyed the protection of Grand Duchess Christine. Like other intellectuals of his circle, he composed verses for court ceremonies and celebrations. He also attended the weddings of Christine and Ferdinand, Henry IV and Marie de' Medici, and Cosimo and Mary Magdalen of Austria. A stalwart of the regime, he wrote eloquent and predictable eulogies. He was a member of all of the important academies and wrote fashionable pastoral comedies that played at court. He also acquired various administrative posts in the government, which were highly desired by those who made their fortune by the grand duke's pleasure. [22]

Buonarroti began restoring his house on Via Ghibellina in 1612. He built a gallery where he displayed some masterpieces of his great-great-uncle. He also asked other artists, including Allori, Cigoli, Fanelli, and Tacca, to decorate the little museum with their sculptures and thus transform the beautiful rooms on Via Ghibellina into a sophisticated and valuable collection of baroque Florentine art. Portraits of the city's historic personages adorned the walls of the house: saints, heroes, princes, and popes. In a picture of a parade hanging high on the wall, one could distinguish the figure of Domenica da Paradiso among the black-and-white Dominican habits. It is to her crystal coffin that we now return, accompanied by Pietro and Michelangelo, artists of the court.

Tacca and Buonarroti examined Domenica's face. They were then taken to the nun's house, where they analyzed the cast, the "image" of the blessed woman. Finally, they gave long, careful inspection to the profile of the mask, which they compared ("contulerunt et collationaverunt") with that of the corpse as if the faces were two philological variations of the same text. Buonarroti swore first, with his hand on the Holy Scriptures:

> I, Michelangelo Buonarroti, having seen and examined the face of the cadaver said to be that of the blessed Domenica da Paradiso, founder of this Convent of Crocetta, having considered the structure and the bones of the face, and having analyzed the cast image of the natural head which was made immediately upon death, believe and state under oath that, by reason of symmetry and resemblance (except for the tip of the nose, which is missing), they are the same.[23]

Pietro Tacca signed and swore next:

> I, Pietro Tacca, sculptor of His Most Serene Majesty, have seen and examined both the face of the cadaver said to be that of the blessed Domenica da Paradiso and the cast image of her face which was made immediately upon death. On the basis of the skills of my art, having looked at and analyzed the appearance, structure, bones, and profile of the one and the other, I believe and state that the face maintains the same natural appearance and look as the original cast, except for the tip of the nose, where the plaster has dried and withdrawn.[24]

According to the "skills" of Tacca's art and the "reason of symmetry," the plaster mask and the corpse's face were the same. The profile, the bones, and the appearance had not changed except for the tip of the nose. The perspective of the face had been rotated in the investigative analysis of the artists; still, seen from above, the front, and the side, the images of cast and face coincided.

AN ANATOMY LESSON

Finally, the body was brought out from under the crystal cover and placed on a table so that it could be examined by the doctors ("ut melius per assistentes et peritos possit inspici, tangi et videri"). The sensory universe of doctors is broader than that of artists, since artists touch only their medium, in this case, plaster, whereas medicine involves a direct tactile relationship with physical bodies. The nuns and the notary lifted the body and put it on the table. The judges asked the physicians to take an oath, reminding them that they would be excommunicated if they failed to report signs of scars and alterations that would indicate either that the tomb had been violated or that preservatives had been applied to prevent the body from decaying. The doctors duly swore to tell the truth, and a judge ordered the notary Centenni to describe the body in writing. Then the judge asked the prioress and the sacristan to undress the body completely, except "its shameful parts."[25]

The two nuns began to remove the clothes from the body piece by piece in front of the witnesses, the judges, and the notary. First they took off the veil, followed by the wimple, the black mantles, the white scapular, the sleeves, and the upper part of the white habit. They left the veil "super pudendis" in place. Finally, they removed the woolen slippers.[26]

Tommaso Centelli conducted a full investigation of the seminaked remains, "omnibus patentis."[27] He lifted the body, turned it over, and inspected the back, "lumbis, costis, scapulis, dorso, et anchis," pronouncing the body to be in excellent condition, "optime conservatum."

With witnesses and technicians surrounding the cadaver, the scene could have been the classroom portrayed in seventeenth-century paintings of lessons of anatomy. In these paintings, the physician talks to the listeners, explaining and gesticulating, about the anonymous body behind him. Meanwhile, the notary writes a description of the anatomical shape on the marble table, recounting its history through physical details. As in the painting, the cadaver in the beatification trial became a text, one provided with a clinical biography didactically illustrated by the word of the commentator and technician.

Smooth as the life-size wax figures, Domenica's body was almost completely covered by dry skin. The flesh was still palpable in many parts of the body: the neck, the cheeks, the lower lip, the chest, the breasts, and the arms. Some parts still retained their original color. Whereas the neck was white, the chest and breasts were rosy. Most noticeably, a red spot and a swelling ("aliquis tumor") marked the skin above the heart. As in contemporary paintings, the corpse was represented through a heroic deformation that accentuated its spiritual mission. Thus, Domenica's throat, whence the prophetic voice had come, and her suffering heart, which had been full of the blood of excess love, were not only intact but also vividly colored. The epicenter of passion, the heart, was swollen, and its potency had left a flaming red mark which the clothes covered. Whippings and hair shirts had produced calluses near the waist. The only signs of decay were the "perforations," which doctors labeled "gnawings" in accordance with then current scientific discussions on the spontaneous generation of worms and the decay of bodies. Fragments of history emerged from these signs. The dead body recounted life, the triumph of the flesh (and therefore of the soul) over dissolution. Only the missing parts—the ears—and the mutilations—a barely attached finger—reminded the witnesses of that moment when the body had passed into death.

Domenica's agony had begun the morning of Saint Jacob's Day, 4 August 1553. After the nun offered her soul peacefully to God, Prioress Angelica del Macchia explained, "It was necessary to call the guards to prevent the crowd from taking not only the flowers but also her clothes. If not for the guards, there would not have been anything left, because everyone wanted something."[28] Had the fury of the faithful led them to take the finger and the ears? We shall never know, although the spectacle of the ritualistic riot foreshadowed, and was necessary to, the canonization.

Compared with the well-preserved body, the clothes were in poor shape. Discolored and corroded, the white habit looked more like a sponge than wool. The black mantle was torn apart, and a large red spot lay on the linen undergarment directly above the heart. The doctors stressed the inverse relation between the clothes and the body, the former being decayed and materially decomposed, the latter full, fleshy, and soft.

The testimony of the first doctor, Antonio Medici, began with this contrast between the clothes and body. After taking an oath on the Bible, he asserted:

> I have seen and examined the body . . . as well as the torn burial clothes, carefully. Neither emits any odor, and I have seen no indication, save for the ears, that the body has been touched by anyone. . . . After examining the sepulcher, I have concluded that no artificial device has been inserted to prevent bad odors from accumulating. . . . There

is no sign of infection or corruption [in the body] except for the perforations, and I do not understand how any body could remain preserved for such a long time. . . . Moreover, I do not recognize the red
spot on the left side of the body as a natural phenomenon.

Doctor Medici also noted that the tattered clothes had not transferred
"the same corruption" to the body. The whole thing is all the more
incredible, the doctor continued, because it was a "complex" body
and "quite fat."[29] The leitmotiv of the following testimonies lay in
these same elements: the frayed clothes that had not contaminated the
body; the unnaturally vivid red spot; the cadaver's intact flesh; and the
many assurances that no preservatives had been added to the sepulcher.

On this foundation, the doctors constructed a more imaginative
language. Let us listen to Niccolò Zerbinelli's testimony.

> I have seen and examined the body in great wonder. It is a natural body,
> not an artificial one, with all its component parts save the ears, which
> are missing, and one finger, which is barely attached to the right hand.
> I have observed that it is a large body of great height and that it has
> never been altered by aromas, liquors, or desiccants. One can tell that
> the body must have been large from the remaining parts of the corpse.
> This is particularly true of the chest, where the skin is detached and
> lifted from the bones. The same manifestation occurs in the arms and
> the legs. The head and the stomach, which decay very easily, do not
> contain any substances, and all parts are here preserved without the aid
> of any artificial means. . . . I have smelled a fragrance . . . so sweet that
> I cannot call it natural. I have also seen a large red spot on the left side
> of the body which extends down to the stomach. Blood turns black
> when mixed with air. Then it disappears little by little, eventually leav-
> ing a spot no longer the color of blood. . . . I will repeat that in this
> case this process is not only unnatural but also miraculous.[30]

The mixture of scientific prose and baroque preciosity is especially
apparent in the sensuality of the flesh being weighed and measured.
And here another corporeal image insinuates itself into the plot of the
story: the contemporary image of plague victims. Their dark cadavers
were recognizable by the swollen, black bubos under their arms and
between their legs. The bodies, piled in the lazarets and in the streets,
emitted a terrible stench about which all complained. Contagion, dis-
coloration, foul odors: the witnesses reiterated that Domenica's body
had transformed these physical qualities into their opposites. The
black color of infested bodies (of bubos and, therefore, of death)
turned into the red of blood, the symbol of life and love. The conta-

gion of the disease became incorruptible flesh, while the stench yielded to a wonderful fragrance.

Giovanni Ronconi and Benedetto Punta testified after Niccolò Zerbinelli. Punta described the miraculous preservation of the body in a string of hyperboles. "I have enjoyed looking at the body," he began. He characterized the color of the blood on the undergarment as "rose-like," a sign of "loving affection" that "flows through the skin—not black and putrid like corpses' blood, but rather alive, full-bodied, and humid." Like a shadow, the picture of a plague victim's ordinary cadaver obscures the profile of this image. Unlike the remains of common people, Domenica's body was "neither drained nor exhausted, but robust and little changed from her normal appearance. The wrinkles on the legs and lower back are very flat; they would not have been so had Domenica been thin, drained, and exhausted." From these observations, Benedetto Punta concluded that a miracle had indeed occurred. He argued that without a soul, "which had maintained all the corporeal elements in harmony before death, these elements would have competed with one another unrestrainedly to cause total decay."[31]

According to the convent doctor, Mario Maccanti, "Her body is like the bodies of salted animals whose flesh retains its substance and color."[32] Maccanti also touched the cadaver, reporting that "the bodily parts are connected to each other in such a way that, when one is touched, all the others move accordingly, a sure sign of the unity of nerves, muscles, and ligaments." Considering that "all things that I have examined are at odds with the nature of corpses," Maccanti agreed with the other witnesses that a miracle had, in fact, taken place.[33] The heroic dimensions of Domenica's body grew from one testimony to another.

MEMORY AND THE EYES

Biographical studies and Sister Angelica del Macchia's testimony indicate that Domenica was a small woman who, although sickly, was able to withstand all kinds of physical pain. She wore a hair shirt, slept on a mat filled with nutshells, and suffered draining hemorrhages.

The ascetic ideal sanctioned the final victory of the aesthetic of ugliness. This ideal presupposed a series of physical transformations during the nun's youth.

As a young adolescent, she was beautiful. Her curly hair looked like gold. She had a wide forehead and sparkling eyes. . . . Her body was shapely and plump, even though she was a peasant. Many thought she was a noblewoman, and her general appearance mirrored her noble soul. She maintained her beauty until the age of twenty-three, even while putting herself through a regimen of privation and punishment, including fasting, keeping vigils, and using chains and whips. Then, fearing that her attractiveness might appear to be the result of artificial means, she asked God to make her ugly. Subsequently, she changed in appearance, becoming pale and losing her natural beauty. . . . Whereas she had once been plump and fresh, she was now so thin and exhausted that she looked like she was made of air rather than flesh.[34]

After viewing Domenica's penitential instruments of torture, Christine of Lorraine, although never having personally met the sister, characterized her as a "weak, listless" woman.[35] The nuns of the convent used to say that the mother superior never ate anything. First she dipped her food in water, and later, as other contemporary saints did, she received her sustenance solely from the Eucharist. Her body therefore posed a constant threat, dangerous to those who attempted to touch it. Sister Maddalena Bonsi, for example, recounted how the arm of a man who had tried to touch Domenica while she was praying withered away.[36] The nuns of the convent were not allowed to come into any physical contact with her. Angelica del Macchia remembered that the Mother

never touched any living creatures or any part of her own body. . . . She never washed her own gloveless hands but instead wrapped a cloth around them. She did not want any of the sisters to wash her hair because she did not want her neck and shoulders touched. However, she was unable to resist allowing someone to cleanse her hair. As a result, she cried in desperation, sure that she had committed an evil act by allowing someone to touch her.[37]

If we recall the scene of exhumation and the analysis of the cadaver described in the testimonies, the doctors' work assumes a tone of veiled desecration, accentuating their and the nuns' differing perceptions of the body. Whereas the nuns stressed the body's indirect power as mediated by the memory and words of the ancient mothers, the doctors broke the continuity of memory and concentrated on the present. To the doctors, attentive examination of the cadaver—by smelling, touching, and seeing—presented a spectacle of "splendid flesh," great height, heavy bodily parts, and such a full chest and shoulders that the skin did not cling to the bones.

This separation between memory and anatomical description poses several problems. First, there is the problem of selectiveness on the part of those observing or recording. We do not have sufficient evidence to state that the doctors' testimony was arbitrary or motivated by dishonesty; rather, their perceptions were oriented by their culture, just as in the case of the nuns. As Pierre Delooz asserts, "Perception selects those elements within a message that correspond to preexisting models transmitted collectively."[38] Thus, the eyes and the act of looking are not neutral sensory activities but are instead organized on the basis of layers of memory and previous visual experience. Not scientifically neutral, the eye sees through the culture of the social group to which the viewer belongs. Although attentive to the semantics of images and a precise internal logic, the eye is even more heedful of symbols. The reading of a message and the ability to grasp the information that message conveys go beyond sensorial boundaries to the articulated ground of social life and history.[39]

The intersection of the two systems, the symbolic and the logical, oriented the doctors' and the nuns' perceptions, bending the sight of the former and the words of the latter toward the religious sphere.[40] The doctors' scientific outlook was therefore conditioned by the different perspectives of Domenica's biography and her position as a cult object, the exemplary figure of an endangered community.

Nevertheless, the doctors' descriptions of Domenica's corpse suggest how deeply her sanctity was rooted in a sensorial code. They considered the physical repercussions of mystical phenomena, such as the swollen heart, not as symbolic manifestations but rather as tangible realities. As A. Vauchez explains, the new criterion for verifying sanctity was popularized in the latter Middle Ages: physiological resemblance to the body of Jesus. Saintly women manifested this tendency more frequently than men; they had nothing besides their bodies at their disposal.[41] Domenica's biographer Father Ignazio de Nente, prior of the Dominican Monastery of San Marco in Florence, was one of the most ardent supporters of the new devotion of the Sacred Heart. Adviser to many important Florentines as well as confessor to the grand duchess of Tuscany, he encouraged among the urban ruling classes the cult of the swollen heart and dripping blood of the body of Domenica da Paradiso.[42]

The ceremonial exhumation opened up a symbolic channel for the witnesses which contributed to the creation around the body of a sort of funereal theater. In the first half of the seventeenth century, the court architect in Florence, Alfonso Parigi, introduced some new choreographic elements in the official funeral apparatus. Previously a draftsman of theatrical scenes, Alfonso abandoned the "old-style funerals," complete with catafalque and columns draped in black, and introduced the new fashion of the "funeral feast," in which the apparatus became more agile and dramatically elegant through a set of moving skeletons and an elevated coffin in a half circle of candles. The clear light stood in sharp contrast to the opaque heaviness of the black columns of the old style.[43] Thus, after the beginning of the century, each illustrious death was also a theatrical death.

Did the exhumation of Domenica da Paradiso's body, the visit of the doctors, and the exposed cadaver belong then to a theatrical play in which already memorized parts were improvised? For the city, filled with death, a theatrical production of the good death was a consoling performance.

7

The Plague

The story of the plague occupied the central part of the canonization proceedings. All the protagonists of this section were lay and of bourgeois origin, and their testimony transferred the narration of events from the public to the private sphere. Whereas the nuns' testimonies revolve around the life of Domenica da Paradiso, and consequently around the fate of the city, the witnesses of the epidemic open their homes to us, describing domestic environments, gestures, and affections.

Testimonies were organized so as to constitute a narrative crescendo culminating in the thaumaturgical efficacy of Domenica. Unlike the earlier accounts, these were not supported by any written texts. Moreover, their truthfulness was based on a chain of cross-references—that is, the links between the various testimonies and the relationships established between the witnesses, Domenica, and the convent community. Gradually, the genealogy of witnesses who were directly related to the saint (the nuns and the grand duchesses) lost ground to a new genealogy whose branches intersected with the protagonists in the convent and in the trial. Domenica's presence was substituted by that of a contemporary, Angelica del Macchia. Angelica's circle of friends and relatives, especially her cousins Lisabetta and Ottavio, provided the most numerous and detailed testimonies. They did not renarrate the biography of Domenica; instead, they confirmed her thaumaturgic powers through concrete reports on recent events. Thus memory turned to the present.

Although testimonies about the plague were not the only ones that concerned miraculous healing, they did constitute a separate part in the documents of the proceedings. In the final analysis, they help explain the connection between the epidemic crisis and the canonization hearings.

BREAD SOUP

On Tuesday, 26 November 1630, Albiera de' Guiducci, the wife of Filippo Samminiati, began her testimony. It was in the Samminiati household in the Borgo Pinti that Domenica had worked as a servant when she first arrived in Florence.

"A few days ago—I think it was before Saint Simon's Day—my daughter, Costanza, who is seven years old, got sick. She had such a high and drawn-out fever that both Doctor Paolo Filiromoli and I believed she wouldn't make it. My sister Maddalena came over and told me to send for a little of the bread that is kept in Domenica's sepulcher and give it to Costanza. I sent my servant Maria to the Convent of Crocetta. There, the good nuns asked her to recite the Salve Regina seven times. They then sent me a piece of bread and a little red cross that they said had touched Domenica's body. When the servant came home, she gave the cross to my little girl, who, saying that she felt better, quickly got up, for the first time in a long while. I prepared a broth from the bread, and she began to feel better and better. She's now completely well. I believe this to be a sign of grace, especially considering that these are strange times, dangerous and contagious, . . . and considering that even the doctor thought she would die."[1]

The following day, 27 November, Albiera's sister Maddalena confirmed the story almost word for word.[2] In the internal development of the various episodes, Albiera's testimony constituted a sort of paradigm. All the other testimonies followed a similar pattern: a relative developed a sudden and unexpected illness, thought to be "malignant"; doctors were unable to cure the sick person; a member of the household, generally a servant, obtained a relic from the nuns; the relic was applied, interrupting the course of the disease through the encounter between the invalid's active devotion and the sacred object; the immediate recovery was expressed as psychological well-being; and a doctor ratified the miracle. In this first testimony the separation between sickness and recovery was transferred into the text with the adverb *prima,* meaning "for the first time in a long while," which marked, both syntactically and symbolically, an upswing in the narration.

Another constant in the narration was the community of women who organized the treatment regimen. This community comprised domestic women who prepared the miraculous soup from the holy bread, the appearance of which was connected to a mixture of ritual and symbolic elements—most importantly and most obviously, those of the Eucharist. Unlike what happened in ancient societies, the sanctified bread, with its gift of salvation, was distributed according to a logic of consumption that, like the provisioning measures introduced in times of crisis, rewarded the poor and suffering. In Domenica's case, bread also appeared to heal miraculously. In 1543, blind Sister Giovanna picked up some bread left on Domenica's plate and "put it over her eyes." She was suddenly able to see again.[3] Whereas Saint Catherine's bread had once saved the city of Siena from famine, Domenica's bread had cured an individual's ailment, blindness, thereby foreshadowing the end of the epidemic.

Claude Lévi-Strauss has observed that while *roasting* meat is a male form of cooking, in that it is connected to outdoor life and to animals of the forests and prairies, *stewing* meat is a role characteristically assigned to women. Placed in a pot, a product of a group's material culture, meat stewed in water belongs to the domestic sphere of what is "inside" and is therefore integral to the female universe. The double mediation of the pot and the water keeps the meat from coming into direct contact with the fire and thus parallels the boundary of clothes, stones, and objects which separates women from the external world of men.[4]

It is not surprising, then, that it was an all-female circle of care and treatment that transformed something boiled in the kitchen by women's hands into medicine.

HEALED "BY A WOMAN"

The soup that Albiera claimed to have made for her daughter introduces us to a type of domestic herbalist's shop in Florence that was run by women. Typically these women, the mothers, wives, and daughters of doctors and herbalists, had been permitted to keep the businesses going when the male owner—their relative—died. Since 1349 the guild statutes allowed "all the women" of a member's family to "work in the same profession in the city of Florence and in the neighboring villages, as long as they neither employed anyone else . . . nor had any apprentices, nor taught the skill to another person."[5] In 1633, Santa, the daughter of Giovanni Peretoli, had a barbershop on the Piazza Pitti, and her mother, Margherita, opened another one on the Ponte Vecchio.[6] Still, during the epidemics only one woman in the city's lazarets was charged with performing the tasks of a male barber (bloodletting, cauterizations): Margherita Lombardi, one of eight men and eight women who helped the doctors at San Miniato, "let blood and cut open bubos, just as a barber-surgeon would." Hence, according to the governor of the institution, she earned "a little more than the average salary."[7]

By the end of the sixteenth century, European medical culture tended to correlate women's treatment of the sick with witchcraft. Significantly, the first French translation of Laurent Joubert's famous text on popular mistakes in medicine was printed in Florence in 1592 and dedicated to Grand Duchess Christine of Lorraine.[8] We want here to stress not the specific tendency to equate female medicine with witchcraft, but rather the progressive expansion of this paradigm to all domestic areas and female spaces, indeed, to the very kitchen implements that women used on a daily basis. One therefore had to avoid not only the "abortionists," charlatans, and other types of ignorant women themselves, but also the pots and vases in which such women had soaked, filtered, and cooked food and medicine from time immemorial.

According to Joubert,

> There are some people who know nothing about medicine, and there are some ignorant women who cannot read or write. However, because they know a few things, such as how to prepare a soup or some other energizing dish, how to make a bed, how to put a hat on a sick person's head, or how to concoct some minor remedies against scabies, smallpox, worms, etc., they think they know everything. They make up all sorts of things with their imaginations in spite of the doctors.[9]

Soup, bed, hat: the treatment of the sick involved harmless objects. Running between the kitchen and the bedroom, women followed an oral tradition of suggestions and advice which Joubert despised, claiming that "they never invented anything. Rather, they learned from doctors, passing on the information to one another. Women never discovered a remedy; everything they used came out of our shops and the shops of our predecessors."[10]

On the contrary, one constant element, almost a topos, appeared already in Albiera de' Guiducci's testimony: the juxtaposition of the doctor's inability to find a remedy with the family woman's success in making—with the help of the servant, the nuns, the holy body of

Domenica, and finally, her domestic instruments—a medicine that cured those for whom, according to science, there was "no hope." We will find this pattern again and again in the other testimonies about miraculous healing. Let us not forget that it had already appeared in Domenica's biography, when, to save Florence from civil strife, the plague, and a siege, she exchanged her own body for the body of the city. On that occasion, too, doctors had made a ritualistic visit that proved ineffective in resolving the crisis.

The conflict between the two groups, the professionals and the traditional healers, was also highlighted by the verses of James Primrose, an English doctor. In the mid–seventeenth century he published another ethnographic compilation of popular mistakes in medicine, extending Joubert's work to the British Isles:

> Loe here a woman comes in *charitie*
> To see the sicke, and brings her *remedie*.
> You've got some grievous cold, alas (quoth she)
> It lies sore in your bones, no part is free.
> His pulse is weak, his urine's colour'd high,
> His nose is sharpe, his nostriles wide, he'll die.
> They talk of Rubarb, Sene, and Agaricke,
> Of Cassia, Tamarinds, and many tricke,
> A pepper posset, *nothing can be bought*
> *Like this i' th' Pothecaries shoppe;* alone
> It cures the Fever, Strangury and Stone;
> If not there's danger, yet before all faile,
> Ile have a Cawdle for you or Mace-Ale:
> Ane Ile prepare my Antimonial Cuppe
> To cure your Maladie, one little suppe
> Will doe more good, and is of more desert
> Then all Hippocrates or Galens Art.
> But loe an *Angell* gently puts her backe,
> Lest such erroneous course the sicke doe wracke
> Leads the *Physitian,* and guides him and,
> *Approves his Art* that God allowes, by him 'tis blest
> To cure diseases, leave them all the rest.[11]

Although its technique of diagnosis resembled that of doctors (heartbeat, urine, alteration of the senses), female medicine was completely external to the professional and commercial circuit. "Nothing that a woman sells can be found in an herbalist's shop," asserted Primrose, and feeling pity was certainly not rewarded with money. In the text, the synthesis of female and popular mistakes culminates in the administration of an "antimonial cuppe," a violent hematinic then very common in England. In order to avoid a deadly conclusion to an illness, the Angel of Poetry finally removes the woman from the bedside and introduces the doctor, whose art was "approved" and "blessed" by God. Thus, recovery is guaranteed by this man's professional skills, not by the superstitious remedies of women; by science, not by the emotion that ignores the law of the marketplace.

Scipione Mercuri catalogued popular medical errors of Italy at the beginning of the century. His overt misogyny overshadowed even that of his French predecessor, Joubert, and his contemporary, Primrose. He argued, "Women . . . should learn to execute doctors' orders and stop interfering with acts that are inappropriate to their condition. Although it is the mistakes of women which bind doctors' hands and feet, making treatments useless, it is the doctors who are blamed if the cure does not work."[12] Women asked untimely questions at each stage of the doctor's treatment. "They want to know the reason behind what has been said and what must be done. . . . In addition, they contest the decisions, saying that it is too early, that the medicine is too strong, or that something else would be better. . . . They even tell how medicine should be administered to the patient, whether in liquid or as a solid, whether in extract or as a pill."[13] According to Mercuri, women's natural curiosity made them vulnerable to the devil, who tempted and seduced many of them. "In ancient times," Mercuri admitted, "women treated women, and it was not customary for a man to treat a woman"; female diabolical curiosity, then, was merely a holdover of some of the competencies that women once enjoyed. Women "used to study philosophy and medicine in order to become doctors, just as men now do. However, today women administer medicine without ever studying, and many are barely able to hold a needle to take care of minor things."[14] This degradation of women's status debased even noblewomen to the level of servants, who "often conspire with their female master against the doctor."[15] The same thing happened in the story recounted by Albiera de' Guiducci. She had found an ally in her servant Maria, who, once Doctor Filiromoli was removed from the picture, mediated between her mistress and the nuns.

The path these texts suggested was dramatically confirmed during the plague outbreak in Milan in 1630. The famous trial against the plague spreaders, which affected every aspect of life in the city for three years, began with the denunciation of a Public Health official, Guglielmo Piazza, by two women, Ortensia Castigliona and Caterina Rosa. The Magistracy's offensive against the reputed plague spreaders directly involved the spaces and instruments of popular and female domestic life. When, in the neighborhood of Porta Ticinese, the magistrate ordered the inspection of some lye found in a pot in the barber Mora's house, Margherita, a washerwoman appointed by the court, swore that it was contaminated and stated that "the best poisons could be prepared from this substance." In large washing pots, "the more one rubs," the more poison is produced.[16]

In contrast, the manuals of popular medicine suggested a plethora of secret remedies that could be prepared in kitchen containers, especially in large all-purpose copper pots such as those used to wash clothes. The compilation by Alessio Piemontese (the pen name of Girolamo Ruscelli), for example, contained a recipe "for plague epidemics" that called for "a big pot made of tinned copper which was deep yet not too big." In this pot, one was to cook "three black spiders, three serpents, three deaf vipers, three frogs, . . . ten tarantulas, and fifty scorpions and other poisonous animals—alive, if possible—over a small flame like one used for soap or stew."[17] Struck by the plague in Milan, Scipione Mercuri, the meticulous cataloguer of all popular mistakes in medicine, cured himself by opening a bubo with a red-hot piece of iron. Suddenly "he felt a silver torrent coming from his heart which reached the little fountain" of his draining bubo.[18] Many writers confirmed the widespread use of this violent treatment. On weak patients, however, it was done with a "flat tool, like the one used by soap makers" and women.[19]

Many of these secrets invented in the kitchen were also stored there. Pantries were full of wax-sealed vases and pots that preserved unguents and potions against various illnesses. Popular practice attributed positive qualities even to those objects and places that science considered with misgiving. In the trial against the Milanese plague spreaders, the motif of the infectious scissors embodied the sense of a besieged domestic area, whose value of reassurance was transformed into its opposite. If women were potential witches, stoves, soap, and interior rooms were dangerous and ambiguous instruments as well, "because the scissors came from all over Milan, infecting sons, husbands, and families."[20]

In 1631 Cardinal Federico Borromeo, stricken by the plague, "refused to be treated by a woman, saying that he would rather die than be healed by a woman."[21]

"I SAW THAT SOMETHING BIG WAS ABOUT TO COME OUT"

The story recounted by Albiera de' Guiducci about the healing of her daughter, Costanza, moved within a historical horizon that, through texts and events, marked a social condemnation of women and the increasingly restricted sphere in which they were entitled to operate. The presence of Domenica da Paradiso, however, seemed to open a glimmer of diversity in the picture's opaque compactness.

Just as Albiera had healed her daughter, so too did Lisabetta Centenni help her husband. Lisabetta's surname suggests a family connection: the link was to Tommaso, the notary of the proceedings and Lisabetta's brother. Lisabetta had been born in Florence thirty-one years earlier and was married to Ottavio Amoni, a notary, who gave his testimony after her. Before she began her attestation, Lisabetta swore on the Bible and stated her economic status. She lived off her husband's earnings and her dowry of three hundred *scudi*. Despite her elevated social position, she was illiterate, so Father Ascanio dell'Ascensione, the Augustinian priest at the canonization hearings, signed on her behalf.

The first episode of healing that Lisabetta remembered had occurred a few years earlier, in 1624, the very year that the archbishop of Florence had begun to gather the documents for the canonization proceedings. It was an important date for Domenica and for the city, although it was a particularly threatening one for the witness, who had been worrying about her husband Ottavio's illness. Lisabetta's words recreate for us the domestic universe characterized by the couple's private suffering. She remembered how they had been confined to the bedroom during that unusually sultry autumn.

> My husband Ottavio was lying in bed with a malignant fever. His sickness had progressed to the point that we were sure he would die. He got weaker and weaker and was in so much pain that no relief was in sight. Also, he was very thirsty. I lost all hope when I noticed that the medicine was not doing any good. He stayed in that condition until 27 September, the eve of Saint Cosimo and Saint Damian's Day, when Sister Angelica del Macchia, currently prioress at Crocetta, sent me a

little piece of bread that had touched the body of Domenica. I made it into a soup and gave it to my husband. He ate it with the greatest devotion. Suddenly, by the grace of God, the fever broke. Generally the fever worsened as the cold night fell, but that evening it didn't. In addition, it didn't even come back later on. His good spirits returned. We were really surprised. . . . Many of our friends knew about this, in particular Niccolò Vanni, who was there.[22]

Although this story was not related to the plague, it foreshadowed others that were, constituting their precedent. Let us examine some of the details in Lisabetta's narration. First, Lisabetta remembered the precise date preceding Ottavio's recovery: 27 September, the eve of Saint Cosimo and Saint Damian's Day. Everyone knew that these saints were the protectors of doctors, and in Florence they enjoyed special popularity because the grand dukes had elected them patron saints of the city. In the Dominican Monastery of San Marco, Beato Angelico painted a cycle of frescoes portraying the lives of the two saints, and later, beneath those figures, Botticelli painted Lorenzo and Giuliano de' Medici. Filippo Lippi completed the linkage of the saints and the grand dukes in his famous tondo in which Cosimo and Damian, holding a surgical kit in their hands, kneel in front of San Lorenzo (symbolizing Lorenzo the Magnificent). These were not the only celebratory paintings; the list goes on to include Lorenzo di Bicci, Ghirlandaio, and Donatello.[23]

These references, however, serve to stress what this exquisitely private citation seems to suggest: political homage, an expression of belonging, a linkage between the remembrance of one's own family and that public and collective memory of the reigning family. For example, Ottavio Amoni, Lisabetta's husband, was not only a notary, but also a minister of the Nove Magistracy. This branch of the Florentine bureaucracy also employed Michelangelo Buonarroti the younger, who worked for the powerful secretary of the regency, Andrea Cioli. As we have seen, a position in the Nove Magistracy was particularly sought after by immigrants from the countryside who wanted to advance quickly in the grand duke's administration. This was precisely the case for Ottavio Amoni, who, born in Colle Val d'Elsa, had recently obtained Florentine citizenship and had married into an important notarial family, the Centenni.[24] Therefore, he was an ambitious provincial eager for a bureaucratic appointment—in other words, a man just like those members of the ruling class who revolved around the regency of Christine of Lorraine and Mary Magdalen of Austria.

Because the memory of Cosimo and Damian alluded to the reigning family and the sacred nature of its government, penetrating the semantic complexity of Lisabetta's mention of them allows one to grasp a surprisingly polemical element. The earliest anthologies detailing the miracles of martyrs attributed to those martyrs the power to cure the faithful with natural remedies—that is, without miracles. Soon, because Cosimo and Damian practiced their skill only for charity, the belief developed that the two brothers had been penniless doctors. Was not the woman healer who had been taken from the bedside of a patient by Doctor Primrose's Angel of Poetry a disciple of anargyric (ἀνάργυροι) medicine? In this case, the miraculous healing recounted by Lisabetta Centenni should be placed within the context of allegorical interlacings that delineated yet another separation between the various possible forms of treatment during epidemics. The soup made of the blessed bread, like the cures of the anargyric healers Cosimo and Damian, was a gift that by definition required no monetary compensation.

The documents from the hearings which touch on the plague insist on the awful opportunistic relationship between doctors and patients, a relationship involving either litigation or submission. To recover by means of official medicine was costly, particularly when one had to avoid the requisite hospitalization. The urgency of the crisis tended to cancel the links that only the community's moral economy and sense of solidarity upheld. Those who worked in the middle and lower ranks of the Public Health Magistracy profited quickly and substantially, in a rapidly developing spiral of social monetarization. Those who could afford to bribe officials did so: the official responsible for locks, so that he would lock only a few rooms in the house; the official responsible for inventorying the confiscated objects, so that he would miss something; the guard responsible for hospitalization orders, so that he would not enforce the regulations; the gravedigger, so that he would not undress the corpses; the barber-surgeon, so that he would not see the bubo; and the doctor, so that he would write a death certificate attributing the cause of death to something other than the plague. The improvised professionalism of some jobs performed by neighbors and acquaintances activated new circuits of expense and earning, reinvigorating animosities and jealousies as well as desires for revenge. What better definition of the hostility elicited by Public Health officials, the *nouveaux riches* of the plague, than Mora's characterization of Commissioner Piazza during the Milanese trial against plague spreaders? "This commissioner was apparently a poor man. He dressed poorly and went out to catch birds. . . . It's true that he made money, and lots of it, after he was appointed commissioner. I don't know how much he really made, but people say that he made tons."[25]

The second important detail in Lisabetta's testimony was a name, Sister Angelica del Macchia, "currently prioress at Crocetta," who provided the blessed bread. Angelica was the cousin of Lisabetta's husband, Ottavio. The two were both born in Colle Val d'Elsa, Angelica in 1574 and Ottavio ten years later, in 1584. The prioress was Ottavio's cousin through her father, the daughter of Lorenzo del Macchia, brother of Judetta, Ottavio's mother.[26] The presence of the notary Amoni and his wife Lisabetta at the canonization hearings can be explained by the family relationship that linked them respectively to his cousin, the prioress of the Convent of Crocetta, and to her brother, the public notary of the proceedings.

Lisabetta thus resumed her testimony with the story of her own miraculous recovery. This time, it was a case of the plague.

> I got a terrible fever and horrible headache on 29 August of this year. I became so sick that I couldn't even get out of bed to go to the bathroom. That very day, I felt a great pain between my left leg and my body. I told my husband about it, and we found a hard red swelling there. It hurt me more than having a baby. My husband, convinced that it was the plague, was very worried because I was four months pregnant. He thought that if I went to the lazaret I would never come back. He said, "Wife, I don't want you to go to the lazaret. I'll call the doctor, but don't tell him that you have a bubo. That way he'll just treat you for the fever." Doctor Francesco della Nave came to see me. He let some blood and prescribed some syrup. Although the fever diminished, the pain from the swelling worsened. My husband decided not to send me to the lazaret and instead gave me a bonnet that had belonged to the blessed Sister Domenica. He said, "This must be your medicine. Place yourself in the hands of the blessed Mother, because I don't know what else to do to save this house from ruin." Faithfully I took it and put it around my neck. I gave myself over to the care of the blessed woman and asked her to cure me of the plague. I got more and more terrified because I heard that two women had died and that their bodies had been dumped in the fields. Finally, about twenty days later, the swelling went down and started to drain. The draining lasted for two months. Then one day I noticed that something the size of my thumb was about to come out. It was hard, and the pain was so bad

that I felt as if my insides were going to burst open. It continued to expel the liquid for more than one month, but today, thanks to God, I am totally healed. This miracle that cured me was due to the help of the blessed Mother, because I did not use any medicine except for the syrup the doctor gave me. He hadn't wanted to prescribe any medicine for me because I was pregnant. My husband also gave me an unguent, but I don't know what it was. Because the plague is so lethal and because I kept it hidden, I should have died and infected my family. There are nine of us, and thanks to God we are all still living. My husband, Ottavio, was the only one who knew the whole story, but he dared not tell anyone about it because there are severe punishments for those who do not report cases of the disease. If Your Excellencies had not obliged me to report this miracle, I wouldn't have told anyone about it.[27]

Lisabetta and Ottavio's transgression revealed the secret agreement that united them in the breaking of Public Health regulations. Like many other citizens, the husband and wife were accomplices, preparing a joint strategy based on precise choices designed to maintain a united and growing family and opposed to and reacting against the epidemic. To Lisabetta, the story of the plague was inscribed in the broader context of hiding the disease, in the sphere of the sacred; it involved not the corruption of sanitary personnel but the defeat of medical science through ridicule, impotence, and even trickery. Domenica da Paradiso directly competed with doctors by offering to the faithful the possibility of avoiding medical therapies and proposing alternatives: bread soup for men and clothes for women. In fact, Lisabetta's healing differed from previous cases, and the thaumaturgical technique changed with the relics involved. Instead of soup, a bonnet was used; thus, not food, but clothes. Medicine must not be swallowed; it should be worn over the sick body, not inside it.

Sister Angelica del Macchia had given the bonnet to Lisabetta's husband. From her testimony we know that an established hierarchy regulated the destination and use of relics. Some were used inside the convent, others outside it; some were for healing women, others for men. The relics in the heaviest demand were the little red crosses, followed by the bread kept in Domenica's tomb. That the bonnet was not mentioned indicates that it was probably not used very often. Perhaps because it was one of the accessories belonging to the blessed woman, its use was limited to the nuns of the convent. In her testimony, Sister Maria Grazia Zambeccari recalled that the relics used by the nuns included the bonnet "and some almonds that were in the cloth on which she rested."[28] Sister Filippa Landi also remembered how she had recovered from a dislocation: "When I was carrying a laundry bag, I felt the dislocation and thought that my kidneys were going to open up." Then she put a bloody bandage, which had been wrapped around Domenica's body, on the ailing part of her own body.[29] Sister Angelica told how wearing "the bloody shirt of the mother who is here in the convent" had cured her when she was young ("doctors said that I was consumptive").[30]

The bonnet given to her cousin by the prioress was therefore a unique relic, to be used in an internal circuit like the one in the convent and in the family connected to it by Sister Angelica del Macchia. The narrative paths increasingly narrowed as the holy body of Domenica, through the network of familial relations, became rightfully part of the family that administered the convent.

The bandages and what was left of the deathbed were, like the shirt and the bonnet, entrusted to the care of women. In his testimony, Ignazio del Nente, Dominican prior of San Marco and one of Domenica's biographers, confirmed that the Mother healed according to practices connected to a chain of celestial healers, a veritable mystical projection of the terrestrial community of his monastery. Domenica healed "through the touches" of the Madonna, Saint Mary Magdalen, and Saint Catherine. Her thaumaturgical effectiveness was embodied in this female genealogy which sanctioned memory and gestures.[31] Even Lisabetta's anguished description of her own illness offered an absolutely feminine perception of the plague. She measured the gravity of the illness by her pregnancy and the delivery pains. The healing she characterized by comparing it to a monstrous delivery, a double of her son who, after the bubo had disappeared, continued to live in her body. The pregnancy explained in extraordinary physical detail the parable Lisabetta utilized to describe her recovery. To be sure, the drainage from the bubo "between her left leg and her body" reminds us of the numerous analogous reports of abnormal deliveries.[32]

The intense passion of the story of Lisabetta, who testified to overcoming fears and secrets and recalled the suffocating ring of death that besieged her home and killed her neighbors one by one, dilated this personal remembrance into an allegory of evil, of personal perception and social aggression. Moreover, her story activated other images belonging to contexts wherein magical and imaginary components were accentuated and made socially explicit.[33]

The emotional quality of her words stemmed not only from the epidemic, but also from her pregnancy, a condition which her culture considered suspended between danger and a temporary state of almost supernatural power. "The many adventures, not all known," of pregnant women increased the risk of ridicule and of mistakes by doctors, whose relationship with women, as we have already noted, was ambiguous, characterized by litigious competition.[34] A large number of reports of clinical cases described doctors visiting female patients for "obstruction," "milt," and "suffocation of the matrix," unable to isolate the mysterious illnesses that disappeared "upon delivery."[35] Full of traps and tricks, the female body was a difficult code to decifer. Even in the case of Lisabetta Centenni, her pregnancy sufficed to divert Doctor Francesco della Nave's attention from the other, by far more dangerous disease she was trying to hide.

"They asked me to visit her," the doctor stated,

> but they did not tell me about the illness. . . . I did not see any sign of the plague. Her heartbeat indicated that she had a fever, so I ordered a bloodletting. Since she was pregnant, I gave her only some syrup without medicine. Had I seen any sign of the plague I would not have done that, because bloodlettings may be dangerous when there is evidence of swelling; the poison is attracted to the vital organs and can suffocate the heart.[36]

In the criminal documents of the Public Health Magistracy, there are many cases of women who were sick twice, both pregnant and plague-stricken. The survivors confessed to the magistrate when, on the basis of secret information, he ordered them arrested. Those cases in which the family was able to hide sick members and thereby avoid hospitalization outlined, within the common practice of hiding the disease, a typically feminine behavior and defense. In this sense, Lisabetta's story was common. Yet it was also exemplary because, among all the episodes we have studied, it was the only time in which this double danger was resolved with the survival of both mother and son. All other pregnant women who did not die of the plague lost the baby. The testimonies of Lisabetta and her relatives, then, reveal the profile of all other women, the network of parallel stories, and the words of defeat and death which enclosed those biographical fragments in memory and in the written record. To ensure that they do not disappear, I will examine one more.

This story does not come from a trial document; rather, the barber-surgeon Carlo Martini reported the episode to the Florentine Public

Health Magistracy. Cold and hostile, he described the case of Francesca Guerri, the wife of Michelagniolo, a "laborer employed by the monks of Vallombrosa," and of Francesca's friends and neighbors, who were guilty of failing to denounce her to the authorities. Three months pregnant and healthy, Francesca returned home after a visit to Santa Maria Novella Hospital only to fall ill. Two days later, "with a bubo between her legs," she died, "having miscarried. Some bubbles appeared, and several women tried to take care of her during her miscarriage and death. Afterwards, they washed and buried her body . . . like one who had not died of the plague." Thus, they buried her in consecrated ground, not in a mass grave. "The women who were present at the woman's death," the barber-surgeon noted, "knew that she had a bubo and had tried to treat it. They did not want to admit how she really died, so they claimed that she had died during a delivery after three months of pregnancy."[37]

This solidarity was not rewarded, however, because Francesca had left her shirt to one of her friends, thereby, through her own affection, involuntarily contributing to the spread of the contagion. Wrapped in the cloth she inherited, the friend went to sleep near her husband and sons, "and it is believed that she spread the plague in her home," killing everyone.[38]

Besides the pregnancy and their illnesses, several other points of contrast marked the stories of Lisabetta Centenni and Francesca Guerri. First, the two women viewed the hospital differently. For Lisabetta, it was an institution to be avoided at all costs because it would ruin the entire family. In Francesca's case it actually confirmed this fear: although she entered Santa Maria in good health, she left sick. Second, the composition of the groups of women treating the sick women differed. Whereas nuns and the prioress of Crocetta aided Lisabetta, female neighbors and peasants assisted Francesca. Third, the clothes and their effect varied: although Domenica da Paradiso's bonnet miraculously healed Lisabetta, Francesca's shirt spread death. Finally, a delivery killed Francesca yet saved Lisabetta, who extracted the plague from her body by herself.

AN ENTERPRISING NOTARY

According to Lisabetta Centenni's testimony, the decision to hide the bubo and resort to home remedies was made after her husband, Ottavio, had found out that she was sick. Thinking of his family's best interests, he declared: "Wife, I don't want you to go to the lazaret."

Not only did this decision correspond to the widespread fear of all medical establishments and the preference for self-treatment, but it also resulted from a particular episode in Ottavio's life. He reported that Lisabetta was actually his second wife. His first wife, Alessandra, had died of typhoid fever in 1620. In 1617 this first marriage had produced a son who was christened Benedetto, after his grandfather.[39] Unfortunately, we do not know whether the boy survived the previous epidemic that killed his mother and many other relatives. In any case, the notary recovered quickly from the loss of his wife and married Lisabetta Centenni about one year later. In 1622 she gave him another son, Giovan Battista.

Although Ottavio had only narrowly escaped the contagion of 1620, he had helplessly witnessed the decimation of his family by the typhoid epidemic. There can be no doubt that his decision to hide his new wife's sickness stemmed from this devastating experience. In fact, he began his testimony by recounting that disaster, revealing as well how attached he was to his family. In particular, he defended himself by tenaciously reconstructing the motives that underlay his actions.

> It was about ten years ago—the year that was full of so many terrible epidemics—in October, that my first wife, Alessandra Ghiosi, fell ill and died. She was affected with a malignant fever, and then many other complications developed. Everybody around her got sick, and altogether ten people died, including a servant named Caterina who came from Rovezzano. A lot of people in Florence thought that my house should be closed. I myself got so sick that I was abandoned by the doctors and given last rites in Santa Chiesa. Sister Angelica, hearing that I was going to be dead within a few hours, immediately went to see the prioress and asked that an oration be said for me. Then she sent me a piece of bread that had been placed over the body of the Blessed Mother. When I received it, I entrusted myself to [Domenica]. After kissing the bread, I made it into soup. As soon as I began to eat it, I felt better and better. The illness subsided, and I was able to rest comfortably that very night, something I hadn't been able to do for a long time. Within a few days I could leave for Colle, my hometown, to breathe some fresh air.[40]

The memory of his suffering at his first wife's death oriented Ottavio's behavior in 1630. The differences between the two epidemics did not seem to be significant: they faded away in the face of an indistinct and threatening horizon. What really mattered was to stick together and confront the disease and the interference of the state. Ten years earlier, cousin Angelica, by sending him the holy bread, had only just managed to save him. She healed him again in 1624, according to Lisabetta, who anxiously followed the course of the disease from her husband's bedside. Ottavio confirmed her story and stressed this miraculous experience. To remember those climactic moments of the disease pained him, and throughout the narration his prose was infused with adjectives that revealed a heightened emotional tension. Despite all the medicine and "bloodlettings," "the disease boiled," filling Ottavio "with weakness and great anxiety." "I tossed from one side of the bed to the other," he recalled, "and I was deliriously afraid that I would suffocate" because the medicine did not bring any relief. Doctor Francesco della Nave had given up all hope.[41] The arrival of the bread from the Convent of Crocetta, its transformation into soup, and the miraculous and intensely felt healing concluded Ottavio's second encounter with illness in a sudden victorious rising.

Finally the notary told the story of Lisabetta and her bout with the plague. Upon his return from Rovezzano, just a few miles from the city, he found his wife in bed, and together they discovered a bubo. This was the second time that Ottavio had mentioned this particular village in his testimony, as if it were a familiar place that he frequented. It was from Rovezzano that, during the typhoid epidemic of 1620, Caterina had come to help him, and it was in the same village that his cousin Piero del Macchia, priest of the Church of San Michele, lived. The notary had gone to register two wills there between 26 and 29 August 1630.

Official notarial protocols enable us to study Ottavio's professional activities and follow his movements during the epidemic.[42] This apparently neutral source, however, suggested, through formulaic expressions, the uncertainties and fears that delimited Ottavio's journeys depending on the worsening and lessening of the contagion. During the three days he spent in Rovezzano, for example, as the mortality rate rose and the plague spread in the summer heat, the people whose wills he recorded were "in good physical and mental condition." One can assume that Ottavio investigated their health, since he feared catching the disease and thereby transmitting it to his family.

He most likely did not expect to find his wife, Lisabetta, already suffering from "a horrible swelling between her leg and body" upon his return from Rovezzano.[43]

"I was struck," he recounted,

> because . . . you were supposed to send the sick people to the lazaret and lock everybody else in the house. I knew that this would ruin my family, so I decided to resort to the Blessed Mother and forsake any human cures. I gave my wife the bonnet that Sister Angelica had given to me. I called the doctor in for the ceremony, telling him that my wife was pregnant and feverish. That way he would say that she did not have the plague and so keep the Public Health magistrates from interfering. The doctor visited her but did not discover the bubo. He prescribed a bloodletting and gave her some syrups, weak ones because of her pregnancy. Finally, as the disease did not let up and my wife experienced some very strong pains, the bubo opened on its own and began to drain a lot. I gave some unguent to my wife and told her to put it on the wound. The drainage continued for a long time, and one day my wife said that a putrid piece which was larger than a thumb had come out.[44]

Thus, it was Ottavio who decided what to do and how to deal with Francesco della Nave, the family doctor. To call him "for the ceremony" so that all formal procedures were properly followed, which would satisfy the magistrate, was motivated by the worry that the family could be ruined.

The notary Amoni's testimony explicated all the passages and thought processes of the other defendants we have encountered who were arrested for hiding a sick relative. The goldsmith Manzuoli, the apprentice Fantasti, the goldsmith Contino, and all others prosecuted for this same crime would be able to see in Ottavio's story motives and attachments much like their own. Moreover, in the Amonis' network of complicity these individuals could identify analogous strategies conceived to preserve the private sphere from the intrusion of the Public Health authorities.

The notary insisted again on his strong feelings for his family, confessing, "Once, I struck a servant who had mistreated one of my sons. She died two weeks later, and people thought that it was because I had hit her."[45] For that action, Ottavio was prosecuted by the Otto and sentenced to one year of exile. He was acquitted somewhat later. This was a man who, in order to protect his son, was ready to kill. Moreover, his position as notary implied that he knew very well what the destruction of a patrimony and a house meant: the residents taken away; the men and women sent to different lazarets; and all their belongings inspected, fumigated, or burnt by the Public Health personnel.

The countless lists of reclaimed, confiscated, stolen, and destroyed objects served as anonymous, macabre reminders (two "dirty" sheets, two "coral necklaces," in addition to documents, jewels, furniture, kitchen tools, etc.) of the already-subsiding epidemic. These poor remains allow us to trace new arguments, testimonies, and notarial acts.

Therefore, for the sake of his family and patrimony, Ottavio lied to Francesco della Nave and gave his wife the bonnet and unguent instead. In the end he told the doctor the truth, who subsequently reported the entire story to the judges. "When he told me what the disease really was, I was astonished that she was still alive and that their neighbors had not been infected. They told me that Amoni had given the woman a bonnet from Domenica da Paradiso." It was truly a miracle, especially considering that, being completely unaware of what the disease really was, the doctor had prescribed medicine that "was the exact opposite of what she needed and would have infected all those who lived with her, causing death."[46] Fortunately, Domenica da Paradiso had once again triumphed over the ritual impotence of doctors.

ORAZIO'S WILL

Unlike her husband, Ottavio, who was cured quickly, Lisabetta took such a long time to get better that no miracles seemed to be at work. We know nothing else about her, because she was confined to the privacy of her bed. Ottavio, in contrast, returned to the city to work and, by so violating Public Health regulations, became a part of official memory. This fact allows us to reconstruct some of his other relationships; in particular, the names of various testators for whom he wrote wills open up interesting vistas. On 5 November 1632, for example, Ottavio drew up the will of Matteo Nicola de Morosi, an overseer who worked at the Convent of Crocetta. On 14 July of the following year he drafted the will of the goldsmith Orazio Vanni.[47] Orazio, the father of Niccolò and Jacopo, was a friend of Ottavio Amoni and Lisabetta. When Orazio was sick, Ottavio and Lisabetta came often to visit him. Jacopo also testified at the hearings, reporting that he frequently went to Ottavio's to exchange news. Members of both families made many statements showing that they cared a great deal for one another: "I and the others in my house had little hope for [Lisabetta]"; and "I stayed there for a long time to see [if the fever would return. The following day] I congratulated [Orazio] on his renewed health."[48] Moreover, both the Vannis and the Amonis were members of the Compagnia del Santo Benedetto Bianco, which met at the cloister of Santa Maria Novella. They attended the same religious ceremonies that linked them to the Dominican order, just as Domenica da Paradiso, her biographers, and the other witnesses at the proceedings were linked.[49] In addition to this, the two families shared a geographical relationship: the Vannis' gold shop was on the Ponte Vecchio, near the offices of the Nove Magistracy, where Ottavio was a minister.

Orazio's will, which was prepared during the pestilence, is one of the most thoroughly representative documents I came across in the course of my research. It is not only representative of its times and of middle-class Florentine society, but it is also revealing of the *mentalités* common to the bourgeois witnesses at the canonization hearings. Reading Orazio's will, therefore, helps us to understand these people's sense of family: its cohesiveness, its lineage, and its sense of honor. It also helps complete the picture of the culture of possession to which all Florentines tenaciously held in the face of the epidemic. Like his fellow citizens, Orazio attributed great significance to the belongings he had accumulated over the years; in essence, they marked the path of his social climb. When, after many years, Orazio finally managed to buy a family vault in Santa Maria Novella "in front of the Ricasoli Chapel," we comprehend the sense and direction of a journey in which the identity of the family group and the shop mutually reinforced one another in a symbiotic binomial relationship. The epidemic was unable to disrupt this social identity based on wealth, this fusion of the consciousness of being and the culture of possession.

Finally, the will brought together people we have already met on different paths, connecting the threads of their stories. Through the testimonies of Pietro Tacca and Michelangelo Buonarroti the younger, the artists of the early Florentine baroque period appeared in the hearings much as lights appear in the dark. Objects and decorations, marked by the taste of the era, took form in Orazio's proud descriptions as he left his possessions to one or another person. Familiar names appeared; besides the Medicis and Pietro Aretino, there was a portrait of Allori and Cigoli, two famous Florentine artists, by Giovanbattista Vanni, Orazio's son. Giovanbattista, the black sheep of the circumspect goldsmith family, worried his father continually; nor did Orazio ever trust his son. According to one biographer, Giovanbattista was a young man "of extraordinary beauty" who possessed an "active and never-ending vitality."[50] Although he showed great promise at an early age, once he began to work under Cristoforo Allori he produced only mediocre paintings and led a dissipated life. Everyone knew that he was financially dependent on his father. Because Orazio "made a lot of money, he gave [his son] installments," which enabled Giovanbattista to go to Parma to study and copy Correggio's frescoes.[51]

The soft Florentine baroque style spread through Giovanbattista to the shop on the Ponte Vecchio. Through his influence, the Vannis' bourgeois solidity was erased and replaced by the paintings of Tacca, Buonarroti, Allori, and Parigi. The contrast, however, was more apparent than real, and Giovanbattista's brush painted the images and places of his family's devotions, as well as those of his friends. In particular, the young artist reflected his family's pious relationship with the Dominican order by paying homage to the saving power of Domenica da Paradiso. He first decorated the chapel of the Compagnia del Santo Benedetto Bianco, then the lunettes of the Chapel of San Antonino, the official protector of the city, and, finally, he painted the portrait of Father Ignazio del Nente, prior of the Dominicans, biographer of Domenica, and witness at her canonization.[52]

Reading Orazio's will provides us with an intimate description of his house:

> all of the linens and blankets, . . . the books, . . . the bed and its decorations, . . . a silk bed cover, white curtains, and other bedroom accessories, . . . Jacopo da Empoli's painting and Boscoli's two pictures of Saint John and Saint Paul resurrecting the dead, . . . six other paintings, including portraits of Giovanni Medici the elder and Pietro Aretino. Portraits of Cristoforo Allori and Cigoli

were painted by Giovanbattista. Orazio wrote that, since Giovanbattista was often away from Florence and his family, "all of the clothes and linens on Giovanbattista's bed should be separated and divided among those whom they fit and those who could use them."

Next comes the shop on the Ponte Vecchio, which he leaves to his two sons, Niccolò and Jacopo, so that they might follow in his footsteps. Besides the shop, Orazio left them a nearby "small store," which was rented out, together with "the benefits and profits that may proceed from the guild's statutes with respect to the shop." "All of the gold and silver, both refined and rough, and the pearls and jewels of all kinds" were left to Niccolò and Jacopo as well. Orazio then explained the vicissitudes that had led him to purchase the shop: "It is now worth six hundred *fiorini,*" precisely the sum with which he had "begun to establish himself as a goldsmith." Since 1612 he had worked with his two sons, and it was with their help that he was able to save twelve hundred *fiorini* for the dowry of his daughter Caterina, who in 1614 married Pietro Comparini.

While the plague was raging in Florence, the goldsmith Vanni drew up the balance sheet of his life, a life that had been enclosed within the walls of his house and shop and would end, should the disease take him, with his remains sealed in the family vault in Santa Maria Novella. The patriarch's memory slowed down when it got to the names of those who had lent him money, those who had drawn up purchasing and property contracts, and those who, like two of his sons, had been loyal to him. He endlessly repeated those figures that concerned dowries, loans, rents, and the interest from the Monte di Pietà, making numbers grow and multiply into a visible ascent of the family fortune. Finally, when he thought about the day when all the debts incurred in the purchase of the shop were repaid, "through the profits, hard work, and fatigue" of his two sons, he calmed down. His entire estate should be left to his two deserving sons.

His other sons, in contrast, the painter Giovanbattista and the priest Lorenzo, had only cost him money and worry. He had always provided them with

> food, clothes, and other necessities, without ever receiving any appreciation or help from them whatsoever. And these expenses had been paid for by the labor of Jacopo and Niccolò. In particular, the sum of 130 *fiorini* had been spent recently to enable Lorenzo to obtain his doctorate. Similarly, Giovanbattista had spent a large sum of money to travel out of the territory of His Most Serene Highness. I provided him with clothes and paid off his debts, yet he has never given me anything in return.

It was a lucky coincidence that the youngest son, Father Serafino of the Dominican order, had renounced his share of the inheritance in order to "serve the Divine Majesty better."

The story of Ottavio Amoni and his wife, Lisabetta, who was miraculously healed by Domenica da Paradiso, requires no further comment. It becomes more comprehensive, however, when compared to the will of Orazio Vanni and the parable of bourgeois success there recounted. These two elements in the large mosaic of the plague shed light on a dark area, showing us that it was not only the lower classes, including artisans, textile workers, and street vendors, who violated Public Health regulations, but also members of the middle class, professionals and bureaucrats.

After the prioress Angelica del Macchia presented her testimony in a tedious repetition of miraculous topoi, the Florentine proceedings ended. The part that concerns us most directly—that which touches upon the plague—concluded with Jacopo Vanni's testimony. Thus, the testimonies of interest to us concerned the Centennis, the Amonis, and some of their friends, that is to say, the enlarged family of Angelica. The centrality of Domenica paled with the arrival of the plague in the trial documents, and her place on the scene was taken over by Prioress del Macchia. While the protagonists of political and court society retold Domenica's story and sang her praises in an implicit exchange of sacred attributes, the middle-class and new-bourgeois protagonists acquired dignity through the devout relationship linking them to their cousin, the prioress.

COSMOLOGIES

On 5 December 1630, a solemn procession bearing the body of San Antonino, the "public protector" and former archbishop, passed through the streets of Florence. Accompanied by the sounds of the city's bells and artillery, the cortege started at the Monastery of San Marco, traversed Via Larga and Via Martelli, and terminated at the duomo. Of all Florence's religious orders, only the Dominicans of San Marco and Santa Maria Novella were present in the cathedral: San Antonino belonged to them.

As with all urban public rituals, men representing both ecclesiastical and secular authority were in attendance. They were carefully placed according to their rank in the hierarchy: the Dominicans; the clergy of the duomo; Archbishop Bardi; four bishops; the canons; the grand duke; the princes Giovan Carlo, Francesco, Leopoldo, and Lorenzo; Duke Salviati; the master of the chamber, Marquis Orso d'Elci; Marquis di Coloreto, majordomo; eight first gentlemen of the court; eight knights of San Stefano; another eight Florentine aristocrats; and, finally, twelve "men of San Martino," the company of paupers founded by San Antonino. According to the chronicler, the prayers "were to be elevated so that the city could assault Heaven and violently snatch away the desperately needed good health." The supplications were characterized almost as a devout raid wherein religious sentiment was imbued with a vaguely militaristic and threatening accent.[53] This parade occurred just as another sophisticated ritual was taking place in the chapel of the Convent of Crocetta and in the chapel of the Pitti Palace: the canonization of Domenica da Paradiso.

Both Antonino and Domenica were linked to the city, to the Dominican order, and to the Medici family. Whereas Antonino was already a saint, the venerated Domenica had not yet been canonized. The hearings and the removal of her body expressed the double polarization of the Medicean cosmology, which acquired particular significance at the recent transition from the female regency of the grand duchesses to the male government of Ferdinand II. The promise to defeat the disease was therefore presented to the Florentine people as a double itinerary that, in the universe of symbols, made explicit the sacred origins of the reigning family. The male Medicis occupied external space in this public demonstration of alliances built around the body of San Antonino at the very time that the female Medicis were showing, in the enclosed space of the convent, the path of recovery through the recounting of the story of Domenica da Paradiso. For the ruling classes, the period of the epidemic harked back to the city's historical past, when the most difficult times were recalled with both their tensions and resolutions. The biographies of San Antonino and Domenica da Paradiso were utilized in this recuperation, emotionally reactivating it. The former was connected to the Cosimian age before the establishment of the principality; the latter to the age of Grand Duke Cosimo, the overcoming of the lethal crisis represented by the Republic, and the subsequent siege of the city.

Antonino Pierozzi was born in 1389, about one hundred years before Domenica Nardini, to a bourgeois family. His father was a notary. Self-taught, Antonino possessed a solid legal background and wrote treatises on ethics and Catholic doctrine. In addition, he obtained several important positions, including diplomatic posts abroad. Significantly, he was also a very good friend of Cosimo the elder. It was because of Antonino that the Dominicans of Fiesole were able to establish themselves in the Monastery of San Marco, which Cosimo

had just enlarged and generously decorated. In fact, Cosimo had reserved a cell for himself in the monastery so that he could be near the
"living saint." Appointed archbishop of Florence in 1446, Antonino
died in 1459, just five years before his friend and benefactor. He was
canonized in 1523 by Adrian VI.

The Compagnia di San Martino was linked to his figure as well.
This company was composed of members of the once-powerful noble
families that had opposed the Medicis. The ruling dynasty had confiscated their wealth and sentenced them to exile, prison, or death. Now
poor and powerless, this company accompanied the body of the saint
in 1630.[54] Thus, support of the republican ideal was reconducted
within the channel of an orthodoxy of might and its generous charity;
any possibility of divisiveness within the political sphere was elimi-
nated by the sight of the ruling class parading in public together. Confronted by a crisis, these leaders had to display unity and loyalty.

Compared to the image of San Antonino, the figure of Domenica
da Paradiso, remembered by low voices within the convent walls, introduces us into a world of private devotion which was, by and large,
female. Domenica's life delineated a model of religious experience
which differed from that of Antonino. Her mystical universe was
rooted in her prophecies and ecstatic experiences, in the orality of
visions and passions of the body. San Antonino's mystical universe
was, in contrast, based on writing and political-diplomatic media-
tions. In his study of communal society, R. Trexler has stressed the
recurrent cult-related presence of personalities peripheral to the religious hierarchy during periods of crisis: "Grave external crisis showed
that only individual religious persons characterized by insight rather
than by membership in a distinct social group could pierce the divine
mind and determine the correct response."[55] In addition, A. Vauchez
has analyzed the feminization of devotion—which, imposed by the
mendicant orders, had been increasingly accentuated since the late
Middle Ages—suggesting particular models of contemplative and
mystical perfection for the faithful.[56] Certainly these considerations
help to explain the utilization of Domenica da Paradiso and the grasp-
ing of this political-symbolic opportunity to begin the canonization
hearings during an epidemic. Yet the nucleus of significance implicit
in the hearings appeared to demolish its compactness, calling attention
to what Michel de Certeau, in his study of seventeenth-century mysticism, calls "les figures du sauvage." De Certeau elaborates:

Dans l'histoire qui mène du sujet mystique du XVIᵉ siècle au sujet économique, le sauvage serait un entre-deux. Comme figure culturelle (voire épistémologique), il prépare le second en inversant le premier, et, à la fin du XVIIIᵉ siècle, il s'efface, remplacé par le primitif, par le colonisé ou par le déficient mental. Au XVIIᵉ, il est opposé aux valeurs de travail, d'économie scripturaire et de classement territorial et social qui se mettent en place par l'exclusion de leurs contraires: il est sans productivité, ou sans lettres, ou sans "état."[57]

Witness of another world, Domenica's presence no longer threatened the established order but rather created a vague atmosphere of nostalgia.

Domenica's life embodied the memory of the countryside where she was born, of the wisdom of simple folk, and of those people's lonely migration to the city. This modest hagiographic profile, filled with bucolic flavor, also stressed the pastoral taste in fashion at the urban court. In the middle of the epidemic, the stories of recovery and miraculous healings delineated an itinerary of female assistance that revolved around a domestic environment and the kitchen utensils used by women on a daily basis. Through prayers to Domenica and the passage of the miraculous soup recipe from the Convent of Crocetta, through the nuns and servants, to the stricken, a cure was obtained. These were heavenly remedies transmitted orally from door to door and from room to room. They created a clandestine chain that somehow violated the regulations the Public Health authorities imposed on the community. In order to be cured by the blessed woman, one had to call the doctor "for the ceremony," just as Ottavio had done, and feed him false information. One had, in short, to hide the sick and treat them at home, despite the law. This transgressive behavior was legitimized, though, by the private and ritualistically miraculous healings.

The chain of recoveries, originating at the Convent of Crocetta and reaching the houses of the city, belonged to a cultural universe opposite to the official one; it appeared like an island where all relationships of buying and selling lost their concreteness and were replaced by the moral economy of the gift. Cousin Angelica, prioress of the convent, supplied the bonnet and bread that healed Lisabetta Centenni and her husband, Ottavio. In contrast, the medical system provided for an institutionalized organization of hospital care, while insuring that all important tasks be performed exclusively by male personnel. Furthermore, both the diffusion of and research into medical understanding were rigorously mediated by the written word. Doctors' prescriptions, herbalists' compilations, Guild statutes, the "Cosimian Provision," and numerous treatises distinguished within precise boundaries licit from illicit substances. The testimonies of barber-surgeons, patients, and herbalists—as we have repeatedly heard—moved within this defined space. The consciousness of having broken out of this space was foremost the consciousness of having violated the regulations established by texts. The miraculous healings performed by Domenica da Paradiso seem to be located, therefore, within a boundary that separated the male from the female sphere. The trial records, moreover, indicate that the dimensions of orality, gratuitousness, and secrecy coincided with female ministrations to sick bodies.

We can see that the public representation of Domenica's life and actions, and the specific textualization of the plague mediated by this representation, made the numerous and often contradictory levels of perception and signification produced by the crisis explicit and comprehensible.[58] Her story, especially the miraculous circuit disclosed by her body, also follows our reading of the chronicles and the official reports into an underground level of significance. It insinuated doubts, broke the thread of the story line, and lacerated the surface of events, texts, and narrations along lines of unsuspected depth.

Notes

INTRODUCTION

1. F. Rondinelli, *Relazione del contagio stato in Firenze l'anno 1633* (Florence: G. B. Landini, 1634). Although there are no detailed figures on death rates, it is commonly believed that the number of deaths was lower than in previous epidemics. See D. Bucci, "Premesse per uno studio sulla peste a Firenze nel 1630," delivered at the conference entitled "Le crisi di mortalità e la società italiana" (Department of Statistics, University of Florence, 1977). In his introduction, Rondinelli writes, "During the first wave, which lasted thirteen months, twelve thousand people in the city and surrounding countryside died. In the new outbreak of 1633, which lasted five months, between six hundred and eighteen hundred people died." Mortality was very selective: "Very few nobles died, perhaps not even twenty-five in the entire eighteen-month period" (p. 24). J. Galluzzi, in *Istoria del Granducato di Toscana* (Florence: G. Cambiagi, 1781), 3:454, tallied 6,921 deaths in the city of Florence during a four-month period. On the figures concerning the region's population, see D. Lombardi, "1629–1631, crisi e peste a Firenze," *Archivio storico italiano* 1 (1979): 44. Lombardi counted between 63,154 and 92,000 inhabitants in the Florentine territory (countryside, dioceses). L. Del Panta, in *Una traccia di storia demografica della Toscana nei secoli XVI–XVIII* (Department of Statistical Mathematics, University of Florence, 1974), suggests that Florence numbered 76,023 inhabitants in 1622. For a comparison of death rates in 1630, see A. Corradi, *Annali delle epidemie occorse in Italia dalle prime memorie fino al 1850* (Bologna: Gamberini & Parmeggiani, 1870), 6:1073–75.

2. Rondinelli, *Relazione*. For a discussion of Rondinelli, see J. Rilli, *Notizie letterarie ed istoriche intorno agli uomini illustri dell'Accademia Fiorentina* (Florence: P. Matini, 1700), pp. 318–21. The preface to the eighteenth-century edition (Florence: J. Guiducci & S. Franchi, 1714), pp. v–viii, is also helpful.

3. Rondinelli, *Relazione*, pp. 42–43. Archivio di Stato, Florence (hereafter ASF), Sanità, Decreti e Partiti, filza 6, fol. 44. The nunzio informed Rome about the contagion in Trespiano in a dispatch on 13 August: Archivio Segreto Vaticano, Rome (hereafter ASV), Segreteria di Stato, Firenze, filza 19, fol. 39.

4. Rondinelli, *Relazione,* pp. 44–45.

5. Ibid., p. 149.

6. Ibid., p. 150.

7. F. Giubetti, *Il Cancelliero di Sanità* (Florence: Z. Pignoni, 1629), p. 2.

The trial documents are contained in ASF Sanità, Negozi, filze 148–56, 166–70, 483. A small group of eight trials is in ASF Otto di Guardia e Balia, filza 1914. These are trials concerning the black market in the Apennines and riots in border towns which occurred in the summer of 1630 before the state of contagion was officially declared. From that moment on, the Public Health Magistracy assumed jurisdiction over criminal trials, which explains why the documents are located in a different series. Research in the documents of the Otto, the ordinary Magistracy, produced no results. Sentences are gathered in Sanità, Decreti e Partiti, filze 4, 6, 7; the grand duke's pardons are in ASF Sanità, Rescritti, filza 37. Some reflections based on preliminary research of criminal behavior in times of plague are in A. Pastore, "Criminalità e giustizia in tempo di peste: Bologna e Ginevra fra '500 e '600," delivered at the conference "Città italiene del '500 tra Riforma e Controriforma" (Lucca, 13–15 October 1983).

8. See J. Revel and J. P. Peter, "Le corps: L'homme malade et son histoire," in *Faire de l'histoire: Nouveaux objets,* ed. J. Le Goff and P. Nora (Paris: Gallimard, 1974), p. 171. Consult as well my article "L'oro, il fuoco, le forche: La peste napoletana del 1656," *Archivio storico italiano* 3 (1981).

9. Sanità, Negozi, filza 148, fols. 692–702; filza 154, fols. 884–85.

10. For a discussion of the culture-resource concept, see H. G. Gutman, *Work, Culture, and Society in Industrializing America* (New York: Vintage Books, 1977), pp. 14–19.

11. Sanità, Rescritti, filza 37, fol. 172. Lombardi, "1629–1631," pp. 34–37.

12. I discuss the theory of the double conspiracy in my article on the Neapolitan plague, "L'oro, il fuoco, le forche," pp. 409–11.

13. V. W. Turner, "Planes of Classification in a Ritual of Life and Death," in *The Ritual Process* (London: Routledge & Kegan Paul, 1969), p. 14.

14. On the use of the categories of expectations and experience as measures of historical time, see R. Koselleck, "La storia sociale moderna e i tempi storici," in *La teoria della storiografia oggi,* ed. P. Rossi (Milan: Il Saggiatore, 1983), pp. 140–58.

15. Sanità, Negozi, filza 154, fols. 481–86.

16. On the institution of the dowry in the legislation of wills, see *Statuta Populi et Communis Florentiae* (Freiburg: Michaelem Kluch, 1778–83), book II, rubric cxxix. A. Pertile, *Storia del diritto italiano* (Turin: Unione Tipografica Editrice, 1893), 4:97–100. N. Tamassia, *La famiglia italiana* (Milan, Naples, and Palermo: R. Sandron, 1910), pp. 289, 291, 293–94.

17. Sanità, Negozi, filza 167, fols. 332–87.

18. Ibid., filza 483, fol. 35.

19. Ibid., fol. 53.

20. Ibid., filza 153, fol. 438.

21. R. Ciasca, ed., *Statuti dell'arte dei Medici e speziali* (Florence: L. Olschki, 1922), p. 80: "To punish those who buy clothes and objects belonging to dead people" (1349, rubric lviii). Changes are recorded on pp. 286 (1375, rubric i) and 290–93 (1376, rubric iii). R. Ciasca, *L'arte dei Medici e*

speziali nella storia e nel commercio fiorentino dal sec. XII al XV (Florence: L. Olschki, 1927).

22. Sanità, Negozi, filza 152, fols. 241–56. The sentence is in Decreti e Partiti, filza 7, fols. 97–98.

23. ASF Notarile moderno, prot. 13392, notary Ottavio Amoni (1620–42), will no. 62.

24. On the articulation of somatic culture, see L. Boltanski, "Les usages sociaux du corps," *Annales: Economies, sociétés, civilisations* 26 (1971): 205–33.

25. R. Trexler, "Florentine Religious Experience: The Sacred Image," *Studies in the Renaissance* 19 (1972): 7–41. Biblioteca Nazionale Centrale, Florence (hereafter BNCF), Magliabechiano, cl. XV, cod. xlviii, *Diligenze usate in Firenze nella peste del 1630;* in this anonymous chronicle, the "resolutive medicine" is the procession of the image of the Madonna dell'Impruneta to Florence. The manuscript *Istorie* (1629–62) by Paolo Verzoni proposes the same resolutive scansion; see Magliabechiano, cl. XXV, cods. cccclxii–cccclxv.

26. Sanità, Negozi, filza 150, fol. 863; Sanità, Rescritti, filza 37, fols. 272–73.

27. From the late Middle Ages, a great rural migration to urban centers characterized Tuscany and affected the biographies of these women; see A. Benvenuti Papi, "Santità femminile nel territorio fiorentino e lucchese: Considerazioni intorno al caso di Verdiana da Castelfiorentino," in *Religiosità e società in Val d'Elsa nel Basso Medioevo* (Florence, Congress of S. Vivaldo, 29 September 1980), pp. 113–14. On their social origins, see A. Benvenuti Papi, "Frati mendicanti e pinzochere in Toscana: Dalla marginalità sociale a modello di santità," in *La mistica femminile nel Tracento* (Todi, International Conference of the Center for Studies in Medieval Spirituality, 1983), pp. 109–35. M. De Certeau provides some general considerations in *La fable mystique* (Paris: Gallimard, 1982), pp. 34–35, 277–79.

28. Galluzzi, *Istoria del Granducato di Toscana,* 3:385; F. Diaz, *Il Granducato di Toscana: I Medici* (Turin: UTET, 1976), pp. 366–67.

29. Diaz, *Il Granducato di Toscana,* pp. 360–64.

30. Ibid., pp. 367–69.

31. See M. Douglas, *Natural Symbols: Explorations in Cosmology* (London: Barrie and Rockliff, 1970); and M. Douglas, ed., *La stregoneria* (Turin: Einaudi, 1980) (*Witchcraft Confessions and Accusations* [London: Tavistock, 1970]).

32. E. De Martino, *Sud e magia* (Milan: Feltrinelli, 1980), p. 72.

33. The testimonies on miraculous healings and the circulation and use of relics are contained in ASV S. Congregazione dei Riti, filza 776, fols. 139–41. A. Vauchez discusses the private and personal devotion of the urban bourgeoisie since the fourteenth century in *La sainteté en Occident au derniers siècles du Moyen Age* (Rome: Ecole Française, 1981), pp. 557–58. R. Firth examines how relics were inserted into a circuit of symbolic exchanges in *Symbols: Public and Private* (Ithaca, N.Y.: Cornell University Press, 1973).

34. S. Congregazione dei Riti, filza 776, fol. 167.

35. Sanità, Rescritti, filza 37, fol. 500.

36. Ibid.

37. See D. Landy, ed., *Culture, Disease, and Healing* (New York: Macmillan, 1977), esp. chaps. 1 and 4.

38. Magliabechiano, cl. XV, cod. xv, *Antidotario di medicamenti di più autori*, 1632.

39. See J. Baudrillard, *L'échange symbolique et la mort* (Paris: Gallimard, 1976).

CHAPTER 1

1. Sanità, Negozi, filza 150, fol. 265.

2. D. Sterpos, "Le strade di grande comunicazione della Toscana verso il 1790," in *Archivio dell'atlante storico italiano dell'età moderna* 4 (Florence: Sansoni, 1977).

3. Sanità, Rescritti, filza 37, fols. 188, 190, 240, 266, 276, 324, 352, 506, on sheep-centered transhumance toward Maremma; fol. 243, on chestnut gathering in Pistoia; fol. 271, on day laborers who descended from Casentino to work the harvest in Maremma; and fol. 275, on the grape harvest. The fear of a connection between deserters and the plague had older roots; see, for example, Giuliano de' Ricci, *Cronaca*, ed. G. Sapori (Milan and Naples: Ricciardi, 1972), pp. 286–87, 291.

4. Sanità, Negozi, filza 149, fols. 222–23. The entire trial is contained in this carton. Henceforth, given the brevity of the acts, I will indicate only the document that refers to the cited trials, without specifying the location of each particular quote.

5. Ibid., fol. 1250.

6. Sanità, Rescritti, filza 37, fol. 157.

7. Sanità, Negozi, filza 150, fols. 271–72.

8. Ibid., fols. 214–15, 250.

9. Pilaster (*hypericum* in Latin) was commonly called the root of Saint Apollonia. It came from Asia and was put in the mouth hot to relieve toothaches.

10. On the physician Giuseppe Rosaccio, who was born around 1530 in Bordenone and died in approximately 1618, see G. Liruti, *Notizie della vita e opere scritte da letterati del Friuli* (Venice: Alvisopoli, 1830) 4:166–69. Two works are of particular interest: *Il microcosmo* (Florence: F. Tosi, 1600), dedicated to Antonio Medici, prince of Capestrano, and *Il medico* (Venice: P. Farri, 1621), which lists his complete works and contains a dedication.

11. Rosaccio, *Il microcosmo*, pp. 63, 65, 67, 70, 72–73.

12. Sanità, Negozi, filza 150, fols. 154–55, 180–81.

13. Ibid., filza 148, fols. 375, 386.

14. L. Mazzoldi, R. Giusti, R. Salvadori, eds., *Mantova: La storia* (Mantua: Istituto Carlo D'Arco, 1963), 3:91–116; L. C. Volta, *Compendio storico-critico della storia di Mantova* (Mantua, 1831), vol. 3; and R. Quazza, *Mantova attraverso i secoli* (Mantua, 1933).

15. Sanità, Negozi, filza 148, fols. 375, 386.

16. On the court of Bozzolo, see E. Marani and C. Perina, eds., *Mantova: Le arti* (Mantua: Istituto Carlo D'Arco, 1965), 3:142. Giulia Cesare Gonzaga reconstructed Bozzolo between 1592 and 1609. On Carlo Scipione Gonzaga, prince of Bozzolo and uncle of Marquis Ferrante de' Rossi, see Volta, *Compendio*, p. 76. On the Florentine and Mantuan branches of the Rossi family, see B. Candida Gonzaga, *Memorie delle famiglie nobili delle province meridionali d'Italia* (Naples, 1876), 4:201–14.

17. Volta, *Compendio*, p. 76.

18. F. Amadei, *Cronaca universale della città di Mantova* (Mantua: CITEM, 1956), 3:493.

19. Mazzoldi, Giusti, and Salvadori, *Mantova: La storia*, 3:109–10.

20. Ibid., p. 111. On the life of Carlo de' Rossi, see A. Valori, "Condottieri e generali del Seicento," in *Enciclopedia biografica e bibliografica italiana*, ser. 20 (Rome: I.E.I., 1943).

21. P. G. Capriata, *Dell'historia libri dodici: Ne' quali si contengono tutti i movimenti d'arme successi in Italia dal MDCXIII fino al MDCXXXIV* (Genoa: G. Calenzano & G. M. Farroni, 1639), pp. 1064–65. On Capriata, see M. Giansante, in *Dizionario biografico degli Italiani*, ed. A. M. Ghisalberti (Rome: Istituto della Enciclopedia italiana, 1976), 19:195–97.

22. Valori, in "Condottieri," mentions the battle at Ostiglia but does not report Rossi's death. No other source discusses his death either.

23. Capriata, *Dell'historia libri dodici*, p. 1066.

24. Quazza, *Mantova*, p. 206.

25. Sanità, Negozi, filza 148, fol. 416.

26. Sanità, Decreti e Partiti, filza 6, fol. 19r.

27. Ibid., fols. 19–20.

28. Ibid., fol. 20v.

29. Sanità, Negozi, filza 148, fols. 417, 420.

30. Ibid., fols. 692–93, 702.

31. L. von Pastor, *Storia dei papi* (Rome, 1931), 13:410. The meeting was held on 12 March 1630.

32. Galluzzi, *Istoria del Granducato di Toscana*, 3:449, reported that the Spanish reinforcements were expressly requested by the two grand duchesses, even though Ferdinand II had promised Richelieu that Tuscany would remain neutral. The Monte di Pietà in Florence had given Spain five hundred thousand *escudos*. The grand duke sent "the usual aid, dispatching the infantry destined for Voltri by sea" in April (p. 450). For the following developments of the Medicean policy during the Thirty Years' War, see A. Panella, "Una lega italiana durante la guerra dei Trent'anni," *Archivio storico italiano* 94 (1936): 3–36; and idem, "Ferdinando II de' Medici mediatore fra i duchi di Savoia e di Mantova per la questione del Monferrato," *Archivio storico italiano* 75 (1917): 166–91.

33. Capriata, *Dell'historia libri dodici*, p. 739.

34. Ibid., pp. 748–49.

35. Ibid., p. 741.

36. Sanità, Decriti e Partiti, filza 7, fols. 28–29.

37. Sanità, Negozi, filza 154, fols. 888–90.

38. Annibale Filangieri courageously fought at the sieges of Casale, Alessandria, Valenza, and Mortara. After the peace of 15 October 1630, he retired to seclusion at the Hermitage of Camaldoli. See Valori, "Condottieri."

39. According to the law, extremely severe sentences were to be imposed on guards who allowed people to cross the border without proper documents. Indeed, these sentences were as stiff as those levied against traitors, "who were burned alive." Guards were also punished, however, if travelers were able to circumvent the checkpoints, whether by luck or by distraction, "as the guards were responsible for the smallest infraction." See Giubetti, *Il Cancelliero di Sanità,* p. 16; on pp. 9–11, Giubetti explains how guards were elected and what they were paid.

40. Sanità, Negozi, filza 154, fols. 884–86, 893–95.

41. This was Ettore Ravaschieri, prince of Satriano; see Valori, "Condottieri."

42. The *parpagliole,* the currency of Piacenza and Lombardy, was worth three Tuscan *soldi.*

43. G. Benzoni, *I "frutti dell' armi": Volti e risvolti della guerra nel 600 in Italia* (Rome: I.E.I., 1980), p. 64.

44. A. Tadino, *Ragguaglio dell'origine et Giornali Successi della gran peste contagiosa . . .* (Milan: F. Ghisolfi, 1648), pp. 50–51.

45. A precise code regulated salaries and the interactions between officers and soldiers in the armies of the grand duchy; see L. Cantini, *Legislazione toscana* (Florence: Albizzini, 1802), 3:12. Cantini explained that each illegitimate action of officers was to be punished: "If a captain of the Bande abuses, by word or action, any soldier, this soldier can appeal to the commissioner, and the conflict will be resolved as between private individuals" without the soldier being punished for disobedience. Cantini maintained that a soldier was entitled to kill if his honor or his family's honor was at stake (pp. 37, 41). Salary regulations are listed on page 30, and the code of the "contingents inscribed in the Bande, and therefore in the service of the state," is outlined on pages 10 and 53. It was illegal for a citizen of the grand duchy to enlist in an army of another state ("Edict of 24 April 1610," 14:350–51), and foreigners were not allowed to enter the grand duchy "with arquebusses" ("Edict of 8 June 1610," ibid., 16:351–54).

46. Sanità, Negozi, filza 148, fols. 536–73.

47. On the legislation concerning mounted guards, see Cantini, *Legislazione Toscana,* 15:236–37. On the mounted guards of Romagna, established in 1618, see page 133. The guards of Pieve San Stefano were established in 1629, the same year as in Valdichiana and Valdinievole. These men were not salaried, were required to be residents of the area they patrolled, and were supposed to maintain their own horse "at their own cost" (p. 121).

48. Sanità, Negozi, filza 148, fol. 1215.

49. San Pier Damiani, *Apologeticum de contemptu mundi,* quoted in P. Camporesi, ed., *Il libro dei vagabondi* (Turin: Einaudi, 1973), p. xxi.

50. Camporesi, *Il libro dei vagabondi,* p. clxxiii. H. Kamen discusses Gia-

cinto Nobili and the picaresque literature of Europe in *The Iron Century* (Guernsey: Cardinal, 1976), pp. 444ff. On marginal people who participated in a counterculture, see B. Geremek, *Les marginaux parisiens aux XIVe et XVe siècles* (Paris: Flammarion, 1976). J.-P. Gutton analyzes the general causes of vagabondage and begging during the Ancien Régime in *La società e i poveri* (Milan: Mondadori, 1977), pp. 13–42 (includes a bibliography) (*La société et les pauvres en Europe, XVIe–XVIIIe siècles* [Paris: Presses Universitaires Françaises, 1974]).

51. Camporesi edited the text, *Il libro dei vagabondi,* pp. 90–165.

52. Ibid., p. 112.

53. The text is in ibid., p. 28.

54. Ibid., pp. 39–40, 133–34.

55. A. M. Cospi, "Il giudice criminalista," in Camporesi, ibid., p. 362.

56. R. Frianoro, "Il vagabondo," in Camporesi, *Il libro dei vagabondi,* p. 163.

CHAPTER 2

1. A. Righi, *Historia Contagiosi Morbi* (Florence: Francisci Honofrij, 1633), p. 70.

2. Ibid.: "Before and during Canis, cleansing is difficult."

3. Ibid., p. 71.

4. M. Ficino, *Il consiglio di M.F. contro la pestilenza* (Florence: Giunti, 1576), p. 3.

5. Ibid., p. 74.

6. *Il ricettario medicinale necessario a tutti i medici e speziale* (Florence: Giunti, 1567), p. 5. Water and dirt are the two pillars on which the entire *Farmacopoeia* is built. They are the foundation of every single medicine: "Simple medicines are water and dirt. Water can be either natural or artificial. Rainwater is natural because it falls from the sky. Well water that is gathered in cisterns, and springwater, whether from sources, wells, rivers, oceans, or mineral baths, are also natural. Artificial water is distilled by any possible means. Groundwater is extracted from the sand of rivers, oceans, or others bodies of water, such as the Lemmia, Armena, Samia, etc. Simple medicines are derived from animals, plants, or things that have been extracted from underground soil and water" (ibid., pp. 2–3). On the whole, ninety-six vegetable extracts, twenty-three metals, and ten animal extracts were suggested for use in the preparation of medicines. Two prescriptions mentioned "the blood of a red man" and woman's milk. On the earliest *farmacopoeie,* see A. Corradi, *Gli antichi statuti degli speziali* (Milan: Rechiedei, 1886), and esp. A. Benedicenti, *Malati, medici, farmacisti* (Milan: Hoepli, 1924–25); see also P. Smit, *History of the Life Sciences: An Annotated Bibliography* (Amsterdam: A. Asher, 1974).

7. Ficino, *Il consiglio di M.F.,* p. 74.

8. S. Rodriguez de Castro, *Il curioso nel quale dialogo si discorre del male di peste* (Pisa: Tanagli, 1631), p. 35; all authors make this assertion.

9. Ficino, *Il consiglio di M.F.,* p. 6.

10. Rondinelli, *Relazione*, pp. 27–28.

11. Sanità, Decreti e Partiti, filza 6, fols. 42r–43; the other ordinances are contained in fol. 286r.

12. Ibid.

13. Sanità, Rescritti, filza 37, fols. 51–52; Sanità, Negozi, filza 148, fols. 975, 991; filza 150, fol. 79; Sanità, Decreti e Partiti, filza 6, fol. 101v; Sanità, Negozi, filza 149, fols. 352, 655; Sanità, Decreti e Partiti, filza 6, fols. 238–39.

14. Sanità, Negozi, filza 149, fols. 1471–72.

15. Righi, *Historia Contagiosi Morbi,* p. 7.

16. Ibid., p. 8. Many historians of the plague have stressed these uncertainties and contradictory diagnoses; see for example, P. Preto, *Peste e società a Venezia, 1576* (Venice: Neri Pozza, 1978), pp. 47–75, 160–86. W. McNeill examines the phenomenon of epidemics within a broad diachronic environmental and demographic spectrum in *Plagues and Peoples* (Harmondsworth: Penguin Books, 1979).

17. Sanità, Negozi, filza 149, fol. 175.

18. Ibid., filza 151, fol. 60. The occurrence of common diseases during periods of epidemic served as alibis for criminal doctors and barber-surgeons. For example, the court doctor Benedetto Punta failed to report the sickness of Giovanni Bassimelli's wife, claiming that she died of eating too many figs in conjunction with drinking "fresh wine" (ibid., filza 150, fols. 1148–49; the sentencing is in Sanità, Decreti e Partiti, filza 6, fol. 142). Punta was not punished because he claimed that he could not recognize the illness. Nevertheless, he was placed in quarantine to prevent him from "going to His Majesty's palace."

19. *Processo originale degli untori nella peste del MDCXXX* (Milan: G. Truffi, 1939), pp. 69, 112.

20. Rodriguez de Castro, *Il curioso,* pp. 35–37.

21. "They cannot transmit [it] to others; therefore it is necessary that, if the disease is in the city, they receive it and retain it, as if they were glands of the society"; Righi, *Historia Contagiosi Morbi,* p. 11.

22. Rodriguez de Castro, *Il curioso,* p. 10.

23. F. Marchini, "De Peste Problemata" in *Belli divini, sive Pestilentis temporis accurata et luculenta speculatio theologica, canonica, civilis, politica, historica, philosophica* (Florence: Sermartelliana, 1633), 25:33.

24. Ficino, *Il consiglio di M.F.,* p. 73. The most illustrious Florentine doctor, Antonio Benivieni (1443–1502), wrote a treatise on the pestilence and preventive medicine. A follower of Savonarola, he treated members of the Florentine aristocracy. For a biographical sketch, see U. Stefanutti, *Dizionario biografico degli italiani,* 8:543–45. G. Targioni Tozzetti provides reports on even the most trivial episodes of the Florentine plague of 1630 in *Notizie degli aggrandimenti delle scienze fisiche accaduti in Toscana* (Florence, 1780), 3:134–35, 144–46.

25. Ficino, *Il consiglio di M.F.,* p. 6.

26. Ibid., p. 30. J.-N. Biraben has compiled a list of remedies against the plague in *Les hommes et la peste en France et dans les pays européens et méditerra-*

néens (Paris and The Hague: Mouton, Ecole des Hautes Etudes, 1975–76), 2:58–62. For the Florentine case, see in particular Ficino's work, Tommaso Del Garbo's *Consiglio,* and Niccolò de' Raynaldi da Sulmona's *Breve consiglio.* Some very interesting remedies are given in Marchini, *Belli divini,* 33:44–57. Marchini also examines images, rings, inscriptions, and incantations that prevented contagion. Only canonical formulas, however, were allowed because they were founded on Psalms, the Gospel, and the Holy Scriptures. On page 47 he records the exorcism against demons pronounced by Federigo Borromeo; this recitation was the only licit treatment. Superstitions and ecclesiastical prohibitions are analyzed in J. Le Brun, *Histoire critique des pratiques superstitieuses* (Amsterdam, 1733), 1:104, 152–53; 2:142–54.

27. Ficino, *Il consiglio di M.F.,* p. 70.

28. *Ricettario fiorentino* (Florence: P. Cecconcelli, 1623), p. 3. Popular texts such as Pietro Ispano's *Thesaurus Pauperum* (Venice: A. Bendoni, 1543) listed inexpensive substances that were thermally efficient. Benedicenti examined the various uses of organic matter, occasionally human, in *Malati, medici, farmacisti,* 2:767. A. Scarpa analyzes the utilization of these medicines in present-day anthropological contexts in *Nozioni di etnoiatria* (Verona: Valdonega, 1962), pp. 290–91. Ficino observed and condemned the practice, prescribed by doctors, of drinking "young men's warm urine." According to Ficino, this remedy was inappropriate for citizens, although he believed that for "peasants," it was actually "expedient." Perhaps this differentiation marked the beginning of a process that, by selecting the quality and origin of medicines while marginalizing some remedies, later became "popular." Ficino distinguished between the rich and the poor based on disparate costs of medicine. The prescription of urine for peasants, though, appears to follow yet another rationale, one internal to a shifting threshold of sensibility. Marchini unreservedly prescribed not only human urine, but also the urine of various animals, such as goats and black hens (*Belli divini,* p. 51).

29. Ficino, *Il consiglio di M.F.,* p. 33; Ficino especially recommended diets based on agar.

30. Rondinelli, *Relazione,* pp. 30–31.

31. Ibid., p. 29.

32. Ficino, *Il consiglio di M.F.,* p. 33.

33. Ibid., pp. 50–51. Benedicenti examined these medical practices in *Malati, medici, farmacisti,* 2:985–87.

34. Benedicenti gave this piece of information in *Malati, medici, farmacisti,* 2:987. In addition, see P. Camporesi, *La carne impassibile* (Milan: Il Saggiatore, 1983), pp. 140–41. The same practice is described by S. Mercurii, *De gli errori populari d'Italia* (Venice: F. Rossi, 1645), book 7, part 2, p. 417. A short biography of Giralomo Fabrizi d'Acquapendente is in B. Zanobio, *Dictionary of Scientific Biography,* ed. Charles Coulston Gillispie (New York: Scribner, 1970), 4:507–12.

35. Benedicenti, *Malati, medici, farmacisti,* 2:990. Benedicenti also describes the use of these techniques in Salerno's medical school until the seventeenth century.

36. Ficino, *Il consiglio di M.F.,* pp. 60–61.

37. Rodriguez de Castro, *Il curioso,* p. 42.

38. F. Bacon, *Historia Vitae et Mortis,* in *The Works of Francis Bacon,* ed. J. Spedding, R. L. Ellis, and D. D. Heath (London: Longmans, 1870), 2:308. Ficino supported many of these practices, which constituted therapies of rejuvenation. He believed that the recovery of good health depended on a cycle of "seasons" in the human body. Bacon opposed Ficino's theory of sympathetic medicine, which stressed the working relationship between the components and the elements of the body: "The conceit of Ficinus to renew the strength of old men by sucking the blood out of the arm of a healthy young man is very foolish. . . . It is an old tradition that a bath made of infant's blood cures the leprosy, and restores the putrid flesh; and some kings have incurred popular dislike on this very ground (Niceforo VII, 33). It is told of Heraclitus that, being afflicted with the dropsy, he covered himself up in the warm belly of a newly slain ox. The warm blood of kittens is used for erysipelas and to restore the flesh and skin." Doctors often put an amputated limb into an animal's body, assuming that the limb would attract the animal's blood. Doctors also placed two halves of a pigeon under their patients' feet to relieve the pain. According to Bacon, these practices were "dirty and loathesome. . . . We must look out for others which may be less disgusting and yet equally useful." A partial translation of Bacon's works, edited by Andrea Cioli, was published in Florence and Venice in 1629.

39. Ficino, *Il consiglio di M.F.,* p. 61.

40. "For their hidden quality, or similarity and affinity with the internal poison"; Marchini, *Belli divini,* p. 54. On therapies designed to heal wounds, consult Benedicenti, *Malati, medici, farmacisti,* pp. 1042–49.

41. Benedicenti, *Malati, medici, farmacisti,* pp. 1018–30.

42. Marchini, *Belli divini,* p. 56.

43. Ibid., p. 57.

44. Magliabechiano, cl. XV cod. xvii, *Modo di adoperare i medicamenti che sono in questa spezieria di campagnia,* p. 80. Particular attention is given to the common diseases of women and children; accordingly, remedies were milder: balsams, distilled water, and unguents.

45. Ispano, *Thesaurus Pauperum,* p. 70. In addition, see A. Piemontese, *De' secreti del reverendo donno Alessio Piemontese* (Venice: A. Gardane, 1580), pp. 23ff. A biography of Piemontese, alias Girolamo Ruscelli, is in G. Melzi, *Dizionario di opere anonime e pseudonime* (Milan, 1863). This edition, preserved in the Biblioteca Nazionale Centrale, Florence, contains the *ex libris* of its original sixteenth-century owner (only partially legible): "I, Antonio di Francesco, called 'Mannone,' a shopkeeper, . . . buy [this book] on 2 March for myself and my friends." On secret compilations of remedies, consult Natalie Zemon Davis, *Le culture del popolo* (Turin: Einaudi, 1980), pp. 340, 359 (*Society and Culture in Early Modern France* [Stanford: Stanford University Press, 1975]). P. Galluzzi examines a more recent period in "Motivi paracelsiani nella Toscana di Cosimo II e di don Antonio de' Medici: Alchimia, medicina, 'chimica' e riforma del sapere," in *Scienze credenze occulte livelli di cultura* (Florence: Olschki, 1982), pp. 31–62.

46. Sanità, Decreti e Partiti, filza 6, fol. 38; Rondinelli, *Relazione,* p. 42. The information arrived in Rome on 13 August; see Segreteria di Stato, Firenze, filza 19, fol. 39, which contains the correspondence between January and October 1630.

47. Rondinelli, *Relazione,* p. 43.

48. Sanità, Decreti e Partiti, filza 6, fol. 44.

49. Rondinelli, *Relazione,* p. 45.

50. Sanità, Negozi, filza 149, fols. 121, 404.

51. Rondinelli, *Relazione,* pp. 44–45.

52. Ibid., p. 145.

53. Sanità, Negozi, filza 166, fol. 833.

54. Sanità, Decreti e Partiti, filza 6, fols. 236–37.

55. Ibid., filza 4, fol. 13v.

56. Rondinelli, *Relazione,* p. 49.

57. Ibid., p. 51.

58. Sanità, Negozi, filza 155, fol. 159v.

59. R. Baehrel examines how the popular classes demanded a Public Health policy controlling the upper classes in "Epidémie et terreur: Histoire et sociologie," *Annales historiques de la Révolution française* 23 (1951): 113–46. Consult also Baehrel, "La haine de classe en temps d'épidémie," *Annales: Economies, sociétés, civilisations* 7 (1952): 351–60. A brief overview of the debate can be found in A. Pastore, "Peste e società," *Studi storici* 20 (1979): 857–73.

60. Sanità, Negozi, filza 152, fol. 215.

61. Ibid., fol. 377; the sentencing is in Decreti e Partiti, filza 7, fol. 29v. The investigation began on 8 November and ended on the twelfth.

62. Sanità, Negozi, filza 152, fols. 505–7, 726–27.

63. Sanità, Decreti e Partiti, filza 7, fol. 48v.

64. This episode occurred at the same time as the events examined by C. M. Cipolla in *Chi ruppe i rastelli a Montelupo?* (Bologna: Il Mulino, 1977). Cipolla's leniency toward the barber-surgeon Coveri is based only on the documents of the Public Health Magistracy, which tended to protect its workers from the ordinary Magistracy. The guards of the Otto arrested Coveri in February and charged him with "carrying a long and a short arquebus," a crime punishable by a fine of twenty-five *scudi*. The barber-surgeon claimed that his work in the countryside necessitated certain precautions and that the weapons "were given to him by the same 'family'"—that is, by the guards. In effect, weapons were often used to compel peasants to "obey and do things like bury the dead, etc."

The episode clearly delineates the conflict between the two magistracies. The charges against the barber-surgeon were aggravated by a report prepared by the grand duke's secretary, Andrea Cioli, who told the Otto that Coveri had attacked a prostitute on Via della Scala with an arquebus. The Public Health Magistracy helped to commute the sentence on 1 March 1630 to two years' exile in Leghorn. Later, Coveri asked the grand duke for a pardon. Another secretary, Giovan Francesco Guidi, used the worsening epidemic crisis to convince the magistrates to allow him to return to his duties in the countryside. The entire story is contained in Otto di Guardia e Balia, Suppliche, filza 2348, fol. 318. Cantini published the regulations governing the use of weapons within the city walls in *Legislazione toscana*, 14:350–51.

65. Sanità, Negozi, filza 150, fol. 87.

66. Ibid., filza 152, fol. 863.

67. Ibid., fol. 2341.

68. See Benedicenti, *Malati, medici, farmacisti*, 1:226–27; and *Ricettario fiorentino*, pp. 50–51.

69. *Ricettario fiorentino*, p. 212.

70. Sanità, Negozi, filza 153, fol. 26.

71. Numerous popular medical treatises mentioned this practice. A vein in the foot was cut to relieve uterine pain, letting the humors flow out of the body. R. Benincasa described the procedure in *Almanacco Perpetuo* (Venice: A. Zatta, 1798), 2:241. A similar episode, recorded in Sanità, Negozi, filza 151, fol. 98, tells how the barber-surgeon Giovanni di Bartolomeo Bruschi was called before the chancellor, who questioned him about the illness and death of Martino, "a member of the choir of the Cathedral of San Lorenzo." Bruschi treated many of San Lorenzo's "priests" and confessed to letting "six ounces of blood from the foot." This confirmed the magistrate's suspicions; indeed, this was an unusual form of bloodletting and was therefore related to an uncommon disease.

72. Sanità, Negozi, filza 153, fol. 37.

73. Ibid., filza 152, fol. 240.

74. Sanità, Decreti e Partiti, filza 7, fol. 76v. Alessandro and Francesco Manzuoli were fined fifty *scudi;* Piero Billi, in contrast, was acquitted.

75. The guild's first statute established the prohibition in 1314, which was confirmed in 1349. The guild condemned all agreements between doctors and herbalists concerning the sale of remedies and the sharing of profits (see Ciasca, *Statuti dell'arte,* p. 187). The guild accepted, however, the fraternization of doctors and herbalists when no profit was involved. Those denouncing herbalists who "prescribed medicine" were entitled to a ten *lire* award. Similarly, the marketing of medicine was strictly controlled.

Until 1560, guild consuls appointed searchers to inspect shops in order to verify the quality of the merchandise and to insure that no poisons were being stored. On 5 September 1561, Cosimo I created the position of *veditore del medicinale*. This official, aided by a doctor, was charged with controlling shops. Medicinal recipes were to be posted on public squares the day before they were sold. The *veditore* carefully examined each prescription and punished all herbalists who neglected to report empty vials. Herbalists' shops in monasteries and hospitals were also carefully monitored. In addition, herbalists could not honor any request other than those signed by doctors or barber-surgeons. Any herbalist who violated these regulations was fined ten *scudi*. The control over doctors' and herbalists' associations became increasingly stringent. Finally, physicians were prevented from placing any orders in shops owned by relatives. The code of 1560 also confirmed previous laws; "medical solutions," in particular, could be prescribed only by the attendant doctor, under a penalty of ten *ducati*. Cosimo's code is contained in *Ricettario fiorentino* and reproduced in its entirety in an appendix entitled "Provisione e capitoli attenenti all'arte delli Spetiali di tutto il felicissimo Dominio Fiorentino, per benefitio della vita humana" (5 September 1561). This particular trial is recorded in Sanità, Negozi, filza 153, fols. 675–76.

76. Sanità, Decreti e Partiti, filza 7, fol. 103.

77. Sanità, Criminale della Sanità, filza 483, fol. 3.

78. Ibid., fol. 25.

79. Ibid., fols. 51–52.

80. Sanità, Negozi, filza 151, fol. 183.

81. Ibid., fol. 608.

82. Ibid., fols. 606–8.

83. Ibid., filza 153, fol. 976. The discrepancy between the total number of people in lazarets and the breakdown by sex follows the source.

84. The official chronicler, Rondinelli, described how pregnant women delivered their babies in the lazarets. They were covered by sheets, which were held by four women. A midwife stood at one side of the bed, while a monk, ever ready to baptize the baby—which was almost always stillborn—hovered on the other. In addition, monks placed their belts on the heads of women who were having difficult deliveries (perhaps an allusion to the breaking of the umbilical cord?). Some pregnant women who died before delivery were cut open so that the fetus might be baptized (*Relazione*, p. 192). Rondinelli examined another connection among pregnancy, plague, and death: "The story narrated by Stella is almost incredible. She worked at the lazaret of San Miniato and remained there while it was open. Laboring as a midwife, she assisted approximately one thousand women. None survived, and only three babies lived" (p. 30).

85. See B. Bennassar, *Recherches sur les grands épidémies dans le nord de l'Espagne à la fin du XVIe siècle* (Paris: S.E.V.E.P.E.N., 1969), pp. 36–47. In addition, consult E. Carpentier, *Une ville devant la peste: Orvieto et la peste noire de 1348* (Paris: Imprimerie Nationale, 1962). S. Clark has examined the relationship between subjectivity and determinism in social historiography in "French Historians and Early Modern Popular Culture," *Past and Present* 100 (1983).

86. Sanità, Negozi, filza 152, fol. 945. The trial is contained in fols. 945–48v, 953–54.

87. Ibid., fols. 126–27, 270.

88. Ibid., fol. 422.

89. Sanità, Criminale della Sanità, filza 43, fols. 13–14, 27, 82.

90. Ibid., fol. 14.

91. Ibid., fol. 56.

92. The trial is recorded in Sanità, Negozi, filza 152, fols. 56–60.

93. Sanità, Decreti e Partiti, filza 7, fol. 25v. The case involving Lorenzo di Francesco Pistelli is in fol. 60.

94. P. P. Giglioli and A. Dal Lago examine the use of this term in sociology in *Etnometodologia* (Bologna: Il Mulino, 1983), p. 32.

95. Sanità, Negozi, filza 154, fols. 1333–36v, 1357.

96. Ibid., fol. 1336.

97. Ibid., filza 151, fols. 1420–22. The testimony of the barber-surgeon Dandino di Niccolò Bargigli is contained in ibid., filza 152, fol. 48: "Somebody I don't know told me that another person in his house was sick, his body covered with tumors. The ill man asked me to take him from the house so that he would not infect anyone else. I wrote a hospitalization order, although I don't recall ever seeing the patient."

98. ASF, Arte dei Medici e Speziali, filza 15, "Matricole dal 23 maggio 1614 al 17 dicembre 1636," 5 March 1632, 13 February 1629, 24 April 1623.

99. Sanità, Negozi, filza 149, fol. 249.

100. Otto di Guardia e Balia, filza 2347, fol. 166, "Suppliche da marzo 1629 a ottobre 1630."

101. Ibid., filza 2350, fol. 345, "Suppliche da marzo 1631 a tutto agosto 1632."

102. Sanità, Negozi, filza 152, fol. 496. See also Decreti e Partiti, filza 7, fol. 67v.: "We mandate that two hundred *scudi* be given to the tailor Bernardo Abbati for his curative powder against the contagious disease. Another five *scudi* shall be allocated so that the man will be provided with a position as Her Majesty desires. We also mandate that the herbalist of Giglio sell the powder at the price of six *cratie* provided that the substance be made precisely according to Abbati's recipe." The correspondence between the herbalist's shop of Santa Maria Nuova and Florentine herbalists is contained in Sanità, Negozi, filza 149, fol. 258: "Cosimo Pitti sent me four ounces and asked for the recipe. . . . The price is one *zecchino* per ounce." Preto analyzes the role of these healers in *Peste e società a Venezia*, pp. 45–108. G.-C. Margolin examines individual charlatans in "Sur quelques figures de charlatans à la Renaissance: Apparence et réalité du charlatanisme," in *Devins et charlatans au temps de la Renaissance*, ed. M.-I. Jones-Davies (Paris: Université de Paris-Sorbonne, 1979), pp. 35–38.

103. "Ordini, provisioni, capitoli attenenti alli Medici, speziali," in *Ricettario fiorentino*. The new guild statutes were approved on 24 July 1556 and confirmed by the code of Cosimo de' Medici in 1562.

104. Ibid.

105. Ibid.

106. Rodriguez de Castro, *Il curioso*, p. 8.

107. Ibid., p. 59. Benedicenti discusses the condition of the territory of Orvieto in *Malati, medici, farmacisti*, 2:1014–16.

108. Rodriguez de Castro, *Il curioso*, p. 59.

109. J.-P. Goubert makes some similar observations in his study of eighteenth-century France, "L'art de guérir: Médécine et charlatans à la fin du XVIIIe siècle," *Annales: Economies, sociétés, civilisations* 32 (1977): 908–26; for an English translation, see R. Forster and O. Ranum, eds., *Medicine and Society in France* (Baltimore: Johns Hopkins University Press, 1980), pp. 1–23.

110. In another supplication, Public Health magistrate Giovan Maria Bardi wrote: "The defendant is convinced that he treated a great friend" (San-

ità, Criminale della Sanità, filza 483, fol. 3). The trial was referred to the grand duke in ibid., fols. 20, 31. C. Klapisch analyzes the meaning of the term *friend* in the fifteenth-century Florentine context in "Parenti, amici, vicini: Il territorio urbano d'una famiglia mercantile del XV secolo," *Quaderni storici* 33 (1976): 953–82. Klapisch defines friendship as "providing services freely, without compensation. . . . In a society where everything was accounted for, love (synonymous with friendship) regulated a parallel system of gifts that were automatically balanced by countergifts of equal value" (p. 970).

111. See F. Cardini, *Alle radici della cavalleria medievale* (Florence: La Nuova Italia, 1981), pp. 47–48, 53.

112. Magliabechiano, cl. XV, cods. xxii, xxx–xxxi, xxxiii.

113. Ibid., cod. xvii.

114. A. Pazzini, *Storia dell'arte sanitaria* (Rome: Minerva Medica, 1973), 2:79. See also L. Rusio, "La mascalcia," in *Collezioni di opere inedite o rare,* ed. L. Delprato and L. Barbieri (1867), vol. 2.

115. Sanità, Negozi, filza 166, fols. 1204–10.

116. J. Habermas, *Strukturwandel der Öffentlichkeit* (Neuwied: Hermann Luchterhand Verlag, 1962).

117. BNCF, MS *Baldovinetti* no. 29, book 2, chap. 6, "Storia della peste seguita in Firenze l'anno 1630. Dalle ricordanze ms. nell'Arcivescovado fiorentino e nella Compagnia della Misericordia."

118. Rondinelli, *Relazione,* p. 49.

119. For the anthropological significance of these terms, see A. Van Gennep, *The Rites of Passage* (Chicago: Chicago University Press, 1960); V. Turner, *The Ritual Process: Structure and Anti-Structure* (Chicago: Aldine, 1969), chap. 3; and V. Turner, *Drama, Fields, and Metaphors: Symbolic Action in Human Society* (Ithaca, N.Y.: Cornell University Press, 1974).

120. Rondinelli, *Relazione,* p. 55.

121. Marchini, *Belli divini,* p. 125: "Everyone in the city talked about whether the secular magistracy had the right to deny burials in churches or consecrated soil to ecclesiastics and illustrious lay individuals."

122. Ibid., pp. 20–21. Although burning the bodies of plague victims was prohibited, they could be covered in tar, sulphur, and calcite, as in ancient Egypt and Ethiopia. This practice accelerated the process of dehydration, preventing bodies from putrefying. The composition of one "mummy" sold in Florence was described by Benedicenti in *Malati, medici, farmacisti,* 1:331ff.

123. Marchini, *Belli divini,* p. 254.

124. MS Baldovinetti no. 29, fols. 7–8.

125. Ibid.

126. See A. Tenenti, *Il senso della morte e l'amore della vita nel Rinascimento* (Turin: Einaudi, 1957), pp. 73–74. See also M. Meiss, *Painting in Florence and Siena After the Black Death: The Arts, Religion, and Society in the Mid-Fourteenth Century* (New York: Harper and Row, 1964); and G. Previtali, *La fortuna dei primitivi* (Turin: Einaudi, 1964), pp. 28ff.

127. G. P. Lomazzo, "Quali pitture vadano collocate ne' sepolcri, cimi-

teri, chiese sotterranee et altri luochi melanconici et funebri," in *Trattato dell'arte della pittura, scoltura et architettura* (Milan: P. G. Pontio, 1585), 5:338–40; republished in *Scritti d'arte del Cinquecento*, ed. P. Barocchi (Milan and Naples: R. Ricciardi, 1973), 3:2492–94.

128. The "gift of tears" enjoyed a broad iconography, being associated with a cult built around numerous saints. On the "gift of tears" see J. Delumeau, *Il cattolicesimo dal XVI al XVIII secolo* (Milan: Mursia, 1976), p. 87 (*Le catholicisme entre Luther et Voltaire* [Paris: Presses Universitaires de France, 1971]). E. De Martino analyzes the assimilation of women's rituals of mourning into the cult of Mary in *Morte e pianto rituale* (Turin: Boringhieri, 1958). See also A. De Spirito, "La comunicazione fra i vivi e i morti: Preliminari e fonti per una ricerca antropologica," *Ricerche di storia sociale e religiosa* 11 (1982): 293–318.

129. G. Boccaccio, *Il Decameron*, ed. C. Salinari (Bari: Laterza, 1971), 1:328–30.

130. Righi, *Historia Contagiosi Morbi*, p. 138.

131. Ibid., p. 139. J.-P. Vernant examines the relationship between a dignified death and open or enclosed spaces in two different cultures in "La belle mort et le cadavre outragé," in *La mort, les morts dans les sociétés anciennes*, ed. G. Gnoli and J.-P. Vernant (Cambridge: Cambridge University Press, 1982).

132. Notarile moderno, prot. 13392, "Ottavio Amoni," will no. 62.

133. Klapisch discusses the strong sense of geographical belonging in fifteenth-century Florence in "Parenti, amici, vicini."

134. ASF, Sanità, Miscellanea, filza 41, fol. 144. Disgust for dirty and disfigured cadavers is a common characteristic of many cultures; see L.-V. Thomas, *Les cadavres: De la biologie à l'anthropologie* (Brussels: Editions Complexe, 1980), pp. 78–97. *Quaderni storici* devoted an entire issue, "I vivi e i morti" (50 [1982]), to the topic of historical cults and specters; see esp. the introduction by A. Prosperi.

135. Sanità, Negozi, filza 152, fol. 241.

136. See S. Cavazza, "La doppia morte: Resurrezione e battesimo in un rito del Seicento," *Quaderni storici* 50 (1982): 551–82.

137. Sanità, Negozi, filza 154, fols. 692–93.

138. Marchini, *Belli divini*, p. 125. The burial of illustrious people was to take place in churches "in providissima fossa cum calce."

139. Sanità, Negozi, filza 153, fols. 900–902. Another trial involving a member of the church, Pallino Pallini, priest at the Anunziata, is recorded in ibid., filza 152, fols. 2378–82; in it, the priest and a notary persuade a dying woman to write a will that is favorable to the priest.

140. This tendency occurred in Naples as well after the plague of 1656. See R. De Maio, *Società e vita religiosa a Napoli nell'età moderna* (Naples: ESI, 1971), pp. 3–20; and G. Galasso, "La peste," *Storia di Napoli* 6 (1970).

141. Sanità, Criminale della Sanità, filza 483, fols. 23, 63.

142. The case of two servants abandoned by their masters is recorded in ibid., fols. 10–12, 30, 84. In the first episode, the owner of a villa sends his sick servant to Florence to live with a relative; later, the relative denounces the

servant to the authorities. In the second story, the master leaves his servant to die in his home and goes to the countryside; both defendants are fined and exiled to Portoferraio.

143. On somatic culture, see L. Boltanski, "Les usages sociaux du corps," pp. 205–33.

144. See A. I. Galetti, "'Infirmitas' e terapia sacra in una città medievale (Orvieto, 1240)," *La ricerca folklorica* 8 (1983): 21–22. See also J.-C. Schmitt, "Le texte hagiographique dans la culture populaire," *Ethnologie française* 10 (1980): 383. De Maio examines the heroism of martyrs in "L'ideale eroico nei processi di canonizzazione della Controriforma," in *Riforme e miti nella chiesa del Cinquecento* (Naples: Guida, 1973), pp. 257–78.

CHAPTER 3

1. Sanità, Rescritti, filza 37, fols. 465–90.

2. Sanità, Decreti e Partiti, filza 4, fol. 3; Sanità, Rescritti, filza 37, fol. 289.

3. Sanità, Negozi, filza 152, fol. 3.

4. Sanità, Rescritti, filza 37, fol. 560. On Ottavio's death, the Public Health officials claimed that their nominee "had been lieutenant of the Florentine Bargello guard for many years and was knowledgeable about the city and guilds." The grand duke, however, refused their choice, so the officials proposed a new candidate on 20 November: "Piero di Giovanni, called 'Rosso,' presently a guard in Florence, has been described to us as a clever man. We have been told that he is very reliable and that he possesses the necessary qualities to fulfill the position's functions" (ibid., fol. 629). The grand duke approved Rosso's appointment on 22 November.

5. "Money and silver pieces" were discovered in Ottavio's house after his death. The magistrate ordered that these items be confiscated to protect the heirs' interests (Sanità, Decreti e Partiti, filza 4, fol. 16v). One hundred *scudi* were deposited at the Monte di Pietà to provide a dowry for Ottavio's daughter, Maddalena. The interest on this deposit, however, was given to her brothers, "who were responsible for Maddalena." The oldest son, Matteo, received the rest of the money. Camarlingo appraised and weighed the gold (ibid., fol. 107v).

6. Sanità, Negozi, filza 152, fol. 109 (continuing in fols. 109–10, 186).

7. The sentencing is in Sanità, Decreti e Partiti, filza 7, fol. 29.

8. Sanità, Negozi, filza 152, fols. 241–46, 253–57.

9. The importance of the cloak can be deduced by the "provisione sopra l'abito civile del dí 5 ottobre 1588." The cloak is here described as a piece of clothing only for "privileged" citizens who are at least twenty-nine years old; it is to be worn only in the morning (Cantini, *Legislazione toscana*, 12:117–20; see also 16:255–60).

10. Sanità, Decreti e Partiti, filza 7, fols. 97–98.

11. Sanità, Negozi, filza 151, fol. 1038.

12. Ibid., fol. 668.

13. Ibid., fols. 1038–40.

14. Ibid., filza 149, fol. 250.

15. On the increasing number of prostitutes who were not registered with the authorities and the deterioration of the living conditions of the lower classes, see Diaz, *Il Granducato di Toscana,* pp. 408–9. See also R. Trexler, "La prostitution florentine au XVe siècle," *Annales: Economies, sociétés, civilisations* 6 (1981): 983–1015; and S. Cohen, "Convertite e malmaritate: Donne 'irregolari' e ordini religiosi nella Firenze rinascimentale," *Memoria* 5 (1982): 46–63.

16. Otto di Guardia e Balia, Suppliche, filza 2348, fol. 288.

17. Ibid., fol. 344.

18. Sanità, Miscellanea, filza 41, 27 October (the documents are not numbered).

19. Ibid.

20. Sanità, Decreti e Partiti, filza 6, fol. 290.

21. Sanità, Negozi, filza 170, fols. 54–56.

22. ASF, Sanità, Testamenti, filza 480, fols. 4–6, 28, "Testamenti et ultime volontà delle persone del Lazzeretto di San Miniato," October 1630.

23. Notarile moderno, prot. 13392, Notary Ottavio Amoni, will no. 44, fols. 52–53.

24. Ibid., will no. 46, fol. 59v.

25. Sanità, Rescritti, filza 37, fol. 671; other episodes related to clothes are in fols. 685, 692, 729–30, 809. In a letter to the Public Health Magistracy, Corporal Rondinelli recounted: "A young man from San Piero a Sieve was hospitalized twenty days ago because he returned from Florence with a bubo. Now they want to release him, burn all his clothes and make him wash in the river. However, he cannot be discharged from the hospital naked" (Sanità, Negozi, filza 168, fol. 980).

26. M. Mauss, *The Gift: Forms and Functions of Exchange in Archaic Societies,* trans. Ian Cunnison (New York: W. W. Norton, 1967), p. 13.

27. Sanità, Decreti e partiti, filza 6, fol. 236.

28. The definition is in Turner, "Planes of Classification," p. 14. This type of community includes all those who experienced the same disease in historical and mythical time.

29. Sanità, Negozi, filza 154, fols. 481–82, 485–86.

30. Sanità, Decreti e Partiti, filza 7, fol. 179.

31. Sanità, Negozi, filza 154, fols. 118, 198, 267, 313.

32. *Statuta Populi et Communis Florentiae,* book II, rubric cxxix. See also Pertile, *Storia del diritto italiano,* pp. 96–100; and Tamassia, *La famiglia italiana,* pp. 281, 291, 293–94. The importance placed on the dowry by the common people is discussed in Tamassia (p. 307). In 1511 dowries were regulated by new provisions assessing their value in accordance with social status; see G. Cambi, *Istoria* (Florence: G. Cambiagi, 1785), pp. 257–58.

33. D. Sudnow analyzes the social practices that defined the conceptual categories connected to death in the modern period in "L'organizzazione sociale della morte," in *Etnometodologia,* pp. 121–43.

34. Sanità, Negozi, filza 154, fols. 1064, 1066–67.

35. Ibid., fols. 685–88.

36. Sanità, Decreti e Partiti, filza 7, fols. 181v–182.

37. Sanità, Criminale della Sanità, filza 483, fol. 6.

38. Ibid., fol. 53.

39. Ciasca, *L'arte dei Medici,* pp. 196–97. These regulations were established in 1375.

40. Sanità, Criminale della Sanità, filza 483, fols. 33, 68, 75.

41. Ibid., fols. 59–62.

42. Ibid., fols. 35, 91.

43. Sanità, Rescritti, filza 37, fol. 635.

44. Rondinelli, *Relazione,* p. 56.

45. Sanità, Negozi, filza 152, fol. 1077.

46. Sanità, Decreti e Partiti, filza 6, fols. 231–32; Sanità, Rescritti, filza 37, fol. 283.

47. Sanità, Criminale della Sanità, filza 483, fol. 43.

48. Ciasca, *Statuti dell'arte,* p. 180 (1349, rubric lviii).

49. Ibid., p. 286 (1375, rubric i).

50. Ibid. See also Ciasca, *L'arte dei Medici,* pp. 119ff.

51. Ciasca, *Statuti dell'arte,* pp. 290–93 (1376, rubric iii).

52. Ibid.

53. *Processo originale degli untori,* p. 93.

54. Sanità, Negozi, filza 153, fol. 757; the trial is recorded in fols. 756–59, 776–77.

CHAPTER 4

1. Sanità, Negozi, filza 148, fol. 683.

2. Ibid., filza 152, fol. 1132.

3. MS Baldovinetti no. 29, book 2, chap. 15.

4. Ulisse was arrested by Ottavio Diligenti, who wrote the denunciation. See Sanità, Negozi, filza 152, fol. 464; the trial is recorded in fols. 465–75.

5. Sanità, Decreti e Partiti, filza 7, fols. 23–24.

6. Luna's report is in Sanità, Negozi, filza 152, fol. 987; the trial is recorded in fols. 988–92.

7. The sentence was promulgated on 30 November. The court condemned Vedovino to suspension from a rope three times "in public." Furthermore, the court punished his accomplices, Cice and Benedetto, "by prohibiting them from serving as guards for as long as it pleases His Majesty. Should they violate their sentence, they will be placed in detention" (Sanità, Decreti e Partiti, filza 7, fol. 69v).

8. Sanità, Negozi, filza 153, fol. 438.

9. Ibid., fol. 439.

10. Ibid., fol. 442.

11. Ibid., fol. 680.

12. The trial is recorded in ibid., fols. 445–50.

13. Sanità, Decreti e Partiti, filza 7, fols. 148–49.

14. Otto di Guardia e Balia (1601–42), filza 1914, no. 73, 20 January 1631. The episode occurred on 3 March 1630.

15. Sanità, Miscellanea, filza 41, 23 October 1630.

16. Sanità, Criminale della Sanità, filza 483, fols. 19, 29, 48, 71 (7 July 1633).

17. A. Manzoni, *I promesi sposi* (Florence: Sansoni, 1928), p. 46.

18. Sanità, Negozi, filza 151, 18 October 1630 (unnumbered folder).

19. Ibid., filza 154, fol. 1342. The sentence, which named only Aurelia di Michele del Brini, was promulgated on 26 July 1631. She was released because "after numerous examinations and many days of imprisonment," she did not change her testimony. The judges believed that her "detention sufficed" for punishment (Sanità, Decreti e Partiti, filza 4, fols. 185v–186.

20. MS Baldovinetti no. 29, book 2, chap. 13.

21. Sanità, Negozi, filza 151, fol. 62.

22. Ibid., filza 150, fol. 87.

23. Ibid., fol. 1126. Even sarcasm expressed the widespread hostility toward Public Health officials. When doctors first appeared on the street visiting well-to-do clients, they "caused surprise and provoked mockery." They dressed in a new grey uniform with red stripes, called a "sanrochino." People in the streets made fun of them and called them names.

24. Sanità, Decreti e Partiti, filza 6, fol. 91.

25. Sanità, Rescritti, filza 37, fol. 1164. His punishment was later commuted to three years' exile, first in Castiglione della Pescaia, then in Pisa.

26. Sanità, Negozi, filza 151, fol. 660.

27. See Landy, *Culture, Disease, and Healing,* esp. chap. 6.

28. R. Baehrel, "Épidémie et terreur," pp. 113–46, and "La haine de classe," pp. 351–60.

29. Sanità, Negozi, filza 152, fols. 162–63.

30. After 1 September 1630 numerous restrictions were imposed on the personnel of the hospital of Bonifazio; see Sanità, Decreti e Partiti, filza 6, fols. 91–92, 202–3, 239. The trial is contained in Sanità, Negozi, filza 150, fols. 948–54. The testimonies of the defense are in ibid., filza 151, fols. 323–32. The sentence of 31 October 1630 is recorded in Sanità, Decreti e Partiti, filza 4, fol. 3: "After he confessed to having twice bought the said meat, . . . Bettoni spent two months in prison. He is now acquitted on the condition that he never return to work in the hospital of Bonifazio." The man had made, after all, only one *soldo* per *liber* of meat.

31. Sanità, Negozi, filza 149, fol. 1328v.

32. Ibid., fol. 977.

33. Ibid., fol. 1621.

34. Ibid., filza 152, fols. 858v, 870.

35. Ibid., filza 150, fol. 532.

36. Ibid., fols. 606, 792.

37. Ibid., fol. 819.

38. Ibid., fols. 852–53.

39. For this classification, see Douglas, *La stregoneria,* p. 19 (*Witchcraft Confessions and Accusations*).

40. The trial is recorded in Sanità, Negozi, filza 150, fols. 855–58.

41. Sanità, Decreti e Partiti, filza 6, fol. 144.

42. Sanità, Rescritti, filza 37, fol. 500.

43. Sanità, Decreti e Partiti, filza 6, fol. 141.

44. Sanità, Negozi, filza 151, fol. 94.

45. Ibid., fol. 923.

46. Ibid.

47. Sanità, Decreti e Partiti, filza 7, fol. 27; the order of release is recorded in fol. 15.

48. Ibid., fols. 42v–43.

49. Ibid., fol. 109.

50. Douglas, *La stregoneria,* p. 23 (*Witchcraft Confessions and Accusations*).

51. Ibid., p. 10.

52. Sanità, Negozi, filza 168, fol. 121.

53. Ibid., fol. 120.

54. Rondinelli, *Relazione,* p. 161. Rondinelli examines the charges of the neighborhood councilmen against Public Health officials on pages 162–63. The complaints were expressed in a very emotional way and focused on forced hospitalizations. Reportedly, the invalids even took with them the "insides and hearts" of those remaining behind. From the lazarets came "an unspeakable stench," "screaming and shouting," and "the inappropriate raucousness" of employees, "making one's sadness more difficult to bear." People were duly outraged and demanded that lazarets be closed.

CHAPTER 5

1. S. Congregazione dei Riti, filza 776, *Florentina beatificationis et canonizationis servae Dei Dominicae de Paradiso ordinis Praedicatorum.* The proceedings were to verify that which was contained in fol. 6: "Quod fuit, erat et est verum communis opinio, antiqua traditio, et indubita reputatio publicum, et notorium, et manifestum, ut testes pro veritate informati latiis testificabuntur de eorum recordatu, et de auditu a majoribus, qui referebant idque audivisse ab eorum antiquioribus, et quod de praedictis semper fuit, erat et est publica vox et fama." P. Brown discusses the importance of sacred bodies within the urban walls during earlier times in *The Cult of Saints* (Chicago: University of Chicago Press, 1981); see also J. Le Goff, "L'immaginario urbano nell'Italia medievale," in *Storia d'Italia, annali* (Turin: Einaudi, 1983), ed. R. Romano and C. Vivanti, 5:9. On the significance of graves as loci of cultural refoundation, see R. Girard, *Delle cose nascoste sin dalla fondazione del mondo* (Milan: Adelphi, 1983), pp. 108–9 (*Things Hidden since the Foundation of the World* [Stanford: Stanford University Press, 1987]).

2. The earliest biography of Domenica da Paradiso, *Vita di Domenica da Paradiso,* was written by her confessor Francesco da Castiglione degli Onesti. The manuscript is kept in the archive of the Convent of Crocetta in Florence. The text was frequently cited during the canonization hearings. On the basis of its contents, Ignazio Del Nente, prior of the Dominican monastery of San Marco, wrote in 1625 the biography entitled *Vita e costumi et intelligenze spi-*

rituali della gran Serva di Dio e Veneranda Madre Suor Domenica da Paradiso, 2d ed. (Venice: M. Miloco, 1664). The first edition was printed in Florence in 1662 and paid for by Paolo del Sera, the same Florentine gentleman to whom the second edition was dedicated. In the early eighteenth century, Benedetto Borghigiani wrote *Intera narrazione della vita di Suor Domenica da Paradiso* (Florence: F. Moücke, 1702). A biographical portrait is also provided in D. Marchese, *Sagro diario domenicano* (Naples, 1676), 4:308–46 (Marchese used Del Nente's *Vita* as his primary source), G. A. Baci, *Vite di alcune sante e venerabili serve di Dio scelte dal sacro diario domenicano* (Florence: C. Bindi, 1707); and S. Razzi, *Vita de' santi e beati di Toscana* (Florence: C. Giunta, 1601). A. Moriconi's recent biography *La venerabile Suor Domenica da Paradiso* (Florence: Scuola Salesiana, 1943) is also helpful. Finally, see the popular anonymous biography *Vita e profezie della venerabile Suor Domenica da Paradiso, religiosa del monastero della Crocetta di Firenze* (Florence: Salani, 1889).

3. J. Le Goff, "Memoria," in *Enciclopedia* (Turin: Einaudi, 1979), 8:1068–1109. See also E. Minkowski, *Il tempo vissuto* (Turin: Einaudi, 1968).

4. S. Congregazione dei Riti, filza 776, fol. 136v.

5. Ibid., fol. 148v. On the beauty of children, see Del Nente, *Vita,* p. 2.

6. Biographers believed that the roles played by Angelina and Filippa were different. Marchese, *Sagro diario,* p. 333, discusses both these women; Del Nente, *Vita,* pp. 83–84, refers to two unrelated women who, jealous of Domenica, attacked her reputation and attempted to kill her. G. Zarri analyzes the subtle dissimilarities between saints and witches in "Le sante vive: Per una tipologia della santità femminile nel primo Cinquecento," in *Annali dell'Istituto storico italo-germanico in Trento* (Bologna: Il Mulino, 1982), 6:431–34.

7. S. Congregazione dei Riti, filza 776, fols. 116–17. Each biographer characterizes the relationship between Domenica and the Samminiati family differently. Del Nente, for example, describes the Samminiatis as amoral people who were reformed by Domenica (*Vita,* p. 84). On the rural migration to urban areas, see Benvenuto Papi, "Santità femminile," pp. 113–14.

8. Marchese, *Sagro diario,* p. 342.

9. S. Congregazione dei Riti, filza 776, fol. 121.

10. Ibid., fol. 151.

11. Ibid., fols. 110, 112, 125.

12. Ibid., fol. 125.

13. Ibid., fol. 238. See also Moriconi, *La venerabile Suor Domenica,* pp. 722–24; and ASF, Conventi soppressi no. 107, "La Crocetta di Firenze," filze 1 ("Libro giornale 1517–75"), 98 ("Filze d'Istrumenti antichi 1486–1583").

14. Del Nente, *Vita,* pp. 114–15. The relationship between Domenica and the ecclesiastical authorities was long and tormented. She was subpoenaed three times by the vicar and questioned about heresy. Her departure from the Convent of Candeli aroused suspicion, and she was interrogated about her ecstasies, mystical raptures, and stigmata. The red cross on her habit could have been interpreted as a reference to her Savonarolean past. Del Nente tried to dispel these rumors, stressing that the insignia had been given to Domenica

by Archbishop Cosimo de' Pazzi (pp. 114–15). On the intricate relationship between Domenica and Savonarolism, see Borghigiani, *Intera narrazione,* 2:337–39; see also Moriconi, *La venerabile Suor Domenica,* p. 343. Domenica's Savonarolism reputedly stemmed from the influence of her confessor Domenico Benivieni, Girolamo's brother, "the official poet of the Piagnoni movement." Upon Benivieni's death, Domenica chose Francesco da Castiglione, the canon of San Lorenzo and tutor of Pier Francesco de' Medici, as her new confessor. L. Polizzotto examines Benivieni's influence on Domenica in "Domenico Benivieni and the Radicalisation of the Savonarola Movement," in *Altro Polo,* ed. C. Condren and R. Pesman (Sydney: Sydney University Press, 1982), pp. 99–102. In 1630–33 the Dominicans still had to defend themselves against charges of Savonarolism; see E. Cochrane, *Florence in the Forgotten Centuries, 1537–1700* (Chicago: University of Chicago Press, 1973), p. 211.

15. Polizzotto, "Domenico Benivieni," p. 111. For Zarri's examination of the waning Savonarolean influence after 1530, see "Le sante vive," pp. 442–43. The Convent of Crocetta occupied the area presently bordered by the streets of Giusti, Pergola, Colonna, and Capponi. The architect Giulio Parigi enlarged and rebuilt the convent in 1620 for Maria Maddalena de' Medici, who became a nun there, dying there in 1633. On the history of the convent, see G. Richa, *Notizie istoriche delle chiese fiorentine* (Florence: Viviani, 1755), book 1, part 2. The convent's main building is now the Archeological Museum; the ecclesiastical community and the archive are located at Varlungo on Via Aretina.

16. S. Congregazione dei Riti, filza 776, fol. 123.

17. Ibid., fol. 125.

18. Ibid., fol. 121.

19. Ibid., fol. 128.

20. Ibid., fols. 143v–144.

21. Zarri, "Le sante vive," p. 421.

22. Borghigiani, *Intera narrazione,* pp. 213–14.

23. R. Bastide analyzes the relationship between trances and mystical ecstasies in *Sogno, trance e follia* (Milan: Jaca Book, 1974). See also Mircea Eliade, *Shamanism: Archaic Techniques of Ecstasy,* Bollingen Series no. 76 (Princeton, N.J.: Princeton University Press, 1964); M. De Certeau, *La possession de Loudun* (Paris: Gallimard, 1980); and G. Lapassade, *Saggio sulla transe* (Milan: Feltrinelli, 1980). J.-M. Sallmann offers some interesting observations on the relationship between sacred thaumaturgy and shamanism in "Il santo e la rappresentazione della santità: Problemi di metodo," *Quaderni storici* 41 (1979): 584–602.

24. Borghigiani, *Intera narrazione,* p. 213.

25. Ibid., p. 99. For a more comprehensive study, see R. von Albertini, *Firenze dalla repubblica al principato* (Turin: Einaudi, 1970), pp. 211–24.

26. Borghigiani, *Intera narrazione,* p. xi.

27. B. Segni, *Storie fiorentine* (Milan: S.T.C.I., 1805), 1:191.

28. Ibid., p. 192.

29. Borghigiani, *Intera narrazione,* pp. 98, 99. On the theme of reciprocity, see *Annales: Economies, sociétés, civilisations* 29 (1974): 1358–80; in particular, see the contributions of Duby and Godelier.

30. S. Congregazione dei Riti, filza 776, fol. 158v.

31. See L. Di Francia, *Storia dei generi letterari italiani* (Milan: Vallardi, 1925), 10:280–84. On the topic of popular satires of medicine, see G. Pitré, *Usi, costumi, credenze e pregiudizi del popolo siciliano* (Palermo, 1889), 1:50. The episodes of Grillo, Doctor Lava Titti, and Santo Sano, who healed the faithful by killing them, were very popular. For a discussion of these stories in Tuscany, see E. Levi, "Paneruzzole di Niccolò Povero," in *Poesia del popolo, poesia di corte* (Leghorn: Giusti, 1915); and A. Mainardi, *Motti e facezie del piovano Arlotto* (Milan, 1953), pp. 153ff. The legend of Santo Sano in southern Italy is discussed by S. Salomone-Marino, "La storia delli miracoli di Santo Sanu," *Archivio per lo studio delle tradizioni populari* 10 (1891).

32. Borghigiani, *Intera narrazione,* p. 98. J. Gil examines the anthropological concept of the communal body in "Corpo," in *Enciclopedia* (Turin: Einaudi, 1978), 3:1096–1160. Niccolò Machiavelli makes an analogy between the body of the city and the human body in *The Prince;* see *Il principe,* ed. S. Bertelli (Milan: Feltrinelli, 1960), p. 21; and Machiavelli, *Discorsi sopra la prima Deca di Tito Livio,* ed. S. Bertelli (Milan: Feltrinelli, 1960), p. 223.

CHAPTER 6

1. S. Congregazione dei Riti, filza 776, fol. 83v.

2. Ibid.: "With the stipulation that no one reveal the time and day [of the hearings] to allow everything to be done in secret, thereby eliminating any crowds and disorder. This was strongly requested to comply with the remissory letters."

3. Ibid.

4. Ibid., fol. 84r.

5. Ibid., fol. 84v.

6. Ibid., fol. 86r.

7. Ibid., fol. 86v.

8. Ibid., fol. 87v: "Anyone who dares to put into or take, steal, or remove anything from the sepulcher, even if for religious purposes." I. Fontanini discusses the evolution of the terminology of sanctity and the officially canonized saint in *Collectio Bullarum et Constitutionum et Diplomatum quas Summi Pontifices ediderunt in solemni Canonizatione Sanctorum . . .* (Rome, 1752). Two years before his death, Pope Urban VIII ordered all his decrees published in one volume: *Urbani VIII Pont. O.M. Decreta servanda in canonizatione et beatificatione sanctorum . . .* (Rome, 1642). R. De Maio discusses the evolution of the laws governing canonization proceedings since the fifteenth century in "L'ideale eroico," pp. 258–59.

9. S. Congregazione dei Riti, filza 776, fol. 87v.

10. Ibid., fol. 88.

11. Ibid.:"recognized masters in the art of sculpture"; "to further clarify and prove the matter."

12. T. De Mauro, L. Grassi, and E. Battisti, "Ritratto," in *Enciclopedia universale dell'arte* (Florence: A. Curcio, 1966), 11:564–67; E. Battisti, "Il Cinquecento," in ibid., pp. 587–92; E. Battisti, E. Cerulli, and L. Sladitz, "Umana figura," in ibid., 14:298–345; and P. Hofer, "Some Little Known Illustrators of Comparative Anatomy, 1600–1626: *De artibus opuscula*," in *Essays in Honour of Edward Panofsky*, ed. M. Meiss (Zurich: Buehle, 1960).

13. J.-P. Vernant, *Nascita di immagini* (Milan: Il Saggiatore, 1982), pp. 124–25 (*Religions, histoires, raisons* [Paris: Maspero, 1979]).

14. G. Vasari, *Opere* (Florence: Milanesi, 1878–85), 3:373.

15. Ibid., 8:88.

16. The wax mask, *notomia di cera*, was very famous in Florence. Sculpted by Ludovico Cardi ("Cigoli"), the mask was reproduced in bronze and became the model for numerous successive copies, including those of Zumbo. See A. Matteoli, *Ludovico Cardi-Cigoli, pittore e architetto* (Pisa: Giardini, 1980); and M. Bucci, *Anatomia come arte* (Florence, 1969). A reproduction of anatomy tables is in A. Hahn and P. Dumaitre, *Histoire de la médicine et du livre médicale* (Paris: O. Perrin, 1962); see esp. the seventeenth-century *Tabulae anatomicae* of Julius Casserius, printed in Venice in 1627. For the relationship between art and anatomy, see G. Wolf-Heidegger and A. M. Cetto, *Die anatomische Sektion in Bildlicher Darstellung* (Basel: Werner & Bischoff, 1967).

17. BNCF, Fondo Nazionale, II.1.454: *Notizie dei ceraioli e lavoratori d'immagini di cera in Firenze;* G. Mazzoni, *I boti della SS. Annunziata* (Florence: Le Monnier, 1923). On the Benintendi family, see G. Gaeta, *Dizionario biografico degli italiani*, 8:540–41.

18. A. Warburg, "Arte del ritratto e borghesia fiorentina," in *La rinascita del paganesimo antico*, ed. G. Bing (Florence: La Nuova Italia, 1980), pp. 117–18, 137–40.

19. *La ceroplastica nella scienza e nell'arte*, 2 vols. (Florence: Olschki, 1977); see esp. M. Praz, "Le figure di cera in letteratura," pp. 549–67. See also M. Praz, *Fiori freschi* (Florence: Sansoni, 1944), and *Il giardino dei sensi* (Milan: Mondadori, 1975).

20. F. Baldinucci, *Notizie dei professori del disegno da Cimabue in qua*, ed. F. Ranalli, (Florence: Batelli, 1846), 4:99. See also Praz, *Il giardino*, pp. 66–67. Tacca, like almost all the witnesses at the proceedings, was a member of the Compagnia di Santo Benedetto Bianco. On Tacca's career as a Florentine bureaucrat, see Cochrane, *Florence in the Forgotten Centuries*, p. 205.

21. F. Baldinucci, *Notizie dei professori*, 4:80.

22. Diaz, *Il Granducato di Toscana*, pp. 413–14. On Buonarroti, see Cochrane, *Florence in the Forgotten Centuries*, pp. 177–78. Buonarroti was one of Galileo's best friends and supporters; see L. Rossi, *Dizionario biografico degli italiani*, 15:178–81. On Buonarroti's home and gallery, see C. De Tolnay, ed., *Casa Buonarroti* (Florence: Arnaud, 1976); and U. Procacci, *La casa Buonarroti*

a Firenze (Milan: Electa, 1967). R. De Maio offers a strong critique of Michelangelo's gallery in *Michelangelo e la Controriforma* (Bari: Laterza, 1978), pp. 456–57.

23. S. Congregazione dei Riti, filza 776, fol. 89r.

24. Ibid.

25. Ibid., fol. 89v.

26. Ibid., fol. 91.

27. Ibid.: "Caput usque ad suturam coronalem est copertum sua cute exiccata non tamen rugosa, interciput est excariatum ita ut craneum appareat. Occipit et nuca sunt cariosa cum suis tamen ligamentis, et carne adhuc palpabile ita ut ad tactum cedat. Aures deficiunt videtur tamen signum ipsarum. Tempora sunt optime conservata, similiter et frons qua et si sicca, attamen sua cute et carne cooperta est levigata, nec ullo modo rugosa. Gena sive malae naturalem formam retinent, carne plena absque ulla carie, supercilia sunt absque pilis, attamen integra, et supereminentia veluti dum viveret. Oculi apparent exiccati, cum pupillis subcilijs, et operculi Nasus usque ad medium in parte ossea, ubi movetur cartilago est integrum. Primae narium sunt exiccatae et compressae, ita ut foramina aperta demonstrant et naturalem formam deturpant in medio ipsius a parte dextera adest caries interfinium vero integrum et si exiccatum. Labrum superius exsicatum, et a parte dextera directum os discooperit quod apparet clausum quatuor dentibus mandibulae inferioris cum duobus hinc inde dimidiatis. Labrum inferius est integrum et adhuc retinet suam crassitiem, sive prochilum mentum es integrum cum sua naturalis forma, cum sua cavitate, sive buccella. Gula est integra cum carie in medio, collum una cum suis nervis, cute et carne adhuc alba optime conservatum. Humeri cum sua carne et cute ad tactum cedente optime apparent conservati. Pectus cum thorace lateribus, mammillis eodem modo cum sua cute, carne et colore optime est conservatum. In sinistra mammilla, sive in sinistro latere apparet caro subrubea, ac si ibi aliquis tumor adfuisset. Stomachus et venter ipsius cum omni regione umbelici sunt valde exsicatae nulla tamen ibi cicatrix aut scissura apparet e lateribus ad cingulum apparet aliqua pars callosa transversa. Ilia sive flanca sunt optime conservata. Sumen et hypocondria apparent sublevata, et ad tactum cedentia seu aliquantulum cariosa. Bracchia cum suis cubilis sunt integra, cum cute et carne rugosa ad suam formam manus vero cum digitis et ungulis sunt exsicatae. Digitus pollex dexterae manus adest pene separatus, in articulo medio ita ut per nervum solummodo coniungitur. Costae sive femora, crures tibiae et pedes cum suis digitis et ungulis ad suam formam cum cute, carne sunt conservatae, in crure tamen sinistro a parte exteriori adest caries longitudinis dimidij palmi, latitudinis vero dimidij circiter digiti, reliquum vero ipsos crurium et femorum est aliquibus partibus cariosum."

28. Ibid., fol. 165.

29. Ibid., fol. 91v. On the symbolism of colors, see F. Portal, *Des couleurs symboliques dans l'antiquité, le Moyen âge et les temps modernes* (Paris: Treuttel & Wütz, 1857).

30. S. Congregazione dei Riti, filza 776, fol. 92r.

31. Ibid., fol. 93r.

32. Ibid., fol. 94.

33. Ibid.

34. Del Nente, *Vita*, p. 2.

35. S. Congregazione dei Riti, filza 776, fol. 123.

36. Ibid., fols. 134–35.

37. Ibid., fol. 151v.

38. P. Delooz, *Sociologie et canonisation* (Liège: University of Liège, Faculty of Law, 1969), p. 11. In addition, for a discussion on the "Antonian phenomenon," see Delooz, "Rapports entre saint réel et saint construit: La sainteté comme construction sociale," in *S. Antonio da Padova fra storia e pietà: Colloquio interdisciplinare su "Il fenomeno antoniano"* (Padua: Messagero, 1977); and W. Christian, *Apparitions in Late Medieval and Renaissance Spain* (Princeton, N.J.: Princeton University Press, 1969).

39. Delooz, *Sociologie et canonisation*, p. 12. See also Vauchez, *La sainteté en Occident*, pp. 625–26.

40. Delooz, *Sociologie et canonisation*, p. 12.

41. Vauchez, *La sainteté en Occident*, p. 517. Meiss analyzes the iconographic theme in *La pittura a Firenze e Siena*, p. 117. See also A. Cabassus, "Coeurs (échange des)," in *Dictionnaire de spiritualité ascétique et mystique*, ed. Marcel Viller (Paris: G. Beauchesne, 1953), 2:1946–51; and O. Herrenschmidt, "Sacrifices symboliques et sacrifices efficaces" in *La fonction symbolique*, ed. M. Izard and P. Smith (Paris: Gallimard, 1979).

42. On Ignazio del Nente, consult *Monumenta ordinis Fratrum Praedicatorum historica* (Rome, 1902), 11:332, 365; V. M. Fontana, *De romana provincia Ordinis praedicatorum* (Rome: N.A. Tinassij, 1670), p. 86; and A. Duval, *Dictionnaire de spiritualité* (Paris, 1957), 3:129–30. On the relationship between the medical profession and religious faith, see P. Segneri, *L'incredulo senza scussa* (Florence: S.A.S., 1960), p. 91; Segneri also examines evidence of divine "signs" as they appear in all parts of the human body. Targioni Tozzetti includes some interesting reflections on the doctors who examined Domenica's body in *Notizie degli aggrandimenti*, 1:353–87. Giovanni Nardi erected a museum of mummies in his house on Via d'Alloro. He opposed the theories of Harvey and Galileo and published *Noctes geniales,* in which, among other things, he discussed whether the stench was a categorical symptom of putrefaction and the case of a young woman who had died of dropsy in ca. 694. The role of doctors was limited to assessing the incurable characteristics of diseases during canonization hearings and verifying miraculous healings; see F. d'Antonelli, *De inquisitione medico-legali super miraculis in causis beatificationis et canonizationis* (Rome: Pontificium Athenaeum Antonianum, 1962), p. 234.

43. O. Berendsen, "The Italian XVI and XVII Century Catafalques" (Ph.D. diss., New York Institute of Fine Arts, 1961); E. Borsook, "Art and Politics in the Medici Court," *Mitteilungen des Kunst Instituts in Florenz* 12 (1965): 31–54; 13 (1967): 95–114; 14 (1969): 91–114, 248–50; and G. Ber-

telà and A. Petrioli Tofani, *Feste e apparati medicei* (Florence: L. Olschki, 1969).

CHAPTER 7

1. S. Congregazione dei Riti, filza 776, fol. 118.
2. Ibid., fol. 120.
3. Ibid., fol. 167v.
4. See C. Lévi-Strauss, *L'origine des manières de table* (Paris: Plon, 1968), pp. 395–403.
5. Ciasca, *Statuti dell'arte,* p. 198 (1349, rubric lxxxviii). Rubric xxxx, p. 148, established that "the daughter of a guild member can become a member herself . . . and does not have to pay dues. The daughter is not, however, entitled to extend her privileges to her own sons."
6. Arte dei Medici e Speziali, filza 15, 4–5 July 1633. On 21 May 1621, Giovanni di Francesco Peretoli, "the barber at Pitti," joined the guild without paying dues "because his father, Francesco Peretoli, had been a member since 3 October 1591."
7. Sanità, Negozi, filza 153, fol. 279. The records indicate that as of 21 May 1621 nineteen women and forty-nine men worked at the lazaret of San Miniato: twelve women were maids, four were washerwomen, and three were wet nurses, including one who handed out medicine. Could this last woman have been Margherita (ibid., filza 156, fols. 926–27)? On the same day, twenty women were working at the hospital of San Francesco: four maids, three washerwomen, one wet nurse, one barber-surgeon, ten nurses, and one surgeon, Alessandra di Francesco Mori. The names of the personnel are listed in ca. 854.
8. L. Gioberti, *De gli errori popolari* (Florence: Giunti, 1592). The dedication to Christine was written by Alberto Luchi, ambassador of the grand duke to the French court. Luchi also translated the text into Italian. The book was first published in Florence in 1578.
9. Ibid., book I, chap. 16, fol. 54.
10. Ibid., book IV, chap. 2, fol. 138.
11. J. Primrose, *Popular Errours: Or the Errours of the People in Physick* (London: W. Wilson, 1651), frontispiece. This book had been published in Latin in 1638 under the title *De Vulgi in Medicina Erroribus;* it was translated into English by Robert Wittie. Doctor Primrose was educated in France, where he read Joubert's text. In his book, Primrose tried to expand on Joubert's work, applying the Frenchman's theories to the English case.
12. S. Mercuri, *Errori popolari d'Italia* (Venice: G. B. Ciotti, 1603), pp. 1–2.
13. Ibid., book III, chap. 13, fol. 149.
14. Ibid., fol. 150.
15. Ibid., fol. 151.
16. *Processo originale degli untori,* pp. 59–60. In his book *La fabbrica della peste* (Bari: Laterza, 1984), F. Cordero focuses on the plague in Milan in 1630.

17. *De' secreti del reverendo donno Alessio Piemontese* (Venice: A. Gardane, 1580), p. 29.

18. Mercuri, *Errori popolari d'Italia,* book IV, chap. 21, fol. 226.

19. As the pestilence was striking Florence, a pamphlet on the therapeutic value of soap was published. See G. Maccioni, *Risposta al parere del sig. G. Marcucci intorno alla qualità del sapon molle* (Florence: Sermartelli, 1630). According to Maccioni, soap could be used to cauterize.

20. *Processo originale degli untori,* pp. 234–35.

21. F. Rivola, *Vita di Federico Borromeo* (Milan: D. Gariboldi, 1656), p. 613.

22. S. Congregazione dei Riti, filza 226, fol. 138.

23. On Cosimo and Damian, see E. Caraffa and M. L. Casanova, *Bibliotheca Sanctorum* (Rome: Istituto Giovanni XXIII nella Pontificia Università Lateranense, 1961), 5:223–27; *Acta SS. Septembris* (Antwerp, 1760), 7:428–55; H. Delahaye, "Les recueils antiques de miracles des saints," *Analecta Bollandiana* 23 (1925): 8–18; A. Pazzini, *I santi nella storia della medicina* (Rome: Mediterranea, 1937); F. C. Husenbeth, *Emblems of Saints* (London: Burns & Lambert, 1850); and J.-D. Jacquet, "Le miracle de la jambe noire," in *Les miracles, miroirs des corps,* ed. J. Gelis and O. Redon (St-Denis: Presses et Publications de l'Université de Paris VIII, 1983), pp. 21–52.

24. ASF, *Consiglio de' Ducento,* filza 151 (Suppliche, 1618–21), fol. 207 (22 January 1619): "Ottavio di Benedetto di Jacopo Amoni informs the Most Serene Grand Duke of Tuscany of the following: Jacopo Amoni, the humble serf of His Majesty, has lived in this city for eighteen years; he has his own house and wife, who was born of a Florentine family, and one two-year-old son. For six years, he has worked in the chancellory of the Nove. He previously served at the Monte delle Graticole and the chancellory of the Parti. . . . Your Excellency, he petitions to be listed among the Florentine citizenry in whichever neighborhood You so choose. He will pay all taxes requested by the city of Florence and will not ask for any reduction on the basis of the location of his goods." The *Cittadinario* provided some interesting information on Ottavio: he moved from the quarter of San Giovanni to the quarter of Santa Croce in 1627, and he had a second son, Giovan Battista, in 1632 (ASF, Cittadinario fiorentino, MS. 419: Consorterie del Quartiere di S. Croce, Lion Nero [1627], fol. 5; Consorterie del Quartiere di S. Giovanni, Vaio [1627], register no. 3, fol. 19). The positions held by the notary are listed in *Raccolta Sebregondi,* no. 129, *Amoni di Firenze.* No information is available after 1638, when Amoni was appointed superintendent at the prison.

26. The family link was established at the opening of the hearings, when all the witnesses were listed in the order that the judges were going to call them. Macchia's family enjoyed a relationship with the Convent of Crocetta: Alessandro, canon of San Lorenzo, became the nuns' confessor after Domenica's death. In 1584 Alessandro witnessed the exhumation of Domenica's body when the church was being restored. Piero del Macchia, Alessandro's nephew, was canon of the Church of San Michele in Rovezzano; Ottavio Amoni dealt with him frequently. Information on the Macchia family is contained in B. Borghigiani, *Intera narrazione,* pp. xiiff.

27. S. Congregazione dei Riti, filza 776, fols. 138v–139.

28. Ibid., fol. 131.

29. Ibid., fol. 199.

30. Ibid., fol. 169.

31. Ibid., fol. 244.

32. All these authors agree that the bodies and diseases of women contain a mysterious element. Besides Joubert, Primrose, and Mercuri, see G. Pasta, *Galateo de' Medici* (Rome: Cannetti, 1792); and T. Garzoni, *Piazza universale di tutte le professioni del mondo, e nobili et ignobili* (Venice, 1586). For a discussion and ample bibliography on the subject, see J. Donnison, *Midwives and Medical Men* (New York: Schocken Books, 1977); see also E. Shorter, *A History of Women's Bodies* (London: Allen Lane, 1983). G. B. Lunadei examines a monstrous delivery in "Lettera intorno a una bambina nata con due teste, con la risposta di Giovanni Bianchi," in A. Calogerà, *Raccolta di opuscoli scientifici e filologici,* vol. 2 (Venica: C. Zane, 1728). See also P. Darmon, *Le mythe de la procréation à l'âge baroque* (Paris: Seuil, 1979). The object that Lisabetta removed from her own body reminds us of the numerous contemporary reports of the expulsion of worms, snakes, and ropes; see P. Camporesi, *La carne impassibile,* pp. 105ff; and G. Penso, *La conquista del mondo invisibile* (Milan: Feltrinelli, 1973), pp. 101–89. In Boccaccio's *Decameron* (p. 326), a young woman dreams that her lover Gabriotto's death was caused by "something dark and horrible" that came out of his body and wrapped around him until death.

33. Landy, *Culture, Disease, and Healing,* pp. 195–230; J. Blacking, ed., *The Anthropology of the Body,* ASA Monograph no. 15 (London: Academic Press, 1977), pp. 111–43. See also E. Evans-Pritchard, *Witchcraft, Oracles, and Magic Among the Azande* (Oxford: Clarendon Press, 1937). The search for "a magical substance" is analogous to Lisabetta's story.

34. Pasta, *Galateo de' Medici,* p. 23. For the contrast of women and doctors, see F. Pona, *La remora* (Verona: B. Merlo, 1630), fols. 23–24.

35. Mercuri, *Errori populari d'Italia,* book III, chap. 26, fol. 174.

36. S. Congregazione dei Riti, filza 776, fol. 142v.

37. Sanità, Negozi, filza 168, fol. 582.

38. Ibid., fol. 705.

39. Cittadinario fiorentino, MS. 419: Consortie di S. Croce, Lion Nero (1627), fol. 5.

40. S. Congregazione dei Riti, filza 776, fol. 140.

41. Ibid., fol. 140v.

42. Notarile moderno, prot. 13392, will no. 48, written in Rovezzano on 26 August. On 3 September Ottavio resumed his job in Florence and prepared a new will in the "herbalist's shop of the Monastery of San Marco."

43. S. Congregazione dei Riti, filza 776, fol. 141r.

44. Ibid.

45. Ibid., fol. 139.

46. Ibid., fol. 143.

47. Notarile moderno, prot. 13392, will no. 62, written on 14 July 1633.

On 27 January 1638 Orazio attached an addendum to the will that left "a full bed" to his grandchildren, Orazio, Filippo, and the yet to be born Niccolò. In Orazio's first will, however, recorded by Amoni on 13 February 1629, the son first mentioned was Lorenzo, a priest. Orazio had expected more than he got from this son. In fact, Orazio paid twelve *fiorini* for the young man's schooling.

48. S. Congregazione dei Riti, filza 776, fols. 141v–142.

49. V. Fineschi discusses the Confraternity of San Benedetto Bianco in *Memorie sopra il cimitero antico della chiesa di Santa Maria Novella di Firenze* (Florence: F. Moücke, 1787), pp. xxvii, 49–50. See also "Notizie della compagnia di San Benedetto 'Bianco,'" MS. 2302, fol. 22, in the Biblioteca Riccardiana, Florence; W. E. Paatz, *Die Kirchen von Florenz* (Frankfurt am Main, 1955), 1:353–62; 3:672–74; and Cochrane, *Florence in the Forgotten Centuries,* p. 217.

50. Baldinucci, *Notizie dei professori,* 4:534–35.

51. Ibid., p. 539.

52. Ibid., pp. 534–48.

53. Rondinelli, *Relazione,* p. 93.

54. R. Morcay, *Saint Antonin* (Tours, 1914), pp. 60ff.; and R. Trexler, "Charity and Defense of Urban Elites in the Italian Communes," in *The Rich, the Well Born, and the Powerful: Elites and Upper Classes in History,* ed. F. Jaher (Urbana: University of Illinois Press, 1973), pp. 64–109. On the confraternity of San Martino, see Trexler, "Charity and Defense," pp. 64–109; on Saint Anthony, see *Acta SS. Maii* (Venice, 1737), 1:310–58; Morcay, *Saint Antonin;* and G. Di Agresti, *Bibliotheca Santorum* (Rome, 1962), 2:87–106.

55. R. Trexler, *Public Life in Renaissance Florence* (New York: Academic Press, 1980), p. 349. On processions as public representation of male political alliances, see page 264.

56. Vauchez, *La sainteté en Occident,* pp. 243–49.

57. De Certeau, *La fable mystique,* pp. 277–78: "During the period leading from the mystic subject of the sixteenth century to the economic subject, the savage would be a descendant of both. As a cultural figure (that is, epistemological), he prepares for the second by reversing the first, and by the end of the eighteenth century he is eclipsed by the native, by the colonized, or by the mentally retarded. In the seventeenth century he is opposed to the values of work, literary economy, and territorial and social classification and so located by the exclusions of these values' opposites: he is unproductive, illiterate, and without 'state.'"

58. Geertz, *The Interpretation of Culture* (New York: Basic Books, 1973), passim.

Archival Sources

Biblioteca Nazionale Centrale, Florence (BNCF)

Magliabechiano. Cl. XV, cod. xv. *Antidotario di medicamenti di più autori.* 1632.
———. Cl. XV, cod. xvii. *Modo di adoperare i medicamenti che sono in questa spe	zieria di campagnia.* After 1651.
———. Cl. XV, cod. xxi. Vincenzo Ferri, *La mascalcia toscana, nella quale s'insegna conoscere la differenza fra tutte le razze di cavalli che sono a nostra notizia et al conoscere e curare tutte le malattie esterne et interne che vengono ai cavalli e tutti i segni loro, l'origine e cure di esse. Aggiuntovi un trattato dove s'insegnano l'operazione manuali che si fanno ne' tumori, ferite, dislocazioni d'ossa et altri mali e un Discorso infine sull'anatomia.* Seventeenth century.
———. Cl. XV, cod. xlviii. *Epistola qua eleganter describit methodum servatam Florentiae pro estirtande pestilentia anni 1633.* Seventeenth century.
———. Cl. XXV, cods. cccclxii–cccclxv. Paolo Verzoni, *Istorie (1629–62).*
MS Baldovinetti no. 29. *Storia della peste seguita in Firenze l'anno 1630. Dalle ricordanze ms. nell'Arcivescovado fiorentino e nella Compagnia della Misericordia.*
Fondo Nazionale, II.1.454. *Notizie dei ceraioli e lavoratori d'immagini di cera in Firenze.* N.d.

Biblioteca Riccardiana, Florence (BRF)

Ms. 2302/22. *Notizie della compagnia di S. Benedetto "Bianco."*

Archivio di Stato, Florence (ASF)

Sanità. Criminale della Sanità. Filza 483. 1633.
———. Decreti e Partiti. Filze 4, 6, 7. 19 Oct. 1630–31 Aug. 1631, 21 June–28 Oct. 1630, 29 Oct. 1630–19 Feb. 1631.
———. Miscellanea. Filza 41. 1630–1720.
———. Negozi. Filze 148–56, 166–70 (1 July 1630–30 Apr. 1631, 1 Aug. 1632–24 Mar. 1633), 465 (*Descrizione delle case e persone. Libro del quartiere di S. Spirito,* 1630), 467 (*Libro delle case serrate del quartiere di S. Giovanni,* 1630–31).
———. Rescritti. Filza 37. 22 Apr. 1630–31 Dec. 1631.
———. Testamenti. Filza 480. 1630.
Otto di Guardia e Balia. Sentenze e voti originali. Filza 1914. 1601–42.

————. Suppliche. Filze 2348, 2350. Nov. 1630–July 1631, Mar. 1631–Aug. 1632.

Arte dei Medici e Speziali. Filza 15. May 1614–Dec. 1636.

Conventi soppressi no. 107, "La Crocetta di Firenze." Filze 1 (*Libro Giornale 1517–1575*), 98 (*Filze d'Istrumenti antichi 1486–1583*).

Magistrato dei Nove Conservatori del Dominio e Jurisdizione Fiorentina. Filza 3996 (*Notizie Istoriche*). N.d.

Consiglio de' Ducento. Filza 151 (*Suppliche*). 1618–22.

Cittadinario fiorentino. MS. 419. Consorterie del Quartiere di S. Croce; Consorterie del Quartiere di S. Giovanni. 1627.

Carte Sebregondi. S.v. Amoni di Firenze. N.d.

Notarile moderno. Prot. 13392. Notario Ottavio Amoni. 1620–42.

Archivio Segreto Vaticano, Rome (ASV)

S. Congregazione dei Riti. Filza 776 (*Florentina beatificationis et canonizationis servae Dei Dominicae de Paradiso ordinis Praedicatorum*). 1630.

Segreteria di Stato, Firenze. Filze 19, 20, 21.

Compositor: Graphic Composition, Inc.
Text: 10/13 Bembo
Display: Bembo
Printer: Braun-Brumfield, Inc.
Binder: Braun-Brumfield, Inc.